Be Ye the Salt of the Earth

Notes To My Graduates

Brenda S. Hanson

Ye are the salt of the earth: but if the salt have lost his savour, wherewith shall it be salted?

It is thenceforth good for nothing, but to be cast out, and to be trodden under foot of men.

Ye are the light of the world. A city that is set on an hill cannot be hid.

Neither do men light a candle, and put it under a bushel,

but on a candlestick; and it giveth light unto all that are in the house.

Let your light so shine before men, that they may see your good works,

and glorify your Father which is in heaven.

Matthew 5:13

"Christianity is not a series of truths in the plural,
but rather truth spelled with a capital "T".
Truth about total reality, not just about religious things.
Biblical Christianity is Truth concerning total reality –
and the intellectual holding of that total Truth
and then living in the light of that Truth."

Francis Schaeffer
Address at the University of Notre Dame
April 1981

Dedicated to my kids

From my heart to yours…
To you, my students, now graduating.
Congratulations on a job well done.
Thank you for all that you have taught me.
For all that you mean to me…

Love and prayers.
Always.

Be Ye the Salt of the Earth

Notes To My Graduates

Brenda S. Hanson

Only fear the LORD, and serve Him in truth with all your heart: for consider how great things He hath done for you.

I Samuel 12:24

Table of Contents

Chapter		Page

May you walk straight in a crooked world.

May you be light in the darkness.

May you stand for what is right.

May you demand truth.

Be bold.

Be peculiar.

Be righteous.

Be Ye the Salt of the Earth.

…grow in grace, and in the knowledge of our Lord and Saviour Jesus Christ.
To Him be glory both now and for ever.
Amen.
II Peter 3:18

Introduction

I'm not quite sure how it happened.

One day in 2009, I was a stay-at-home mom, not looking for any extra duties.

The next, I was standing in a classroom on a warm August morning…teaching. I was nervous and over my head. But, I knew standing there that I had found a special place and a special people.

I had found, or more accurately had been given, both a calling and a family.

It is a high calling. A serious responsibility. An exceeding great joy.

And, truly a blessing.

Teaching has changed my life.

You, my students, have changed my life.

You have challenged me and chiseled me and encouraged me.

You have seen me at both my best and my worst.

We have shared good days and bad days, happy days and sad days, mediocre days and exceptional days.

In April, 2011, I buried my only child, as God surely knew I would, and in my path He placed kids…my students. And with you, my students, has come purpose and enthusiasm and joy and memories.

Now you are traveling on. You are beginning the next chapter of your lives. This is exciting and scary all at the same time. Our world needs righteous men and women, young people who are willing to stand for truth and glorify God with their lives. You are called by the great Creator and Redeemer God to lives of excellence and beauty in the midst of a crooked and depraved generation.

You are marked with a high calling. For you are to be a peculiar people. You are to be salt. You are to be light. Be who He has called you to be…and always understand that He will equip you for whatever He has called you.

Walk by faith. Walk worthily. Be steady in an ever shifting world, and may your steadiness be built on the foundation of God, His character, His Word. May you know Him and the power of His resurrection, and may you be willing to share in the fellowship of His sufferings.

Remember, greater is He that is in you than he that is in the world.

Remember, you are more than conquerors through Christ Jesus our Lord.

Remember, the battle has been already won.

We know the end of the story. Victory in Jesus.

As for this book, this is my heart to you. It's chaotic. The words on the pages that follow are from many different seasons of my life…some are prayers…some are devotions…some are random thoughts…some were written on easy days…more were written on tough days. It's all mixed together, for that is what life so often is like, a mixed up mess.

But, in the midst of the mess is our God with a plan and purpose.

Whatever the circumstances of life, God is the same day by day, year by year, season by season. Whatever you may face, God can be trusted.

Always. For He is great. And He is good.

These are the words I would have shared with my daughter.

I give them to you, my kids.

Congratulations as you graduate!
Truly, you are loved.

And the LORD God formed man of the dust of the ground,
and breathed into his nostrils the breath of life;
and man became a living soul.
Genesis 2:7

January

"Gravity explains the motions of the planets,
but it cannot explain who sets the planets in motion."
— Isaac Newton

"All of humanity's problems stem from man's
inability to sit quietly in a room alone."
— Blaise Pascal, Pensées

JANUARY 1

Heavenly Father,

Lord, it is You who makes things new.

It is You, through Christ, who makes what is dead alive and brings new life to the broken hearts of sinners.

I pray for new birth and new life for my students. May each be born again, born of the Spirit, saved and forgiven through Christ Jesus who died for us.

May each be clothed in Christ's righteousness, clean and white.

This is my prayer…broken lives made whole…newness of life…victory in You…

Forever.

The chains removed…freedom from bondage…repentance and humility.

Hope.

For all eternity.

You and more of You for each person in our families now and in the generations yet to come.

Glory to God in the Highest and on earth peace…peace with You, Lord and then peace one with another.

JANUARY 2

One of the clichés I've had people say to me over the years is, "God will never give you more than you can handle." I know this is always said with the best of intentions. But, I wonder, is it true? Is it biblical?

When I think about Noah and Abraham and Joseph and Moses and David and Elijah, I think about how they often were given more than they could handle. It wasn't they who handled it, it was God. They were part of God's plan, and He used them in mighty ways, but ultimately it was God's strength and sovereignty that fought the battle and won the victory. Not theirs.

There have been times when I've challenged people to back up this comment with Scripture. Inevitably, they always quote I Corinthians 10:13: *No temptation has overtaken you that is not common to man. God is faithful, and He will not let you be tempted beyond your ability, but with the temptation He will also provide the way of escape, that you may be able to endure it.* As I've studied that verse, I've noticed that the verse tells us that "*HE will also provide the way of escape.*"

Could it be that God **does** give us more than we can handle, and then He comes alongside and instructs and leads and loves and shows us the way that, in **HIM** and by **HIM** we can come through the trials of life refined and beautiful?

As a new year begins, I stand at the threshold of the unknown. We all do. We plan and dream, and all that is good. But, the truth is, we don't know all that this year will bring. There will be joys and sorrows and laughter and tears and memories and challenges and surprises and painful moments and wonderful moments....and some of us will face things that we never imagined and that we cannot handle.

As I look back on my life, I realize the value of those overwhelming moments, those moments standing at a crossroads. I know it is only because of God and **HIS** handling of those moments that I ever came through. Whatever this new year brings, I am His and He is mine.

Happy New Year to all of you, and may it be well with your souls.

JANUARY 3

How prone we are to praise God when the burden is eased, and prone to forget to praise Him when it is not.

Is it possible that our praises to Him are sweeter when raised while we are yet in the fire of affliction or walking through the valley of the shadow of death?

Is He any less worthy of our praises when the storm is still raging?

The God who felt the bitter sting of rejection, the tearing of His flesh, and who shed His blood for me is worthy of my praise always.

He deserved praise from my lips and from my heart on the day Sarah drew her last breath as much as on the day she drew her first.

I choose to praise Him for who He is and for what He does.

I choose to praise Him because of His very nature and character: all-powerful mighty Creator and Redeemer God, perfect in holiness and unending in love.

I praise Him because He is, and was, and is to come.

I praise Him because He is greater than any circumstance, greater than any fiery trial, greater than any tragedy or failure or disappointment. Therefore, I will "rejoice always, pray continually, give thanks in all circumstances....I will bow down in worship and kneel before the LORD our Maker; for He is God and we are the people of His pasture, the flock under His care."

JANUARY 4

Dear Lord,

I pray for those in our families who struggle. There are so many kinds of struggles. Some are self-created and some are the result of life in a fallen world. Sickness abounds. Physical illness is frequent. Emotional fractures run deep. Financial stress is real. Broken relationships litter the battlefield of life. There are spiritual battles going on this very minute.

The battles are real. For some, the pain is constant.

There are struggles to be endured. Whatever challenges we face this year, may You, Lord, use those challenges to grow us up in the faith and draw us near to the only lasting solution, You. I pray for those who are lonely. Afraid. Deceived. Confused. Weary. Defeated. Oppressed. Overwhelmed. Distraught and distressed. Fearful and worried. In bondage to sin. Help us, Lord. Give us eyes to see and ears to hear that You are greater than all. Help us to believe and to trust You and have peace with and in You...the peace that passes all understanding…the peace that comes from You and is in no way dependent on our circumstances. Teach us how to cast our cares upon You and humbly, with empty hands and open hearts, reach toward You and the nail-scarred and outstretched arms that You extend.

Father, reach toward us. Reveal Yourself. Be manifested in our thoughts and our lives, and help us to understand, that even though You are not completely comprehensible to our finite minds, You are real and victory is possible. Victory is promised in You. There is hope, and His name is Emmanuel, Wonderful, Counsellor, Everlasting Father, and Mighty God.   Help us to know, and help us to come to You, Bread of Life and Living Water.

JANUARY 5

Mark and I stopped at Mom's house this morning. My seven year old nephew, Sam, was visiting. Sam asked if I wanted to go for a ride on Mom's golf cart. "Sure," I said, and we jumped on the golf cart and headed out behind the barn.

It's easy to talk on an electric golf cart. They are very quiet.

In our conversation, I shared with Sam how I get up early in the morning, and settle in on my kitchen floor with a cup of coffee and the Bible. I shared how I read God's Word and pray.

His response? "You could be a priest!"

Out of the mouths of babes, right? I chuckled and tousled his brown hair and let him in on the truth…God's Word tells us we can all be priests: *And they sung a new song, saying, Thou (Jesus) art worthy to take the book, and to open the seals thereof: for Thou wast slain, and hast redeemed us to God by Thy blood out of every kindred, and tongue, and people, and nation;* ***And hast made us unto our God kings and priests: and we shall reign on the earth*** *{Revelation 5:9-10}.*

I, Sam, you…we can be kings and priests…not because we sit on our kitchen floor in the morning and read the Bible and pray…but because of Jesus Christ who *"wast slain, and hast redeemed us to God by His blood."*

I open God's Word and cultivate quiet time with Him not for the purpose of making myself a king or a priest...but because Jesus Christ has already made me so.

JANUARY 6

I am thankful for believers bold enough to proclaim both halves of Biblical truth.

We were traveling through Lancaster, PA and I spotted a sign outside a church that read, "the gift of God is eternal life."   And, I was bothered.   For that is only half of the verse. In its entirety, this verse proclaims, *"For the wages of sin is death; but the gift of God is eternal life **through Jesus Christ our Lord**."*

The sign outside the church announced only half the truth. Yes, *"the gift of God is eternal life,"* that is half of the truth. But half-truth is no truth at all. *"(T)hrough Jesus Christ our Lord"* is the second half...and both halves are required for total truth.

I am grateful when believers are bold enough to speak both halves, bold because they love the Lord and bold because they love people.

Truth may be politically incorrect. But, it's still truth. Jesus, and He alone, saves.

JANUARY 7

Been thinking about how God's Word both comforts me and at the same time rubs me uncomfortably raw.

Truth.

Truth is the only real comfort.

Truth is…God is good all the time.

Truth is…God owes me no explanation.

Truth is…God is in control and is sovereign over all.

Truth is…God has a plan that is bigger than my understanding of it.

Truth is…God's everlasting arms are under me.

Truth is…God sees me in my low estate.

Truth is… God is my refuge in the storm.

Truth is…the pain is temporary and even purposeful.

Truth is…the blood of Christ has redeemed me.

This same truth of God's Word can also rub me **uncomfortably raw** as He sands down the idol of self and conforms me more and more into the image of His Son.

God's Word is light…

And where that light reveals sin, I am to be painfully uncomfortable.

Truth should rub me raw.

This, too, is comfort…even if it's uncomfortable.

If I can read about God's holiness and purity and yet remain comfortable in my sin and comfortable with the darkness of the world, something is dangerously wrong.

Thank You, Father, for both comforting me and making me uncomfortable. Both your comfort and the raw wounds of your work and Word in my life reflect Your love, Your mercy, and Your grace.

JANUARY 8

Jesus wants me to love others. He wants my love to be active and sacrificial. Forget about vague and mushy love. He's looking for real and messy "into it up to your elbows" kind of love.

Jesus said in Matthew 25: *Then, the King will say to those on his right, 'Come, you who are blessed by my Father; take your inheritance, the kingdom prepared for you since the creation of the world. For I was hungry and you gave me something to eat, I was thirsty and you gave me something to drink, I was a stranger and you invited me in, I needed clothes and you clothed me, I was sick and you looked after me, I was in prison and you came to visit me.' Then the righteous will answer him, 'Lord, when did we see you hungry and feed you, or thirsty and give you something to drink? When did we see you a stranger and invite you in, or needing clothes and clothe you? When did we see you sick or in prison and go to visit you?' The King will reply, 'I tell you the truth, whatever you did for one of the least of these brothers of mine, you did for me.'*

Jesus does not say, "Love others when it is convenient" or "Love others when it is fun" or "Love others as long as you don't have something else to do" or "Love others only when they think and live exactly like you do" or "Love others only when you agree with the sort of people they are" or "Love others when you are well enough rested."

Jesus tells us to love others like He loved us.

Well, He died for us.

Jesus taught that when we love others, we are really loving Him. When we care for others, we are really caring for Him.

John tells us in I John 3: *This is how we know what love is: Jesus Christ laid down His life for us. And we ought to lay down our lives for our brothers. If anyone has material possessions and sees his brother in need but has no pity on him, how can the love of God be in him? Dear children, let us not love with words or tongue, but with actions and in truth.*

JANUARY 9

Jesus said in John 13:34, *A new command I give you: Love one another. As I have loved you, so you must love one another. By this all men will know that you are My disciples, if you love one another.*

Jesus said in Luke 6:27-36: *But I tell you who hear me: Love your enemies, do good to those who hate you, bless those who curse you, pray for those who mistreat you. If someone strikes you on one cheek, turn to him the other also. If someone takes your cloak, do not stop him from taking your tunic. Give to everyone who asks you, and if anyone takes what belongs to you, do not demand it back. Do to others as you would have them do to you. If you love those who love you, what credit is that to you? Even sinners love those who love them.*

Love is not about a warm feeling toward another person, it is about identifying a need that a person has and then determining, with the Lord's guidance, whether you have the gifts, talents, resources to help meet that need. God does not, for our own good and the good of the world, want us to merely live our lives separate from the rest of the world, comfortable in front of the television but unwilling to reach out to others. Of course, God created us with limitations. We require sleep and rest. We have some skills but not others. God does not expect us to be God, and we cannot do everything and meet all needs. That is why we must listen for God to guide us into how to love. We must not let our limitations become excuses to fail to love.

Above all, love each other deeply, because love covers over a multitude of sins. Offer hospitality to one another without grumbling. Each one should use whatever gift he has received to serve others, faithfully administering God's grace in its various forms. If anyone speaks, he should do it as one speaking the very words of God. If anyone serves, he should do it with the strength God provides, so that in all things God may be praised through Jesus Christ. To him be the glory and the power for ever and ever. Amen (I Peter 4:8-11).

Put on therefore, as the elect of God, holy and beloved, bowels of mercies, kindness, humbleness of mind, meekness, longsuffering; Forbearing one another, and forgiving one another, if any man have a quarrel against any: even as Christ forgave you, so also do ye. And above all these things put on charity, which is the bond of perfectness. And let the peace of God rule in your hearts, to the which also ye are called in one body; and be ye thankful (Colossians 3:12-15).

Loving others does not mean accepting and tolerating sin. If anything, loving others includes confronting sin and also includes allowing people to experience the consequences of sin. The thing about this, though, is that the love needs to be present as the sin is confronted, as the consequence is endured. Love does not cease to exist because sin is present. We would all be destined for hell if that were the case. Confronting sin without a loving heart will fail. Jesus often reached out in love prior to confronting the sin. A patient spirit with an ear always turned in God's direction with lots of prayer is what is needed here. To confront sin in another individual, you must yield to God's guidance and God's timing on the matter. You are not God. You are his servant and you, too, are a sinner.

There is no excuse….if you are a Christian who believes in Jesus Christ as your Savior, the Bible is clear: we are called to love. His way.

JANUARY 10

From *The Deeper Christian Life* by Andrew Murray [1]

"The first and chief need of our Christian life is fellowship with God.

"The divine life within us comes from God and is entirely dependent upon Him. As I need every moment afresh the air to breathe, as the sun every moment afresh sends down its light, so it is only in direct living communication with God that my soul can be strong.

"The manna of one day was corrupt when the next day came. I must every day have fresh grace from heaven, and I obtain it only in direct waiting upon God Himself. Begin each day by tarrying before God and letting Him touch you. Take time to meet God.

"To this end, let your first act in your devotions be setting yourself still before God. In prayer, or worship, everything depends upon God taking the chief place. I must bow quietly before Him in humble faith and adoration, speaking thus within my heart: 'God is. God is near. God is love, longing to communicate Himself to me. God the

Almighty One, Who worketh all in all, is even now waiting to work in me and make Himself known.' Take time, till you know God is very near.

"When you have given God His place of honor, glory, and power, take your place of deepest lowliness and be filled with the Spirit of humility. As a creature, it is your blessedness to be nothing, that God may be all in you. As a sinner, you are not worthy to look up to God; bow in self-abasement. As a saint, let God's love overwhelm you and bow you still lower down. Sink down before Him in humility, meekness, patience, and surrender to His goodness and mercy. He will exalt you. Oh! Take time to get very low before God."
From <u>The Deeper Christian Life</u> by Andrew Murray [1]

<u>JANUARY 11</u>

I came to realize a few years ago that, unless I die first, I will experience loss and the death of some of those I love. There is no avoiding this. That seems obvious, doesn't it? Obvious, perhaps, but readily ignored in our younger years.

I'll never forget the day this reality sunk in. Sarah had a stroke in 1998 when she was a year and a half old. Following that, everything changed. I left my job to be home with Sarah. Mark went to school and earned his CDL to drive tractor-trailer. Sarah cried all the time. She lost every physical skill she'd developed. No longer able to sit, roll, use her arms, sleep normally, she was inconsolable.

I tried to develop a routine. Sarah usually slept pretty good between 4:00 AM and 9:00 AM. When she woke, she was usually a little more calm, with less crying, than she would be later in the day. Following our morning activities, I would lay Sarah on the living room floor to watch TV. I would often make a cup of tea and then step outside for a quick walk to the small creek behind our house. Escape. These walks became a precious time of the day for me.

Quiet time with God.

One day as I walked, the thought came to me, "Wow, unless I die first, I will lose people close to me, people I love." Such an obvious fact of life shouldn't seem so shocking. But, it was. And, it made me feel afraid. I know that day will come when the phone will ring, and it will be bad news on the other end. Even though I believe in heaven (and hell), and in Christ, I felt afraid at this new, and yet old, reality.

Now time has passed, and here we are years later, 2004. During sharing time and prayers at Church, the list of people suffering from cancer or other medical problems continues to grow. Sometimes I feel like crying. I know God loves us, but the effects of sin (sickness, death) are at times unbearable. I look around, and

I see people who have experienced so much more loss than I. Despite my faith, I wonder how anyone gets through tragedy and loss. But, they do, and I will when the time comes.

Bear with me…when I was a little girl, I loved licking the raw cookie dough off the beaters. Mom would always leave a little bit extra on them just for us kids. Somewhere along the line, I stopped licking the beaters because I grew afraid that the raw eggs in the cookie dough could make me sick.

I think I'm going to start licking the beaters again.

I'm tired of being afraid.

Tragedy and loss will come. Avoiding the raw cookie dough will not stop it. I can't control this. I need God, His presence, His assurance.

He gave and He gives….the time to praise has come….for fear cannot live in songs of praise and victory that we raise to God Omnipotent who reigneth.

Praise God for every breath…for life…. Praise God for His victory over sin and death through Jesus' blood shed on the cross.

Praise God for raw cookie dough and the boldness to lick the beaters.

JANUARY 12

I love You, Lord, my God and Father, my peace and righteousness. Jehovah Shalom, I raise to You in prayer my beloved students. More than anything, I pray for them to be humble and right with You, through Christ. I pray for their hearts to seek and their minds to desire You. First. Early. Often.

Father, Your goodness endures continually.

Lord, are there any that have not made You their salvation and their strength? Any who are trusting in the abundance of riches and possessions rather than You? I know You know. And, more than that, I know You know what to do and when to do it.

I pray for my students now and in the generations to come, to be like green olive trees in the house of God with deep well-nourished roots of spiritual truth.

I trust in the mercy of my God forever and ever. I will praise Thee forever, Lord, because Thou hast done it: And I will wait on Thy Name; for it is good before Thy saints.

JANUARY 13

I didn't realize it was a big deal until I was half way through the project. Mark was at work, Sarah was napping, and I decided it was time to move the old blue chair out of the living room and down to the basement.

Doesn't sound like a big deal, does it? But for me it was. That old blue chair ended up in our living room late one night in March, 1998, a month after Sarah suffered a stroke. She was a mess, and she cried most of her waking hours. Since the stroke, she'd had a terrible time falling asleep and staying asleep. Smiles, naps, and full-night's sleep were things of the past. In their place were misery and uncertainty and exhaustion.

Day after day, night after night Sarah stayed awake and cried. And cried. And would wake up easily when she did finally fall asleep. The only way to stop her from crying was to hold her and walk while bouncing her in my arms. For hours. She would usually fall asleep around 4:00 AM and sleep for 3-4 hours. But until 4:00 AM arrived, we were on the move.   We didn't know if this situation was ever going to get better. The only thing we knew for sure was that Sarah would get bigger.

One night, I could handle it no longer. I called my Mom and asked her to come over. I woke up Mark (he helped through the night the best he could, but he needed to go to work every day). I told him I was going to bed. He and Mom took over. That night, Mark went down to the basement and dragged up an ugly, old royal blue fuzzy-cloth-covered rocking chair.   Its color matched nothing in the living room. Or anywhere else in the house for that matter. It had been in the basement for a reason, that's how ugly it was.

For seven years, the ugly royal blue rocking chair sat in our living room.

The ugly blue chair became a very good friend.

Hours were spent in it, holding and rocking Sarah.   At first, I had to rock her vigorously to get her to sleep. Then, once she fell asleep, I would ever so slowly stop rocking and very cautiously stand up and carry her back to her bed.   I learned to appreciate and enjoy Sarah in that ugly blue rocking chair. Of course, I always loved her, but life was hard in those days, and having energy to appreciate and enjoy her was a rare treasure.

Now here we are seven years later.

Sarah sleeps all night long in her very own bed now. She laughs and smiles and loves life very much. She's had more battles since that night seven years ago: surgeries, leukemia, chemo, seizures. But she just keeps making it all worthwhile. And, enjoyable. She has a good life. We have a good life. She is blessed. We are blessed. God was always with us, even when we wondered if that was so. He was right there, the whole time. And He even provided an ugly blue rocking chair to help us along the way.

JANUARY 14

I spilled milk on my Bible today. Quite a lot of milk, actually. My Bible, open and lying on the kitchen island while I was preparing some sort of meal, me rushing around trying to get too many things done at the same time. And thus the spill, the result of rushing and my innate gift of clumsy. The milk crashed all over the island, down its sides and into those oh-so-hard to clean decorative crevices on drawer handles and hinges. And, it washed all over my Bible.

Spilled milk helped me understand that I, by God's great grace, have grown.

Not so long ago, there would have been no open Bible on my kitchen counter.

I felt a tug to pat myself on the back. I was sure that God was pleased with me. Is it OK to pat oneself on the back? Especially in the realm of spirituality? Was I bordering upon Pharisaical self-exaltation?

Clearly, I am being dramatic. But, the question remains, how does one handle recognizing spiritual growth in one's self without becoming a Pharisee? How prone we are to develop a self-righteous pride as we grow spiritually. Yet, such pride is itself a sign of shallowness, not spiritual depth.

Knowledge of the Lord needs to be wrapped in awe of the Lord.

It is essential for we Christians to examine ourselves and to recognize, honestly, where we are at spiritually. Failure to do so is dangerous. Failure to do so prevents us from accurately determining God's purpose for our lives. We must assess whether we are growing or not. We must assess where we are gifted and where we are not. We must assess where there are spiritual strengths and where there are spiritual weaknesses. We must actively seek. We must actively listen for His voice, found in His truth, about our lives.

It's about honesty. An honest examination is not proud.

It's about gratitude. A grateful examination is not proud.

If I see signs in my life that I have become more Christ-like, REJOICE!

With rejoicing must come reflection. I need to ponder myself in the light of God's great presence in order to understand how I am to relate and interact and be salt in this world. To best serve God and others, I need to grasp where I am and how big God actually is in my life. Introspection is an essential exercise in scaling the heights of higher spiritual ground.

Complete spiritual maturity is never obtained on our earthly pilgrimage. God can never be big enough in our lives on this earth. Failure to spiritually thrive is a risk we all face, daily. The dangers of backsliding and drifting are ever present. We are, truly, prone to wander. The devil prowls like a devouring lion, and we believers are the prey he seeks.

Stay close to the Savior. Be honest. Be humble. Grow. Rejoice!

JANUARY 15

From *Foxe: Voices of the Martyrs* [2]

Justin Martyr (ca. AD 100 – 165)

"For all his intelligence, Justin Martyr never quibbled with the prospect that he, too, would die violently at the hands of the Roman state. In his day and time, execution was more or less the expected means of passing from this life to heaven. After all, a Roman magistrate need only order the smallest reverence toward the emperor or their pagan deities, the shortest nod of worship, and the faithful Christian, utterly refusing, was condemned. Justin might have anticipated such a fate, but he lived into old age (for his era) before the choice confronted him.

"Justin was a scholar devoted to ideas, debates, and arguments – by modern standards undramatic, yet immensely significant for the early church in the decades after the apostles. Born to a pagan family living at the site of ancient Shechem in Samaria, this bright lad mastered the writings of the Stoics and the Platonists, the best minds of Rome and Greece. Unsatisfied and yearning for the peacefulness of truth, he responded to the witness of an unknown 'old man,' and around age thirty committed his life and mind to Jesus Christ, who alone taught 'the one sure worthy philosophy.'

"Thereafter Justin employed his mind to spread the truth with zeal and determination. Armed with passion for God and the tools of ancient rhetoric, he debated with Jew and

Gentile the merits of the gospel, the truth of the Messiah, and the coming judgment of the one righteous and merciful God. It is often said that Justin was the first Christian thinker after Paul to grasp the universal implications of Christian faith: God's love reached to all; the resurrection of Christ was a once-for-all answer to sin's horrendous judgment.

"Strong in faith and articulate in early theology, Justin did not neglect the horizontal view. He was astute and appreciative of culture, and knew, as a sociologist might today, the times and people who comprised his dynamic world.

"He taught that one can find truth in the philosophies of pagans; God had given pagan philosophers a glimpse of truth through the mercy of Christ. But the glimpse was only foretaste, not substance. The pagans cannot fully find truth until they come to Christ, as Jesus is the Reason, the Logos of the universe come to Earth. Justin's breadth would pave the way for other Christians to recognize the good, the true, and the beautiful in non-Christian cultural works and writings. With courage and conviction, Justin's 'apology' for the faith affirmed that only Christ was Lord and refused all compromise with lesser gods.

"He resented the widespread notion that Christians were traitors, immoral, weak, or rebellious. A large part of his work described the social benefits of faith. The followers of Jesus should be admired and promoted as model citizens, he told the Roman authorities. Because of faith, because of the goodness of Christ, these Christians gave the state its noblest strength. 'We are in fact of all men your best helpers and allies in securing good order.' But he warned: 'don't demand that they bow before falsehood.'

"And just that demand sealed Justin's fate after thirty-five years of teaching and preaching (he never held an official church office). Early in the reign of Marcus Aurelius, Justin and six others were arrested and brought before the prefect Rusticus. Justin was the group's spokesperson, of course; but as soon as he began his confession and defense, the prefect, obviously bored at the prospect of a sermon, made the fatal demand to renounce Christianity and bow before Caesar. Everyone refused, and Rusticus pronounced the standard brutal sentence. Soon after, Justin and his fellows were scourged and beheaded, but the truth was not silenced. 'The lover of truth ought to choose in every way, even at the cost of his own life, to speak and do what is right, though death should take him away,' Justin wrote at the beginning of his <u>First Apology</u>. 'You can kill us, but cannot do us any real harm.'"

From <u>Foxe: Voices of the Martyrs</u> [2]

JANUARY 16

Born again. Freshly born faith spilling over and into the lives of all who come in contact with the newly saved. The gift is so new to them. The joy is so exciting. They are on fire for God and His Word and truth. It is so beautiful.

God blesses me daily in so many ways, but recently He blessed me with a reminder of the enthusiasm and joy that are meant to mark the lives of those washed by the blood of the lamb, Jesus Christ.

Ramon came into our daughter's hospital room and shared the news. He was born again! He told us how the Spirit had been all over him awaking him to things eternal and causing him to ponder the destination of what he innately knew was his eternal soul. One recent day, he had been driving alone in his car and a sudden urgency came upon him. In heart and mind he was confronted with the reality that life is frail, and – trembling - he wondered where his soul would go should he have a car accident and die that very minute. He was convicted in his conscience that he needed Jesus Christ to save his soul and forgive his sins. Ramon repented of his sins. He trusted the blood of Jesus to wash clean the deepest stains.

It is a beautiful thing when God interrupts our lives with His truth. With His presence. With Himself.

God always desires to give His children good gifts. I was saved a long time ago. And, sometimes I forget to be enthused. My faith becomes common and ordinary to me, and I need a reminder of just how wrong that is. Ramon's enthusiasm and hunger for God were contagious. He told us that he prays asking God to fill him with knowledge like a sponge getting filled with water.

I pray for Ramon. I pray for the enthusiasm to continue and to bear fruit. I pray to become more like Ramon, fresh and excited about what God is doing. We are prone to becoming lukewarm in our faith. Often, the new born believer ages into the long time believer who has tired of God and forgets to stand in awe before the Holy Creator, giver of life, designer of the universe, redeemer of man's soul. Distractions take hold. Faith is choked by worries. Disappointments and troubles come as frequently to the believer as to the non-believer. Sometimes even more. Ramon, like each of us who trust in Christ as Savior, needs to daily be aware of the human tendency to drift from God and toward self, the world, and the old way of thinking and living.

Spiritual maturity is different from physical and worldly maturity. Our physical bodies grow, and as they do we prepare to move away from our parents and live our lives separate from them. In the world, maturing is a process of becoming self-sufficient and independent. Conversely, spiritual maturation, is the opposite, for it involves a process of moving ever closer to our heavenly Father and becoming more dependent upon Him and less dependent upon self.

Worldly maturity involves self-promotion. Spiritual maturity involves surrender. Worldly maturity involves selfish gain. Spiritual maturity involves loss of self. Worldly maturity is proud. Spiritual maturity is humble. Worldly maturity stands in awe of self and the accomplishments of the flesh. Spiritual maturity bows low and worships deeply the God of heaven and earth.

May we stand this day in awe and wonder of the Creator and Redeemer God!

May we be like Ramon…amazed and undone in the presence of holiness.

JANUARY 17

A couple years ago, I was baking in our kitchen. The radio, tuned to 930 AM, was playing in the background. The "Dr. Laura Show" was on, and a caller named "Nancy" was speaking. She introduced herself as a wife and mother with a dilemma regarding an abortion she'd recently had. Her dilemma was whether or not she should be accepting the sympathy of family and friends who she had misled into believing she'd had a miscarriage rather than an abortion. As the conversation unfolded, she attempted to justify the abortion. Finally, she stated, "I believe we did the right thing. The baby was diagnosed with Down syndrome. I believe Down syndrome is an error. God doesn't make errors, so having the abortion was the right thing to do."

I froze.

The adrenaline was pumping and any potential compassion toward the caller vanished. This is personal.

We have a daughter with Down syndrome. And hydrocephalus. And a heart defect. And a vascular disorder that led to strokes which led to spasticity and the inability to perform any activity independently. And a feeding tube. And diapers for the rest of her life. And acute lymphocytic leukemia. Through it all, I had never, ever, ever thought of Sarah as an "error".

I stormed around my kitchen railing against the caller for the next fifteen minutes.

Well, does God make errors? My immediate response would be, "That's a stupid question, of course God doesn't make errors. He's God, after all." But, that's perhaps not a thoughtful response. Some might argue that the creation of Lucifer, the great angel who fell and became the evil Satan, was an error.

Some might argue that God's decision to allow free will was an error. There are those who would ask, "If God doesn't make errors, then why are there natural miscarriages in many early pregnancies?" Because God is all-knowing, all-powerful, and all-present, I have to believe that the above examples are not errors, but somehow part of God's great and mysterious plan.

A plan, by the way, of which He owes me no explanation.

Does God make children with Down syndrome? Is attaching that little bitty microscopic piece of extra genetic information to chromosome 21 (or chromosome 13 or chromosome 18), part of God's plan?

It's an easy question to answer. Yes, He does make children with Down syndrome.

Of course, if you are choosing to be miserable that you have a child with Down syndrome, then this would lead you to blame God, rather than thank Him, for your child. Whether you are happy or angry or disappointed that your child was born with a birth defect (or anything else – blue eyes, red hair, a big nose, a girl rather than a boy, a boy rather than a girl, lots of hair, no hair), God is the creator of life – all life. You can decide to blame Him or praise Him for that life and the struggles and joys that come with it. Whatever your choice, I believe that God knows, creates, and loves all children…in the womb and out.

Is Down syndrome an error? Scientists would tell you, yes, it is. They would point out that Down syndrome is the result of extra genetic material, i.e. an abnormality or mistake. I guess it depends on what glasses you are wearing to look at life. Wearing the glasses of secular science, you will see Down syndrome as a genetic and random error. Once the secularist glasses are removed, it becomes less a matter of fact and more a matter of choice whether or not Down syndrome is an error.

Sarah's Down syndrome and other medical struggles have a meaningful purpose that I, as a parent, am responsible for helping her discover and then fulfill. Such discovery is made over time with prayer and faith and an honest sharing with God of all the events, sorrows, joys, decisions that occur. Discovery of one's purpose is a process not only for "normal" people, but for people with Down syndrome as well.

What are some of the possible purposes for the life of a person with Down syndrome? The answer is as beautifully complex and varied for those with Down syndrome as it is for those not. Children with Down syndrome, just like normally developing children, experience life. They have the potential for teaching us the joys of successes. They remind us to be thankful for our health and life and capabilities – because each one of us, really, is just one car wreck away from being disabled ourselves. They offer us the chance (in C.S. Lewis' words) of "becoming heroes". When a difficult or heart wrenching situation crashes into our lives and we rise to meet it (however long that may take) and deal with it and grow because of it, we have become heroes. The purposes of a person with Down syndrome are as meaningful and diversified and unique as purposes for anyone. Again, it's a matter of choice. Will we look for purpose or will we be passive victims to life events?

Ultimately, our most important purpose in life is to love God, grow in trust in Him, and glorify Him with our lives, whether they are "normal" lives or disabled lives. People with Down syndrome can do that just as well as we, the normal population, can. Sometimes maybe even better.

Will Sarah have Down syndrome when she goes to heaven? It doesn't even matter. God is more concerned with the condition of our souls than He is with the condition of our bodies

As for the caller to Dr. Laura's show, I don't know for sure, but she might have missed out on her purpose for life. At the very least, she missed out on the opportunity to become a hero to her child and a great example to others. The error that was made was not God's, but hers, and I pray she seeks His forgiveness, which He will freely give the repentant heart.

JANUARY 18

I looked at the clock. It was 2:50 AM. Perhaps it was Mark's snoring. Perhaps it was the quiet creaks and groans of the house. Whatever the cause, I had just woken and already my brain was going hundreds of miles an hour over the details, small and large, of the upcoming day. I lay there, one minute plotting the organizational plan for the next day and the next scolding myself that it was almost 3:00 in the morning and I should be sleeping.

Brain clutter. Too much to think about. Too many things to do. For myself, brain clutter is the result of believing everything I have to do is just as important as everything else I have to do. Prioritizing is a problem for me. Just can't seem to get the hang of it. Thus, I claw through life thinking I MUST get through my long list of things to do! The result is thinking about the next thing I "need" to do before even completing the thing I am doing. The result is day after day speeding by like a bullet. The result is exhaustion.

I don't like brain clutter. But, it's a choice. Do I want to continue living in the fog of a hectic life or do I want to live with peace and clearness of mind? Assuming my choice is peace and clearness of mind, then practice must begin. The habit of being too busy and preoccupied is a tough one to break, and, following the choice to live a more meaningful life, it takes discipline. There will be days of total relapse. There will be days of triumph. There will be days in between. Practice is the key.

I have to change how I frame life. I have to change how I think.

The fact of the matter is this: I can NOT do everything. Any attempt to do everything is arrogant and foolish. God did not design us to do everything. He doesn't expect us to do everything, and I would guess He may even feel rather disturbed when I start thinking I'm so important. God designed us with unique gifts and unique challenges for His purpose in our lives. As much as I can give lip service to that obvious fact, it will take practice to get it sunk deeply down into my heart and mind. God also designed each of us with specific limitations and dependency on both Him and other human beings. Because of this, we need to become masters in prioritizing – and becoming a true master means listening for God's direction.

It boils down to arrogance. Apparently, I live like I have to do everything because I think other people can't get it as right as I can. Arrogance. It is really foolishness. Idiocy. Jesus never overlooked the capabilities of other people. Daily, I do. Daily that makes me an arrogant idiot. Would I have noticed the capabilities of Peter as Jesus did? Jesus was able to look at Peter, the man who denied him three times, and see potential. Jesus identified Peter's talents and capabilities. Then, He gave Peter the time and the chance to use those qualities to the fullest. The same with Paul. Would I have seen Paul as a person capable of leading the early church? But, Jesus did. Jesus knew the truth. The truth is each person has gifts and potential. Jesus trusted the growth of His church on earth into the hands of human beings. He never forgot the capabilities of spirit-filled individuals. He was not arrogant or impatient.

Listen, and He will lead.

JANUARY 19

Dear Father,

I pray, Lord, that You will be our dwelling place throughout all generations. From everlasting to everlasting, You are God! May the truth of who You are grow deep roots in our lives, our thinking, the very fiber of our being.

Lord, our iniquities are before You. Our secret sins are in the light of Your presence. They are no secret to You. Our days pass away quickly. Teach us, everlasting Lord, to number our days aright, that we may gain a heart of wisdom. Satisfy us in the morning with Your unfailing love. Only You can satisfy our real needs...the need for salvation, truth, guidance and counsel...straight from Your Throne.

We attempt to satisfy our needs in so many unsatisfying ways. Foolish we are apart from You! Condemned we are apart from You! An encounter with You, Lord, always changes us. We will encounter You, one way or another. And when we do, we will be either consecrated and made holy, or we will be consumed.

Have compassion, Lord, and save those whose feet are currently being licked by the flames of Your righteous wrath and consuming fire. May we experience the need to worship You in the beauty of holiness. You are worthy of all honor and praise and glory! Give us moments of silent awe and an eternity of bountiful worship to the One worthy from everlasting to everlasting.

January 20

From <u>The Deeper Christian Life</u> by Andrew Murray [3]

"I fear there is a terrible, terrible self-satisfaction among many Christians;

"They are content with their low level of life.

"They think they have the Spirit because they are converted, but they know very little of the joy of the Holy Ghost and of His sanctifying power.

"They know very little of the fellowship of the Spirit linking them to God and to Jesus.

"They know very little of the power of the Spirit to testify for God, and yet they are content...

"Oh, friends, do not be content with that half-Christian life that many of you are living, but say, 'God wants it, God commands it; I must be filled with the Spirit.'"
From <u>The Deeper Christian Life</u> by Andrew Murray [3]

January 21

It's been a good day. Father, You have been near. I pray for my students. I pray for our families. I pray that today each has had a good day, not because everything has fallen in pleasant places, but because Your presence is real to them and the grandeur and majesty of who You are lights their paths.

I pray especially today, Lord, for marriages. For purity. It's hard to be married, but when we grasp and come to agree with You and what You say about marriage, our marriages improve and become useful. Help us to forget about the fallacy of happiness and to instead strive for the holiness that You know is best for us. Help us to honor You in our marriages and to embrace the goal and beauty of glorifying You in them, even when they are troubled and even when the going is tough. If we go with You, we are not going alone.

Father, purge from our minds, our hearts, and our homes anything impure and replace the lusts of the flesh with the truth and counsel of the Spirit. Protect marriages. May they endure and thrive under Your watchful care and wise guidance.

Jesus, You are the One who renews and revives. Praise Your holy name!

JANUARY 22

Today is the anniversary of the Roe v. Wade Supreme Court decision...

In May, 1996, sitting in a darkened ultrasound room, my husband and I heard life changing words. The doctor came in, gently placed his hand on my shoulder, and said, "Your baby will be born with birth defects."

And she was. Sarah was born with Down syndrome, hydrocephalus, and a heart defect. For fifteen years, our sweet girl faced mountains of medical battles, including a debilitating stroke, acute lymphocytic leukemia, and frequent seizures. Sarah never spoke. She never walked. My daughter never threw her arms around my neck and whispered, "I love you, Mommy" in my ear. I never heard the pitter-patter of excited feet running down the hall in eager anticipation on Christmas morning. Instead, for fifteen years, I changed Sarah's diapers, pushed her wheelchair, brushed her hair, bathed her, programmed her feeding tube pumps, and administered all kinds of meds with all kinds of side-effects for all kinds of medical conditions.

And, for fifteen years, I loved like I never knew I could. Sarah's smile melted me. Her joy stunned me. Her appreciation amazed me. Her courage shocked me. Her life humbled me.

I gave birth to a child many would have chosen to abort. My life, as the result of choosing life, was harder. But far richer! My life, as the result of choosing life, was different than I'd expected it to be. But, so much better! In choosing life, I walked away from a career to embrace a role that paid no dollars. Yet my cup of joy ran over! Day after day, trial after trial, my husband I were abundantly rewarded by the child who shared our home and our lives.

Was I afraid in May, 1996 when our doctor breathed out those life changing words, the words that the life growing in my womb was not the life we expected? You bet! I was more than afraid, I was terrified. I had no idea how to do what I was being asked to do. I had no idea what the future held. How was I to learn to care for a very special and medically frail child? I was young, I was disappointed, and, yes, I was scared.

But, a mother's love is stronger than fear. And God's love is greater yet. I praise God, who makes no mistakes, that when He asked me to be Sarah's mother, my trembling heart breathed out, "Yes." God, who knit Sarah together and asked us to care for her was also the God who showed us the way. Throughout the journey, He carried us. Every step of the way, He was there. Never, ever did He forsake us or leave us. When the days were difficult, in God's grace, we discovered not only the ability to do what we needed to do, but also joy, purpose, and treasures rich and real.

Fifteen years after she was born, Sarah died. Together, we shared fifteen beautiful years. It's true that many of those years were difficult and challenging. Yet, without reservation I can say that each was valuable and that every day, the tough ones included, were days worth living and days precious and meaningful beyond words.

Sarah lived life well. And as a result of the life she lived, we are richer.

We have been abundantly blessed. The day will come when I will hear Sarah's voice for the first time. And on that day I will, face to face, thank and praise the Lord Jesus for Sarah, and His complete utter and undeserved favor and goodness to her, to me, to us. He makes no mistakes, and I praise Him for the extra chromosome that changed our lives forever for the better .

JANUARY 23

Special children bring special joy...In 2008, I wrote...

I can't believe Sarah will soon be twelve years old. The past decade plus has really flown by. It has not been an easy decade. But, it has been a treasured, precious, and spiritually profitable decade. I walk into Sarah's bedroom to get her ready for the day.

Little Sarah, not so little anymore, looks up at me from her bed. She smiles her sweet smile and makes her sweet happy sounds. Sarah speaks no words, but her smile says everything my heart could wish to hear.

Sarah has faced many battles. But, just as many victories. Perhaps not victories as the world would define them, but victories none-the-less. Victory such as joy even in struggles. Victory like love from a beautiful little girl we call ours. Blessings too many to count. I am blessed to be called Sarah's mom. Triumph as priorities that don't matter are replaced by those that do. And, life is a priority. We must stand up for those who cannot stand up for themselves. We must speak for those who have no words. We must guard life. Sarah's life. Every life.

I reach down to Sarah and give her a hug. And, then I remind her of something very important. I remind her that Psalm 139 tells us that she was *fearfully and wonderfully made,* and that God *knit her together in the womb* and *saw her substance.* I remind Sarah that God was there, knitting her together, when that extra chromosome became part of who she is. I remind her that it matters not that her physical body is disabled, she was and is "fearfully and wonderfully made." God makes no mistakes. She is no error of nature.

My fearfully and wonderfully designed child is here, and she is here with purpose. We are not on an aimless journey. There is a reason. And, there is work to do. There are frightened, expecting parents out there who have just been given "bad" news that the ultrasound shows this or the amniocentesis diagnoses that, or the early AFP test reveals a possible problem. There are professional people and family and friends around them, many who think they are being compassionate and well-intentioned by counseling these frightened parents to abort their child.

The world wants us to believe we would be better off if that disabled child is not born. That we don't have what it takes to care for and raise a special child. We are tempted to think that, if this child won't have a normal life, why have life at all? We are frightened and anxious about how a disabled child will affect our plans and our lives and our finances. The world wants us to believe this child is an accident and that abortion is the simple answer to solve the "problem." But, this is not a problem to solve. This is a life!

As with any child, a disabled child will have and will bring both joy and sorrow. As with any child, a disabled child will achieve milestones, will experience successes and failures. The accomplishments may be different, but there will be accomplishments. And, you will find, as I have found, that as your disabled child achieves a developmental milestone or overcomes an obstacle or succeeds in defeating a barrier, your joy will be great.

Special children bring a special joy.

God doesn't slip up while He is "knitting together" children in the womb. There are no mistakes in His design. The developing child, whether disabled or "normal" is precious. Twelve years ago, I would never have thought I could do what I am doing. Today, I can imagine no greater privilege."

JANUARY 24

Life. On Saturday, we received a bill from a radiology group who had read some of our Sarah's radiology films (we never met them, of course). The dates of service on this bill were September 19, 2001 and December 18, 2001, nearly two years ago! The proper insurance information was provided on those dates to the medical group, and yet here we are, almost two years later, holding a bill in our hands. As much as I wanted to, I could not call the billing company until Tuesday afternoon.

So, I placed the bill on the table, and waited for Tuesday.

Tuesday arrived. The mail came. Guess what…another bill, from the same billing company, but from another radiologist (same medical location), for a more recent date of service (5-3-03). This radiologist had read Sarah's bladder ultrasound films (we never met him, of course). As usual, I had provided all the proper insurance information at the time services were rendered, yet a bill arrived none-the-less. But, this bill was different. This bill was on pink colored paper rather than blue colored paper. As I read the pink paper, I started to fume. The pink paper was sent as a warning, for the next step will be a collection agency. How am I to understand this…a service provided two years ago which is yet unpaid (despite my responsible handling of the matter) is not causing collections threats, but a service provided less than four months ago is?

I felt very frustrated because I had done everything I was supposed to do. To make a long story short, it was Tuesday afternoon, and I could now call the billing company. So I did. Guess what? They blamed the insurance companies. Thus, I called the insurance companies. I got an answering machine at one and no answer at another (I let the phone ring at least thirty times, and yes, it was the right number). Since it was nearly 5:00 PM, I decided that anybody who actually did answer the phone at that time of the day would mess up everything anyhow, so it would be better to wait, as much as I hate such loose ends, until tomorrow.

With the nonsense of the phone calls tabled until tomorrow, I decided to step outside and breathe deeply of the beautiful summer day. As I walked out the door, I noticed my garden. I hate gardening, but I love my garden, and I have worked hard this year tending it. I planted a rose bush and have been babying it. I spent time learning how to properly plant it, how to care for it, what to do to protect it once winter marches in, how to keep the bugs from eating it up. However, my poor beloved rose, while surviving, is not thriving. It is stick-like spindly and sickly looking despite my best efforts.

How surprised I was, then, when I stepped out my door, to behold two blooming pink roses atop my skinny rose bush. They were the most beautiful roses I had ever seen. Yet, they were more than roses. They were reminders. Two bills. Two roses. A choice to make. Certainly the bills needed to be dealt with. But need they wreck the rest of this God-given day? Need they be the first thing I think of when I wake up tomorrow morning? The roses reminded me, no, they need not be. Deal with the bills, but keep focused on the roses and all of God's good gifts to us.

JANUARY 25

Lord,

Help me to be useful when I encounter hurting people.

May I speak with restraint and wisdom and love.

I ran into some old friends today.

About three years ago their son committed suicide.

They talked about it. Told me they were coping.

I was reminded as we visited not to assume that everyone grieves the same way.

God has blessed me with joy.

He prepared me for Sarah's death.

He has made it possible for me to experience joy even in sorrow…

Yet, I must be sensitive.

While there is absolute truth, there are relative experiences…and one person's walk is different from another person's…and the journey through grief is unique to each.

It would be cruel for me to expect that everyone else's experience with grief is similar to mine.

There are many ways that hearts can break.

My friends who buried their son, they know the gospel. They know truth.

They didn't need a sermon today.

They didn't need to hear my story today.

They needed a listening ear, and so I listened to my friends.

They needed a shoulder to cry on. So I gave them my shoulder. And now I pray for them…in God's time…to experience joy…the joy of walking with God along even difficult paths.

JANUARY 26

Dear Father,

Transform me!

Renew me!

Give me a heart of flesh.

I pray for a heart that wants to know Christ and the power of His resurrection and the fellowship of sharing in His sufferings.

I want such a heart to beat within me.

May this be the desire of my life…to KNOW Christ!

Father, there is such power in this knowledge, in the reality of Christ's resurrection. Help us to know that power and experience the miracle of salvation.

Everything, everything, everything is LOSS compared to the surpassing greatness of knowing Jesus Christ.

This is truth. Make it, Lord, reality in my life, my husband's life, the lives of each in our sweet family, and in the lives of my students.

Jesus, Your name is a refuge. May Your name ever be upon our lips.

JANUARY 27

Heavenly Father,

I raise my voice to You, a new song I bring, a song of praise to You, Creator of heaven and earth and all that is therein!

Father, I pray for eyes to see and for ears to hear. My eyes, my ears, not of my physical body only, but of my spirit, help them to work as they ought. I pray for each soul in our families to have eyes that see and ears that hear You and Your truth.

Protect our hearts from waxing cold and growing hard. Protect us from becoming dull of hearing. When our eyes see and our ears hear, by Your grace, give us understanding in heart and mind. Heal troubled and confused minds and calm our anxious hearts with the truth of who You are and all that You can accomplish in a life…salvation, security, newness of life.

There is a day of harvest soon to come. It is a day when the tares will be separated from the wheat and cast into a furnace of fire where there will be wailing and gnashing of teeth. Lord, may each person in each of our families be part of Your family. Lord may we be wheat, not tares, growing for You. May we each be ready when the harvest comes. May we be the righteous shining forth as the sun in the Kingdom of the Father. The wicked one day will be severed from the just. Through the precious blood of Christ, may we be of the just, clothed in Christ's righteousness and justified fully and forever.

Jesus, Your Name is Righteous….and to You I sing a song of praise!

JANUARY 28

"They didn't even appreciate it."

"If I had it all to do over again, I wouldn't have because they weren't even thankful!"

Are we called to help only the appreciative and grateful?

As Christians we already know the answer to that question.

Why are we to help the unappreciative?

Jesus did.

Sometimes it is we who are the unappreciative and the ungrateful.

When we are kind to the undeserving, it is peculiar.

We are called to be peculiar.

To sow seeds.

To be salt and light.

To remember how much we have been blessed.

To demonstrate our gratitude to God by willingly giving to those who are ungrateful to us.

Help us, Lord, for we are a selfish people.

JANUARY 29

Dear Lord,

How grateful I am to You! How glad I am to know Your Name. How truly I do believe that You will not forsake me. I pray for my students. I pray for our families, near and far. You, Lord, know the true needs of each. You know each well. To each, Father, reveal Yourself.

May they know to seek You. May they trust in You. May they believe You are who You say You are. May they believe Your promise that You will not forsake those who seek and trust You.

You know the many things we are tempted to trust in besides You. None of these can save. This is a truth that must pierce and challenge us and ultimately change us. It is truth requiring repentance, a new heart, a turning away from anything that we trust in or boast in other than You. Help us to turn toward You, determined to gaze intently upon Your holiness, beauty, and perfect character. Recognizing, as we gaze upon You, how unclean we are and how deeply we need the cleansing blood of Christ.

Help us to make this turn and look full in Your face. On You, the Solid Rock, we can be saved and build eternal futures and purposeful lives to Your glory!

JANUARY 30

From <u>The Deeper Christian Life</u> by Andrew Murray [4]

"God wants us to learn the lesson that when we fall, then we can cry to Jesus, and at once He reaches out His hand. Remember, Peter walked back to the boat without sinking again. Why? Because Christ was very near him. Remember, it is quite possible, if you use your failure rightly, to be far nearer Christ after it than before. Use it rightly, I say. That is, come and acknowledge, 'In me there is nothing, but I am going to trust my Lord unboundedly.' Let every failure teach you to cling afresh to Christ, and He will prove Himself a mighty and a loving Helper. The presence of Jesus restored! Yes, Christ took him by the hand and helped him, and I don't know whether they walked hand in hand those forty or fifty yards back to the boat or whether Christ allowed Peter to walk beside Him. But this I know, they were very near each other, and it was the nearness to his Lord that strengthened him....do believe that it is possible for the presence of Jesus to be with us every day and all the way. Your God has given you Christ, and He wants to give you Christ into your heart in such a way that His presence shall be with you every moment of your life...

"Who is willing to lift up his eyes and his heart and to exclaim, 'I want to live according to God's standard?' Who is willing? Who is willing to cast himself into the arms of Jesus and to live a life of faith – victorious over the winds and the waves, over the circumstances and difficulties? Who is willing to say this, 'Lord, bid me come to Thee upon the water?' Are you willing? Listen! Jesus says, 'Come.' Will you step out at this moment? ...Oh, come out of the boat of past experiences at once; come out of the boat of external circumstances; come out of the boat, and step out on the word of Christ, and believe, 'With Jesus I can walk upon the water.'"
From <u>The Deeper Christian Life</u> by Andrew Murray [4]

JANUARY 31

Snow day tomorrow? Maybe...

I just took a walk outside, down to the creek behind the house. When I turned and looked back at the house, it was shrouded in a cloud of blowing snow. Big flakes were falling, the wind was blowing, the trees were bending, and snow was flying both from the sky and from the ground as the wind picked it up and carried it horizontally across the yard. Beautifully blizzard-like!

The only sounds I heard in the back yard were the blowing wind, the running creek, and an occasional bark from some excited dog in the distance. As I walked, I prayed. I prayed for my family to all be safe in this weather. I thanked

God for my family, my friends, my students. I thanked God that I have a warm home to walk into, a soft bed to sleep in, clothes to wear, and food to eat.

I was walking in a storm, but nearby was shelter. I praised God for that. I looked to the sky. I could see neither moon nor stars. They were hidden behind snow and low, heavy clouds. But, I knew that behind the clouds and behind the snow, the moon and stars were still there. And I praised God that even when I can't see the moon and stars, I know they still are and they still are where they are supposed to be. And, I praised the God who hung the moon and stars in place! I praise Him that even when I can't see Him, I know He still is. He is still there, even in the storms.

As I walked toward the house, toward the warmth and comforts waiting for me, I prayed for faith to love God more than I love things. I prayed that, should the day ever come when I must do without the comforts, the house, the food, the stuff, that I would still be a person who would praise Him…that being His girl, washed in the blood of Christ, forever certain of my everlasting position in Him, would be enough to cause me to sing a song, a song to Him.

January's Apologetic Moment...Contend for the faith

Do Starting Assumptions Matter?

When I was a student, long ago and far away, none of my science teachers spoke about starting assumptions and presuppositions. I guess the starting assumptions were assumed true, making discussion of them unnecessary.

Let's consider them...

What were (are) some of the starting assumptions in secular science?

Naturalism – only natural explanations are allowed.

Materialism – only matter exists.

The rationality and orderliness of the universe do not require an explanation, they simply are.

The universe is billions of years old.

Darwinian evolution is true and the science is settled.

Science always involves objective measurements and objectivity.

Religious faith is an enemy of science.

Are there problems and consequences with these starting assumptions?

Indeed.

Let's consider some of the flaws of these assumptions...

Assumption: Scientific explanations must be framed within materialism and naturalism – only naturalistic explanations are allowed. FLAW: God is automatically excluded. Even if God is a logical, reasonable explanation, He must be excluded because He is not a naturalistic, materialistic explanation.

Assumption: The rationality of the universe does not require an explanation, it simply is. FLAW: From where arose the orderly laws from which we are able to even have science in the first place? Why is the universe rational and orderly as opposed to chaotic and unpredictable?

Assumption: The universe is old, at least 14 billion years, and our solar system is 4 billion years old. FLAW: What is the actual evidence for an old universe? What about evidences (such as lunar recession, the predominance of spiral arm galaxies, short period comets, thermal equilibrium of the universe) that are better explained by a young universe?

Assumption: Darwinian evolution is true and the science is settled. FLAW: Darwinian evolution applies its assumptions to its evidences. For example – Darwinian evolutionists claim homology (similar structures in different kinds of animals) demonstrates a common ancestor. But, homology could also be logically explained by a common Creator rather than a common ancestor. Other issues that are problematic and that undermine the arguments used in support of Darwinian evolution include: the Cambrian explosion, lack of transitional forms in the fossil record, the origin of life in the first place, the presence of information within DNA…from where came this information?

Assumption: Science always involves objective measurements. FLAW: This is simply not true. There is science that is observable and measurable, with which we are all familiar. Then there is science that is based on models and interpretation. This is forensic (or historical) science. This type of science is necessary when something can't be repeated…such as a murder. Or the origin of the universe, the origin of the planet, the origin of life. Since these events were one-time events, they cannot be repeated. Thus, we study them from a distance, trying to make sense of what we observe. This requires interpretation. And interpretation always involves assumptions and bias…which is ok…but we must be honest about this.

Assumption: Religious faith is the enemy of science. FLAW: Sometimes religious folk are even disrespectfully referred to as "flat-earthers." Superstition may be an enemy of science. But religious faith is not. **It was Christianity that brought the world out of the Dark Ages. The founding fathers of many of the fields of science were Bible-believing, God-fearing men who were using the brain God gave them to learn about the world in which God placed them. Here are a few of them…**

Francis Bacon (1561-1626):	Scientific method
Johann Kepler (1571-1630):	Scientific astronomy
Robert Boyle (1627-1691):	Gas dynamics
Isaac Newton (1642-1727)	Laws of motion, law of universal gravitation
Carolus Linneaus (1707-1778)	Taxonomy
William Herschel (1738-1822)	Galactic astronomy
John Dalton (1766-1844)	Atomic theory
Georges Cuvier (1769-1832)	Comparative anatomy
Humphrey Davy (1778-1829)	Thermokinetics
Michael Faraday (1791-1867)	Electromagnetics
Samuel F.B. Morse (1791-1872)	Telegraph
James Joule (1818-1889)	Thermodynamics
Rudolph Virchow (1821-1902)	Pathology

Louis Pasteur (1822-1895)	Bacteriology, pasteurization, biochemistry
Gregor Mendel (1822-1884)	Genetics
Henri Fabre (1823-1915)	Entomology
William Thompson (Lord Kelvin)	Absolute temperature
Joseph Lister (1827-1912)	Antiseptic surgery
Joseph Clerk Maxwell (1831-1879)	Electrodynamics
William Ramsay (1852-1916)	Isotopic chemistry, element transmutation

What about the Christian worldview? Does it, too, have starting assumptions?

Indeed!   Starting assumptions are unavoidable.   The difference between the biblical worldview model and the secular science worldview model is that we acknowledge the existence of starting assumptions. We are honest about our presuppositions.

One of our starting assumptions is that God is allowed to be considered as an explanation. We assume that an intelligent, rational God could – logically – create an orderly universe. We assume that an intelligent, rational Creator could – logically – create complex life. We assume that an intelligent, rational Designer could – logically – impose information into DNA.

We acknowledge the Bible is authoritative, and thus we start on and stand upon His revelation.

Yes, we do have starting assumptions.

But let's be clear: both models – the biblical creation science model and the secular Darwinian evolutionary model – require faith.

Let's just be honest about that as we go about the business of living and learning.

Beware that thou forget not the LORD thy God.
Deuteronomy 8:11a

February

"Atheism turns out to be too simple.
If the whole universe has no meaning,
we should never have found out that it has no meaning..."
— C.S. Lewis

FEBRUARY 1

Not ten minutes ago, I stepped out of our basement door and into the dark crispness of an early February morning. All was quiet. All was calm. Alone, but not alone. I breathed the chill air deeply, and I smelled the freshness, the cleanness of the snow and cold around me. And I remembered. I breathed in memories, I drifted back decades ago…

A teenage farm girl, alone but not alone….walking in the woods, snow to the knees, the world quiet and calm, the smells crisp and clean…this same teenage farm girl after evening chores lacing up white skates with metallic blades and skating clumsily on a slick driveway between house and barn, under a clear sky with diamond stars hung in the heavens by a gracious, beautiful God.

Life was quiet back then.

The only sound was silver blades slicing through icy ground. Alone, but not alone. And I breathed the cold deeply and memorized the smell of clean. And I sensed God's presence in the pure quietness of this farm girl's heart.

Here and now, over thirty years later, I stand beneath the same stars. I breathe deeply God-given air into God-designed lungs. Memories wake and tears well and balance and then slip from corners of grateful eyes.

I lift hands, and I praise the Creator of the stars and the Redeemer of my soul. I look back on life, and I see God always with me, always calling me to Him, His plan much greater than mine.

I was a slow learner of His great truths. He remained faithful to me even when I was not to Him.

My God pursued me...from a farm house and open fields on Partridge Road, to the campus of a secular suburban college, to the world of the working and down the aisle of marriage. He saw my tears of joy when I became a mother and held for the first time my beautiful girl. He saw my tears of sorrow when I laid this beloved child in a grave.

Alone, but not alone.

He knew me and knows me well and still.

And as I stood this morning, hands held up and tears sliding down, I felt humbled....humbled by memories of an unchanging, faithful God who pursued me and has given me life and life eternal.

FEBRUARY 2

Dear Father,

We are just getting home. Mark and I went today to visit Mark's 90 year old uncle. He's old, and he's hard. Lord, what You say about salvation seems to him to be foolishness. But God, You are the all-powerful One, the God of miracles. Salvation is ALWAYS a miracle. As only You can, Father, soften Uncle's heart and draw him to You. I pray for all the hard-hearted in our family. You know them. They are trusting in themselves and their own perceived goodness. Or they are trusting in the church pew they warm each Sunday and neglect the rest of the week. Or, they are trusting in the lie that all go to heaven when life is over. Or, they foolishly think they have lots of time. Or, they wickedly love their sin more than they love You, and they bristle at the idea that You have the right to judge them.

Only You completely and accurately know each heart. Only You know what it will take. Soften hard hearts. Open blind eyes. Unstop deaf ears. Turn these hearts, eyes, and ears to You. Turn these souls to You. Make the gospel make sense to them. Make it real. And urgent. And necessary. This is not too hard for You to do, Lord! There is nothing too hard for You! Make the miracle of salvation a reality in hearts, minds and lives of the many this year in this family. Praise Your Holy Name!

In the Name of Jesus, the One who reconciles...the ONLY One who can reconcile.

FEBRUARY 3

October, 2006. 9:00 PM.

Bedtime for Sarah. She was snuggling with her Dad in his recliner, and her eyes were growing heavy. I picked her up and headed to her room. I laid her on her bed and sat beside her.   Sarah and I had recently started to read a Psalm every night at bedtime. Sometimes, I'm so tired I just want to skip it, get her quickly settled in, and head back to the living room and the couch and the television and escape for a few moments before I nod off myself.

Reading a Psalm to Sarah, though, always ends up blessing me. Exhaustion slows me down, and I can see what I might not always see when I'm in a hurry at the beginning of the day. Tonight, I read Psalm 3 to Sarah. *Lord, how are they increased that trouble me! Many are they that rise up against me. Many there be which say of my soul, There is no help for him in God. But thou, O Lord, art a shield for me; my glory, and the lifter up of mine head.*

I stopped. Stunned.

How had I read Psalm 3 in the past and missed this? *But thou, O Lord, art a shield for me; my glory, and the* **lifter up of mine head**. You see, Sarah is 10 years old, but we still need to carry her to bed. We still need to change diapers. Sarah had a stroke, from a rare disease called "moyamoya syndrome" when she was 20 months old. Since then, Sarah has depended on us for her every need moment by moment, day by day. She cannot sit independently or stand or walk or use her arms very well. She even has a hard time keeping her head up. So you see, the words, **lifter up of mine head** mean something quite literal to me, to her.

We finished reading the Psalm, and then we prayed. One of the things we prayed for that night, and have prayed for since that night, is for God to be the lifter up of Sarah's head.   Praying for this specific need, using God's specific words reminds me that it is God who controls not only the entire universe, but our very own bodies. It is He who is sovereign over all. Will this prayer, prayed in faith using the name of Jesus, bring healing and strength to Sarah's neck muscles?   She will, indeed, be whole and healed in heaven, but whether or not God chooses to lift her head here on earth, well, He owns that decision. I will trust Him to do what is best, understanding that "best" does not always mean "healed and normal." I will trust that it is true when the Bible states, *And we know that in all things God works for the good of those who love Him, who have been called according to His purpose (Romans 8:28)....and when Jesus states, I have told you these things, so that in me you may have peace. In this world you will have trouble. But take heart! I have overcome the world (John 16:33)......and Surely I (Jesus) am with you always, to the very end of the age (Matthew 28:20b)*. I will walk by faith that these promises are true no matter the circumstances, and it will matter not whether Sarah's head is lifted on this earth or in heaven to come.

The blessing of Psalm 3 has continued for me. Yesterday, I was busy. I seem always to be busy, and generally by mid-afternoon, as Sarah arrives home from school and Mark arrives home from work and as time closes in on needing to get dinner prepared, dishes done, baths taken and given, my energy starts to dwindle, and I sometimes feel pressed upon with too many tasks and never enough time.

On this particular day, I had just put Sarah in her stander, dinner was cooking, Mark had just left for the store to get a few groceries, and I was walking quickly out to the weedy wild area behind our house to dump some compost that should have been dumped earlier in the day. It was windy and cold out. I didn't bother with a coat - who has time? As I walked, the words of Psalm 3 came to me...*lifter up of my head.* And, I started to understand. God wants to be the lifter up of my head as well as Sarah's. Sarah and I, our needs are different, but the promise and the presence are the same. Sarah needs God's touch to strengthen her physical body. I need God's touch to strengthen my spiritual journey. My head needs to be lifted so that my eyes will be always upon HIM...whether I'm vacuuming, cooking, cleaning, washing dishes, caring for Sarah, caring for my husband, visiting with a friend, encountering an enemy, running late, having a good day, having a bad day...whatever the task and the work at hand or the condition of my life, my eyes need to be fixed upon Jesus. God wants to lift up my head, off the stifling things of this world and onto His high and abundant promises.

With my head lifted, and my eyes upon Him, those things that would overwhelm in the world take their proper position and Jesus takes His...the author and finisher of my faith, my strength and my shield, my joy and my peace, my counselor and comforter, my Savior in a fallen world.

FEBRUARY 4

Dear Father…The Hope of Israel and God Most High…

I pray, Lord, for the heart of a humble servant to beat within me.

Through Your grace, may my soul be a soul that glorifies You and rejoices in God my Savior. Thank You, Father, for the great things You have done for me. Thank You for the great things You are doing. You called. I heard. I believed and embraced and received the truth…I am a sinner who needed a Savior to bear the unbearable price of my pride, my selfishness, my idols, my foolishness. My sin. You bore them and because You have, I have crossed over from death to life. I am no longer condemned. I know a time is coming when the dead will hear the voice of the Son of God and those who hear will live. Jesus will judge and those in the grave will come out. The righteous ones clothed in Christ's garments and washed clean in His blood will rise to live. The rest will rise unto condemnation. They may have done many mighty and good deeds, but apart from Christ these good deeds are filthy and useless.

Father, I am grateful for Your great salvation. I am grateful that it does not depend on my being good enough. I can never meet Your standard apart from Christ. There is no such thing as our good outweighing our bad, for it is all wicked and impure if Christ is not in it. I pray for all those in this family who are trusting in themselves and a perception of their own goodness. Reveal to them, Lord, the danger they are in. Reveal this, Father, before it is too late and grant them willing spirits and tender hearts to hear and receive and embrace the truth.

In Jesus' Name…the Servant of God and Man of Sorrows…

FEBRUARY 5

I've been so tired lately.

Unconfessed sin.

Exhausting me.

I was alone in the house this morning. Mark had gone to men's prayer at church. I was getting ready to exercise. I was in the middle of putting my hair up in preparation for my work-out, when grief flooded over me.

Not grief over losing Sarah…

But grief over all the times I could have been a better mother…all the times I could have been more patient, more tender, more attentive, more sacrificial.

I loved Sarah. We enjoyed our time together.

But I know my heart and its bitterness, and I know I had my share of selfish and unkind moments.

I know I could have been a better mom.

And now she's gone.

For the lost moments, I grieve.

I stood in my bathroom…overcome. I was in the vice grip of the Holy Spirit, being held in the purifying fire of godly sorrow that leads to repentance. Right there, I fell to my knees. I cried and cried and prayed.

I confessed my sin.

And God took it. He threw it in the depths of the deepest sea…removed…as far as the east is from the west. There is now no condemnation. For I am in Christ Jesus the Lord. White as snow. Assured that this is a burden I no longer have to carry.

It is finished.

His blood is sufficient.

The idol of unconfessed sin has been cast down and its power broken.

Praise God!

When my tears ebbed and the time to stand up from the floor came, I could picture my God stooping down to lift me up. Out of the miry clay, He raised me up. From my low estate…into His eternal arms.

FEBRUARY 6

Dear Father,

The sun is shining brightly today. Like You, Lord. You always are shining. Your glory cannot be measured or contained. I pray, Lord, For Your light and truth to shine powerfully upon the lives, minds, hearts, thoughts of each in our family. May Your truth burn through to the darkest corners and blaze into the most unkempt and neglected crevices of each of our lives. Help us to be people who hold our lives out to You, who acknowledge both Your sovereign right and perfect ability to judge our lives, our words, and the intents of our hearts.

I stood today next to my child's grave. I was reminded of the terrible brevity of life. For each, it will soon pass. May this be a family of people prepared for that moment, for that appointed day when we breathe our last and enter eternity. Heaven or Hell awaits. May the urgency of this truth push us forward unto salvation and then unto witnessing and testifying of the gospel of Jesus Christ, the Way, the Truth, and the Life!

Jesus, You are the Righteous Judge and Redeemer, and in Your name I pray…

FEBRUARY 7

1997....It has been 14 months since Sarah had her stroke. This past year plus has been a year of devastating losses. And, a strange year of growth. It is not my intention to write about my emotions over these 14 months – but they will show up anyhow.

Peter and Paul tell us to rejoice in our suffering (Romans 5:3, Romans 12:14, I Peter 3). These words used to mean (not that I ever really thought much about suffering before), that I should be joyful when I suffer and happy because of the suffering. Their words mean something different to me now.

I will never be able to feel joyful that my daughter had a stroke. What I am joyful about is that, somehow, God has drawn me close to Him. I am rejoicing that the Lord is near, not that my child struggles.

I am hungry to know God now in a way I never felt before. Sadly, I don't think I would ever have experienced such hunger had Sarah remained strong and healthy. That makes me angry at myself sometimes. I want to understand the Lord better. Actually, I want to understand Him completely. But, one of the first things I had to learn is that I am not going to understand as completely as I would like. Not all of my questions will be answered. That is so frustrating to me, but I guess that is part of the definition of faith – believing even when there are nagging questions and doubts. Perhaps especially when there are questions and doubts. And truly, if God were completely comprehendible, He then would be a small and limited God...for our minds are small and limited...but my Creator and Redeemer God is not at all small...and thus those moments in which I fail to comprehend Him completely are ultimately moments of His greatness and my smallness.

And so, by faith I walk, and in those moments when I feel really crazy and overwhelmed, I think about Psalm 46. Over and over I repeat the verse that says, *Be still and know that I am God....*

And crazy leaves and God's peace...because of His presence...arrives.

FEBRUARY 8

Dear Father...The Lord is my rock...

I pray for Your strong and solid call to be heard by me, my husband, our family. Call us, even to the point of irritation, because irritation leads to action, and may we take action in Your direction. May the call of salvation, the gospel of Christ be heard and may those who hear, Lord, respond in humble brokenness falling before you. You heal the broken. You uplift the fallen.

Please, Lord, call. Please, Lord, be active in very obvious and unavoidable ways to all in our family. Make it absolutely impossible to ignore You or overlook You. May events, be they joyful or sorrowful, point the lost and dying souls in this family toward the cross. Bring them each, Lord, to Calvary and to that fount that washes clean and completely saves even the vilest. And, remind the proud, those who doubt they are vile, that before You their pride is one of the vilest sins of all. I pray for all those who are church-going folk. Keep them from trusting in their outward goodness. Trust not in church attendance for that cannot save!

Salvation is found in Christ alone. Not baptism. Not tithing. Not church membership. Certainly not in religion. May each in our family sit in pews of churches in which the full counsel of God is proclaimed and the gospel expressed. May our family hear it, and may each truly know and walk upon the path of deliverance bought and paid for by the blood of Jesus Christ.

Protect us, Lord, from any church that fails to proclaim the reality of sin and the need for the Savior. The way is narrow! Call clearly, Lord, each soul of our family to You. Draw them to you. This is my plea and may this plea ever rise before You, Holy Lord, Creator and Savior.

In Jesus' Name, the Rock strong and solid…

FEBRUARY 9

The Earth is full of the goodness of the Lord. *By the word of the Lord were the heavens made; and all the host of them by the breath of His mouth…Let all the earth fear the Lord: let all the inhabitants of the world stand in awe of Him. For He spake, and it was done; He commanded, and it stood fast (Psalm 33:5b, 8, 9).*

I sure do love winter! There is something about winter that quietly reveals the truth that, yes, *the earth is full of the goodness of the Lord.*

I know, I know, some (perhaps most) are reading this and thinking, "What kind of a nut are you? Winter is awful!" Others may be reading it and thinking, "Sure, that's easy for you to say. You can stay home whenever you want. You don't have to drive in it to work every day!" Well, it's true.....I may be a nut, and no, I'm not forced into driving in this weather or working in this weather...but, if possible, grit your teeth and read on anyway...

There are simple things in winter that whisper volumes about the goodness of the Lord. I have never seen a more beautiful shade of blue than a blue winter sky on a sunny winter day against clean white snow. There is no blue in the world quite like it. When I look at that deep blue against that pure white, I stand amazed that God created colors. Yes, beautiful colors everywhere! Can you imagine our world without these precious shades and hues? Can you imagine a sunset without the variety of all the oranges and pinks and reds and yellows? Do you know that God designed these colors and the electromagnetic spectrum of which they are a part?

Yes, the earth is full of the goodness of the Lord!

This morning I bundled up in my husband's worn out brown jacket and took my morning walk behind the house, down by the little creek that winds its way across our backyard. In the summer, this little creek is but a big mud puddle full of stagnant water, tangled weeds, and happy mosquitoes. But, in the winter, the water runs sweetly by, and the trees and tangled brush that appear chaotic in the summer now are hidden or decorated with snow, white and pure. It was peaceful. I could hear Route 16 traffic in the near distance, but there behind the house and away from the rush of the cars and the trucks, the goodness of the Lord was falling from the sky in the shape of unique hexagonal snowflakes. Can you believe that God designs gloriously intricate snowflakes? What a creative God is He!

A couple weeks ago, we had a little warm up for a day or two. The snow on the ground reacted to the warm up. When I walked over it, the snow would crunch beneath my feet, and it seemed that walking on it was like walking on crème Brule in which the brittle, thin top layer would quietly break beneath my feet with each step taken. Just as the top layer of crème Brule gently breaks beneath a spoon.

Yes, the earth is full of the goodness of the Lord.

And, finally, there is hot chocolate on a cold winter day after being outside. You know, hot chocolate on a summer day is just not the same as hot chocolate on a winter day. The warmth of hot chocolate on a winter day is comforting and a reminder that we have an all-powerful, sovereign Lord who wants always to warm us on our cold days, befriend us on our lonely days, and guide us on our days of struggle and wonder.

It's true, the earth is full of the goodness of the Lord...blue skies against white snow, snowflakes gently falling, snow like crème Brule, hot chocolate. Yes, it really is true, the earth is full of the goodness of the Lord! A manger in Bethlehem where God became flesh, a lonely garden where Jesus cried out for strength to endure, a hill upon which a cross was raised and redemption made possible, blood running through the veins of Jesus in life and willingly shed for sinners in death, an empty tomb from whence the Savior rose...the ultimate victory for those who believe, for those who take the Savior's outstretched, nail scarred hand.

And someday, this same God who came in the flesh to save repentant sinners, will come again. Next time as King. He will reign in might and majesty forever, and the goodness of the Lord that we now experience will become the redemption of a fallen earth.

Yes, the earth is full of the goodness of the Lord!

FEBRUARY 10

From <u>Holiness</u> by John Charles Ryle [5]

"The first thing I have to say is this: true Christianity is a fight! True Christianity! Let us mind that word 'true'. There is a vast quantity of religion current in the world which is not true, genuine Christianity. It passes muster, it satisfies sleepy consciences; but it is not good money. It is not the real thing which was called Christianity eighteen hundred years ago. There are thousands of men and women who go to churches and chapels every Sunday, and call themselves Christians. Their names are in the baptismal register. They are reckoned Christians while they live. They are married with a Christian marriage service. They mean to be buried as Christians when they die. But you never see any 'fight' about their religion! Of spiritual strife and exertion and conflict and self-denial and watching and warring they know literally nothing at all. Such Christianity may satisfy man, and those who say anything against it may be thought very hard and uncharitable; but it certainly is not the Christianity of the Bible. It is not the religion which the Lord Jesus founded, and His apostles preached. It is not the religion which produces real holiness. True Christianity is a 'fight'.....

"Let us remember that some have seemed good soldiers for a little season, and talked loudly of what they would do, and yet turned back disgracefully in the day of battle....

"Let us remember that the eye of our loving Saviour is upon us morning, noon and night. He will never suffer us to be tempted above that we are able to bear. He can be touched with the feeling of our infirmities, for He suffered Himself being tempted. He knows what battles and conflicts are, for He Himself was assaulted by the prince of this world. Having such a High Priest, Jesus the Son of God, let us hold fast our profession (Heb. 4:14).

"Let us remember that thousands of soldiers before us have fought the same battle that we are fighting, and come off more than conquerors through Him that loved *them. They overcame by the blood of the Lamb, and so also may we. Christ's arm is quite as strong as ever, and Christ's heart is just as loving as ever. He that saved men and women before us is the One who never changes. He is 'able to save to the uttermost' all who 'come unto God by Him.' Then let us cast doubts and fears away. Let us follow 'them who through faith and patience inherit the promises', and are waiting for us to join them (Heb 7:25; 6:12).*

"Finally, let us remember that the time is short, and the coming of the Lord draweth nigh. A few more battles and the last trumpet shall sound, and the Prince of Peace shall come to reign on a renewed earth. A few more struggles and conflicts, and then we shall bid an eternal goodbye to warfare and to sin, to sorrow and to death. Then let us fight on to the last and never surrender. Thus saith the Captain of our salvation: 'He that overcometh shall inherit all things; and I will be his God, and he shall be My son'" (Rev. 21:7).
From <u>Holiness</u> by John Charles Ryle [5]

FEBRUARY 11

Here I sit. It's a rainy day. The house is peaceful.

Out the window, I glimpse cars speeding by on Route 16.

Life. It's so fast-paced.

I'm grateful for the calm and the quiet of my home in the middle of a very noisy world and a very busy life.

Lord, I do want to hear your voice. But, I get so easily distracted. I am more of a Martha than of a Mary, but as I get older and as I more easily tire, I am learning how to be like Mary, how to sit quietly at Your feet, soaking in Your presence. It's not my natural tendency, as You already know.

Lord, thank You for Your great patience with me.

Lord, I can be so foolish. I have an idol. It's called "my schedule." It's a schedule filled with good things... church things... Christian school things... but it's still just a schedule and it's not supposed to be more important to me than You are. Could it be that some of the most dangerous idols are the "good" ones? Forgive me, Lord, that I so often forget about You in the hectic rush of life. Help me, Lord. I need Your pace to overpower mine.

Lord, thank You for Your undeserved patience with me.

Lord, I'm tired. I am struggling to keep up. I am unable to keep up with all that is expected of me. Remind me of truth. The truth is, I need to follow You and You only. I need to do the work that You have designed for me. I need to find Your priorities and purpose for my life. Not everyone else's.

And to do that, I need to meet with You. In a quiet place. Every day.

FEBRUARY 12

What to do with "them"?

"Them" being those statements Jesus made that many modern Christian churches are now avoiding, ignoring, rationalizing, minimalizing. "Them" statements include words in red (i.e. spoken by Jesus) about a literal hell. "Them" statements include words in red (i.e. spoken by Jesus) about He being the exclusive way to eternal life with the Father. "Them" statements include words in red (i.e. spoken by Jesus) about the sacred nature of marriage between a man and a woman. "Them" statements include words in red (i.e. spoken by Jesus) about the way being narrow and few there be that find it and about people who think they are right with Him but are not and when the time comes they will be turned away and cast out.

"Them" statements, well "them" are hard to reconcile if "your" plan is to pave a broad and wide path that leads every one of every imaginable philosophy and belief system into heaven.

Truth is, we are not God. We don't get to decide, even though we sometimes think we do, what is true about the path to eternal life in heaven.

Sorry.

The final word rests with God, and He has given His final word and His truth in the Bible. Not everyone believes that. But, God is bigger than everyone, and what you or I believe has really no impact or influence on God's truth.

FEBRUARY 13

It just made me sad to watch. I was sitting at the kitchen table, drinking a cup of coffee. I was busy with paperwork, but had the television on for some background noise. "Good Morning America" drew me away from the paperwork when the news anchor began a story about Down syndrome...

A new prenatal test to screen for Down Syndrome...in the first trimester.

You see, my husband and I have a nine-year old daughter with Down Syndrome. Sarah is a blessing, and a gift from God in our lives. Sarah is a joy. She never feels sorry for herself. She has taught me more about faith, courage, hope, purpose, and priorities than any talking, walking person whose path has ever crossed mine. To say it's been easy would be a lie. To say that there are no bad days would be a lie. It is not all milk and honey and peaches and cream. There is a lot of work to do. There is a lot of worry to fight off. But nothing I have ever done in my life has ever made me feel so useful or given me so much meaning as taking care of my daughter.

My husband and I were thrilled when we found out I was pregnant with Sarah. I was 26 years old. It was a wonderful pregnancy. We decided to skip the prenatal blood test (AFP test) when it was offered. Besides the fact that I was considered a low-risk pregnancy, neither my husband nor myself would have ever considered terminating my pregnancy no matter what the diagnoses.

When I was seven months pregnant, my OB/GYN did an ultrasound as part of his protocol for all his pregnant patients. The ultrasound was abnormal. The mid-line of Sarah's head was not mid-line. She had hydrocephalus. Other appointments were scheduled with specialists and geneticists. More ultrasounds, a bunch of amniocentesis', and more difficult news... heart defect and Down Syndrome. As soon as Sarah's lungs were mature, she was delivered C-section on a beautiful June day in 1996.

She was absolutely, spectacularly wonderful. It took three months before our baby could come home from the hospital. But, home she came, and we just fell more and more in love with her every day. More medical problems came along. We dealt with each one the best we knew how. We grew used to doctors and nurses and medical appointments. We learned how to use feeding tubes, central venous lines, infusion pumps, and catheters. We've had to spend time thinking about the very obvious fact that our daughter could die. That reality has not led to despair, instead it has led to joy at every day that we are blessed to care for, learn from and share life with our girl. She has a good life. We have a good life. It certainly is not the life we expected. But, over time, it has become even more than the life we expected. We have learned that life is about more than convenience and comfort and ease. It's about doing the right thing.

So, there I sat this morning snapped to attention at the news story on "Good Morning America". According to the story, there is a new screening test, to determine if a baby may have Down Syndrome, available around the eleventh week of pregnancy. The anchor on "Good Morning America" wrapped up the story with the comment that such an early pregnancy screening tool results in more choices and options being available for women.

I just sat there sad.

The only reason to screen for Down Syndrome that early in pregnancy is to offer abortion. I know there are many people out there who would say, "Well, just because you and your husband have been able to handle your situation, doesn't mean that everyone can." I know that. But, I think that American women and American families have been deceived into believing that they cannot do things that they just might be able to do. And these things that they just might be able to do, i.e. care for a child with special needs, could possibly be the whole reason for their existence, and if they abort that baby, they abort that perfect opportunity to grow into the best person they can be. There is no question about it, special needs' children can be hard on a family's finances, straining on a marriage, and physically and emotionally exhausting. But, American people are underestimating their ability to cope and grow and handle the difficult situations of life. They are allowing themselves to be deceived into the belief that "choice" in the form of abortion makes their life better, or at least more simple. It does neither.

Down syndrome is not just an extra chromosome. Down syndrome is an opportunity. And, I embrace my daughter with Down syndrome and all her other medical problems as the best experience of my life, and the best gift God has ever given to me.

FEBRUARY 14

Dear loving and merciful Father,

It's Valentine's Day.

Help me to love You. Help me to love others. I love my family and, Lord, it is my heart's desire for them to each love You. Help us, Lord, to be like the wise virgins – the ones who were prepared for the coming groom, the ones whom the groom found waiting and ready with oil in their lamps upon His arrival (Matthew 25).

Lord, truly, we know neither the day nor the hour when You will come again or the day and the hour when our lives here will end. Protect and save all in our family, Lord. May they not die apart from You and the cleansing of Christ's shed bled. The horror of death apart from You! To hear the words, *"I tell you the truth I don't know you!"* and have the door to the wedding banquet forever closed. The horror it will be!

I pray for all in my family now and in generations to come. May each be prepared with oil in their lamps. May each be ready. Waiting. Watching. Clothed in wedding garments that make them fit for the feast and the marriage, garments of righteousness purchased by Jesus Christ. This is the cry of my heart and the plea of my lips on behalf of all my family. My people.

In the name of the Bridegroom, Jesus Christ.

FEBRUARY 15

From Foxe: Voices of the Martyrs [6]

Alban (304 AD)

"Alban lived near Verulamium, a town in Roman Britain situated near the modern city of St. Albans in Hertfordshire on what is now park and agricultural land. A pagan and a soldier in the Roman Army, Alban became the first Christian martyr in Britain...

"In 303, the emperor of the Eastern Roman Empire, Diocletian, published his edict against the Christians. At some point, Alban gave shelter to a Christian priest who was fleeing the authorities. Impressed by the priest's lifestyle and devotion, and through their many conversations, Alban was converted to Christ and baptized.

"Hearing that the priest was in that vicinity, the local magistrate sent soldiers to search for him. As they approached Alban's cottage, he changed clothes with the priest, wearing his hooded cloak, and was arrested instead. Alban was brought before the magistrate as he was offering sacrifices to the pagan gods. Seeing that the prisoner was Alban and not the priest, the magistrate became enraged that Alban had freely offered himself to the soldiers in place of his guest.

"The magistrate ordered Alban to be dragged to the pagan gods and ordered the punishment for Alban that the priest would have received, if Alban had indeed become a Christian. Alban declared, 'I worship and adore the true and living God who created all things.'

"Alban, who had voluntarily given himself up to the persecutors as a Christian, was not in the least afraid of the magistrate's threats. Instead, he openly declared that he would not obey the government's commands. Then the magistrate said: 'Of what house and stock are you?'

"Alban replied: 'What business is if of yours of what lineage I am born? If on the other hand you desire to hear the truth of my religion, know that I am now a Christian and devote myself to Christian service.'

"Angered even more, the magistrate ordered Alban to be beaten, hoping that he would recant. But Alban patiently endured the torture. Realizing that Alban was determined to confess Christ, he ordered him to be beheaded.

"Alban was taken out of the town Verulamium to the top of the hill across the river. The place of his beheading is where St. Alban's Cathedral now stands. The most probable date for Alban's martyrdom is 304.

"Alban, thus, became the first martyr in Britain. The second was the executioner that was ordered to kill him, who after hearing his testimony became a Christian on the spot and refused to follow the order. The third was the priest, who after hearing that Alban had been arrested in his place, hurried to the court to turn himself in and save Alban."
From <u>Foxe: Voices of the Martyrs</u> [6]

FEBRUARY 16

For many years, I allowed lies to dominate my thoughts about the nature of God. I fit the mold of a modern sort of spiritual person. I was a person who believed the "do what works for you as long as it doesn't hurt me" mentality. Relative truth seemed reasonable and absolute truth arcane. Such a mentality relieved me of any responsibility of sharing the gospel if such sharing would make another person – or me – uncomfortable.

But, the truth is very often uncomfortable. And the truth is…we are unworthy to stand in the presence of a Holy God.

We live in a political and social climate where our "rights" and "entitlements" are of epic proportion. But, truly, we have neither rights nor entitlement – on our own merit – to stand in the presence of Holiness.

This is truth that is these days neglected. We have forgotten our unworthiness. We compare ourselves to one another, and feel quite confident in our goodness. We fail to see ourselves in the light of His perfection and absolute moral standards. We become apathetic and indifferent to the concept of sin. Once we dismiss sin, we dismiss our need for the grace of God expressed in Christ.

Yet, the Bible tells us clearly that, unless we are covered by Jesus' blood on the cross, we are unworthy and will not spend eternity in the presence of God Almighty:

*There is no difference, for **all have sinned and fall short of the glory of God**, and are justified freely by His grace through the redemption that came by Christ Jesus*

(Romans 3:23,24).

But He (Jesus) continued, 'You are from below; I am from above. You are of this world; I am not of this world. **I told you that you would die in your sins; if you do not believe that I am the one I claim to be, you will indeed die in your sins'** *(John 8:23-24).*

Jesus said, 'For God did not send His Son into the world to condemn the world, but to save the world through Him. Whoever believes in Him in not condemned, **but whoever does not believe stands condemned already because he has not believed in the name of God's one and only Son'** *(John 3:17, 18).*

He will punish those who do not know God and do not obey the gospel of our Lord Jesus. They will be punished with everlasting destruction and shut out from the presence of the Lord and from the majesty of His power on the day He comes to be glorified in His Holy people and to be marveled at among all those who have believed (2 Thessalonians 1:8-10).

Exodus 20: The Ten Commandments…God is a HOLY God:

And God spake all these words, saying, I am the LORD thy God, which have brought thee out of the land of Egypt, out of the house of bondage.

Thou shalt have no other gods before me.

Thou shalt not make unto thee any graven image, or any likeness of anything that is in heaven above, or that is in the earth beneath, or that is in the water under the earth.

Thou shalt not bow down thyself to them, nor serve them: for I the LORD thy God am a jealous God, visiting the iniquity of the fathers upon the children unto the third and fourth generation of them that hate me; And shewing mercy unto thousands of them that love me, and keep my commandments.

Thou shalt not take the name of the LORD thy God in vain; for the LORD will not hold him guiltless that taketh his name in vain.

Remember the sabbath day, to keep it holy.

Six days shalt thou labour, and do all thy work: But the seventh day is the sabbath of the LORD thy God: in it thou shalt not do any work, thou, nor thy son, nor thy daughter, thy manservant, nor thy maidservant, nor thy cattle, nor thy stranger that is within thy gates: For in six days the LORD made heaven and earth, the sea, and all that in them is, and rested the seventh day: wherefore the LORD blessed the sabbath day, and hallowed it.

Honour thy father and thy mother: that thy days may be long upon the land which the LORD thy God giveth thee.

Thou shalt not kill.

Thou shalt not commit adultery.

Thou shalt not steal.

Thou shalt not bear false witness against thy neighbour.

Thou shalt not covet thy neighbour's house, thou shalt not covet thy neighbour's wife, nor his manservant, nor his maidservant, nor his ox, nor his ass, nor any thing that is thy neighbour's.

Matthew 5: Jesus expands the Ten Commandments to include sins of the heart:

(Jesus said), Ye have heard that it was said of them of old time, Thou shalt not kill; and whosoever shall kill shall be in danger of the judgment: **But I say unto you, That whosoever is angry with his brother without a cause shall be in danger of the judgment***... Ye have heard that it was said by them of old time, Thou shalt not commit adultery:* **But I say unto you, That whosoever looketh on a woman to lust after her hath committed adultery with her already in his heart.**

Like it or not, we stand naked and helpless before a Righteous Judge.

Our pride recoils. For we want to be able to save ourselves.

Stop. Consider His holiness. Review His standards.

See your helpless estate before the eyes of the all-knowing, all-seeing, all-powerful Creator God.

FEBRUARY 17

Being "good" in the eyes of the world is simply not good enough to get into heaven. "Good" in the eyes of the world basically is defined as not breaking laws (at least not those that affect other people), not interfering in other people's business, doing charity work from time to time, and working hard. The basic premise is that you can do whatever you want as long as you don't hurt somebody else. The truth is, though, **sin hurts God**.   Check out the Ten Commandments sometime. Every time we break one of these commandments, we hurt God (even if we don't break the laws of the world). Like it or not, whether the world wants to tell us this or not, and even if we never break a single law of the world, we are sinful beings.

It is hard now-a-days, at least in our society, for people to understand and recognize sin. And, that is a dangerous situation for a person's eternal soul. Why is it dangerous? Because the first step in coming to God for salvation in Christ is recognizing the need. The true need is that sin needs to be washed off our souls, and only Jesus can do that washing permanently and completely. But, if we do not understand that we are sinners, then we are at risk.

If we believe we are already clean, we will not come to Jesus.

And, if we don't come to Jesus, we will die in our sins.

Apart from Jesus Christ, all our righteous acts are filthy rags (Isaiah 64:6).

But, if we confess our sins, He is faithful and just to forgive us our sins and to cleanse us from all unrighteousness (I John 1:9).

We should be…we must be…completely undone by the holiness of God.

FEBRUARY 18

Many people believe that there are multiples path to enter the Kingdom of Heaven.

But, what does Scripture say?

Jesus said, "I am the way and the truth and the life. No one comes to the Father except through me" (John 14:6).

For there is one God and one mediator between God and men, the man Christ Jesus (1 Timothy 2:5).

Jesus answered and said unto him, Verily, verily, I say unto thee, Except a man be born again, he cannot see the kingdom of God (John 3:3).

He that believeth on the Son hath everlasting life: and he that believeth not the Son shall not see life; but the wrath of God abideth on him (John 3:36).

I used to believe that somehow all religions are the same. I believed this because I wanted to. It let me off the hook. It made things less complicated. But then I started to seek rather than to assume, and what I found when I sought was eye opening and life changing.

Ultimately I discovered that Christianity is unique among the religions of the world. At the center of Christianity is the cross – God invading humanity. He does it all. This is unique among the faiths: God reaching out to mankind to rescue and God becoming Man to redeem man.

No, all the faiths are not the same.

No, there are not multiple ways to heaven.

If there could be other ways to heaven, why would Jesus suffer such a horrible death on pagan cross? If there are other ways, the cross is foolish! The words of the Apostle Paul in the book of Galatians express this: *I do not ignore or nullify the [gracious gift of the] grace of God [His amazing, unmerited favor], for if righteousness comes through [observing] the Law, then Christ died needlessly. [His suffering and death would have had no purpose whatsoever] (Galatians 2:21, Amplified).*

If there could be other ways to heaven, why did Jesus, after His resurrection, instruct His disciples to *go and make disciples of all nations, baptizing them in the name of the Father and of the Son and of the Holy Spirit (Matthew 28:19) and He (Jesus) said to them, 'Go into all the world and preach the good news to all creation. Whoever believes and is baptized will be saved, but whoever does not believe will be condemned.' (Mark 16:15-16).*

If there could be other ways to heaven, why would the early disciples change so drastically? Almost all of the original disciples were transformed from whiny, cowardly, doubting men into men willing to suffer, face torture and die horrible deaths for the sake of speaking and teaching the truth of Jesus. Why would they bother to face persecution and painful death earlier than necessary if there were some other way to reach God?

Make no mistake, I have wanted to find ways to believe that all people, regardless of their faith, go to heaven. I have scoured the Bible looking for these longed after loopholes.

But, instead of finding loopholes, I found the holiness of God. And before His holiness, I trembled. And, before His holiness I fell humiliated in my filthy rags. But God, whose love is high and deep and wide and long, remembered me. He stooped down….and redeemed me. Unworthy me. Now I am one of His treasured possessions, a jewel He prizes.

World…you can keep your loopholes. For I have found – or been found by – Jesus Christ, Lord of lords and King of kings…the way, the truth, the life.

FEBRUARY 19

People sometimes overlook God's holiness and prefer to look just upon His love and grace. But, that's a mistake. To know God, one must know both of His love and of His holiness. An idol is carved when you magnify one of these attributes over the other.

The holiness of God offends because we people types tend to believe we are pretty good, and being pretty good should be good enough to earn heaven. These are the folks who think God should just "get over" sin or at least modernize the definition to fit with the times….forgetting that God (and His standards) are the same yesterday, today, and forever.

Rejecting or minimalizing God's holiness diminishes the size of God in our already diminished vision of truth. It causes us to think of God on terms we can understand, and reduces God to an image of us. It makes us think of God as "the big guy in the sky" or "the man upstairs." Such a reduction is dangerous and flawed.

God is holy, and He owes us no explanation for that truth.

God's holiness actually enhances His love. It makes His love for us that much more amazing. For to love us, He had to bridge a gap unbelievably and painfully wide. And He did. When His love is understood in the light of His holiness, words fail and all we can do is fall before Him in brokenness and praise His Holy Name. Holiness and Love…these are not opposite sides of God's character. These attributes are completely bound one with the other…each enhancing the other.

God's holiness and love are truly beyond my comprehension. That is what makes God God….He and His ways are beyond me. Yet, He reaches into history and into my life and makes is possible for me to be His.

Faith flows from brokenness before the one true and holy God who loves.

Everything seems so complicated, politically and socially, in our country now. If we are unhappy with a decision that has been made at school, with our jobs, our health care, our applications for services or financial programs, we can appeal the decision. We have grown so accustomed to the idea that appeal is possible and that red tape is unavoidable in our now heavily bureaucratic nation, that the simplicity of God's salvation plan eludes many. Too many. There are no bureaucrats to go through, no being put on hold waiting for customer service, no red tape. The road is simple but narrow: Jesus Christ is the way to God and eternal life in heaven.

And, remember, there is no appeal process beyond the grave.

<u>FEBRUARY 20</u>

From <u>Holiness</u> by John Charles Ryle [7]

"Like us, He was born of a woman. Like us, He grew and increased in stature. Like us, He was often hungry and thirsty, and faint and weary. Like us, He ate and drank, rested and slept. Like us, He sorrowed and wept and felt. It is all very wonderful, but so it is. He that made the heavens went to and fro as a poor weary Man on earth! He that ruled over principalities and powers in heavenly places, took on Him a frail body like our own. He that might have dwelt forever in the glory which He had with the Father, amid the praises of legions of angels, came down to earth and dwelt as a man among sinful men. Surely this fact alone is an amazing miracle of condescension, grace, pity and love.

"I find a deep mine of comfort in this thought, that Jesus is perfect Man no less than perfect God. He in whom I am told by Scripture to trust is not only a great High Priest, but a feeling High Priest. He is not only a powerful Saviour, but a sympathizing Saviour. He is not only the Son of God, mighty to save, but the Son of man, able to feel. ....

"Had my Saviour been God only, I might perhaps have trusted Him, but I never could have come near to Him without fear. Had my Saviour been Man only, I might have loved Him, but I never could have felt sure that He was able to take away my sins. But, blessed be God, my Saviour is God as well as Man, and Man as well as God – God, and so able to deliver me; Man, and so able to feel with me. Almighty power and deepest sympathy are met together in one glorious Person, Jesus Christ, my Lord."
From <u>Holiness</u> by John Charles Ryle [7]

<u>FEBRUARY 21</u>

Dear Father,

Paul asked an amazing and essential question in Romans 7:24. He cried out, *Who shall deliver me from this body of death?* Isn't this something we all struggle with? Isn't this the common cry of all mankind of all the ages come and gone and yet to come?

We will all die. Father, may we wrestle with this reality, and may our wrestling lead us to the foot of the cross with a heart and mind heavy with repentance and then to the door of the empty tomb with a heart and mind joyful in victory and freedom!

Paul answers his own question in the next verse. He asked, *WHO would deliver?* He answers, *Jesus Christ our Lord.* That is the answer! Jesus Christ, the all-sufficient One, He alone is able to deliver these bodies of death.

I pray for our family. I pray for my students. Help each to wrestle with the reality of death. Help each to wrestle well and wrestle until they are completely broken before You, Lord. And then, save them and raise them to victory. I thank God through Jesus Christ our Lord!

In Jesus' Name…the Savior…Immortal Son of God and Son of Man

FEBRUARY 22

I would rather be watching mindless television right now. Sitting here at the computer is making me think, and I think I've thought enough for one day. It has been a tumultuous day in my head. I am tired. I am overwhelmed.

Our daughter has leukemia. She is in remission, but needs to continue chemotherapy for another 20 months.

Sarah should be getting her chemotherapy medication every other week. We tried that. It was a disaster. The dose was too high for her to handle, and she landed frequently in the hospital. The oncologists reviewed her situation and decided it would be best to significantly reduce the dose and administer it once each week. We were all very hopeful that this would get us on the consistent track that we were promised maintenance chemotherapy would be. After some initial problems were resolved, it looked like we were at that hopeful place. Sarah had her small dose of chemo for 3 weeks in a row! Then, last week her counts were just a bit below the required threshold for giving the chemo. By this week, I had no doubt that Sarah would be ready to go. It's odd what we parents with kids with serious illnesses become hopeful for. Hopeful for chemo?

Anyhow, the nurse was at our home this morning to draw blood off Sarah's PICC line. The blood would be taken to the lab to check Sarah's white count, hemoglobin, platelets. If the counts were good, and I assumed they would be, Sarah would get her chemo.

It was a beautiful day in February in Western New York. It was in the 40s and sunny and just a hint of spring could be felt. I kept busy while Sarah was at school. At 2:45 PM, I went to school and picked Sarah up. We came home. The answering machine was blinking. It was Julie, the oncology nurse, calling to let us know that Sarah's white count was 1.1 and she was neutropenic. In other words, Sarah's white count was still too low for chemo. Making it worse was that the counts were even lower than last week despite holding the chemo.

I simply could not believe this mess. It's not that I want my child to have to endure the rigors of chemotherapy. It is that I want my child to remain in remission and get this all done and over with. And, it sure would be nice if there could be some sort of organization and consistency in managing this treatment stuff. Nothing can be planned under these circumstances. Ever. Our lives revolve around CBCs, nurses, oncologists, methotrexate, central lines.

It stinks. Totally.

Blessedly, Sarah doesn't always know that it stinks. Unless she has caught the latest germ floating around, she tends to handle her low counts with relative ease, and she certainly is happy to skip the poison we call chemotherapy. She watched some television while I gave her some fluid in her feeding tube. I catheterized her. I flushed her PICC line. I hugged her and she smiled her big, happy smile at me and made her happy sounds to let me know she'd had a good day at school.

My mind was restless. Anxious. I wanted so badly to control the uncontrollable, and figure out what we could do differently so that all the chemo stuff could be more consistent. My mind was racing. I wanted to talk to Julie or the oncologist or at least a pharmacist who understood these meds. I wanted to talk to the neurologist to find out if Sarah's seizure meds were affecting her counts. Should these meds be decreased? Are they contributing? How do we know? Do we really want to go through the work and difficulty of transitioning some sort of new seizure med with probably the same side effects as these current meds? I called Julie. She was gone. I called the pharmacist. I called the neurologist. Too late, just got Tom on the answering machine and left a message. I even called family members with medical backgrounds looking for answers that, simply put, were not available.

I felt so desperate to figure this out. And, absolutely ill-equipped to do so.

As my mind ran in circles, I worked with Sarah. I completed range of motion exercises on her. Then, I strapped her into her stander. The stander is a piece of equipment that Sarah uses to bear weight on her legs....it does just what it says...it lets her stand. Sarah has always loved her stander until recently. She is developing contractures in her hamstrings, and that makes it painful to straighten her legs...thus her growing distaste for using the stander. I know she needs surgical releases of those hamstrings. I also know that there is no way an orthopedic surgeon is going to operate on her while she is undergoing chemotherapy and has lousy white counts. I know we just need to wait it out at this point. But, as I kneel on the floor behind my little girl trying to get her into a piece of equipment that she has always loved, and now is starting to hate, I am overcome by this situation. I start to cry. I pray. For so long, I have prayed. And, in general, I feel we live a blessed life with a blessed child who is just an awesome treasure and gift from the good Father above. But every once in a while, I just wish the circumstances would line up a little bit better. I didn't know what to pray at that moment. I do not want to be a pessimist. I have fought hard to remain an optimist, but today on the floor that optimist was feeling pretty beat up.

Romans 8, hid in my heart came to my mind: *Who shall separate us from the love of Christ? Shall trouble or hardship or persecution or famine or nakedness or danger of sword?.....For I am convinced that neither death nor life, neither angels nor demons, neither the present nor the future, nor any powers, neither height nor depth, nor anything else in all creation will be able to separate us from the love of God that is in Christ Jesus our Lord.*

Today has not been a good day. It doesn't have to be, though, to experience the love and closeness of Christ. In all my sadness on that floor kneeling behind my little girl struggling to stand in her stander, I simply prayed, "God, please help me to trust you. I'm trying so hard to figure this out all on my own, and I know I don't have to. I don't always know how to trust you. Help me to trust you." I could have prayed for God to get Sarah's body making white cells. I could have prayed for God to manage Sarah's seizures. Believers are told to go boldly to the throne of God with specific requests and to persist in prayer and that the excruciating details of our lives mean something to God. But, I have prayed all those prayers, and I know God knows Sarah's needs. What I really need help with here is not Sarah's medical situation. What I really need help with is trusting God to handle what sometimes seems to be an unendingly difficult situation. I have grown to know it really is not about the circumstances as much as it is about the attitude, but sometimes applying knowledge to the reality of our daily lives is much more difficult than expected.

Since the difficult days are not going to disappear, what am I to do? This is more than theory and doctrine. What am I to do so that I trust God?

My mind just kept going back to Romans 8: *Who shall separate us from the love of Christ?* It all hinges on truth. Filling my mind and my life with truth.

Who shall separate us from the love of Christ? Shall cancer or low white counts or seizures or danger of relapse? For I am convinced that neither chemotherapy nor contractures nor the risk of stroke, neither infection nor central line, neither death nor life nor anything else in all creation will be able to separate us from the love of God that is in Christ Jesus our Lord.

Amen.

Now, I'm going to go get a good night sleep, and see if the optimist within will rise with the morning sun. Thanks to the Son, I know we will go on. We will face tomorrow...but first we must get through today. And while getting through the tough days may feel ever so lonely, the truth is...God is here...and the yoke I bear, He bears with me.

FEBRUARY 23

Jehovah,

Your Word says, there is, thanks to Christ, no condemnation to those who are in Jesus, to those who walk not after the flesh, but after the Spirit.

Lord, I deserve Your condemnation!

But here I am, Yours in Christ. I am forgiven and no longer condemned.

Instead, I am free! I no longer walk after the flesh.

Oh, the flesh still grips and confuses me, no doubt.

But, its power over me has been broken.

Its power to condemn me is no more. Jesus has borne the condemnation for me. He has done what I never could do. He, and He alone, has saved me.

And, I no longer stand condemned.

God's righteous wrath has been satisfied by the sacrifice of Jesus Christ. For me.

Lord, I pray for everyone in our family who is still in condemnation. Make each aware of the weight hanging over them and the eternity awaiting them. Reveal insights regarding the wrath to come and the awful, everlasting price of deserved condemnation. Then, in Your amazing power and overwhelming mercy, deliver them. Plant their feet on Calvary. Show them the cross. Show them Your blood. Your mercy. Your truth.

Burn an understanding of Your holiness upon their hearts.

Any who are depending on their own holiness are standing in condemnation.

They are still walking in the flesh.

May they desire to walk in the Spirit. May anything less than a saving relationship with You, a relationship in which they possess You and You possess them, leave them exhausted, unsatisfied, completely aware of their lost condition and their filthiness. May they tremble in the light of Your pure righteousness.

In the Name of The Lord, my Righteousness…

FEBRUARY 24

"All love aside," my husband said, "that person was just stupid!"

My dear husband, Mark, was referring to the gentleman at the gas station who yelled at my husband for pulling in front of him. Per my husband, he did not see the gentleman in the tiny Chevy Corsica behind the woman in the Explorer SUV. Mr. Chevy Corsica pulled around Mark, up to another pump, rolled down the window, and yelled at him.

Earlier in the day, we had attended church. It was a lovely service and sermon based upon I Corinthians 13…you know the passage: *"love is patient, love is kind…"* Pastor, of course, spoke of the importance of loving our family, our brothers and sisters in Christ, those in need. But, he also spoke of the essential importance of loving those who are difficult to love, those who are irritating or cold or selfish. We are called to love these difficult, irritating, cold, selfish folks the same way that we are called to love those easy to love. We are called to love those who are having bad days as well as those who are having good days.

There is no putting "all love aside."

It is precisely these moments of which my husband complained when we most have to strive and succeed at applying God's word and truth to our daily lives. Christian and non-Christian alike, we are all prone to protect our territory and prone to taking another person's bad mood personally. Is that what God wants from us? Are we supposed to spend our time and effort guarding our personal space and our rights? In the Sermon on the Mount, Jesus tells us, *There is a saying, 'Love your friends and hate your enemies.' But I say: Love your enemies! Pray for those who persecute you! In that way you will be acting as true sons of your Father in heaven. For He gives His sunlight to both the evil and the good, and sends rain on the just and on the unjust too. If you love only those who love you, what good is that? Even scoundrels do that much. If you are friendly only to your friends, how are you different from anyone else? Even the heathen do that.*

Even the heathen love the lovable. Even scoundrels love those who are easy to love. We are called to be different, and not to "put love aside" just because someone is behaving unlovable.

Applying God's instructions in our lives takes effort on our part. We are surrounded by and pounded upon by the rules and ways of the world. We are very prone to adopt those ways and make them our own. Choosing God's way takes intent for it does not come easily or naturally to us. And, we tend to mirror the behavior of those around us. Thus Mark's behavior reflected the behavior of the bad mood man in the Chevy Corsica. Mark let that happen. He let this world and its rules guide his decision. "You aren't nice to me, so I won't be nice to you." I, too, am like this. Sometimes he and I are like this to each other.

The difference our demonstrations of love make in the lives of other people is not always obvious. So what! Do it because you are told to do so by God, and God does know what He's talking about. He's not telling us to love the difficult and the grumpy just because it's a nice thing to do. He's commanding us to do so because He loved us when we were difficult and grumpy and worse.

We can't control others. But we can choose to act God's way and play by His rules. It may not be noticed immediately by others, but God will always see, and it will please Him when we, out of hearts of gratitude for His love to us, strive to walk worthily. Sometimes it will be noticed by man. Sometimes it may even make a difference in another person's life.

We are salt and light.

As we love the unlovable, the salt preserves…the light shines…and we grow in Christ-likeness.

FEBRUARY 25

Pride has held me captive this year.

I have been proud, but I have called it "grief" and have allowed myself to wallow and get away with it.

Grief has become an excuse for pride. Pride has become a springboard for irritability. Irritability has become a tendency to avoid others. Love for others is waxing cold in my heart.

This is sin.

The uncovering of this sin in my heart has been steadily proceeding over this past month. It all started with a James McDonald message on the radio. He was speaking about how we saved people can sometimes view the unsaved as nuisances. My ears perked up. I know this to be true. I am guilty. A few days later, I was at prayer meeting, and Tabea prayed about having an outward focus. It wasn't aimed at me, but God used her prayer to hit my hardening heart. Then, a few days after this I received an e-mail from my friend, LuAnn. Her e-mail was about she and Karen and I...how each of us relates to our mothers...how each of us can be haughty in our responses and expectations. I was stunned.

I confess, Lord. I have been self-centered. I have had an inward focus. My heart has been hardening. I have been irritable. I haven't been "seeing" people as I ought. I may be able to hide this from others around me, but God, I cannot hide this from You. Nor should I. You, Lord, are well aware of the condition of my heart and mind. Forgive me. I repent. I turn away from this, and I turn to You. I lay my life before You. Thank You for revealing darkness in my thinking. Continue to expose. Otherwise I will not grow into the new creation I am in You. Thank You for salvation. Thank You for the Holy Spirit, for indwelling me. Thank You for loving me.

Create in me, O Lord, a new heart.

Renew a steadfast spirit within me.

Return to me, O Lord, the joy of salvation.

FEBRUARY 26

Jehovah-Jireh,

Life seems heavy today. Keeping up with it all, understanding it all seems truly more than I can bear. How many in our family feel heavy and burdened and unable to keep up? Are there many? Really, we people who live side by side can know very little about one another.

When it's all boiled down, our heaviness is rooted in lack... lack of time... lack of money... lack of knowledge... lack of energy... lack of vision... lack of salvation... lack of humility... lack of gratitude... lack of faith.

The law of the Spirit of life in Christ Jesus hath made me free from the law of sin and death.

Did you hear that??!! FREE! Free from the law of sin and death. I am free, and yet I live burdened! God forgive me when my burdens are self-created bundles of pride, self-righteousness and perceived self-importance.

Self is heavy...there is no freedom in self.

Jesus, You offer us salvation and freedom. Yet, we so often choose the bondage of sin, self, tradition, death. The flesh cries for more and more and we become burdened and heavy laden trying to satisfy what can never be satisfied with stuff. Help me to live free! May all of us in this family come under the law of the spirit of life in Christ Jesus...where there is deliverance, where chains are broken, where bondage is destroyed and freedom from sin and the flesh echoes forth.

In the Name of the Lord who Provides...

FEBRUARY 27

Two paths before us. One appears easy and comfortable and the other difficult and exhausting. Most of us, if we had the choice, would choose the easy path. I am no exception.

Most of the time, the difficult paths we walk are not the paths of our choosing. We must walk them, none-the-less, and along the way, the only control we often have is the power to decide our attitude and our response to the tough times and where or with whom we will place our faith.

When Mark and I found out I was going to have a baby, we were thrilled. If God had spoken face-to-face with us and asked, "So would you like to have a healthy baby or a chronically ill and severely disabled child?" which path do you think we would have chosen?

Like most, we would have chosen health and ease. Praise God, He did not give us the choice! Praise God, who sees beyond our circumstances and always knows best, even when we doubt Him. He blessed us with Sarah and the difficult path.

We all have our "Sarahs" don't we? Whatever your "Sarah" may be, it is my prayer that you would understand God knows you and all your "Sarahs".

And He loves you and can make your "Sarah" of great value. Lean in. Lean hard. On Him. Your full weight, the weight of your burdens...He can handle them...cast your cares upon Him. He will sustain you. Humble yourself under His righteous right hand. He will lift you up.

FEBRUARY 28

Dear Lord,

How great You are! You are the Rock that is indeed higher than I! You are the safe place where I may continually resort. When the waters of life are rough and choppy and when storms threaten to drown, I can hide in you.

Lord, the law cannot save. We cannot stand before You in our own goodness, for we are not good. The law, rules, being "good enough" cannot save because we cannot be "good enough." Our flesh cannot meet the demands of Your holy law and Your perfect standards.

Praise You for Jesus. You sent Your Son in the likeness of sinful flesh. He became man, and He in His perfect obedience to the law, condemned sin in the flesh. Because of Him, what the law could not do, can still be done. Through Him. The righteousness of the law shall be fulfilled in us, who walk not after the flesh, but after the Spirit.

I pray for our family. Help each to walk after the Spirit, and may the righteousness of the law, accomplished through the life, death, burial, and resurrection of the Son You sent, be fulfilled in them.

Any who are trusting in the deeds of their flesh are condemned and will face Your righteous judgment. The need for the Savior is real. And, praise God, the Savior is real! Come, family, come and be saved. Thank You, Lord, for sending Your Son. Thank You, Jesus, for becoming flesh. Praise You for what You have accomplished, of which I, unworthy, am a beneficiary.

In the Name of the Lord who Sanctifies…

FEBRUARY 29...FOR THE LEAP YEAR...

From *Holiness* by John Charles Ryle [8]

"But what if your heart be right with God, and yet you are pressed down with a load of earthly trouble? What if the fear of poverty is tossing you to and fro, and seems likely to overwhelm you? What if pain of body be racking you to distraction day after day? What if you are suddenly laid aside from active usefulness and compelled by infirmity to sit still and do nothing? What if death has come into your home, and taken away your Rachel or Joseph or Benjamin and left you alone, crushed to the ground with sorrow? What if all this has happened? Still there is comfort in Christ. He can speak peace to wounded hearts as easily as calm troubled seas. He can rebuke rebellious will as powerfully as raging winds. He can make storms of sorrow abate, and silence

tumultuous passions, as surely as He stopped the Galilean storm. He can say to the heaviest anxiety, 'Peace, be still!' The floods of care and tribulation may be mighty, but Jesus sits upon the water floods, and is mightier than the waves of the sea (Ps. 93:4). The winds of trouble may howl fiercely round you, but Jesus holds them in His hand, and can stay them when He lists. Oh, if any reader of this paper is broken-hearted and care-worn and sorrowful, let him go to Jesus Christ, and cry to Him and he shall be refreshed. 'Come unto Me,' He says, 'all ye that labour and are heavy laden, and I will give you rest' (Matt. 11:28)."
From <u>Holiness</u> by John Charles Ryle [8]

From <u>Night of Weeping</u> by Horatius Bonar [9]

"Affliction is our fullest opportunity for glorifying God. It is on earth that He expects to get glory from us, glory such as angels cannot give, glory such as we shall not be able to give hereafter. It is especially in sorrow and under infirmity that God looks for glory from us. What a God-honoring thing to see a struggling, sorrowing child of earth cleave fast to God, calmly trusting in Him, happy and at rest in the midst of storm and of suffering! What a spectacle for the hosts of Heaven! Now then is the time for the saints to give glory to the Lord their God. Let them prize affliction as the very time and opportunity for doing so most of all. Ah, surely it is one which an angel might covet, which an archangel would gladly stoop to were that possible! They can glorify God much in Heaven amid its glory and blessedness, but oh, not half so much as we can on earth amid suffering!"
From <u>Night of Weeping</u> by Horatius Bonar [9]

February's Apologetic Moment...Contend for the faith

What is a Biblical Worldview?

Excerpt from <u>How Now Shall We Live?</u> by Charles Colson and Nancy Pearcey [50]

CREATION
God spoke the universe into existence and created humanity in His image.

FALL
The human condition is marred by sin.

REDEMPTION
God in His grace provided a way to be reconciled to Himself.

RESTORATION
We are called to bring these principles into every area of life and create a new culture.
(p. 37)

"Our choices are shaped by what we believe is real and true, right and wrong, good and beautiful. Our choices are shaped by our worldview. The term *worldview* may sound abstract or philosophical, a topic discussed by pipe-smoking, tweed-jacketed professors in academic settings. But actually a person's worldview is intensely practical. It is simply the sum total of our beliefs about the world, the 'big picture' that directs our daily decisions and actions." (pp. 13, 14)

"The basis for the Christian worldview, of course, is God's revelation in Scripture. Yet sadly, many believers fail to understand that Scripture is intended to be the basis for ALL of life. Christians often think in terms of a false dichotomy (separation), allowing our belief system to be reduced to little more than private feelings. Evangelicals have been particularly vulnerable to this narrow view because of our emphasis on personal commitment. On one hand, this has been the movement's greatest strength, bringing millions to a relationship with Christ. But this emphasis on a personal relationship can also be evangelicalism's greatest weakness because it may prevent us from seeing God's plan for us beyond personal salvation. Genuine Christianity is more than a relationship with Jesus, as expressed in personal piety, church attendance, Bible study, and works of charity. It is more than discipleship, more than believing a system of doctrines. Genuine Christianity is a way of seeing and comprehending ALL reality. It is a worldview.

"The scriptural basis for this understanding is the creation account, where we are told that God spoke everything into being out of nothing (Genesis 1 and John 1). Everything that exists came into being at His command and is therefore subject to Him, finding its purpose and meaning in Him. The implication is that in every topic we investigate, from ethics to economics to ecology, the truth is found only in relationship to God and His revelation. God created the natural world and natural laws. God created our bodies and the moral laws that keep us healthy. God created our minds and laws of logic and imagination. God created us as social beings and gave us the principles for social and political institutions. God created a world of beauty and the principles of aesthetics and artistic creation. In every area of life, genuine knowledge means discerning the laws and ordinances by which God has structured creation, and then allowing those laws to shape the way we should live.

"When we truly grasp this, we are compelled to see that the Christian faith cannot be reduced to John 3:16 or simple formulas. Christianity cannot be limited to only one component of our lives, a mere religious practice or observance, or even a salvation experience. We are compelled to see Christianity as the all-encompassing truth, the root of everything else. It is ultimate reality." (pp. 14, 15)

"We must show the world that Christianity is more than a private belief, more than personal salvation. We must show that it is a comprehensive life system that answers all of humanity's age-old questions: Where did I come from? Why am I here? Where am I going? Does life have any meaning and purpose? The church's singular failure in recent decades has been the failure to see Christianity as a life system, or worldview, that governs every area of existence. This failure has been crippling in many ways. For one thing, we cannot answer the questions our children bring home from school, so we are incapable of preparing them to answer the challenges they face. For ourselves, we cannot explain to our friends and neighbors why we believe, and we often cannot defend our faith. And we do not know how to organize our lives correctly, allowing our choices to be shaped by the world around us. Most of all, our failure to see Christianity as a comprehensive framework of truth has crippled our efforts to have a redemptive effect on the surrounding culture. As agents of God's common grace, we are called to help sustain and renew His creation, to uphold the created institutions of family and society, to pursue science and scholarship, to create works of art and beauty, and to heal and help those suffering from the results of the Fall." (pp. xi and xii)

"To engage the world requires that we understand the great ideas that compete for people's minds and hearts. The culture war is not just about abortion, homosexual rights, or the decline of public education. These are only the skirmishes. The real war is a cosmic struggle between worldviews – between the Christian worldview and the various secular and spiritual worldviews arrayed against it. This is what we must understand if we are going to be effective both in evangelizing our world today and in transforming it to reflect the wisdom of the Creator." (p. 17)

"What is the major challenge today? In the broadest categories, the conflict of our day is theism versus naturalism. Theism is the belief that there is a transcendent God who created the universe; naturalism is the belief that natural causes alone are sufficient to explain everything that exists. The most fundamental questions reflect these categories:

Is ultimate reality God or the cosmos? Is there a supernatural realm, or is nature all that exists? Has God spoken and revealed His truth to us, or is truth something we have to find, even invent, for ourselves? Is there a purpose to our lives, or are we cosmic accidents emerging from the slime?

"These two major systems are utterly opposed, and if we are going to defend the truth effectively, we must grasp their full implications. Naturalism is the idea that nature is all that exists, that life arose from a chance collision of atoms, evolving eventually into human life as we know it today. In its broadest sense, naturalism can even include certain forms of religion – those in which the spiritual is conceived as completely inherent within nature, such as neo-pagan and New Age religions. **By contrast, Christianity teaches that there is a transcendent God who existed before the world existed and who is the ultimate origin of everything else. The universe is dependent at every moment on His providential governance and care.**

"MORAL RELATIVISM. In morality, naturalism results in relativism. If nature is all there is, then there is no transcendent source of moral truth, and we are left to construct morality on our own. Every principle is reduced to a personal preference. By contrast, the Christian believes in a God who has spoken, who has revealed an absolute and unchanging standard of right and wrong, based ultimately on His own holy character.

"MULTICULTURALISM. As a consequence of relativism, the naturalist treats all cultures as morally equivalent, each merely reflecting its own history and experience. Contemporary trends like postmodernism and multiculturalism are rooted firmly in naturalism, for if there is no transcendent source of truth or morality, then we find our identity only in our race, gender, or ethnic group. But Christians can never equate truth with the limited perspective of any group. Truth is God's perspective, as revealed in Scripture. Hence, while we appreciate the cultural diversity, we insist on the propriety of judging particular cultural practices as morally right or wrong. Furthermore, Christians regard the Western tradition and heritage as worth defending; that is, to the degree that historically it has been shaped by a biblical worldview.

"PRAGMATISM. Since naturalists deny any transcendent moral standards, they tend to take a pragmatic approach to life. Pragmatism says: Whatever works best is right. Actions and policies are judged on utilitarian grounds alone. By contrast, the Christian is an idealist, judging actions not by what works but by what ought to be, based on objective standards.

"UTOPIANISM. Naturalists generally embrace the Enlightenment notion that human nature is essentially good, which leads to utopianism. Utopianism says: If only we create the right social and economic structures, we can usher in an age of harmony and prosperity. But Christians can never give their allegiance to utopian projects. We know that sin is real, that it has deeply twisted human nature, and that none of our efforts can create heaven on earth. Heaven is an eschatological hope that will be fulfilled only by divine intervention at the end of human history. In the meantime, the human propensity to evil and disorder must be hemmed in by law and tradition.

"THIS-WORLD-PERSPECTIVE. Naturalists consider only what happens in this world, this age, this life. But Christians see things from an eternal perspective. Everything we do now has eternal significance, because one day there will be a judgment, and then it will become evident that our choices in this life have consequences that last into eternity." (pp. 20-21)

"As we begin the new millennium, the mission for Christians is nothing less than becoming men and women of 'another type.' We must be men and women who will dare to wrest Christianity free from its fortress mentality, its sanctuary stronghold, and establish it once again as the great life system and cultural force that acknowledges the Creator as sovereign over all. We must be men and women who understand that the task is much more than launching spasmodic crusades to fight one battle or another. We must be men and women who see that the struggle is one of first principles. 'If the battle is to be fought with hope and with a hope of victory, then principle must be arrayed against principle.' We must understand opposing views as total life systems and then 'take our stand in a life system of equally comprehensive and far-reaching power.'

"Dare we believe that Christianity can yet prevail? We must believe it…When the church is faithful to its calling, it always leads to a reformation of culture. When the church is truly the church, a community living in biblical obedience and contending for faith in every area of life, it will surely revive the surrounding culture or create a new one." (pp. 36-37)

From <u>How Now Shall We Live?</u> by Charles Colson and Nancy Pearcey [50]

Behold, the heaven and the heaven of heavens
is the LORD's thy God, the earth also, with all that therein is.
Deuteronomy 10:14

March

"I believe in Christianity as I believe that the sun has risen:
not only because I see it, but because by it
I see everything else."
— C.S. Lewis

MARCH 1

Yesterday, Mark and I went to the last girls' home basketball game of the season...and the last home game for the five seniors on the team. Right before the game, each of these senior girls was called up front and, with their parents, honored and recognized.

I sat in the bleachers, and I choked up. As I write these words even now, I'm crying. It's more than a basketball season ending. It's a season in their lives ending, and a new one beginning. It's sad and exciting all at the same time.

Why am I crying? Oh, there are probably lots of reasons, and let's be honest here and admit that one of them is that I will never have a daughter who will be applauded for her successes or who will graduate or walk down the aisle toward a waiting groom. These are things I will never experience, and there is pain in that.

And then there are these beautiful senior girls, young woman now, who I have watched grow up before my very eyes these past four years. I cry because I love them. And, I am going to miss them.

And there is the reality that life is hard, and that each of these young women has already had to deal with hard and broken things in their lives. At their young and tender ages, each has already had to face a loss or a brokenness or a disappointment or a sorrow of some sort. That breaks my heart and chokes me up.

What I have learned on my own life's journey is that life is hard...the old farmhouse burning down, Grandpa's death in a car accident, my Dad's sudden death from a stroke, family that could go years without talking to us and we without talking to them, struggles in marriage, burying my Sarah, and the consequences through the years of selfish or worldly decisions I have made…yes, life is hard.

But, I have also learned through these hard things – some self-created and some not – that God is good. All the time. God is enough. Always. He is the Blessed Controller of all things, and He is worthy of all praise and glory at all times and in all places. I have learned that rejoicing is a choice and that it is a choice that can be made even when we are crushed and crying. I have learned that being grateful in the storm delivers a knock-out blow to Satan. I have learned that, in Christ, I am more than a conqueror!

More than anything else, I pray my seniors will begin the exciting new chapter of their lives READY. Now is the time when they will either make this faith truly their own or drift from it. What they really believe in their hearts about You, Lord, is what will determine the way in which they shall go.

My prayer is that they believe and hold on with both hands to the truth of who You are….that your grace truly is sufficient…that Your name really is a strong tower…that You are good – all the time. May these young woman leave CBCS really, truly, in the depths of their hearts and minds believing these things about You so that when the circumstances and experiences and distractions of life may seem to speak otherwise, they will know what they know and they will know Who they know, and they will endure.

Equip them, Lord. Prepare them. Help them to face life always with you, and may they be more than conquerors through Christ Jesus who loves them with an everlasting love that is high and wide and long and deep! And, may they know that I, too, love them….

MARCH 2

Adonai,

It seems most of the world "minds the things of the flesh." Concerned about self and convinced of their own goodness, most people live their lives, the lives that You, Lord, give and sustain, ever mindful of the flesh and generally convinced that, somehow, they will be entitled to stand before You and live with You in heaven.

But, I know Your Word speaks differently. You tell us we cannot be good enough. We desperately need You. We desperately need Your Son. But, pride or stupidity or procrastination often keeps us minding the flesh and ignoring the Spirit.

I pray for our family. May they fight the flesh and start to mind the things of the Spirit. Our flesh, even as I write this is aging and wearing out and is useless in obtaining salvation. May we be people who are after the Spirit – striving, seeking, following hard and early and often after the Spirit of the Living God.

MARCH 3

He brought me to the banqueting house, and His banner over me was love (*Song of Solomon 2:4*). This verse may be the very reason the Lord led me to Song of Solomon...with some resistance on my part I must add. Always, it has been a book that has made me uncomfortable. It is just so intimate and passionate!

We say things like, "God is love," and then we proceed to picture God as stoic and cool, forgetting that love really does mean intimacy and passion and union.

My beloved is mine, and I am His (*Solomon 2:16*).

The time has come for me to really love and be loved by the Lord, not just to know about His love, but to be in His love...His intimate, passionate love.

I am His. He is mine.

MARCH 4

Jehovah-Shalom,

A choice lies before us. What shall we chose? Death or life? Enmity or peace? *For to be carnally minded is death. To be spiritually minded is life and peace.* Father, may Your will become our will so that we can choose, deliberately, to lay aside our carnal thoughts and to hold tightly the spiritual.

The carnal mind is enmity against God. The carnal mind rages against You and denies that You have authority, right, and even the obligation, to judge. Unfortunately for the carnally minded, it is not necessary for them to agree to Your authority and judgment. You shall judge with or without their consent. There is enmity between You and them. But, it need not be so, for You not only are the Righteous Judge, You are the all-sufficient Savior! You have made the way. In their carnality, they see no value in Your law. They scoff at the cross. Yet, deep within, they know, because we all know, they and we have violated Your law.

We need the cross.

Subject our minds to Your law, O Lord. Replace the power of the world's ways with the truth of Your righteous law. And sharply pierce our consciences so that we will have a clear understanding of our guilt before a holy God. May godly sorrow sweep over us as we stand, and then fall, at the foot of the cross with repentant hearts and minds ready to embrace forever the Savior who has bled on our behalf. Forever and through all things, may we be and become spiritually minded and choose life and peace.

In the Name of the Lord our Peace...

MARCH 5

"Brenda, what do you really control?" I heard this question rattle around in my head as I walked this morning.

When it's all said and done, what do I really control?

Well...not much.

Truly, the only control I have is whether or not, in this minute and this circumstance of life, will I seek God or not seek God?

But you know what?

It's enough...

And this is liberating!

If all the energy I spend trying to control what I really can't is focused on what I can – seeking God – then I am free! I am now able to rest.

And I am so tired. Rest sounds so good.

The details get sloppy and confusing sometimes. Chaos seems common...but all the sloppy, confusing, chaotic moments of my life are securely within the framework of God's sovereignty. He is the Blessed Controller.

Seeking Him is the smartest, safest, sanest thing I can strive to do.

MARCH 6

Elohim,

Praise You, mighty Creator God who sustains all things! For You we were created. In You, we live and move and have our being. How differently we would think our thoughts, speak our words, and live our lives if this we truly believed!

In Romans 8, we are admonished that *They that are in the flesh cannot please God.*

Cannot!

Scripture does not say, "They that are in the flesh doing evil things cannot please God." NO! Merely "in the flesh." In the flesh, we can do some wonderfully kind, properly motivated in the world's eyes, sweet and sacrificial service unto one another. BUT, if we are "in the flesh," we **cannot** please God, even if we are doing good and kind things.

Our flesh must be crucified with Christ. It must die so that we can live and so that the Spirit of God can dwell in us. If we do not have the Spirit of Christ, we are not God's.

We are none of His apart from Christ.

Relying upon the flesh, whether indulging it or disciplining it, whether using it for evil or for good, is fatal to the spirit.

Open the eyes of all in our family who depend upon and trust in their flesh, abilities, good works, sacrifices instead of depending upon You. Give them sight. Give them life in the Spirit and a hunger to know You as You really are.

In the Name of God, Creator, Author of life, and Authority over all…

MARCH 7

El Shaddai,

How I love our family! How I long for them to walk in the light of Your truth. I know You, too, love them. And, I believe You are All-Mighty El Shaddai and that You are All-Powerful to save!

Our bodies are dead because of sin. Death is the wages of sin, and death pulls us ever closer day after day. It is never satisfied. There is no discharge from this war, from this enemy.

Even at birth, our bodies begin to die.

The clock is ticking. It is a clock we are absolutely helpless to stop. Ignore it we may, but we ignore it at our own eternal peril. Death yawns before us.

It is all around us.

Death need not have the final say! You see, *if Christ be in you, the body is dead because of sin, but the Spirit is life because of righteousness (Romans 8:10).*

We can live! Lord, help the dying to know that life is possible. Eternal life with You, through Christ. Lord, You raised Jesus from the dead, and if Your Spirit abides in us, You who raised up Christ from the dead shall also make alive these mortal bodies by Your Spirit dwelling in us.

Father, thank You for saving me. Thank You for Your Spirit dwelling in me. Pour Your Spirit and Your truth into the lives of our family. I plead on their behalf.

In the Name of God Almighty, the All Sufficient One…

MARCH 8

Abba Father,

Help us to know You as You really are.

Thank You that we have capacity to know You.

As are all things, such capacity flows from the river of Your grace.

Capacity we have. But, have we desire?

Is it the cry of our hearts to know You? I dare say, with great sorrow, that it is not.

Father, in Your grace and mercy, bless us with the will to mortify the deeds of the flesh, to die to self, and come to You. If we live after and strive to satisfy the flesh, we will die.

Indeed, we are already dead.

But, if through the Spirit we mortify the deeds of the body, we shall live. *For if ye live after the flesh, ye shall die: but if ye through the Spirit do mortify the deeds of the body, ye shall live. For as many as are led by the Spirit of God, they are the sons of God. For ye have not received the spirit of bondage again to fear; but ye have received the Spirit of adoption, whereby we cry, Abba, Father. The Spirit itself beareth witness with our spirit, that we are the children of God: And if children, then heirs; heirs of God, and joint-heirs with Christ; if so be that we suffer with Him, that we may be also glorified together. For I reckon that the sufferings of this present time are not worthy to be compared with the glory which shall be revealed in us (Romans 8:13-18).*

Foolishly, we often believe we are Your children and Your heirs when we are not. This is one of Satan's deceptions: whispering into the lives of the lost that somehow we are all God's children. This is a great lulling deception causing many to ignore the true wooing of the Spirit of God.

We are only Your children if we are adopted into Your family through Christ. Once adopted, the Spirit comes to dwell within and to lead.

Those led by the Spirit of God are sons of God.

Bless all in this family with truth. Reveal any deception within a heart that becomes a stumbling block to the necessary and available adoption. May we all awake from slumber and walk in Your light and be led by Your Spirit.

Father I pray…

MARCH 9

Abba Father,

Truly, how great You are! Truly how present You are! How I long for each soul in our family to live, saved, in Your greatness and with an awareness of Your presence. How differently we would live, how differently we would speak if we truly realized that You, Righteous Judge, see and hear all.

Righteous in You, righteous because of You and what You have accomplished through Christ, we need not fear. We no longer need to be in bondage to fear as long as we have received the Spirit of adoption and have been grafted into the Family Tree.

Indeed, we all are born Your creatures for You have created us.

But, we are not all Your children.

We must be adopted into Your family in order to be called children of God, and in order to have the privilege of crying "Abba, Father" unto You.

The adoption becomes final when Christ's blood is poured over our lives and upon our sins. As He atones, we become Your children and You our Father. How beautiful is the blood of Christ whereby we may be adopted into Your family! How great the cost, how steep the price You paid...the blood of Your Son shed for me!

I pray for the adoption of each person in this family, for each soul to have the adoption sealed by the blood of Christ. Free from bondage and free from fear of death.

Father, I pray...

MARCH 10

From *Knowing God* by J.I. Packer [10]

The Majesty of God

"Our word 'majesty' comes from the Latin; it means 'greatness.' When we ascribe majesty to someone, we are acknowledging greatness in that person, and voicing our respect for it: as, for instance, when we speak of 'Her Majesty' the Queen.

"Now, 'majesty' is a word which the Bible uses to express the thought of the greatness of God, our Maker and our Lord. 'The LORD reigns, He is robed in majesty... Your throne was established long ago' (Psalm 93:1-2). 'They will speak of the glorious splendor of your majesty, and I will meditate on your wonderful works' (Psalm 145:5). Peter, recalling his vision of Christ's royal glory at the transfiguration, says, 'We were eyewitnesses of His majesty' (2 Peter 1:16)....

"But this is knowledge which Christians today largely lack: and that is one reason why our faith is so feeble and our worship so flabby. We are modern people, and modern people, though they cherish great thoughts of themselves, have as a rule small thoughts of God. When the person in the church, let alone the person in the street, uses the word 'God', the thought is rarely of divine majesty....

"Today, vast stress is laid on the thought that God is personal, but this truth is so stated as to leave the impression that God is a person of the same sort as we are – weak, inadequate, ineffective, a little pathetic. But this is not the God of the Bible! Our personal life is a finite thing: it is limited in every direction, in space, in time, in knowledge, in power. But God is not so limited. He is eternal, infinite and almighty. He has us in His hands; we never have Him in ours. Like us, He is personal; but

unlike us, He is great. In all its constant stress on the reality of God's personal concern for His people, and on the gentleness, tenderness, sympathy, patience and yearning compassion that He shows toward them, the Bible never lets us lose sight of His majesty and His unlimited dominion over all His creatures."
From <u>Knowing God</u> by J.I. Packer [10]

MARCH 11

Jehovah-Shammah,

I miss Sarah.

I miss taking care of her.

I miss walking into her room in the morning and seeing her pretty eyes looking at me, waiting for me.

But, as great as my sorrow may be, my love for You is growing greater still. Thank You, that, by Your grace, I can say, and mean it, that You are good. And You are good all the time! *The LORD is good, a strong hold in the day of trouble; and He knoweth them that trust in Him (Nahum 1:7).*

Suffering, indeed, is an unwelcomed companion we all, saved and unsaved, have in this life.

May I suffer well.

Lord, may your children suffer well, and when I suffer, may I suffer with Him, Your Son and my Savior, that I may be also glorified together with Him.

*Adoption. Inheritance. Suffering. Glorified…*Beautiful words are these when You, Lord, are the Master and the Potter. May all in our family share in Your inheritance. May they suffer well. May they be glorified together with Christ.

This is truth: You are the foundation of all that matters.

Prevent us, Lord, from our vain attempts to build on flawed and useless foundations that cannot save and will not endure. May Your presence be so powerful in each of our lives that we will not be distracted by the flawed foundations that the world offers. How these manmade foundations glitter and entice us with their sparkling exteriors! But within they are rotten. Make Your presence powerfully real and known to our hearts and minds so that we can withstand the temptations and stand with confidence and endurance upon Your eternal foundation.

In the Name of the Lord who is there and promises His presence…

MARCH 12

Jehovah-Rapha,

Beautiful are Your words! How amazing You are! You led me, over and over, to share the words of Romans 8:18 with Sarah in the months just before her death, the death that we did not see coming: *For I reckon that the sufferings of this present time are not worthy to be compared with the glory which shall be revealed in us.*

I used to sit next to Sarah and read this, and remind her of the truth – glory awaits!

At her wake, these were the words on the little cards, whatever you call them, at the funeral home. This is the verse referenced on the plaque next to the lilac bushes planted in her memory at church.

I love these words.

I believe them even in the moments when I doubt.

I love You, Lord! How good You have been to me. How good You have been to Sarah. And, truly, *I do reckon that the sufferings of this present time are not worthy to be compared with the glory which shall be revealed in us!*

Hallelujah!

Lord, pour Your Spirit and Your rich saving truth upon the hearts and into the minds and lives of each person in this family. Grip them, Lord, with the great and glorious truth that all, apart from You, must be reckoned useless to save. All else must be reckoned dead so that You can save and so that we can live forever with You.

These bodies of flesh are useless unless they are reckoned dead to sin and alive to You. In our suffering, Lord, draw us near. Speak. Guard and protect us, and give, Father, a passionate love for You that lifts us high above the broken details and suffering of life. Glory shall be revealed! We cannot really understand this mysterious promise, but we can seize it, possess it, and make You our own and then soar, renewed, upon eagles' wings!

In the Name of the Lord who heals…

MARCH 13

Jehovah-Sabaoth,

It's coming. I'm waiting. I know that You will restore this broken world and the broken bodies and lives of Your children. Thank You for saving my soul and for making me Your child. As I await the great restoration and glorification of my body, may I earnestly expect You at any moment; may You find me waiting, ready, and serving well.

This planet groans. It is wearing out. Even the innocent suffer. All creation is in bondage to corruption. The consequences of sin, indeed, are steep and affect all. Sin impacts even those incapable of sinning. Thus, creation groans. But, deliverance has been promised, and liberty, glorious liberty, awaits the children of God and this groaning planet!

Bring groaning, Lord, into the lives of our family. Bring the right kind in the right doses and at just the perfect time with the purpose of pointing proud hearts toward You. Within the light of Your truth, crush haughty hearts! Pound them into humility! It takes humility to come to You and admit that the need is great...so great that we, of our own efforts, cannot accomplish it. Sometimes humility comes only in the dense moments of deep groaning. It is then that one's perceived ability to save one's self becomes an obvious illusion and the reality of the cross becomes hope unbound!

In the Name of the Lord of Hosts, who is our deliverer and helper...

MARCH 14

Jehovah-Nissi,

So many needs! Before I opened this journal to write these words, I was praying, interceding for others... Kendra and Chloe... sick children each with cancer... Cheri's husband on a ventilator following yesterday's surgery... Kristen whose mom died last summer and now she is battling cancer... Earl whose leg was amputated thanks to complications of diabetes... Laura facing false accusations and a life unraveling and uncertainty about the future... Jackie walking in spiritual darkness...

Needs. Everywhere. Serious physical, emotional, relational, financial, and deep spiritual needs.

Truly this is a groaning world, and we who participate will, no doubt, groan.

For the saved, though, our groans are temporary. We travail, we hurt. But, we also hope. We know as we wait, that redemption is coming, the adoption already final will be finalized, and the inheritance shall satisfy and endure. You, Lord, are the inheritance! You are the All in All and above all.

Father, save our family. Hear our groans. Meet our deepest needs. May we face You and fall before You and call You Lord and Savior, Master and King!

Salvation and victory, Father! This is my prayer for our loved ones.

Lord, I groan on their behalf.

In the Name of the Lord our Banner, who gives the victory…

MARCH 15

From Foxe's Voice of the Martyrs [11]

William Hunter (1555)

"Provide all the incentives a young adult might want – those were the bishop's tactics. Just offer the lad what he needs and doesn't have. Offer him money. Offer him a bit of public honor. That's enough for any boy. He'll take it. London's Bishop Bonner was confident. He knew the mind of London's youth. But Bonner, trying to buy William Hunter's obedience, instead brought the judgment of history upon himself and his queen.

"William Hunter's case was clear enough. Raised in a Christian home, he learned the Bible and loved it. He trusted God and distrusted the established church. The charge against him was just as clear. Queen Mary had decreed that everyone in London must take Mass. No ambiguity there. But young Hunter did not take Mass. Even in the big city, he could hide only so long.

"The lawbreaker was finally caught. He explained to the sheriff that reading the Bible, even alone, was worship. He had obeyed the edict, just not in the edict's required way. Then the bishop got involved, even though he certainly must have had more important responsibilities. Who was this young boy? Why should he be petulant? Failing to coax him by money, Bonner had William Hunter placed in the stocks. For two days Hunter crouched in the wood frame without food or water. Now will you obey the Queen? No? To Newgate prison then. No honor awaits you there.

"For the next nine months William Hunter carried chains around the dismal prison – all for reading a Bible, for not taking the Mass, for defying the Queen's express order. By February 9, 1555, Bishop Bonner had troubled himself enough with this boy. Still no? Then back to Brentwood with you, your home village, to be burned as a heretic.

"On March 26, with Psalm 51 on his lips, William Hunter, Bible reader, age nineteen, died in the fire lit by bailiff Richard Ponde, acting on orders of the state.

"As the wood ignited, William's brother yelled to him, 'Think on the holy passion of Christ, William, and be not afraid of death.'

"The sheriff said to his convict: 'I would no more pray for you than for a dog.'

"'I am not afraid," William replied.

"Today a monument in Brentwood carries this message:

> *William Hunter. Martyr.*
> *Committed to the flames March 26 MDLV.*
> *Christian Reader, learn from his example to*
> *value the privilege of an open Bible.*
> *And be careful to maintain it."*

From *Foxe's Voice of the Martyrs*"

MARCH 16

El Roi,

It's true, we do not always know how to pray. We do not always know what will be the best for us and others. It's true, we do know what we want right this moment. But, that is not always the best and most profitable path for us.

Thank You, Lord, that the Spirit also helps us. Because we are so often spiritually sick and infirm, our vision is impaired and myopic, and our prayers remain small, selfish, malnourished and short-sighted. We know not what we should pray for as we ought. But, praise You Lord! *For the Spirit itself maketh intercession for us with groanings which cannot be uttered* (Romans 8:26).

Truly, all we need to do is groan.

And You know already our real and deepest needs expressed in the groan.

Father, help us to become people for whom our real needs, known by You, become our real and dearest desires. For then, we will know how to pray. We will know how to live. And above all, when our need, as known by You, matches the desire known by us, we will find You – ever waiting to save and ever willing to welcome us home to the place of perfect rest found in You alone.

Oh, Lord, the blessings of salvation! How great they are! Indwelt by the Holy Spirit...God with me. Mysterious, amazing, and powerful. The Holy Spirit knows me completely. The Holy Spirit knows You, Lord, completely...this is a powerful combination. The Spirit can intercede perfectly, and the Spirit's intercession will be according to Your will, God. The Spirit will intercede, bringing my needs before the throne of God, and these prayers will align with God's will.

I have access to the will of God through the presence and power of the Holy Spirit.

This is a gift reserved for the saints...those who have been saved by the blood of Christ.

I have been saved by the blood of Christ. I am, thus, a saint.

I praise You, Father, for such a gift, and I pray that all in our family will become saints...that they will each come to Calvary, to the great efficient and sufficient fount of salvation, and be made clean and whole and free. And then, as they cry, "Yes, Lord," the Spirit will come to dwell, to intercede, and to connect them to Your perfect will, the best for their lives. Help us, Lord, to know the Holy Spirit's power and presence in our lives.

In the Name of the Living God who sees and acts on our behalf...

MARCH 17

El Elyon,

It is a beautiful and sunny day here in Delevan, NY. There is life in the spring air. There is freshness and newness. Praise You, Father, for the newness of life that You offer, that You are.

Lord, Your Word says ALL things work together for GOOD (Your glory and our best) to those who LOVE YOU and are the CALLED according to YOUR purpose. Our love for You must be supreme, and we must be seeking Your will no matter where it leads, even if it leads through surging waters and raging seas of turmoil.

Good comes to those who love You and are called according to Your purpose. Good comes from all circumstances when You, Lord, are the center and on the throne of our lives. Oh, this is so hard for us to believe! We struggle to understand, and the details of how this works out in our particular lives and specific trials seem mysterious.

But, praise God, I believe!

I have experienced Your goodness in all situations. And that includes Sarah's death. Often through tears, I proclaim in my heart that ALL things work together for GOOD to those who love You, Lord, and are the called according to Your purposes. Thank You for helping me love You. Thank You for calling. Thank You for Your great, although sometimes mysterious, purpose in all things that I walk through.

In the Name of God Most High, the exalted and sovereign One...

MARCH 18

El Olam,

Your foreknowledge, the truth that You already know, and have always known the beginning from the end is the anchor of Your promise that all things work together for good to those who love You and are called according to Your purpose.

"The called," foreknown by Thee, O Lord, are predestined to be conformed into Christ's image. *Called...justified...glorified*...already accomplished even if not yet experienced. Thank You, Lord, for calling me, justifying me, and glorifying me...the work is complete, the fullness of it already known by You, and someday to be fully known by me. Christ's great sacrifice flows seamlessly into Christ's great accomplishment...obedience to You and salvation for us!

O what a Savior! Hallelujah!

Father, conform me more and more into the image of Your beloved Son. May this be the desire of my heart, may this be the desire of each person in our family...to be shaped into the likeness of Christ. It is only His nail scarred hands and precious blood that can save! May everyone in this family be called to know this great truth and to seize it and to seize You, through Christ, as their own. May each be justified. And glorified. Our glory is Your glory, and Yours is ours. Your glory reflected within and upon us, the redeemed, is then reflected back to You and to those around us. Your essence with us, shining through us forever and always, this is what it looks like…a glimpse of glory.

O what a Savior!

May the great miracle of justification and glorification reach deeply into the minds and hearts and souls of our family, of me. May we be firmly planted in the rich soil of Your truth, and anchored securely in the depths of Your great salvation.

From the foundation of the world, You, O Lord, the One who inhabits eternity, have known those who would be Yours. I praise You for Your foreknowledge. I praise You for justification. I praise You for glorification!

In the Name of the Eternal God, without beginning and without end…

MARCH 19

Jehovah,

Thank You, Lord, that You are for me. If You are for me, then victory is mine already. Circumstances cannot defeat me, if You be for me. I can be in the grip of the worst circumstances with no clear way out and no end in sight. And, yet, if You be for me, You will prevail, and I through You shall overcome.

Lord, nothing is more powerful than You! You are Almighty. And, You are for me! I dare not shrink back. My Lord is for me, and He is able, and thus I daily MUST discard fears, doubts, lingering insidious anxieties, and shadows of sorrow. I am called to live life in a BIG way, above these defeating circumstances. My life is not big. My life should not and shall not and literally cannot be big. But, the way I live life must be big because the God I serve is the All-Powerful El Shaddai. He is Elohim and El Olam and El Roi.

He is my all in all, and if He be for me, who can be against me?

Protect me Lord. Protect our family, and be for them, Lord. Stand, I pray, Father, on their side and fight on their behalf. Fight for their souls. Save them in the raging battle and deliver them from sin and pride, from Satan's lies, and from the flames of an unquenchable hell.

In the Name of the ONE WHO IS…self-existent…always has been and always will be…

<u>**MARCH 20**</u>

From <u>**Knowing God**</u> *by J.I. Packer* [12]

God Only Wise...

"What does the Bible mean when it calls God wise? In Scripture, wisdom is a moral as well as an intellectual quality, more than mere intelligence or knowledge, just as it is more than mere cleverness or cunning. For us to be truly wise, in the Bible sense, our intelligence and cleverness must be harnessed to a right end. Wisdom is the power to see, and the inclination to choose, the best and highest goal, together with the surest means of attaining it.

"Wisdom is, in fact, the practical side of moral goodness. As such, it is found in its fullness only in God. He alone is naturally and entirely and invariably wise. 'His wisdom ever waketh,' says the hymn, and it is true. God is never other than wise in anything that He does. Wisdom, as the old theologians used to say, is His essence, just as power, and truth, and goodness, are His essence – integral elements, that is, in His character.....

"God's almighty wisdom is always active, and never fails. All His works of creation and providence and grace display it, and until we can see it in them we just are not seeing them straight. But we cannot recognize God's wisdom unless we know the end for which He is working. Here many go wrong. Misunderstanding what the Bible means when it says that God is love (see 1 John 4:8-10), they think that God intends a trouble-free life for all, irrespective of their moral and spiritual state, and hence they conclude that anything painful and upsetting (illness, accident, injury, loss of job, the suffering of a loved one) indicates either that God's wisdom, or power, or both, have broken down, or that God, after all, does not exist.

"But this idea of God's intention is a complete mistake: God's wisdom is not, and never was pledged to keep a fallen world happy, or to make ungodliness comfortable. Not even to Christians has He promised a trouble-free life; rather the reverse. He has other ends in view for life in this world than simply to make it easy for everyone.

"What is He after, then? What is His goal? What does He aim at? When He made us, His purpose was that we should love and honor Him, praising Him for the wonderfully ordered complexity and variety of His world, using it according to His will, and so enjoying both it and Him. And though we have fallen, God has not abandoned His first purpose. Still He plans that a great host of humankind should come to love and honor Him. His ultimate objective is to bring them to a state in which they please Him entirely and praise Him adequately, a state in which He is all in all to them, and He and they rejoice continually in the knowledge of each other's love – people rejoicing in the saving love of God, set upon them from all eternity, and God rejoicing in the responsive love of people, drawn out of them by grace through the gospel.

"This will be God's glory, and our glory too…"
From <u>Knowing God</u> by J.I. Packer [12]

MARCH 21

Dear Lord,

You are Logos…the Word made flesh…the Truth in skin…

I love Your Word, Lord. I love the beautiful and real way You reveal Yourself in Scripture. Your written Word is the balm of truth that will heal the most broken of hearts and broken of lives. It is Your Word that will crack the hardest of hearts. It is a double-edged sword intended to piercingly reveal the truth of who You are and of who we are. I love You, Lord, the Living Word, Logos, God in the flesh.

God, how can I thank You for sending the LOGOS, the Word, Your Son? How can I thank You that You spared Him not? How can I thank You that You delivered Him up for me? There is but one way to thank You, and that is to receive You, and to be delivered by the One who was delivered up for me, for us.

Any response other than embracing the Logos, this great gift, amounts to rejecting the gift. Lord, seize each person in our family in such a way that they will seize You. You who spared not Your own Son…You who gave Him to us…You who will freely give us all things…You hold out this great gift, and we so often and so foolishly walk by You and past You as if there is something greater than You.

Fools are we!

There is nothing, no one greater. There is no greater gift. And there is no greater gift-giver than You.

What promises are poured over, upon and into our lives in that moment when we grip the hand of the Son You gave and say, "Yes, I will be made whole. Yes, I will be clean. Yes, I will seek Your forgiveness and admit how deeply it is needed!"

This is what You offer to a lost and dying world.

You offer life.

You offer wholeness. Cleanness. Forgiveness.

You offer Your very flesh, spared not and given for us!

In the Name of The Word…

MARCH 22

Dear Lord,

You alone justify. It is only because You have laid our deserved punishment upon Your Son that we can stand before You justified and forgiven. Not at all by our own works or any goodness within us. We can stand in Your presence because Your Son willingly poured out His life and allowed His body, cold and dead, to be laid in a lonely tomb.

That is why I am justified.

All because of You and You only. Christ is worthy! He is worthy to condemn us. He is worthy to save us. He can rightfully judge and condemn, and He can rightfully judge and save. Indeed, we will all be judged by this worthy, righteous God. Some will be judged and declared righteous because they accepted Christ. Many will be judged and condemned because they rejected Christ.

Where are you, dear reader?

Judged you will be. Guilty you are.

Who shall pay the price?

Christ or you?

With all my heart, I plead…let Christ pay your debt! Your debt is steep. You cannot pay. Do not let your pride deceive you into thinking you can.

Christ alone can satisfy the righteous wrath of the Father and settle the account against you. Come. Today.

In the Name of God…Consuming Fire…

MARCH 23

Dear Jesus, my Savior, my King,

Life is fleeting. A year ago today, we took Sarah to a number of doctor appointments…neurosurgery, cardiology, oncology. Each declared her well. She was stable and doing fine. Within 3 weeks, she would be dead. Yes, life is a fleeting shadow, a blooming flower that fades and withers. A mist…here and soon gone.

I praise You, Lord, for life despite its brevity. I praise You, Lord, that in You is life everlasting. Lord, You experienced death. You became flesh, subject to the same pain and suffering that we are. Like Sarah, there was a moment when You breathed Your last breath and Your heart stopped. You died. For me. And You rose again. For me. And You, Jesus, are now at the right hand of God making intercession. For me. For us.

Lord, may all of us in our family recognize the true nature of life…it is precious, it vanishes quicker than we imagine. Do not, Lord, allow any of us to neglect the truth that we are dying. May we each die prepared to meet You. May we each die forgiven, clean, and saved, robed in Your white garments of righteousness.

Jesus, intercede without ceasing on behalf of our family. Make intercession for all who are lost in our family. Intercede for their salvation. Jesus, You are alive and at God's right hand. Thank You that You are mighty to save. Save all in this family.

In the Name of Jesus the Savior…

MARCH 24

Dear Eternal Father,

You are the great I AM, and I cry out to You for help!

Help me to wrestle.

This day I am struggling.

The details of the struggle are not as important as the mere reality of, "I struggle." Common to all man is struggle. Help us Lord to understand that the battles always include a behind-the-scenes spiritual front. Help us to wrestle well and win the victory on the spiritual front even if we suffer loss and defeat on the physical. Temporary physical defeat is really no defeat at all for the child of God. The real war is always spiritual, and my God is always greater than the enemy.

Tribulation, distress, persecution, famine, nakedness, peril, sword…How frightening is this world! But, for the saved, we need not fear. These things shall not and cannot separate the child of God from the love of Christ! We may feel, in our pounding hearts, confused minds, and exhausted bodies that we have been separated. But that is untrue!

God has said these things shall not separate us from Him. If God has said, then it is so.

Let us hold fast.

I pray, Lord, in all the fears and trials and dilemmas our family may face, may we find You and be Yours.

In the Name of the Great I AM…

MARCH 25

What if God is real?

What if God really did create?

What if He truly does see and know all we think and say and do?

What if God does have the right to establish standards of morality?

What if He really is holy?

What if He really does love me?

What if He really is King with the right to rule and reign?

What if we really will someday stand before Him and give an account?

What if the existence of God actually is the best explanation for the complexity of DNA and cells and stars and a rational universe?

What if God really did humble Himself and put on flesh and walk among us and hang on a cross and lie in a tomb?

What if Jesus Christ really did rise from the grave?

What if all His promises are "yes" in Christ?

What if someday every knee really will bow and tongue confess that Jesus Christ is Lord?

What if it's all really true?

Are you ready?

MARCH 26

Dear Lord, Creator and Redeemer,

I love You, Lord. And, I am persuaded that neither death, nor life, nor angels, nor principalities, nor powers, nor things present, nor things to come, nor height, nor depth, nor any other creature, shall be able to separate us from the love You have poured out when the blood spilled from Your Son's veins on our behalf.

What more needs to be said? Romans 8 opens with freedom from condemnation, praise the Lord! Romans 8 closes with the guarantee that NOTHING anywhere at any time under any condition can separate us who are Yours from You. Freedom and security. Praise the Lord!

How I love this chapter of the Bible. How I loved to read these holy words and beautiful promises to my sweet daughter. What a privilege I had to be the one to call her, "Mine," and cover her with Your Words during the years of her life. I pray, Lord, that Your Words, Your truth, Your very presence would cover our family and lead each one to the freedom and security found at the cross, the place where we can never, ever be separated from You.

In the Name of the Good Shepherd...

MARCH 27

Dear Father,

It has been a difficult and a lonely day. I do believe You are well aware of these troubles and the heartache that accompany them. Lord, help me to respond to the tough days the way Mary did. With confidence in You, Mary proclaimed, *My soul doth magnify the Lord, and my spirit has rejoiced in God my Savior...For He that is mighty hath done to me great things; and holy is His name (Luke 1:46-49)*. May this be the cry of my heart to You, my Father. As You regarded Mary's low estate, regard mine, and help me to obey as Mary obeyed You and simply said, *Behold the handmaid of the Lord; be it unto me according to Thy word (Luke 1:38)*.

Mary trusted You despite confusing circumstances that appeared impossible to overcome. Help me to trust You with such depth and faith. In the midst of sorrow and loneliness, help me to trust that You will provide safe landing to this child of Yours.

I don't know all the details of the trials and struggles individual members of our family may be facing. The human condition it seems so often includes conflict and strife, and this family is no exception. Wherever our family may be, whatever they may be experiencing, whatever they may be enduring, Lord, may they find You on the journey. May they be like Mary and give it all to You and submit willingly while rejoicing in the conflict and trusting You implicitly in the storm.

In the Name of the One who is the source of all.

MARCH 28

Dear Father,

My heart floods with thoughts for my nephews, nieces, grandchildren, and students…

May they each now and as they grow love You, Lord. Be their strength. Father, be their rock, their fortress, and their deliverer. Be the One in whom they take refuge. You are a shield and it is in You only that salvation is found. May these precious children and young people grab a hold of the horns of Your salvation and hold tightly to You through all that they may face. Lord, You are worthy of all praise. It's You who saves us from our enemies, the greatest of which is sin. I pray that welling from their hearts will be praises lifted to You and a plea from each one for Your salvation, graciously extended through the bleeding hands of Your Son.

Help us to live life with the faith of Shadrach, Meshach, and Abednego. They knew how to live straight in a culture that was wicked and perverse. These men were surrounded by adversity and threatened with death. Yet, they stood for You, determined that dying while standing for You was better than living while denying You.

Help us in this family to become like these faithful men. Nourish us with Your truth so that we grow bold to stand for You, intentional in our walk, and absolutely committed to persevering without shrinking back. Were these men afraid? Probably. But they were driven not by fear but by belief and principle.

They believed You are who You say You are, Lord, and that You would do what You had promised. They believed.

May we be a believing family and people that are unshaken even by fiery furnaces and other terrifying circumstances. May we become people capable in today's culture, of saying, *If we are thrown into the blazing furnace, the God we serve is able to save us from it, and He will rescue us from your hand, O king. But even if He does not, we want you to know, O king, that we will not serve your gods or worship the image of gold you have set up.*

May our faith rest solely upon You, Lord. May our faith in You never waiver, even if our circumstances are grueling. May we be a people of grit and determination with the iron of truth running through our veins. May we be a people convinced of Your goodness – no matter the fiery trial – now and in generations to come.

In the Name of the One who is our Strong Tower and Refuge, Mighty to save and Faithful to deliver…

<u>March 29</u>

Dear Father,

It's early morning. The eastern sky is just beginning to show the beautiful colors of a sunrise. How amazing, mighty and loving You are, God, to create colors of such variety and beauty! How wonderful You must be to make us with the ability to both see and appreciate the colors You have designed!

Lord, I pray that our family would be a family that stands in awe of who You are and what You do! May we stand still before You today and worship You in silent awe. When we look at the stars, the sun, the moon, the seas, and all that is therein, when we contemplate the cosmos, the world around us, and the complexity of even a single cell, may we humbly adore You. Protect us from overlooking the power that is behind our world and the power that sustains it and us.

Father, help us to have honest and good hearts. May we have ears to hear Your Word and hearts and minds that are ploughed and prepared for Your Word to be planted within. May we nurture and cherish Your Word and may Your truth grow deep, strong roots into the lives of each. May we be saved and able to hear the Word, keep it, and bring forth much fruit with patience.

In the Name of the One who is the source of the sun and the moon and the starry host of heaven…

MARCH 30

From <u>Knowing God</u> by J.I. Packer [13]

Goodness and Severity

" 'Behold therefore the goodness and severity of God,' writes Paul in Romans 11:22. The crucial word here is 'and'. ...

"Never, perhaps, since Paul wrote has there been more need to labor this point than there is today. Modern muddle-headedness and confusion as to the meaning of faith in God are almost beyond description. People say they believe in God, but they have no idea who it is that they believe in, or what difference believing in Him may make.

"Christians who want to help their floundering fellows into what a famous old tract used to call 'safety, certainty and enjoyment' are constantly bewildered as to where to begin: the fantastic hodgepodge of fancies about God quite takes their breath away. How on earth have people got into such a muddle? What lies at the root of their confusion? And where is the starting point for setting them straight?

"To these questions there are several complementary sets of answers. One is that people have gotten into the practice of following private religious hunches rather than learning of God from His own Word; we have to try to help them unlearn the pride and, in some cases, the misconceptions about Scripture which gave rise to this attitude and to base their convictions henceforth not on what they feel but on what the Bible says. A second answer is that modern people think of all religions as equal and equivalent – they draw their ideas about God from pagan as well as Christian sources; we have to try to show people the uniqueness and finality of the Lord Jesus Christ, God's last word to man.

"A third answer is that people have ceased to recognize the reality of their own sinfulness, which imparts a degree of perversity and enmity against God to all that they think and do; it is our task to try to introduce people to this fact about themselves and so make them self-distrustful and open to correction by the word of Christ. A fourth answer, no less basic than the three already given, is that people today are in the habit of disassociating the thought of God's goodness from that of His severity; we must seek to wean them from this habit, since nothing but misbelief is possible as long as it persists.

From <u>Knowing God</u> by J.I. Packer [13]

MARCH 31

Then the Philistine said, this day I defy the ranks of Israel! Give me a man and let us fight each other! On hearing the Philistine's words, Saul and all the Israelites were dismayed and terrified…When the Israelites saw the many, they all ran from him in great fear…

David asked, *Who is this uncircumcised Philistine that he should defy the armies of the Living God?…The Lord who delivered me from the paw of the lion and the paw of the bear will deliver me from the hand of this Philistine!*

David said to the Philistine, *You come against me with sword and spear and javelin, but I come against you in the name of the Lord Almighty, the God of the armies of Israel, whom you have defied. This day the Lord will hand you over to me.*
(from I Samuel 17)

I have fears.

These are my uncircumcised Philistines.

I struggle with sin in my life.

These are my uncircumcised Philistines.

I look around. I see sin, lies, blasphemy in the world.

These are uncircumcised Philistines.

David knew his position and rights and duties in the Lord.

Do I?

So often, I am like Saul and the Israelite army, terrified and trembling, fearing the Philistine instead of the Lord.

I need a dose of David.

I, like him, must learn to cry out, "Who is this uncircumcised Philistine who dares to defy the army of the living God!" Like David, I need to remember the power and the sovereignty of the Lord over Goliath.

I need to call uncircumcised Philistines what they are, and go forth in faith in the living God whose I am.

March's Apologetic Moment...Contend for the faith

Can They Both Be True?

Compromise.

That was what my college years were all about.

One of the areas in which I compromised was my belief system about origins...nerdy sounding, perhaps...but highly consequential nonetheless.

In college, I held really fat, well-documented, beautifully illustrated textbooks in my hands. I sat in lecture halls with professors referred to as "Dr." such and such...men in glasses who rarely smiled and spoke long words into complicated sentences. It all seemed so, well, smart. Reading these books and listening to those professors, I decided Darwinian evolution was true. Had to be, right, with such high sounding words and lofty arguments and sophisticated people spouting the party line?

I grew up believing that the Genesis account of Scripture was real and accurate.

In college, I changed. I compromised. I graduated from college believing that BOTH the Genesis account of Scripture and Darwinian evolution were real and accurate. My worldview shifted, and I held onto the combined belief that "evolution is true and God caused it." Formally, such a compromised view is called "theistic evolution."

This worldview diminished my view of God...and of His holiness...and of His commandments...and it made me comfortable with compromise in my personal life.

If Genesis is compromised, the seriousness of sin is compromised.

If the seriousness of sin is compromised, the gospel is compromised.

It becomes easier to sin when Genesis is small.

But, this is not an essay about the ugly consequences of a flawed worldview. It is an essay about the logical and scientific errors that make it impossible – if one is intellectually honest - to reconcile the book of Genesis and Darwinian evolution

You see, Genesis and Darwinian evolution (including cosmic evolution and chemical evolution) are not compatible.

Simply put, they cannot both be true.

In order to reconcile these two belief systems, something must give. What ends up giving is Genesis.

Let's consider some specific examples in which Genesis and Darwinian evolution are not compatible....

In the Genesis account, plants are made before the sun.

In the evolutionary account, the sun comes first.

These can't both be true.

In the Genesis account, the earth is young, less than 10,000 years.

In the evolutionary account, the earth is old, at least 4 billion years old.

These can't both be true.

In the Genesis account, the earth was created before the sun and stars.

In the evolutionary account, the sun and stars were created before the earth.

These can't both be true.

In the Genesis account, man was created and death came as the result of man's sin.

Thus, there was no death before man.

In the evolutionary account, death existed for millions of years before man evolved.

These can't both be true.

In the Genesis account, God declares His creation "very good" prior to the disobedience of man which ushered in death. If the evolutionary account is true, then death came before man. If this is so, can God accurately declare His creation "very good?" Either creation was "very good" because man's sin had not yet marred it or there was death before man and creation was not "very good."

Consider what evolutionary theorist and philosopher David Hull had to say about this: "Whatever the god implied by evolutionary theory may be like, He is not the Protestant God of waste not, want not. He is also not a loving god who cares about his productions. He is not even the awful god portrayed in the book of Job. The god of the Galapagos (evolution) is careless, wasteful, indifferent, almost diabolical. He is certainly not the sort of god to whom anyone would be inclined to pray."[51]

In the Genesis account, creatures were made by a common Designer.

In the evolutionary account, creatures evolved from a common ancestor.

These can't both be true.

In the Genesis account, creatures were made according to their kind with the ability to adapt within genetic limitations.

In the evolutionary account, adaptation is without limit as long as there is ample time for the mechanisms of natural selection and mutations to act.

These can't both be true.

In the Genesis account, diversity in creation reflects the creative power of the mind of God who designed creation with purpose.

According to the American National Association of Biology Teachers (representing the evolutionary account), "The diversity of life on earth is the outcome of evolution: an unsupervised, impersonal, unpredictable and natural process of temporal descent with genetic modification that is affected by natural selection, chance, historical contingencies, and changing environments."

These positions can't both be true.

In the Genesis account, a catastrophic global flood explains the voluminous fossil record and geologic strata.

In the evolutionary account, uniformitarianism explains the voluminous fossil record and geologic strata.

These can't both be true.

In the Genesis account, death is an enemy.

In the evolutionary account, death is a necessary ingredient, for it fuels survival of the fittest and survival of the fittest fuels evolution.

These can't both be true.

In the Genesis account, there is a rational explanation for the origin of matter, space, and time. That rational explanation is an eternal God that exists outside of matter, space, and time.

In the evolutionary account, there is no rational explanation for the origin of matter, space, and time. There are hypothesis – such as quantum fluctuations – that are suggested. But, these hypothesis require just as much faith, perhaps more, than does the Genesis account.

These can't both be true.

In the Genesis account, there is a straightforward literal story of creation. In the Genesis account, the word "Yom" is used to describe each day of creation. The word "Yom," when paired with a number (such as first day, second day, third day, etc.) means "24-hours."

In the evolutionary account, "Yom" cannot mean a 24 hour period. In other words, creation scientists claim Genesis is literal and theistic evolutionists claim that Genesis is mythical or allegorical.

These can't both be true.

If the Genesis account is true, man is responsible for death and man needs a redeemer.

If the Darwinian evolution is true, man is not responsible for death and man needs no redeemer.

The Genesis account and the Darwinian evolutionary account are opposing worldviews.

They cannot, if one is intellectually and spiritually honest, be reconciled.

At least let's be honest about that.

And said, Naked came I out of my mother's womb,
and naked shall I return thither: the L ORD gave,
and the L ORD hath taken away;
blessed be the name of the L ORD.
Job 1:21

April

"I am trying here to prevent anyone saying the really foolish thing that people often say about Him: I'm ready to accept Jesus as a great moral teacher, but I don't accept his claim to be God. That is the one thing we must not say. A man who was merely a man and said the sort of things Jesus said would not be a great moral teacher. He would either be a lunatic — on the level with the man who says he is a poached egg — or else he would be the Devil of Hell. You must make your choice. Either this man was, and is, the Son of God, or else a madman or something worse. You can shut him up for a fool, you can spit at him and kill him as a demon or you can fall at his feet and call him Lord and God, but let us not come with any patronizing nonsense about his being a great human teacher. He has not left that open to us. He did not intend to."
— C.S. Lewis, Mere Christianity

APRIL 1

And out of the ground made the LORD God to grow every tree that is pleasant to the sight, and good for food; the tree of life also in the midst of the garden, and the tree of knowledge of good and evil…And the LORD God commanded the man, saying, Of every tree of the garden thou mayest freely eat: But of the tree of the knowledge of good and evil, thou shalt not eat of it: for in the day that thou eatest thereof, thou shalt surely die.
(Genesis 2:9, 16, 17)

Isn't it funny – or wickedly horrifying – that one of the first things we think of when we read this passage in Scripture is, "Well, why did God even put that tree of the knowledge of good and evil in the Garden?" And, whether we admit it or not, many of us may wonder in the back of our minds if God is really so good after all. Would a good God really put a test like this before frail us?

Yes, yes, I know the standard response a mature Christian is expected to make: "God didn't want people to be robots programmed to love and forced to choose Him. He wants our love freely given to Him. Thus, something to choose beside Him was necessary….thus the tree of knowledge of good and evil."

But, my real point here is, why do we even wonder this in the first place? Why do we zero in on this, as if God set us up to fall? Are we still looking for excuses to sin? Are we still trying, like Adam, to lay the blame on God?

This is loophole mentality.

Fight it!

God planted every tree that is pleasant and good, including the tree of life, in that perfect garden. Probably hundreds or thousands or hundreds of thousands of luscious, beautiful trees and the food that they produced awaited Adam and Eve.

There was no lack.

There was no need.

There was no physical hunger.

There was plenty, for God provided abundantly....perfect beauty, perfect food, perfect fellowship, perfect union.

And one rule with which to prove our love and obedience.

They failed.

We continue to fail.

We are Adam and Eve.

Yet somehow, despite all the great goodness God freely gave, they then and we now continue to question and wonder why God planted that old tree of the knowledge of good and evil in the first place. We continue to blame God. We accuse God, missing the reality of God's sovereign holiness...and revealing with this very accusation the pride still alive and well within mankind individually and corporately.

APRIL 2

It's getting to be that time of the year again...the anniversary of Sarah's death.

How gracious God has been to us. I look back at the days leading up to her death and the months immediately following, and I stand in awe of His goodness to us, to her.

Sarah, my sweet little lamb, now safely in the arms of Jesus, the Great Shepherd.

I live with a beautiful, heart-breaking and heart-healing contrast...One weekend in April, on a Saturday cold and rainy, we buried Sarah. On the next weekend in that same April, we celebrated the glorious resurrection of Jesus Christ, the Perfect Lamb of God.

I knew then, and I know still now, that God gave me a gift putting these two very different events, one of sorrow and one of joy, so closely together. The stark contrast was a sweet reminder of the great hope I have in Christ.

There is no hope eternal apart from Jesus. He gave Himself for us. Not just to save us, but to fill us, to overflow our lives with His abundant presence and peace. Apart from Him, hope is not eternal, but merely temporary escape from our reality and pain. But in Him, through Him, because of Him there is hope that is real and secure and everlasting, the type of hope that gives purpose to pain and meaning to trials, the type of hope that fills emptiness with perspective.

Yet, it's more than hope.

It's identity.

Don't we all ask, "Who am I and why am I here?" Yes, I am Dave and Sharon's daughter. Nancy and Bear's sister. Mark's wife. Sarah's Mother. I am a grandmother. Teacher. Friend. But above all and before all these, I am a child of the King, a child of the Great Creator God who, in mighty power, spoke the universe into being. This all-powerful and sovereign God needs nothing from me. I have nothing to offer Him. Despite my smallness compared to His greatness, He loves me. He treasures me. He cares. He knows me. Every detail….He is aware of every need, He grieves every sin, He sees me and hears me and knows my heart, every bitter and selfish beat of it. For this, broken me, He died. And therein is my value rooted in Him and nourished with His life's blood. He the Vine, I the branch.

I have been bought with a price, the blood of Christ, and I am no longer my own, but His. Redeemed. Reconciled to the Father, and in Him I live and move and have my being.

Identity. I am His and He is mine.

Nothing shall separate me from the love of God in Christ Jesus. Neither death, nor life, nor angels, nor principalities, nor powers, nor things present, nor things to come. Neither height nor depth, nor any other creature shall be able to separate me from Him. Ever. Because He bought me. I am His. Forever.

What a Savior!

For me, He died. He saw me in my low estate. He knew I could not free myself from the bondage to sin. He knew I could not afford the price of sin, a payment rightly demanded by a righteous and holy God.

So He came.

Deity put on humanity.

And He suffered. Died. Bled. He sacrificed His life for mine, and poured out His blood in place of mine. Beautiful propitiation!

What victory! For He is now alive, and in His life I share and in His victory I walk. In Him I am more than a conqueror. Any battle I fight now or in the future I fight from a position of victory, and the battle is already won.

There is no other hope eternal. There is no other way to the Father but through this, the bleeding Son. There is one mediator between God and man. One mediator. Jesus Christ, resurrected, the Way, the Truth, the Life.

I celebrate Easter because I serve a risen King!

So three years later I prepare again for that stark, yet sweet, contrast…On Sunday, April 13 I will remember the exact slow-motion moments of Sarah's death. I will hear the violent sounds of CPR on her tired heart. I will feel the crush of doctors and nurses who pushed us into the back of the hospital room when she coded. I will smell the sterile smell of an ICU. I will remember touching her hair for the last time. I will remember her skin beginning to grow cold. I will remember walking into our home for the first time without her and barely being able to breath as I did so.

But God…weeping may endure for a night, but joy comes in the morning.

And on Sunday, April 20, the morning will come, and with it the joy of knowing Jesus my Savior. And I will celebrate! He's alive! Where, O death, is your sting? Where, O grave, is your victory? Sin, hell, death, the grave are defeated in the veins of Emmanuel, King of kings, and Lord of lords, Savior mighty in power, Savior coming again. There is no hospital room that can take what I have with Him away from me. He fills me to overflowing with His goodness to me.

Easter is not meant to be merely a tradition or a cultural habit.

Easter is about relationship of fallen man with redeemer God, and it shouts out, "Seek Him while He may yet be found!"

I celebrate Easter because of who He is and what He does. I celebrate Easter because I love Him. And I love Him because He first loved me.

May today be the day of salvation for all who are seeking Him!

APRIL 3

Common sense isn't quite so common anymore. Much less the public expression of it, which takes both effort and courage. Let's talk climate change for a moment. Is climate change really an impending doomsday? Is it, if it exists at all, really a manmade phenomenon? These questions are certainly politically incorrect. But are they scientifically incorrect?

Recently the IPCC (Intergovernmental Panel on Climate Change) published a report that sent television news anchors into the murky deeps of hyperbole. News anchors everywhere proclaimed, based on the presumed settled science of the IPCC report, that we are on the brink of extinguishing ourselves as we continue to plunder and abuse the planet upon which we live. Is the science, however, really settled? Is there truly a consensus within the scientific community that climate change is a fast approaching Armageddon for which man is to blame?

It takes but a little effort to discover that there is not consensus among scientists on this topic. True, the microphone of the modern media and education machines may not give equal play time to those scientists who dissent from the politically expected interpretation of data and computer generated climate models. That, however, does not mean that there is no disagreement. The science is not settled. Don't take my word for it. Research the work of Ph.D. meteorologist Roy Spencer. Or physicist S. Fred Singer. Or take the time to read the Non-governmental International Panel on Climate Change (NIPCC) response to the IPCC report.

And in your research, don't forget to follow the money. To whom is grant money being rewarded? Integrity in the field of science requires that scientists pursue discovery and truth. Agenda driven money poured into scientific inquiry has, at the very least, the potential of corrupting the process.

I was an elementary student in the 1970s. I was told our planet was heading toward a deep freeze. My daughter, a couple decades later, was told a dangerous warm up was on the way. But, when the actual temperatures failed to comply with the predictions of the computer models, the "inconvenient truth" of global warming stood before the rebranding committee and came forth as nebulous "climate change."

There is an assumption that if the climate of the planet is changing it is the fault of man. This assumption needs to be challenged. The Montreal Protocol of 1987 became international policy when this faulty pre-supposition was not confronted. The Montreal Protocol called for the phase out of CFCs (chlorofluorocarbons). Use of CFCs had allowed for efficient and safe refrigeration. The political world held the flawed belief that the "hole" (it was actually a seasonal thinning) in the ozone layer over Antarctica was man's fault and in man's control. There was little public conversation about the fact that the "hole" was actually discovered in the 1950s by a scientist named Dobson well before CFCs came into widespread use. There was little discussion in political policy making circles about the fact of the annual polar vortex or that Mt. Eurebus (in Antarctica) was spewing 365,000 tons of chlorine each year into the atmosphere compared to the 7500 tons released worldwide annually by CFCs. In the end, science did not win out. Neither did mankind as this international protocol has certainly had negative effects, most especially upon the poorest people of our planet, those for whom more expensive refrigeration options can lead to no refrigeration options, which leads to the inability to store food which can easily, in Third World countries lead to death.

And then there is (or was) DDT. This insecticide, used from 1944 – 1972, prevented more human death and disease than any other chemical in recorded history. Millions of people in the Third World were protected from mosquito-borne malaria. But then came Rachel Carsen's book <u>Silent Spring.</u> This book was an appeal that energized an environmental movement and proved pivotal in leading a charge to ban DDT use in the United States and to reduce its use worldwide. Carson's book was lyrical and emotional. It was not, however, scientific. And millions of people in Third World countries have prematurely died since DDT has fallen into disfavor.

There is much at stake. I pose these questions: If you believe that climate change is a manmade phenomenon, why do you believe this? Have you really actively pursued knowledge and sought truth on this topic? Do you know the name and credentials of even one scientist who signed his or her name to the IPCC report? Or do you believe because you have simply heard it over and over from others who have heard it over and over? If you were asked, "What evidence do you have that supports the belief in man-made climate change" what would be your response? Would you offer evidence, or just a regurgitation of the words and talking points you have heard others speak? Man is to be a good and caring steward of creation. I'm just not sure that the modern environmental movement is actually about the environment.

APRIL 4

April 4, 2012

To my beloved students…

It was one year ago today that we drove Sarah into Children's Hospital. She was admitted with pneumonia, and 9 days later, the Lord called her home. I have to guard my thoughts. It would be very easy to let discouragement or doubt or loneliness or thoughts of "unfairness" to get the better of me. But, I always reminded Sarah that in Romans 8 we are told that we, who know Christ, are *MORE THAN CONQUERORS!*

On my drive to school most mornings, I listen to the same song. It helps prepare my mind for the day. It reminds me that I am not alone. It reminds me that we must "press on" and that victory is the proper position for a child God. Don't ever forget that we can experience victory even while bearing a burden. Here are some words from the song, "Through the Fire," by the Crabb Family...

So many times I've questioned certain circumstances
And things I could not understand.
And many times in trials,
Weakness blurs my vision
And then my frustration gets so out of hand.
Oh, but it's then I am reminded
I've never been forsaken
And I've never had to face one threat alone
Then the spirit rises up in me

He never promised that the cross would not get heavy
Or the hill would not be hard to climb.
He never offered our victories without fighting
But He said help would always come in time.
Just remember when you're standing in the valley of decision
And the adversary says "Give in"
Just hold on
Our Lord will show up
And He will take you through the fire again.

You know, I pray for you guys. And, my prayers for you are very much like my prayers were for Sarah. I don't pray for you to be happy. I don't pray about your physical health or material prosperity. I pray for you to be HOLY. I pray for you to know Christ and the power of His resurrection and to share in the fellowship of His sufferings. I pray that you will be young men and women who seek the Lord with all your hearts, minds, and strength. I pray that you will be spiritually alive and spiritually vibrant and growing in your knowledge of the Lord and how He is specifically working in your lives. I pray that your lives will honor God, reflect His glory, and that no matter what you go through in life that you will stand firm in the confidence of who God is, what God had promised, and who you are in Him. My prayer is that you will trust Him and lean on HIM and HIS understanding.

No matter what your position may be in the world, never forget that you are important to God, that you have been given gifts by Him to use to bring Him glory. Don't ever forget that God has a plan for you, and that He has meaningful work for you to do. In the eyes of the world, Sarah was small and had very little to offer. The Lord blessed me one day with a beautiful quote that I came across in a devotional, and it was a quote that I often shared with Sarah: "There are people too big for God to use. But, there are no people too small."

No matter what you are called to do, no matter how unnoticed it may be by the world, do it well, unto the Lord. That's how you live a big life, a valuable life.

APRIL 5

Been thinking...my joy used to be more noticeable. But it was shallow. I am more serious and sober minded these days. Are sober mindedness and joy opposites?

Perhaps in the eyes of the shallow world, yes. But, not so in the reality of God's Kingdom. Sober mindedness is necessary because the spiritual dangers are real. There is an enemy of which to be aware, and there is a war in which to engage. To face these, we must be serious. And joyful. Is it possible to be both at the same time?

I am serious because the battles are real.

I am joyful because the victory has been guaranteed!

I am more than a conqueror through Him!

Thus, I face the enemy and fight the battles with both a sober and rejoicing mind.

God is big and holy and real and loving and sovereign. He is Creator, Sustainer, Redeemer. He is El Shaddai and Elohim and Jehovah Nissi. He is righteousness. He is the All-mighty Conqueror who knows my name and has rescued me from the dominion of darkness and made me His child. The mighty cross and the empty tomb are life and freedom.

Thus now my joy is real. There is depth that was impossible in my shallow younger years. My joy looks different now because I am different now. My joy is stronger, strong enough to exist side-by-side and hand-in-hand with sober mindedness.

My joy is alive and well because it is growing deep roots in the soil of truth, nourished by the very character of Creator God, my Redeemer, my Love.

APRIL 6

Dear Father,

On Christmas we celebrate God becoming flesh. And on Good Friday, we remember how that very flesh was slain. Lamb of God slain upon a bloody cross, a death so horrible and undeserved, and yet so completely necessary to redeem the souls of men.

When I think about Sarah being buried, I am very aware that her physical body is alone in a dark and cold grave. You went, Jesus, to a dark and cold tomb on my behalf. Lord, help us this day to think about what You have done for us! We don't think about this as we ought! Instead, our minds race and grow weary thinking about our possessions, our jobs, our entertainment, our money, our time or lack thereof, our families. Us. We. Mine. Me.

Fools! Sooner than we know, our souls will be required. Where we have laid up treasure will then be revealed. Are we laying up treasure in heaven? Are we seeking Your Kingdom? Are we exalting self or exalting You? The true nature of our hearts and motives will soon be disclosed. Where, will our treasures be found? What will have been our motives?

Life is more than food. The body is more than clothes. We toil for food and drink and pleasure, and all the while we cannot even add an inch to our height. We live and breathe and eat and drink and laugh and cry because You, Lord, allow us this! And yet, how little we think of You and how often we think of ourselves and our stuff.

Lord, it is Your good pleasure to give us the Kingdom. You died so we could be part of your Kingdom. But so often, we live like atheists who have no interest in You or Your Kingdom. God forgive us and God help us to get ourselves off our minds and fix our thoughts upon You.

In the Name of the One who is the source of life...

APRIL 7

Friday, April 6, 2012 GOOD FRIDAY

Dear Father,

In less than an hour, we will be at church, worshipping You with a somber eye on the cross upon which You bled and died. Help us, Lord, to take seriously Your sacrifice on our behalf. Pierce us with the truth of what You went through for sinful man. Lord, I pray that You would literally force our minds off ourselves and instead open our minds and eyes to BEHOLD THE MAN, God bleeding and dying upon a cross. May Your sacrificial, substitutionary death become REAL to us, both saving us and affecting everything in our lives from this moment forward.

Godliness with contentment is great gain! We are a discontented people. We grumble and demand our way and refuse to believe that You are sufficient. We take matters, including our salvation, into our own feeble hands. The results are tragic. Salvation may elude us or we it. Victory is short-lived and not our normal position. The bottom line is, we need You. But, how much energy do we put into that compared to the attention we give to the matters of the world and the flesh?

We brought nothing into this world. And it is certain we can carry nothing out. Yet, we live as if we can, and spend so much time and energy on stuff. Save us, Lord, and make this a family of godly, contented people who recognize the great value of a relationship with You and the great beauty of resting in You. Praise Your Name! Worthy is the Lamb!

APRIL 8

Dear Father,

You know our frames. You know how easily we become bewildered. You know how swiftly we crumble when difficulties cross our paths. Father, may we know You as crucified Savior and risen Lord, and may we tremble in Your presence. Tremble in awe. Tremble in gratitude. Tremble in utmost respect. Tremble in anticipation of how You are working all things out in Your perfect way and perfect timing. Tremble in excitement at knowing You and the power of Your resurrection and knowing that You have plans for us!

May this be a family, Father, in which each of us is looking honestly and earnestly for Jesus the Nazarene. Honest, determined seekers will find Him and will discover through Him and His torn flesh the way the truth and the life.

Jesus, You have gone on ahead of us. You have prepared the way. You are sitting at God's right hand and You will come again. You will come as Judge and King.

Save each person in our family, Lord. Save the lost! Make of us disciples willing to follow You and to go out and preach everywhere the truth of who You are and how You save!

Lord, I plead that You would make Your presence powerfully known in my life and the lives of our family. Jesus, stand among us and speak. Help us to hear.

I pray that the peace You came to give, peace with the Father, peace within, and peace with one another, would surround us and protect us and, like a blanket, cover us.

May we look upon You, Jesus, and see Your hands and feet. You are real! You are alive! Equip us to touch and see and know and believe that You, Lord Jesus, are the risen Savior who bore the Father's wrath for me.

Open our minds to understand Scripture. Open our minds to desire Scripture. Everything that was written about You in the law and the Prophets and Psalms has been and is being fulfilled.

What was foretold happened. The Messiah came. The Messiah suffered. The Messiah rose from the dead on the third day. Repentance and forgiveness of sins is being preached in Your name, Jesus. This began in Jerusalem and has swept the world.

Yet not all hearts have been swept. Many hear and refuse to believe. Pride is a powerful enemy of the everlasting souls of men.

May the power of the resurrection, through the active work of the Holy Spirit, reach the hearts, minds, spirits of all in our family. As only You can, open the minds of the lost to understand and to desire Scripture and to understand and to desire You.

APRIL 9

Sunday, April 8, 2012 EASTER

Dear Father,

I serve a risen Savior! Praise You, Father, for the resurrection of the Son – a guarantee of my own resurrection. Christ's blood bought me, and His resurrection secures me. Jesus' sacrificial death and victorious resurrection justify me. I am made right with You, Lord, because of the cross and the empty tomb from which my suffering Savior arose a victorious Redeemer.

May we and our families be like the women who went that Sunday morning to the place where Jesus' dead body had been laid. They went looking for Jesus.

May we go forward looking for Jesus. May we be willing to go where You lead to have more of Him. When these women heard that Jesus had risen from the dead, they believed and were filled with joy. They hurried to tell others!

Father we are so guilty! We possess a certain callousness toward the cross and the resurrection. They seem far away. Sometimes we even think of them as boring, if we think of them at all. They don't seem to always fit with our "real" lives, so we take for granted the reality of Your sacrifice and what You really went through. We keep it at arm's length. Perhaps we've heard the gospel so many times that the thrill has worn off. Perhaps we were never thrilled by the gospel at all. How very sad!

God, open our eyes! God, as You met the women at the tomb, so meet us on the way and remind us of the reality of You. Open our eyes to see You…to see You crucified and we each with a hammer in our very own hands pounding in a nail…and to see You risen…glorious, beautiful, victor over the enemies of sin and death. May we see ourselves…bound in heavy chains apart from You…wearing filthy rags apart from You. May we see ourselves…free in You…clean in You.

And may we rejoice and proclaim, "He is risen! He is risen, indeed!"

APRIL 10

From *A Dangerous Grace* by Charles Colson [14]

Did Man Create God?

"The influential German philosopher Ludwig Feuerbach believed that God was made in the image of man, a creation of the human mind. So did Sigmund Freud. 'A theological dogma might be refuted (to a person) a thousand times,' he wrote, 'provided, however, he had need of it, he again and again accepts it as true.'

"Is religion just a psychological prop? Consider the nature and character of the God revealed in the Bible. If we were making up our own god, would we create one with such harsh demands for justice, righteousness, service, and self-sacrifice as we find in the biblical texts?

"Would the pious New Testament religious establishment have created a God who condemned them for their own hypocrisy? Would even a zealous disciple have invented a Messiah who called His followers to sell all, give their possessions to the poor, and follow Him to their deaths? The skeptic who believes the Bible's human authors manufactured their God out of psychological need has not read the Scriptures carefully." *From A Dangerous Grace by Charles Colson* [14]

APRIL 11

Dear Father,

It's early. Mark and I will be leaving soon for Florida. Just the two of us. We haven't gone on a trip like this in almost 15 years. Thank You that we can go and do this. Help us, Lord, to honor You on this trip, to keep our gaze upon You and to enjoy and appreciate one another.

I pray, Lord, for our family. May we and they, Father, recognize Christ's voice in our lives. In the gospel of John, You speak to Mary Magdalene as she is crying. You speak her name, and she recognizes Your voice. May we, too, be familiar with the voice of the Good Shepherd.

Speak to us, Lord, help us to hear. I pray for You to breathe upon us and fill us with the Holy Spirit.

Life in Your name, Lord, is my prayer for myself, my husband and our family.

Draw us this day ever closer to You. Keep us near to Your heart. Praise You for the length and breadth and height and depth of Your love that opens the door of salvation to repentant souls.

I love You.

In the Name of the One who is the source of love…

APRIL 12

Dear Heavenly Father,

Stand, Lord, I pray on the shores of our lives and bear with us when we are slow to recognize You and shallow in our understanding of Your greatness.

Thank You, Father, for being incredibly longsuffering toward us.

We get busy and distracted on our little fishing boats that we call "life," and all the while You are on the shore calling us to Yourself and preparing to feed us, nurture us and spend time with us. May all in this family have that moment when we, like Peter, jump out of the little boats we are in and swim eagerly to the shore upon which You stand.

As You asked Peter, Lord, may You ask each of us, "Do you truly love me?'

Do we? Do I? Do we truly love You, Lord? Are You supreme above all in our lives? I think most of us could honestly answer that question with a "No." No, Lord, most of the time You do not occupy the throne of our lives because we have foolishly and wickedly set idols in Your place and upon Your throne.

Help us, Lord, to examine our thoughts, our words, our deeds, our motives, the intents of our hearts and wonder, "Are You, Lord, beloved above all in my life? Do I truly love You as I ought?"

Father, may this question fall upon us and linger long and hard until we have answered it. Honestly.

And then, help us to love You. Show us what that looks like.

APRIL 13

This day is the anniversary of Sarah's death.

Soon after Sarah died, a package arrived in our mail. In it I found a book. It was a book written by a group of moms who had each buried a child. Most of their children were between the ages of 15 – 25, and their deaths occurred in a variety of ways including illness and tragic accidents.

This book helped me. But, not in the way you may expect.

The moms in this book were moms without hope. They were not women who were surrendered to God. If they mentioned God at all, it was with anger and disappointment, or it was a vague and distant generic kind of god.

As I read this book and each mom described her unique experience with grief and the "shadow grief" (their term) that has followed them ever since, I decided I did NOT want to be like them.

They spoke of how they felt justified to be selfish.

They spoke of how God had stolen something from them.

They spoke of how they each went to psychics to try and communicate with their children.

They said they could not even bring themselves to wear colorful clothing anymore, and they choose to wear black, brown, or other dark and somber colors.

It was a sad book to read.

Of course, there was sorrow in reading of the death of each beloved child.

But, the deepest sorrow was the hopelessness of these grieving moms.

Real and everlasting peace and solid comfort comes only from truth.

I pray that these moms will come to the truth that God loves them, knows them, and can give them beauty for ashes at the foot of the cross and victory at the empty tomb of Christ the Savior…..

As for me, I will wear yellow, and orange, and pink, and purple.

I grieve, but I grieve as one with hope.

Praise the Lord, O my soul, and all that is within me….Bless His Holy Name!

APRIL 14

Saturday, April 14, 2012

Dear Father,

A year ago yesterday, You called our sweet Sarah home. She has now experienced what I have yet to. She has made the journey across Jordan ahead of me. I don't understand what it must now be like for her. It is mysterious, and honestly, frightening to us left here on this side of the Jordan. It's all about faith, isn't it, Lord? I do not know the details. Instead, I know You. Do I trust You and who You say You are in Your Word? I do!

And yet, I tremble at what I don't fully understand. *I know that my Redeemer lives, and that in the end, You Lord, will stand upon the earth. After my skin has been destroyed, yet in my flesh I will see my God. I, myself, will see You, God, with my own eyes! My heart yearns for You, Lord (Job 19:25-27).* Sarah's skin has been destroyed, yet in her flesh she will see You, God! O, Your blessed assurance, how beautiful, Father!

May our family and each one therein yearn for You, God. May we each be prepared to stand on the bank of the chilly Jordan and face death.

The Redeemer lives!

Use my child's life and her death to confound the wise and the mighty of this world – that they may see that their wisdom and might, apart from You, is death. May others be hungry for you, reminded of You and their need for You when they remember my child.

Lord, may the preaching of the cross be real to me and my family. May our hearts be prepared to hear and receive this preaching in truth. May we not be like those who are perishing. May we be of the saved who experience the cross as the POWER of God. Use Sarah's death to cause our families to think about their own deaths and to examine themselves in truth.

Lord, use our sufferings. We lay these sufferings on your foundation – the foundation of Jesus Christ, who Himself suffered. I ask for Your grace and strength so that I can build my life on Your foundation. May I build for Your Kingdom. May my efforts produce gold, silver, and precious stone.

In the Pre-eminent Name of Jesus…

APRIL 15

From Foxe: Voice of the Martyrs [15]

John Nesbit (1685)

"John Nesbit was a fighter, a soldier in the Thirty Years War on the Continent, a warrior among the Scottish Covenanters. But he suffered scars and wounds of the heart nearly more severe than those of the body. By the time he was captured and tried, he was already taking leave of the struggles he had seen on earth and was eager for Heaven.

"When Nesbit returned from war in Europe, King Charles II had begun to impose his will on Scotland and the Scottish church, a will opposed by the determined free-church Covenanters. They resisted any king as church-head and the king's priests as intermediaries. The Covenanters believed with equal ferocity in Christ alone as head of the church and armed resistance as the right of all who seek to worship that way. The Covenanters would not bow to Charles without a fight.

"But Nesbit had other business, too. He married Margaret Law and they raised a family. He kept a handwritten New Testament passed on to him from a great-grandfather who was one of the barefoot preachers sent to England in the fourteenth century by John Wycliffe. He studied, learned, worked, prayed, and often hid from Charles's dragoons.

"But John could not hide forever. Severely injured on the field at Rullian Green, he was left for dead, but he escaped and recovered. He fought again at the Battles of Drumclog and Bothwell Bridge, both Covenanter disasters, which Nesbit survived after a brave fight. By then he was marked and a bounty was put on his head.

"To draw him out from hiding, the king's troops forced Margaret and the children out of their home. Unable to secure shelter that winter, she died of exposure. A daughter and son followed her. Nesbit apparently found them as his daughter was being prepared for burial. His surviving son later wrote this account of it: 'Friends were putting his little daughter in her rude coffin. Stooping down, he kissed her tenderly, saying, 'Religion does not make us void of natural affection, but we should be sure it runs in the channel of sanctified submission to the will of God, of whom we have our being.' Turning to a corner where two of his sons lay in a burning fever, he spoke to them but they did not know him. He groaned, saying, 'Naked came I into this world and naked I must go out of it. The Lord is making my passage easy.'

"He buried his family and quickly went into hiding again. For two years he evaded his captors, despite the growing price on his head. Then one day, in the company of three others, a squad of dragoons led by a Captain Robert, John's cousin, surrounded them. A brief fight followed. Nesbit's three colleagues were injured, then executed. John, however, was worth more alive than dead. He was taken to Edinburgh, where he told his prosecutors that he was more afraid to lie than to die; that he was more willing to give his life than even they were to take it.

"Quickly convicted, John was sentenced to be hanged. A few days before his death, he called aloud in prayer, 'O for Friday: O for Friday! O Lord, give me patience to wait Thy appointed time.' In prison he wrote his Last and Dying Testimony: 'Be not afraid at His sweet, lovely and desirable cross, for although I have not been able because of my wounds to lift up or lay down my head, yet I was never in better ease all my life. He has so wonderfully shined on me with the sense of His redeeming, strengthening, assisting, supporting, through-bearing, pardoning, and reconciling love, grace, and mercy, that my soul doth long to be freed of bodily infirmities and earthly organs, that so I may flee to His Royal Palace.'

"On the gallows he recited from the eighth chapter of Romans, then dropped and was gone. A warrior's heart was home at last." **From <u>Foxe: Voice of the Martyrs</u>** [15]

APRIL 16

Monday, April 16, 2012

Dear Father,

A year ago today, we buried Sarah. On a dreary and rainy day her body was laid in the cold ground until the trumpet sounds. In the twinkling of an eye, the dead will be raised incorruptible. It is a mystery, but in You, Lord, the mystery will one day be revealed. Our spirits will be reunited with a changed and immortal body – a body that will be glorious for the saved and a body that will endure the rigors of hell for the unsaved. Either way, a body changed to never die again. I pray, Father, that every person in my family will be saved, born again, and redeemed by the blood of Christ. At the last trumpet, may their bodies be raised immortal to eternity with You.

Death is an enemy. The grave is never satisfied. Daily, thousands die. Day after day death stalks and shadows us. The grave continues to demand more. We shall all die.

I pray that in our family, we shall all die in You! For in You, Lord, death has lost its sting and the grave will not have the final say. You, Lord, are triumphant over the terrors of death and in You, alone, we too can rise victorious and take the inheritance that is ours through Christ…life eternal, life abundant, life glorious.

May the last trumpet sound soon, Lord. Come, Lord Jesus!

You, LORD, reign and are robed in majesty!

You, Father, are armed with strength. Sarah's death does not diminish Your majesty or Your strength. Your throne was established long ago, and You, Mighty LORD, are from all eternity.

The seas have lifted up, O LORD, the seas have lifted up their voice and their pounding waves. But mightier are You, LORD, than they. You are mightier than the thunder of the great waters. You are the LORD on high and You are all-mighty. Your statutes stand firm. Holiness adorns Your house for endless days, O LORD.

When our families think of Sarah, turn their minds and hearts to Your everlasting power and might. Reveal to them Your sovereignty and that You, LORD, reign in majesty and rule in victory. When Sarah's life and death cross their minds, Lord lay eternity upon their hearts and cause them to tremble in acknowledgement of their own deaths yet to be. Cause them to seek You and to find You and to know You as You really are. Use Sarah's death, Lord, to advance Your Kingdom in our family.

Praise Your Name! Sing unto the LORD a new song!

In the Name of the One who is the source of new birth, new life, and life everlasting…

APRIL 17

Dear Father,

I lift my eyes to the hills. Where does my help come from? Lord, my help comes from You! You are the All-mighty Creator of heaven and earth. And, somehow and for some reason you care about me. You will not let my foot slip. You watch over me and slumber not. You, who watches over Israel, will neither slumber nor sleep. Our eyes grow weary and our bodies grow weak. But not You, O Lord! You do not grow weary or weak.

Thank You, Father, for watching over me. You are my shade in the heat of day and in the heat of trials. Neither sun nor moon nor the wicked plans of evil man can harm me because I am Yours and You will keep me and watch over my life. You watch my coming in and my going out, and are familiar with all my ways.

Now and forevermore You are my Savior and my helper and my strong tower and the rock that is higher than I! I love this deep and intimate relationship You and I share. What a privilege to be Your child. May all in our family, Lord, know despair, deep and dark despair, if they have not yet grabbed the horns of Your altar and fallen before You at the cross. In the darkness of the trials so often required to break the proud, Lord, shine Your beautiful light and rescue any who are perishing in our family.

APRIL 18

To the One True and Almighty God, Creator of heaven and earth,

I sing for joy to You, LORD! I shout aloud to the Rock of my salvation! I come before You, LORD, with thanksgiving, and I extol You with music and with song.

LORD, You are the great God, the great King above all! In Your hands are the depths of the earth, and the mountain peaks belong to You. The sea is Yours, for You made it, and Your all-powerful hands formed the dry land.

LORD, I bow down in worship! I kneel before You, LORD and Maker. For You are my GOD, and I am a sheep of Your pasture. I am part of the flock under Your care. There is no better, safer place to be than in Your flock and under Your care.

Protect my heart from hardening. Keep my heart ever soft toward You and my ears ever opened to Your voice. Soften the hearts and open the ears of every person in my family. Soften the hearts and open the ears of my students now and in the years to come. Draw them to Your flock, LORD, carry them safely to Your pastures. Seek them. Buy them. Make them each Your own.

Father, how easily our hearts go astray. How easily we listen to the lies of the flesh and the world – the enemy within and the enemy without. Guard our hearts and our minds, and lead us through the valleys and along the rocky paths safely to Your perfect rest. The joy of the LORD is my strength!

APRIL 19

Dear Father, Maker of heaven and earth,

Shine forth, LORD, shine forth! Rise up, O Judge of the earth and reveal Your power and righteousness to those who are foolishly self-righteous. In the light of Your purity, LORD, expose our utter impurity.

Who is senseless? LORD, You know, You alone know! In ways that only You can accomplish, teach the senseless to take heed. Remind and instruct the foolish that their foolishness will profit them nothing on the day of their deaths.

You are GOD who implanted the ear. You will hear! You are GOD who formed the eye, and You will see!

You are mighty and sovereign to discipline nations, and You will punish the unrighteousness of man. There is no knowledge You lack, LORD. Indeed, You know the very thoughts of man. Indeed, You know that the thoughts of man are futile. We need Your thoughts, LORD, for ours will not lead to salvation.

Blessed is the man You discipline, O LORD. Bear down upon us, LORD, with loving discipline intending to reclaim the lost and bind the wounds of the broken. It is in discipline that gaping raw wounds of sin are healed and hope is found. Blessed, O LORD, is the man You teach from Your law. Lay upon the hearts of each person in our families Your beautiful law, the law that leads to the cross and the blood of the Savior that satisfies the law and opens to us the gate of heaven.

In the Name of Jesus, Maker of heaven and earth…

APRIL 20

From *A Dangerous Grace* by Charles Colson [16]

Contemporary Christs

"There's a growing trend to recast Jesus to fit a modern secular perspective. And theologians are leading the pack. Just listen to some of the titles hitting the bookshelves.

"Anglican Bishop John Spong wrote <u>Born of a Woman</u>, offering the preposterous suggestion that Mary was raped – and that the virgin birth was concocted by the church as a cover-up.

"Divinity professor Barbara Theiring authored <u>Jesus: The Man</u>, in which she says Jesus didn't die on the cross, He was just poisoned. He was revived and went on to marry and raise three children.

"In <u>The Historical Jesus</u>, Catholic theologian John Crossan argues that Jesus didn't rise from the dead. Instead His body was buried in a shallow grave, Crossan says, where it was dug up and devoured by dogs.

"Taken together, books like these can create a widespread climate of opinion that the Bible is simply a collection of myths and errors. Even evangelical Christians may gradually accept the same principle and begin to separate faith from facts. The Bible is true in is spiritual message, they say, but full of errors in its history.

"**But Scripture never separates faith from facts**. In I Corinthians 15 Paul explicitly argues that if Christ was not physically raised from the dead, our faith is worthless. Besides, once you accept in principle that Scripture can be wrong, you start performing surgery on the text. You sort out certain historical details and stack them in a pile marked 'believable,' label the rest 'unbelievable' and dump them out.

"But surely this is illogical. It's all the same text. If the Bible is reliable on some facts, why does it suddenly become unreliable on others?

"**No, the Bible must be accepted in its total message**. Otherwise, all we're doing is remaking Jesus to fit our own personal prejudices."
From <u>A Dangerous Grace</u> by Charles Colson [16]

APRIL 21

Dear Father, the God of Abraham, Isaac, and Jacob, the Lord who is unchanging and ever faithful,

I sing to You, LORD, a new song! May all the earth break forth in song unto You. I lift my voice and praise Your Name, Father. Through joy and truth and well-timed words, may I proclaim Your salvation day after day. May my life proclaim Your salvation. I declare Your glory and Your marvelous deeds!

LORD, I have only a small audience. I am unimpressive and unimportant in the eyes of this world. But, GOD, I love You. I trust You. In the places where I am, may I always be declaring Your glory.

Father, You are great and most worthy of praise. You are to be feared above all gods, for all the gods of the nations are but senseless and impotent idols. But You, LORD, made the heavens. Splendor and majesty are before You and strength and glory live in Your sanctuary. There is glory, LORD, due Your Name. Equip me to ascribe glory to You. I worship You in the splendor of Your holiness.

I tremble before You. I pray that each person in our families, now and in the generations to come, will tremble before You. I pray for the earth itself to tremble before You.

The LORD reigns! What You, LORD, have established cannot be moved. You will judge the people with equity. You will judge the world in righteousness and the peoples in truth. There is no hiding from Your righteous judgment. May I and our family be clothed in Christ's righteousness. That is the only way to escape Your wrath and the literal place called hell we deserve.

I pray for Your return, Jesus. Then the heavens will rejoice and the earth will be glad. The sea will resound and all that is in it. The field will be jubilant, and the trees of the forest will sing for joy. They will sing before the LORD! Come, Lord, I pray.

In the Name of Jesus, the God of Abraham, Isaac, and Jacob, the Lord who is unchanging and ever faithful…

APRIL 22

Today is earth day.

Today and every day, I choose to worship the Creator rather than the creation.

I praise Him for speaking the earth into existence, for giving me life and making me a living soul created in His image.

For by Him were all things created that are in heaven and that are in earth, visible and invisible, whether they be thrones, or dominions, or principalities or powers: all things were created by Him and for Him. And He is before all things, and by Him all things consist (Colossians 1:16-17).

The earth is the Lords and the fullness thereof; the world, and they that dwell therein (Psalm 24:1).

By the word of the LORD were the heavens made; and all the host of them by the breath of His mouth...Let all the earth fear the LORD: let all the inhabitants of the world stand in awe of Him (Psalm 33:6,8).

For the invisible things of Him from the creation of the world are clearly seen, being understood by the things that are made, even His eternal power and Godhead; so that they are without excuse: Because that, when they knew God, they glorified Him not as God, neither were thankful; but became vain in their imaginations, and their foolish heart was darkened. Professing themselves to be wise, they became fools, And changed the glory of the uncorruptible God into an image made like to corruptible man, and to birds, and four footed beasts, and creeping things.   Wherefore God also gave them up to uncleanness through the lusts of their own hearts, to dishonour their own bodies between themselves: Who changed the truth of God into a lie, and worshipped and served the creature more than the Creator, who is blessed for ever. Amen (Romans 1:20 – 25).

APRIL 23

Last night at church, Nate and Erin shared the testimony of their son. He was born with a complicated heart defect and passed away when he was 8 months old. Nate and Erin shared both the story of their beautiful son's life and how God has worked in theirs through this storm and sorrow.

For me, the pictures they showed pierced my heart. He was a beautiful baby! These pictures brought back memories of Sarah's infancy in the intensive care unit at Children's Hospital of Buffalo. The white hospital receiving blankets with the striped blue borders...the ventilator tubing...ECMO machines...picc lines...post-surgical heart protocol with the chest still open due to swelling....the percussion equipment used for chest physical therapy. All of this, Mark and I are familiar with, and seeing these pictures brought big tears to my eyes as I remembered, and quite honestly, longed for those days. They were difficult days, to be sure, but they were days when Sarah, although sick, was here, and I could touch her, kiss her cheek, and stroke her pretty brown hair. I miss those days. I miss my Sarah. I cried with loneliness and my arms ached to hold my child.

After the Sunday night service, Mark and I came home. We turned on the television for a few minutes. I made some hot chocolate for myself before I went to bed. I went to bed, but I couldn't sleep. Around 11:00 pm, I climbed out of bed and stumbled in the dark down the hall and into the living room and our couch. I lay down and pulled the blanket, Sarah's blanket, around me. As I expected and hoped, our cat, Jo, jumped up and snuggled tightly into my arms. I lay on the couch, wondering, "What is victory?"

Victory does not mean forgetting. It does not require that I forsake the joys and struggles of Sarah's life or the sorrow of her death. Victory does not mean that I refuse to cry as if tears somehow negate triumph and usher in defeat.

Victory does not mean that I deny the searing pain of loss, the jagged edges of grief, or the deep loneliness birthed straight from the womb of Sarah's death. Victory is not about ignoring these realities and playing make-believe.

Victory is not about will-power. It is not found in an attempt to conjure up the strength to get through the day or to withstand the temptation. Victory is not, and cannot be, about my own supposed abilities.

Victory does not mean that I walk around skipping and happy all the day long. When I write this word, "happy," the picture I see is one of a laughing person whose circumstances are comfortable and pleasant. I picture a sort of selfish silliness in the type of happiness to which I am referring. It is shallow because it is based on the moment and has no greater perspective than self and the getting what it wants at that particular moment. It is without depth, very fickle, and in no way a true indicator of real victory.

Victory does not mean that I merely return to the life I had before Sarah. It is not about remaining the person I was before she came into my life or before she left my life.

Given these things that victory is NOT, what then is victory?

Victory means that even as I remember, I press on. When I remember my child, there will be moments when I laugh and moments when I cry, and really not much separates the two. I carry with me memories of a season of life now over. Victory is remembering that season with a willingness to persevere into the next.

Victory means that as I experience a broken heart and aching loneliness, that I KNOW I will come forth as gold. Victory always involves refining. And refining is painful. The dross must be removed and the pure, precious metal remain. The furnace of affliction must be hot to remove impurities, but when it is all done, what comes forth from the fire is valuable and has been drawn out by the loving master gold smith, the Lord Himself, who knows the perfect temperature necessary to refine me without destroying me. Victory is believing that, through the fire, I will come forth as gold.

Victory is found in brokenness before the Lord. It is coming to Him crushed and empty and completely aware that my own will-power and self-effort, while at times able to temporarily relieve, can never truly deliver me. Victory is acknowledging that there is a real, spiritual enemy from which I need deliverance, and understanding that this needed deliverance can come only from the Lord. Sarah's death is not my enemy. Satan and his insidious deceptions are. Satan whispers lies about God's character. He tries to plant doubt. He attempts to stir up conflict. He encourages me to give in to imaginations and to set up high places in my mind and life with Sarah's death as an idol. Satan is a liar and the father of lies. He is a thief who has come to kill, steal, and destroy. He is the enemy. I dare not think I can handle him alone with my limited will-power, positive thoughts, and worldly ways. Victory is recognizing this enemy and leaning hard on the Lord, leaning my full weight upon Jehovah for His deliverance in His perfect timing.

Victory means that I must deliberately CHOOSE gratitude. When I purpose in my heart to be thankful, I experience joy. Yes, the tears may be burning my cheeks, but when I say in my heart and with my mouth, *"The LORD giveth, the LORD taketh away. Blessed be the name of the LORD,"* I deliver defeat to the enemy and joy takes root in my life. Every time I choose to say "thank you," those roots of joy grow deeper still. Joy sown in the soil of a grateful heart will grow into a mighty oak. Under the shade of this mighty oak, I may cry buckets of tears, but as I choose to praise God in the groaning, I quench the fiery darts of the adversary and deliver a blow, in the strength of the Lord, to Satan's deceitful lying mouth. Gratitude is, indeed, a mighty weapon in the arsenal of victory.

Victory means recognizing, although I will never again be the same person, that potential exists to be this day conformed more and more into the image of Christ. I will never again be the same! Indeed, that is a very good thing! I want to become, truly and really, that new creation that I can be in Christ. There are new songs to be sung. The melodies, while now different, can yet be beautiful. I will choose this day to sing unto the Lord a new song. I will choose this day to share in the fellowship of Christ's sufferings and ever cling to the promise that, as His child, I also share in the power of His resurrection. So weep, sad eyes, weep if you must. But on the days when the tears flow, even then, my heart beats with the truth that I am God's child through Christ, and as a child, I am an heir, and the riches of God's kingdom, of God Himself, are mine, and this sorrowful valley through which I walk is not the end of the journey. Victory is!

Oddly enough, I cannot experience victory without experiencing a battle. The easy, comfortable, pleasurable moments of life do not challenge me to seek the Lord as I ought. How do I know if I have faith if I never am asked to exercise it? How do I know what victory is if I never encounter a battle? Trials, tragedies, temptations, troubles are all unpopular. These are things we strive hard to avoid.

And yet, it seems they are somehow profitable and often unavoidable pre-requisites to a victorious life. Thus, I must, even with tears in my eyes, embrace these struggles, and praise the Lord for them.

Victory is not an accomplishment. Victory is a person, and His name is Jesus Christ. I am His and He is mine. In all the challenges, I am His and He is mine. Through all the tears, I am His and He is mine. In any rejection or disappointment, I am His and He is mine. Through the deep waters and storms of life, I am His and He is mine. In any sickness I face, I am His and He is mine. At all the gravesides upon which I have stood and yet will stand, I am His and He is mine. At the moment of my own death, I am His and He is mine.

APRIL 24

Thinking about...how I can rest in the goodness of God in loss and sorrow as well as in gain and joy...for God's presence is as real in the death of a saint as in the life of a saint. Some children recover from life threatening illnesses. And when they do, we talk about how God has answered prayer and poured out His blessings. But, some children do not recover. My child didn't get better. But...God. He was and is still present. He was and is still answering prayer. He was and is still pouring out blessings.

I may not always understand the sovereignty of my God. But I will, by His grace, always cling to and proclaim His goodness in spite of and whatever the circumstances. I will not limit my all-powerful God by narrowly defining His blessings and expect that He must answer prayer my way.

His ways are not my ways. His ways are better and bigger.

And I rest. I abide. In His goodness.

APRIL 25

Took a bike ride this morning down to the cemetery. Standing there in the cool morning air, I sensed God's goodness. I stared at the dates on Sarah's stone: one a date of birth and the other a date of death. And I remembered that God knows both and that He knew both even before Sarah was conceived. My eyes drifted over to the stone bearing my name and Mark's. Just dates of birth etched in that stone. Someday the dates of death will be chiseled in, for there is no discharge from that war.

But, I felt joyful. Peaceful. Confident. God already knows those dates. I have been reconciled to the Holy God who knows all things already.

How prone we are to allow our experiences to dictate our beliefs and understanding of life, our worldview. How unnatural it seems to these bodies of flesh within which we dwell to allow God to dictate our beliefs and understanding and worldview.

It's true, our experiences sometimes do seem to contradict what we are told we are supposed to believe about God…that He is all-powerful, good, loving…that He is even these things when there is sickness, death, tragedy, brokenness in this world. What will guide us? Through what will we filter reality? Will we choose our experiences? Will we choose our physical senses? Or will we choose God and His Word?

My experiences include the death of a beloved child. Shall this loss become my identity?

No!

My identity is in the Savior! He has been merciful and gracious to me. He has convinced me that He is good despite Sarah's death. He has revealed to me that He is always good. And He has assured me He loves me even though Sarah died.

I believe.

And my identity is in Him.

APRIL 26

Dear Mighty, All-Knowing God, the LORD who inhabits eternity, and who is and was and is to come,

Praise and bless Your Name! I am Your servant, Lord. Teach me the way and the joy of serving You well and living and dying as Your bond slave. I praise Your Name. Let Your Name be praised, O Lord, both now and forevermore.

From the rising of the sun to the place where it sets, praise Your Name! You are exalted over all the nations. Your glory, Father, is above the heavens. Who is like unto You, the One who sits enthroned on high, the One who stoops down to look on the heavens and the earth? You raise the poor from the dust, and You lift the needy from the hopeless ash heap. You seat them with princes. You settle the barren woman in her home as a happy mother of children.

All praise to You, Lord, that although my children are not here, they still are. And I am still their happy mother....one day to be reunited with the child I knew and held and to be introduced to the child who died in my womb. Praise the LORD!

Death is real and must be faced. May we in this family be well aware of our spiritual poverty and our complete inability to save ourselves. Raise the spiritually dead in our family, LORD, to life. Life in You, the One who stooped down and walked among the ash heaps of this world. May the spiritually destitute know their destitution and turn from darkness to light. Plunge them and their awful sins and their pride under the cleansing fountain of the blood of Christ.

In the Name of Jesus, All-Knowing God, the LORD who inhabits eternity, and who is and was and is to come...

APRIL 27

Dear LORD, my Shepherd, my Bread of Life, my Living Water,

I praise the LORD! May the LORD be praised from the heavens! Be praised in the heights above. May all Your angels praise You. May heavenly host praise You...sun, moon, and shining stars. Highest heavens, burst forth in song and praise unto the LORD, the LORD who commanded and the stars were created, the LORD who sets them in place. God, creator of gravity and orbits and spiral galaxies and light years....Praise Your Powerful, able to create all out of nothing, Name.

Praise You, LORD from the earth. From ocean depths to mountain peaks, be praised, O LORD. Wild animals and all cattle, small creatures and flying birds, kings of the earth and all nations, princes and all rulers, young men and maidens, old men and children, let them praise Your Name, O Great and Mighty LORD. Your Name is exalted. Your splendor is above the earth and the heavens.

You have raised up for Your people a horn, a strong One, a King. He is the praise of all His saints, of Israel, the people close to His heart. Jesus is the Horn of Salvation, the Rock of Ages, the Perfect Lamb, worthy to set us free. I pray for our families to stand upon the Rock of Ages and to KNOW salvation.

In the Name of Jesus, my Shepherd, my Bread of Life, my Living Water...

APRIL 28

Dear God, Lord of Righteousness and Truth,

I will exalt You, my God the King! I will praise Your Name forever. I will praise You. Every day. I will extol Your Name forever and ever. Lord, great You are and worthy of all praise. Your greatness is unfathomable. We will pass it on and declare it to the generation coming behind. I will speak of Your glorious splendor and majesty, and I will remember Your wonderful works. I proclaim Your great deeds. And, as I celebrate Your abundant goodness, I will joyfully sing of Your righteousness.

LORD, gracious and compassionate You are. You are slow to anger and rich in love. You are good to all, and You have compassion on all You have made. May those You have made respond to Your compassion with a plea for Your undeserved mercy. You are both compassionate and righteous. You, LORD, are righteous and pure in all Your ways. You are near to all who call upon You. Help our family to call upon You, LORD, and be safe from Your righteous wrath. Safety is found in Your compassionate and perfect blood shed on our behalf and in our place. But to dwell in that place of spiritual safety, we must be under the blood and our hearts must beat to the tune of repentance and confession.

You are near to those who call on You in truth. Breathe Your truth, LORD, into my life and this family. Over all, You watch. You know those who love You. And You know those who do not. You know those who are wicked and still unclean in their sin, pride, and self-righteousness. Father, I pray, rescue the lost from the broad path and save them. My mouth will speak in praise of You. Let every creature praise your Holy Name forever and ever. Amen.

In the Name of Jesus, Lord of Righteousness and Truth...

APRIL 29

Dear All-Knowing, All-Wise LORD, the Lion of the Tribe of Judah,

Praise You, LORD! O my soul, praise the LORD. I will praise You, LORD, all my life. Whatever circumstances I face, I will praise You. When the enemy comes in like a flood, I will praise You, LORD, because You have raised up a standard and beneath Your banner, I am safe. When the enemy presses in hard, I know You, Father, are all the stronger and the battle is Yours.

I will sing praise to You, my God, as long as I live. I will not put my trust in this world, in princes, in mere mortal men who cannot save. These are nothing! Their plans will come to nought.   Their lives will end, and they will return to the ground. But You, O LORD, and Your holiness, righteousness and perfect plan shall endure. I am blessed because my help is the God of Jacob and my hope is the LORD God, the Maker of heaven and earth, the sea and everything in them, the LORD, who remains faithful forever.

Father, You uphold the cause of the oppressed. You give food to the hungry. You set prisoners free and give sight to the blind. You lift up those that are bowed down. You love the righteous. You watch over those in foreign lands and sustain the fatherless and the widow. You frustrate the way of the wicked. You, LORD, are mighty in power and complete in knowledge. You are perfect in wisdom. You reign forever. For all generations, You God, the God of Zion, reign in might! Praise You, LORD.

In the Name of Jesus, the All-Knowing, All-Wise LORD, the Lion of the Tribe of Judah…

APRIL 30

From *A Dangerous Grace* by Charles Colson [17]

Everything Under the Son

"An associate of mine was having lunch with a staffer from another Christian ministry when their conversation touched on the subject of recycling programs. My associate commented that Christian ministries should be the first to recycle, but her companion burst out, 'What is it with you? Not everything is about God, you know!'

"Sometimes I get letters telling me that in my writing I should stick to devotional issues: After all, not everything is about God, is it?

"Let me show where that line of reasoning leads.

"I know a Christian business executive who attended a three-week course in business ethics at Harvard. The course gave him some practical pointers for ethical conduct, he said. 'I can sum it up: When you're making a serious business decision, never do anything you think might end up in the newspapers.'

"I can only conclude that this man left his faith at the door when he walked into the classroom. Despite his apparent Christian maturity, he didn't realize that he had consumed a blitz course in secular utilitarian ethics: Ethics is about not getting caught.

"This lack of discernment is not unusual. A Search Institute survey found that only one out of three Christians believe that Christianity should have any effect on how they live.

"Christians need to realize that every decision they make reflects their core values. Choices about voting, budgeting, marriage, and movies are all philosophical issues. Christians who don't have a distinctively Christian philosophy will easily be suckered into living by the world's philosophies. Like my friend at Harvard.

"This is why church pews may be full on Sundays, but secular values dominate our culture. America's halfhearted religion leaves plenty of room for an anti-Christian value system."

From _A Dangerous Grace_ by Charles Colson [17]

April's Apologetic Moment…Contend for the Faith

Origins Matter…From Whence Came Matter, Space and Time?

"It was 1916 and Albert Einstein didn't like where his calculations were leading him. If his theory of General Relativity was true, it meant that the universe was not eternal but had a beginning. Einstein's calculations indeed were revealing a definite beginning to all time, all matter, and all space. This flew in the face of his belief that the universe was static and eternal. Einstein later called his discovery 'irritating.' He wanted the universe to be self-existent - not reliant on any outside cause – but the universe appeared to be one giant effect…" [52]

Where did it all come from? At the heart of science, is the quest to discover causes. What caused the universe? This one-time event cannot be repeated. It cannot be directly observed. Rather, we study the origin of the universe in a forensic and historical manner. We seek models that fit wh at we observe today as we look back, trying to figure out how it all happened.   The best model may not be able to explain everything, but it will be a model that fits well and is rational and logical.

Let's get logical.   Everything that had a beginning had a cause.   This is the law of causality and it underlies everything in science.   We could not have science if we did not have causality (which leads to predictability and rationality in the universe).   We now know that the universe had a beginning (this is based on the second law of thermodynamics, the red shifts of the expanding universe, and cosmic background radiation).   **IF everything that had a beginning had a cause AND the universe had a beginning, THEN the universe had a cause.**

So what?   Well, for atheists (including Darwinian evolutionists) this is a problem.

Why is it a problem for atheists? Well, it means that something has to exist OUTSIDE of matter, energy, time, and space. The CAUSE of matter, time, and space must logically exist OUTSIDE of these things. Otherwise, these things created themselves, and that is not logical. *"In his book* The Creation Revisited, *Dr. (Peter) Atkins (an atheist) struggles mightily to explain how the universe could come into existence, uncaused out of nothing. But in the end he finds himself trapped in self-contradiction. He writes, 'Now we go back in time beyond the moment of creation to when there was no time, and to where there was no space.' At this time before time, he imagines a swirling dust of mathematical points which recombine again and again and again and finally come by trial and error to form our space time universe…(this) is not a scientific theory but is actually self-contradictory pop-metaphysics. It is pop-metaphysics because it's a made-up explanation – there's absolutely no scientific evidence supporting it. And it's self-contradictory because it assumes time and space before there was time and space."* [53]

How well does the Biblical model fit the question of origins? **IF an all-powerful, eternal God exists, THEN He could be a rational First Cause of the universe and the matter, time, space it contains.**

What follows is an excerpt from I Don't Have Enough Faith to be an Atheist *by Norman Geisler and Frank Turek* [54] *:*

"Atheists are quick to ask the age-old question, 'Then who made God? If everything needs a cause, then God needs a cause too!'

"The law of causality does not say that EVERYTHING needs a cause. It says that everything that COMES TO BE needs a cause. God did not come to be. No one made God. He is unmade. As an eternal being, God did not have a beginning, so He didn't need a cause. 'But wait,' the atheist will protest, 'if you can have an eternal god, then I can have an eternal universe! After all, if the universe is eternal, then it did not have a cause.' Yes, it is logically possible that the universe is eternal and therefore didn't have a cause. In fact, it is one of only two possibilities: either the universe, or something outside the universe, is eternal. The problem for the atheist is that while it is LOGICALLY possible that the universe is eternal, it does not seem to be ACTUALLY possible (second law of thermodynamics, red-shifted planets, cosmic background radiation)...So by ruling out one of the two options, we are left with the only other option – something outside the universe is eternal.

"What is the First Cause like? From evidence alone, we know the First Cause must be:

> *Self-existent, timeless, non-spatial, and immaterial (since the First Cause created time, space, and matter, the First Cause must be outside of time, space, and matter). In other words, the First Cause is without limits, or infinite.*

> *Unimaginably powerful, to create the entire universe out of nothing.*

> *Supremely intelligent, to design the universe with such incredible precision.*

> *Personal, in order to choose to convert a state of nothingness into the time-space-material universe.*

"These characteristics of the First Cause are exactly the characteristics theists ascribe to God...

"If there is no God, why is there something rather than nothing? This is a question that we all have to answer. And in light of the evidence, we are left with only two options: either NO ONE created something out of nothing, or else SOMEONE created something out of nothing. Which view is more reasonable?

"The most reasonable view is God. Robert Jastrow (astronomer, evolutionist and agnostic) suggested this when he ended his book <u>God and the Astronomers</u> with this classic line: 'For the scientist who has lived by his faith in the power of reason, the story ends like a bad dream. He has scaled the mountains of ignorance; he is about to conquer the highest peak; as he pulls himself over the final rock, he is greeted by a band of theologians who have been sitting there for centuries.'"
From <u>I Don't Have Enough Faith to be an Atheist</u>, by Geisler and Turek [54]

Teach me Thy way, O LORD; I will walk in Thy truth:
unite my heart to fear Thy name.
Psalm 86:11

May

"You can never learn that Christ is all you need,
until Christ is all you have."
— Corrie ten Boom

MAY 1

As I was reading God's Word this morning, a verse jumped out at me: *Gather my saints together unto me; those that have made a covenant with me by sacrifice (Psalm 50:5).*

And here we find the definition of the word, "saint."

A saint is a person who has made a covenant with God by sacrifice.

And what is the sacrifice? Jesus Christ.

....His body broken on the cross...His blood poured out to pay for sin.

Mine. Yours.

My sin. Your sin.

That is the only all-sufficient sacrifice in which we must hope and to which we must cling.

If we do, then saints we become. His saints.

We become saints because Jesus Christ performed a miracle on our behalf.

The God of Creation became the God of Redemption. God, who needs nothing from us, died for us. God, who is perfectly holy, died for us the unholy.

The Creator, Redeemer God is a purifying fire.

In His presence we will either be consumed or consecrated. To be consecrated by Him means to be set apart for Him. It is He who makes us special and valuable, not we ourselves. It is He, through His sacrifice, who makes us saints, not we ourselves.

We are without hope apart from Him.

I pray that you are washed in the blood of the Lamb, clean and pure.

Consecrated.

One of His saints.

MAY 2

And Abel, he also brought of the firstlings of his flock and of the fat thereof. And the Lord had respect unto Abel and to his offering (Genesis 4:4).

In other words, Abel gave obediently to God of his first and best. God approved. God expects us to trust Him enough to give Him our first and our best and our everything in all things.

How often I fail!

I am much more like Cain most of the time. I give what is convenient and expect approval and blessing although I have sacrificed nothing and forget that all I have is from the Lord in the first place. One hundred percent comes from Him: the money I possess, the skills I have, the energy to apply those skills, the time I have. It all comes from Him.

He gives it all. He asks for the first and the best to be given back. Not because He needs it. But, because He wants to know our love and our trust is in Him, not His stuff.

Yet, more often than not, we, like Cain, give to God our way rather than His.

Then we pout when He doesn't pat us on the back.

And, lest we forget, God knows about giving His first and His best....*For God so loved the world that He gave His only begotten Son (John 3:16).* To an undeserving world, out of love for sinful selfish man, to satisfy the righteous wrath of a holy God, He gave. His Son. His first. His best. For me. May we have respect and awe unto the Lord for His offering!

May I, through God's grace, lay aside the powerful Cain within me that clings so tightly to "my stuff," "my time," "my needs," "my wants," and "my rights."

May I learn from Abel.

Thine, O Lord, is the greatness, and the power, and the glory, and the victory, and the majesty: for all that is in the heaven and in the earth is Thine; Thine is the kingdom, O Lord and Thou are exalted as head above all. Both riches and honor come of Thee, and Thou reignest over all; and in Thine hand it is to make great, and to give strength unto all. Now therefore, our God, we thank Thee and praise Thy glorious name. But who am I and what is my people, that we should be able to offer so willingly after this sort? For all things come of Thee, and of Thine own have we given Thee (I Chronicles 29:11-14).

MAY 3

And I (God) said unto you (Israel), I am the Lord your God; fear not the gods of the Amorites, in whose land ye dwell: but ye have not obeyed my voice (Judges 6:10).

And, today here in America, we are dwelling among Amorites.

There are so many gods in this country now in which we dwell. **Government** has become a god that we expect to meet our needs and solve our problems. **Environmentalism** and worshiping the created rather than the creator is the rising religion of this age. **Naturalism and materialism** are the gods of secular science. **Humanism and secularism and moral relativism and situational ethics and Darwinian evolution**, and all the consequences spawned by such sweeping ideas and anti-God worldviews…these are some of the gods in today's culture.

Convenience. Careers. Comfort.

My stuff. My rights. My time. My choice. My body. My life….

Me, me, me and more of me….

Yes, we are among the Amorites and their many gods.

Worse yet, sometimes we are the Amorites.

Forgive us, Lord, that we have not obeyed your voice. Forgive us Lord, that we no longer fear and honor you as we ought. Turn the hearts of our leaders and our individual hearts to You…the only truth and answer here in the midst of such perplexity and danger.

MAY 4

May God speak to me, to my heart and my mind, as I read His Word, and as I spend time with Him.

Lord, I want to know you!

I want to share in the fellowship of your sufferings.

I want to know the power of the resurrection in my life.

I want to be led by the Holy Spirit.

Lead me. Speak to me. Show me the changes that need to be made so that I can and will hear You in the midst of a crooked and perverse generation, in a loud and noisy world. Help me to be peculiar.

Yours. Always.

The FEAR of the LORD is the beginning of knowledge (Proverbs 1:7a).

His delight is in the law of the LORD, and in His law doth he meditate day and night. And he shall be like a tree planted by the rivers of water, that bringeth forth his fruit in his season (Psalm 1:2-3a).

MAY 5

How can it be that God is real and powerful and good and loving when so often the trials and tragedies of life scream otherwise? It is a mystery, a question no man can fully answer because no man's vision is big enough or vocabulary deep enough to grasp and describe the glory of God.

All I know is that HE IS bigger than the stuff we face. Period. His understanding is infinite, and ours is not. He sees the big picture. We catch glimpses.

Perspective matters.

A perspective that holds only earthly things will brim with earthly sorrows of a fallen, groaning creation.

A perspective that embraces the One True God of Creation, the One True God of Redemption will see beyond pain. It is a perspective of hope.

And thus I can declare with confidence that God is real and powerful and good and loving. Even as I stand at my child's grave.

This is the day the LORD has made! I WILL rejoice and be glad in it!

Today, tomorrow, always I will glorify God. I will enjoy Him forever.

Be excited about this God who is greater than our greatest need and deeper than our deepest trial.

MAY 6

Dear Father, Great and Powerful Healer, God Mighty to Save,

I praise You! I sing to You, O LORD, a new song. I praise You in the assembly of the saints. Let Israel rejoice in their Maker. Let the people of Zion be glad in their King. I praise Your Name, Lord, with dancing, and I make music to You.

May my life be a melody which You write.

Thank You, LORD, that You take delight in Your people, that You crown the humble with salvation. May we who are crowned with Your salvation rejoice in this honor and sing for joy upon our beds. In health and in sickness, may we rejoice. In life and in death, may we, crowned in Your great salvation, rejoice.

Praise You, O LORD! I praise God in His sanctuary. Praise Him, mighty heavens. You, LORD, are the One who creates, the One who sustains, and the One who can righteously judge. You, LORD, have the right, ability, and duty to carry out the sentence written against sinners and against the wickedness of this world and the wickedness within each of us.

O, LORD, I praise You for Your mercy and Your compassion. Apart from these, I would be rightfully condemned and consumed. I praise You, LORD, for Your acts of power and for Your surpassing greatness. Be praised, LORD, with the sounding of the trumpet, with harp and lyre, with tambourine and dancing, with strings and flute, with clash of cymbals and resounding cymbals!

Let everything that has breath praise You, my God and Savior. Praise the LORD!

In the Name of Jesus, Great and Powerful Healer, God Mighty to Save...

MAY 7

Dear Father in Heaven, the One who was, who is, and is to come, the great I AM,

One year ago, I wrote a prayer in this journal. Now, this journal is full. I have poured out my heart to You, Lord, and pled for Your mercy on behalf of our family. I trust Your sovereign goodness and know that, in the end, all will be as You would have it to be.

Praise be to You, O LORD, God of our father Israel, from everlasting to everlasting. Yours, O LORD, is the greatness and the power and the glory and the majesty and the splendor, for everything in heaven and earth is Yours. Yours, O LORD, is the Kingdom. You are exalted as head over all. Wealth and honor come from You; You are the ruler of all things. In Your hands are strength and power to exalt and give strength to all. Now, our God, I give You thanks and praise Your glorious Name.

But, who am I, and who are my people, that we should be able to give as generously as this? Our days on earth are like a shadow, without hope. But with You, LORD, I have hope, true and real. All I have, all I am, belongs to You, LORD (I Chronicles 29:10-20).

Make my life a sanctuary. Make my life a sweet aroma of Your truth and goodness. I know, my God, that You test the heart. O, LORD, God of Abraham, Isaac, and Jacob, keep my heart pure before You. May my heart forever desire You and be loyal to You.

Who am I, LORD, that You would choose me? I am nothing. You are all. Have Your way, O LORD, in my life. I am Your bond slave. I am Your child. I am Yours. You are mine.

In the Name of Jesus, the Name that is above every name…The One who was, the One who is, the One who is coming again…The great I AM…

MAY 8

Favor is deceitful, and beauty is vain: but a woman that feareth the LORD, she shall be praised (Proverbs 31:30).

"Fear of the LORD" – this is a quality good to possess, a quality to be highly desired. To tremble before a Holy God is a proper position, a pleasing response to all-consuming God. God doesn't want me to cringe and cower, for His Word says to come boldly to the throne of grace. That kind of fear, the cringing kind, causes a person to want to flee and hide – as impossible as it is to flee an all-knowing God! He wants our fear of Him to draw us near to Him. This kind of fear is different, unusual to the human mind and experience.

As humans, we avoid fear. We work hard to eliminate the causes of our fears. We think of fear as something to battle against, an enemy. But, the "fear of the LORD" is a fear in an elevated and unique category. It is different. It is other. It is necessary. It is "respect," but more than respect. It is "awe," but more than awe. Words, fail to adequately communicate "the fear of the LORD."

Maybe, I am complicating what is simple. If we see God as He really is – omnipotent, omniscient, omnipresent, holy, sovereign, eternal, immutable, Creator, Sustainer, Redeemer, Savior, King, gracious and merciful – if we see Him, then we see also ourselves, and the response that follows must be a humble acknowledgement of His greatness. His otherness. He is big, we are not. He needs not. We need always.

This is the "fear of the LORD": knowing Him as He really is, acknowledging Him for who He really is, and trembling....yes, trembling even as we run or stumble into His open arms and fall into His nail-scarred hands, proclaiming Him LORD of not just the universe, which indeed He is, but also LORD of our lives, individual and small.

Serve the LORD with fear, and rejoice with trembling (Psalm 2:11).

The lofty looks of man shall be humbled, and the haughtiness of men shall be bowed down, and the LORD alone shall be exalted in that day (Isaiah 2:11).

MAY 9

In Acts 3, a lame man is healed.

Why was this lame man healed and my Sarah not?

Why was Peter able to so confidently declare to the lame man that God would restore to him his legs, his health? I would never so boldly expect, much less proclaim to someone disabled or sick that God would heal him in that moment. Does this mean that my faith is too small? Am I, like Peter, supposed to be proclaiming physical healing?

I don't think so.

Peter could boldly proclaim because Peter was being boldly and specifically led by the indwelling Holy Spirit. My proclamation in Sarah's life was no less bold, but it was different. The Holy Spirit never led me to believe Sarah would be healed. Thus boldly proclaiming that she would walk and talk would have been merely proclaiming my own desire and would have been followed by deep disappointment and confusion. What the Holy Spirit taught me to proclaim, over time, was that God is good. Always. His grace is sufficient. Always. He gives His strength day by day. One day at a time. Manna every morning. This was and is my bold-like-Peter proclamation.

Sarah was not healed, but God's mercy to her and love for her was as deep and mighty as it was for the lame beggar in Acts 3. And, His work in her life, and thus in mine, was just as great, even if less known.

As I read Acts 3 this morning, I asked, "For what purpose could it be that the lame beggar was healed and Sarah not?" Could it be that in both situations similar purposes may be woven into the story? When the lame man was healed, the people who knew him *were filled with wonder and amazement (Acts 3:10)*. Could it be that this same outcome may be accomplished both in the life of the healed beggar and the death of my Sarah?

The God of Abraham, and of Isaac, and of Jacob, the God of our fathers hath glorified His Son Jesus (Acts 3:13a). How true this is both in the healing of the lame man and in the death of Sarah...God is still the same....He remains the God of Abraham, Isaac, and Jacob....

The details, the places, the times were different. But God was the same, and His purposes stood then and stand now and will always stand. And ever good are they, even if mysterious, the purposes of this great unchanging God of Abraham, Isaac, and Jacob.

My God.

God can always heal. But, we limit Him when we shrink the definition of "heal." How prone we are to assume He is only answering our prayers and loving us if He heals. Sometimes true healing and wholeness of life and completeness of purpose comes through a broken body. His was, after all, broken for us.

God loved Sarah who died as much as he loved the beggar He healed. His love continues to flow high and wide and deep and long in both health and sickness, and in both life and death. We think small about God when we condition His love upon our circumstances.

MAY 10

From *The Problem of Pain* by C.S. Lewis [18]

"The relation between Creator and creature is, of course, unique, and cannot be paralleled by any relations between one creature and another. God is both further from us, and nearer to us, than any other being....But at the same time, and for the same reason, the intimacy between God and even the meanest creature is closer than any that creatures can attain with one another. Our life is, at every moment, supplied by Him: our tiny, miraculous power of free will only operates on bodies which His continual energy keeps in existence – our very power to think is His power communicated to us. Such a unique relation can be apprehended only by analogies: from the various types of love known among creatures we reach an inadequate, but useful, conception of God's love for man.

"The lowest type, and one which is 'love' at all only by an extension of the word, is that which an artist feels for an artefact...We are, not metaphorically but in very truth, a Divine work of art, something that God is making, and therefore something with which He will not be satisfied until it has a certain character. Here again we come up against what I have called the 'intolerable compliment'. Over a sketch made idly to amuse a child, an artist may not take much trouble: he may be content to let it go even though it is not exactly as he meant it to be. But over the great picture of his life – the work which he loves, though in a different fashion, as intensely as a man love a woman or a mother a child – he will take endless trouble – and would, doubtless, thereby give endless trouble to the picture if it were sentient. One can image a sentient picture, after being rubbed and scraped and recommenced for the tenth time, wishing that it were only a thumbnail sketch whose making was over in a minute. In the same way, it is natural for us to wish that God had designed for us a less glorious and less arduous destiny; but then we are wishing not for more love but for less."
From *The Problem of Pain* by C.S. Lewis [18]

MAY 11

It's funny what we think as we go about the mundane tasks of life. I was just down in our basement, cleaning and changing the cat's litter box, sweeping the floors. And thinking. And praying while I cleaned and swept.

I was praying for my students, praying for them, and us, to recognize the unique and real danger that "churched kids" face....the danger of taking it all for granted, the danger of growing bored with the Lord and His Word, and the danger of knowing all the expected things to say and do and yet remaining cold hearted and lukewarm and able to hide it behind the very words and deeds for which we often pat you on the back.

How my heart cries out to You, Lord! Help my kids to really, really know You, want You, hunger for You with passion rather than mere duty. They need to radically own it, and sadly I doubt all do.

It's vain repetition: speaking and doing what is expected even while the heart itself is careless and could care less. Growing bored with God, and yet acting and speaking words that are traditionally expected and smiled upon by we, the older ones.

While my Baptist brethren may disagree, I am beginning to understand that communally praying the Lord's prayer, surely, must be less vain repetition than the day to day responses we often give one another!

May we be cautious not to pat the backs too vigorously of the students who know the expected things to say and do while in our presence.

MAY 12

Thinking about failures.

I don't like to fail.

Failure makes me feel embarrassed, and to me embarrassment is near to the top of my list of distasteful and disliked emotions.

But God...He is teaching me the value of failure. He is chiseling away at my mind and bringing a new and necessary understanding that, for a person like me – a person who is proud - failures are good and spiritually beneficial.

I know it to be true that I, in the presence of my own successes and accomplishments, will cling to them like gods. They will become idols to this proud mind. But they are worthless. Dangerous. And the way to crush them is to dash them upon the stones of failure.

Me, without failure, would result in me without God.

And so my flesh hates to fail because my flesh is puffed up and haughty.

But my spirit, confronted by God's Spirit, knows I need to be brought low. I need failure if ever I am going to know God and depend upon and exalt Him as He deserves.

As I need to beware of my successes becoming my idols, I need also to beware that my failures, too, can become strange idols. Worthless idols, whether germinated in success or failure, have the potential to become my identity.

And therein is tragedy...identity in anything other than the LORD.

Failure, the supposed flip side of success, can still become proud. It is the other side of pride, but pride none-the-less. Self-puffed up or self-defeated, either one is pride.   Whenever "self" is front and center, self remains an idol, an idol that must be diligently dashed down and crushed.

True identity comes only when self suffers a mortal blow.

For self and God cannot co-reign. One and one only can occupy the throne of a life.

Oh, how blessed can be the failures of life!

MAY 13

Rebuked.

I sat in the sanctuary, listening to the Sunday evening message of Pastor Paul Phillips. And I was humbled.   Pastor Phillips wasn't speaking directly to me, but the Spirit of God was, and I was rebuked.

The topic? The doctrine of salvation and positional truth.

Positional truth (who we are in God through Christ) and experiential truth (what we feel or what we go through) are not the same. Positional truth is the truth about WHO WE ARE in Christ from the moment of salvation. Positional truth is truth no matter what we feel. It is always true no matter what we experience. An example of positional truth is found in Romans 6:2: *How shall we, that are dead to sin, live any longer therein?* The positional truth: in Christ, I am dead to sin. However, that doesn't mean, experientially, that I will no longer sin. What I will experience will be an ongoing battle with sin. Yet, positionally, I am no longer a sinner.

Rather, I am a saint who still sins.

Pastor Phillips moved the message to application, and used the example of an addict, specifically a person addicted to crack. He spoke of how, should this person embrace Christ and be saved, he is positionally a SAINT immediately, and no longer a sinner, even if he still sins.

He said something along these lines: "Let's say this man comes to Christ and continues to struggle with this addiction. Does that mean he is not saved? No. we cannot expect those who are new in the faith to immediately shed the sins they are struggling with. Sometimes a person is immediately delivered, and what a wonderful thing when that is the case! But, it is not always the case, so get used to that reality when dealing with people and yourself! This person, perhaps still using crack, is positionally dead to sin. Does this mean we ignore the sin and anything goes? No. But what we need to do is to disciple this person regarding who God is, not demand that the person immediately shed the sin."

Demanding the person to stop the sin is focusing on the person. What is needed is discipleship…helping the new believer develop a BIG view of our great God, a view that grows bigger than the addiction, a view that equips the believer to walk in victory and freedom. How we all – new and old believer alike – must strive to live in the reality of who God is and what God does.

But it takes time and tender care….

Salvation first, and then discipleship followed by transformation.

The transformation of life and behavior (experiential truth) does not always, or even often, happen at the moment of salvation. But, the positional transformation does….the sinner is dead to sin even if he continues to sin.

The Christian response, especially for a new believer is discipleship focusing on GOD rather than on the person.

Transformation – often with great pain – will come if the person is truly seeking. But the focus must be God. Always God.

My focus isn't always God. I often look at other people through the eyes of a Pharisee, expecting the transformation before the salvation. Such thinking is the thinking of all the other religions in the world, a religion based on works. And we Christian are prone to think like that.

And therein was the rebuke.

MAY 14

I had to give one of my students his PSAT scores today.

They were not such good scores.

I wondered what his response would be?

Would he be defeated and discouraged?

He was neither.

May his response to failure become my response to failure....

For my student said to me, "I need to know where I'm really at so I can begin to get better and work on what really needs to be worked on."

Huh?

Such maturity as such a young age?

My student chose to not feel sorry for himself.

He chose to think like a conqueror.

He chose to look at a Goliath and respond like a David.

He handled it.

His response was one of strength and enthusiasm and perseverance.

He is on the verge of great growth.

MAY 15

From Foxe: Voice of the Martyrs [19]

Robert Thomas (1839 – 1865)

"*An isolated Asian government, an aggressive American skipper, and a Welsh missionary armed with Bibles all came together at one spot in September 1865. The foreigners had come too far, their supplies were too thin, and they were overwhelmed. They all perished, including the missionary-interpreter Robert Thomas, the first Protestant to minister in Korea, and the first Protestant to die there.*

"*Robert Thomas was born in Wales in 1839, the son of an independent church minister. He studied at London University; and with his wife Caroline, he was commissioned by the London Missionary Society for work in Asia. A five-month-long voyage put the young missionaries in Shanghai, where Robert quickly learned Mandarin. He was assigned as a schoolteacher in Beijing. But the Hermit Kingdom, as Korea was then called, was on his heart.*

"*Robert found a way. In 1864 or 1865, he slipped into Korea loaded with Chinese language Bibles provided by Scotland's National Bible Society, and as many Korean language as he could obtain from contacts in China. For four months he traveled and preached, though heavily disguised. Only a year earlier, the Korean king had turned against Christians, killing about 8,000 Roman Catholics in a purge of 'foreign religions.' Robert's successes brought joy, but his heart sank when Caroline suddenly became ill and died.*

"*In the summer of 1865, an American entrepreneur, W.B. Preston, with the help of a British business firm, launched an expedition designed to open trade with Pyongyang. They supplied a former U.S. navy ship, renamed the* General Sherman. *Thomas offered his services as translator and packed cases of Bibles for his second expedition to this tightly controlled kingdom.*

"*The journey was a missionary's nightmare. The ship captain, under pressure from Preston, ignored Korean orders to turn back. Instead, at high tide, the* General Sherman *steamed upriver. It appeared to be a direct threat to the already testy Dae Won Kun, who apparently believed the ship was an effort by Catholics to reestablish their mission. He ordered his army to kill the ship's crew.*

"*Now stuck on a sandbar, the crew of the* General Sherman *had cannon and rifle in their favor, but time favored the Koreans massed on the banks of the river. Captain Page even took one of the Korean negotiators as hostage, but to no avail. After two weeks of gunfire, Korean troops sent burning barges against the American ship. Its crew fought the blaze, but unable to contain it, they jumped overboard into the waters and the waiting swords of the Koreans. Some reports claim that Thomas made it to shore with Bibles, which he offered to the soldier who killed him.*

"*The* General Sherman *sank into the river, its iron ribbing and anchor all that remained. Thomas's executioner did indeed take that Bible offered to him, and used it to wallpaper his house. Amazingly, guests read the writing of that strange book so casually displayed. The soldier's nephew was converted and became a pastor.*

"*Today forty percent of South Korea is Christian. However, little is known about the church in Pyongyang. North Korea is as isolated and closed to public worship as in the day of Robert Thomas. But that too will change. Then, stories of the martyrs of Pyongyang will be told for the first time, and Thomas's sacrifice – his kneeling on the shore to offer a Bible – will be among the stories of faith gratefully recalled and remembered.*"
From <u>Foxe: Voice of the Martyrs</u> [19]

MAY 16

For as long as I can remember, I've known about China's one-child policy. I've heard about it on news reports, read about it in magazines, and occasionally it has been mentioned in conversations. Of course I've always believed that such a policy is wrong. But, it seemed so far away.

Today, though, I was reading "National Review" and the subject came up. And for the first time, I sensed the reality of the evil of this man-centered, man-made, man-destroying policy. When one really thinks about the details of what is going on here – forced abortions and unforced abortions, forced sterilizations and even infanticide – what does this wickedness do to the soul of the society upon which it is thrust?

Do those involved in the propagation and application of this policy ever consider the consequences? Do they even think about the lives they are ending, the families they are destroying, the God they are mocking, or the core of wickedness that is driving the policy? Or is it just routine to them now?

Someday they will stand before the God that today they refuse to recognize, and He will demand an account. Each will appear, clad in the darkness of his deeds, before the light of the Holy God of all creation....the One who saw all they did with the hands He gave them.

This policy is systemic evil! Yet we Americans and even we Christians, myself included, think little about it. Perhaps because it is far away. Perhaps because it seems there is little that we, individually, can do. Perhaps because there is just something everywhere you look that needs battling and we can't battle everything every moment.

The more I thought about it today, though, the more I realized this is possibly one of the greatest evils ever...and yet our level of outrage is nearly nonexistent. We should be abhorred! We should be crying out to God for justice. We should be praying for these babies – the least among us - and the mothers in whose wombs they are conceived and the fathers who planted that seed....that these parents stand up and refuse, even if at great cost, to continue any longer in this darkness.

We should be in anguish over this.

I imagine Satan smiles every time a Christian is reminded of this one-child policy and yet does not cry out to God with an anguished plea. Horror exists. It should pierce our hearts and drive us to our knees.

MAY 17

I need to remember we are living in Babylon.

I forget that sometimes because I spend much of my life with brothers and sisters in Christ.

But the broader culture is not Christian.

And of that I need be aware, both to remain vigilant to stand up for God's truth and to remain vigilant to see the opportunities that a dark world provides for light to shine.

How do we make sure that the influence is going from Church to culture rather than culture to Church?

We, the Church, need the Holy Spirit all the time.

Otherwise the culture will influence us more than we influence it.

And that is tragic for both.

MAY 18

Don't be like Lot.

In Genesis 12, Abraham included Lot when he sojourned to the land of Canaan.

In Genesis 13, Abraham and Lot were together in Bethel. Both had flocks and herds and tents.   But they needed more space. So Lot was given the chance to choose which way to go. Lot looked at the plain of Jordan and its lushness, and he chose this lushness.

Later in Genesis 13, Lot dwelled in the cities of the plain. He pitched his tent toward Sodom.

In Genesis 14, Lot dwelt in Sodom. He no longer was gazing at Sodom from afar. He was in the midst of it.   While at Sodom, Lot was captured by enemies. Abraham rescued him.

In Genesis 19, Lot sat at the gate of Sodom. In other words, he had become an important man within the wicked city.

Later in Genesis 19, God is in the process of rescuing Lot from the destruction and righteous wrath that Sodom would soon experience. But Lot lingered. God needed to take him by the hand.

It was all God and His mercy.

No, don't be like Lot.

Don't pitch your tent toward evil.

Don't dwell comfortably in the midst of evil.

Don't sit in the gate of evil.

Don't linger.

At least Lot didn't look back as his wife did....

Don't be like Lot's wife, either.

She looked back.

That backwards glance was a reflection of her heart, a heart that desired Sodom, the world.

Don't desire the world.

MAY 19

God is doing awesome things in our world. How could He not, for God in His very character and nature is awesome. May I not be like those, who when Jesus literally walked among them, limited Him to the expectation of a sociopolitical revolution.

His presence and His work are about much more than merely establishing men of faith in positions of power and toppling evil political regimes. These things will, indeed, one day happen, and when they do, there will be no mistaking God's sovereign hand or the sword of His Word.

But for now He restrains Himself politically and yet continues to pour Himself out, His Spirit poured upon me, daily bearing the load. His Spirit transforming lives of those not perhaps in power or positions of influence – thus it sometimes seems to we who are waiting and watching that His presence and work are muted. But they are not! He is present! And He is working! Lives ARE being transformed and souls ARE being saved, and while this may not be reported in the sensationalism of modern news and social media, there are angels in heaven rejoicing when even the least of those among us cry out and claim Jesus Christ as Lord and Savior.

Miracles are still occurring, and salvation is always a miracle, always supernatural. Always awe-inspiring.

In His timing and in His mysterious ways, His truth is marching on and great things are every day done by Him.

We have no right to be discouraged merely because His ways are not ours.

MAY 20

From *The Problem of Pain* by C.S. Lewis [20]

"When Christianity says that God loves man, it means that God loves man: not that He has some 'disinterest'...concern for our welfare, but that, in awful and surprising truth, we are the objects of His love. You asked for a loving God: you have one. The great spirit you so lightly invoked, the 'lord of terrible aspect', is present: not a senile benevolence that drowsily wishes you to be happy in your own way, not the cold philanthropy of a conscientious magistrate, nor the care of a host who feels responsible for the comfort of his guest, but the consuming fire Himself, the Love that made the worlds, persistent as the artist's love for his work and despotic as a man's love for a dog, provident and venerable as a father's love for a child, jealous, inexorable, exacting as love between the sexes. How this should be, I do not know: it passes reason to explain why any creatures, not to say creatures such as we, should have a value so prodigious in their Creator's eyes....

"The problem of reconciling human suffering with the existence of a God who loves, is only insoluble so long as we attach a trivial meaning to the word love, and look on things as if man were the center of them. Man is not the center. God does not exist for the sake of man. Man does not exist for his own sake. 'Thou hast created all things, and for Thy pleasure they are and were created' (Revelation 4:11). We were made not primarily that we may love God (though we were made for that too) but that God may love us, that we may become objects in which the Divine love may rest 'well pleased'. To ask that God's love should be content with us as we are is to ask

that God should cease to be God: because He is what He is, His love must, in the nature of things, be impeded and repelled by certain stains in our present character, and because He already loves us He must labour to make us lovable. We cannot even wish, in our better moments, that He could reconcile Himself to our present impurities....What we would here and now call our 'happiness' is not the end God chiefly has in view: but when we are such as He can love without impediment, we shall in fact be happy."
From <u>The Problem of Pain</u> by C.S. Lewis [20]

MAY 21

And they shall be mine, saith the LORD of Hosts, in that day when I make up my jewels; and I will spare them, as a man spareth his own son that serveth him (Malachi 3:17).

These are the words that Pastor Phillips read to us and Sarah, standing at her bedside in the ICU, just a couple of days before she, much to my surprise and yet also completely expected, died.

I read these words from Malachi, and they stirred my memory, sharply bringing into focus the days immediately preceding Sarah's death. Oddly, my memory of that time is not only sharp – I can picture the details as though I am still there – the memories are beautiful. It was a time in my life when God's presence was undeniably real to me. I knew Him, and I knew He was with me, and I knew I was not alone, and I knew He was enough. I wasn't trying to impress any one. I wasn't trying to do anything in my own strength. I was completely stripped of any self-consciousness and the fear of man. I was exposed and naked and raw and vulnerable – but in this condition, I knew God's presence in a very special way as He day by day provided and carried me through.

Why does this God awareness fade as the pain fades?

Is that the normal human experience, or just mine? I miss the days of grief because they were days when I was alive to God's presence and was sharply sensitive to Him in the details of my life.

Now the grief has dulled, and so, too, has my sensitivity to Him.

I'm back to struggling with the fear of man. I'm back to trying to do things in my own strength.

I'm back to letting the lesser things become the bigger things.

So today, I found myself strangely remembering with fondness and longing the days of sorrow and grief.

MAY 22

How often do I speak words that glorify God? I think probably rarely.

For words to glorify God, must they be words about God or directly to God? Are the words we speak one to another about day to day life separate from God-glorifying words? They probably are, but do they have to be? Are they supposed to be? Is this dichotomy Godly? I doubt it...

Can I learn to speak God glorifying words in any and all situations?

Regardless of the topic, the focus of my heart and mind is to be God, and from this peculiar focus flow God-glorifying words.

But I know the truth about my heart and mind.

The default setting of my heart and mind is myself. In the secret places of my emotions and my mind, what so often motivates me is me.

What if the words spoken from my tongue are God-glorifying, but the heart behind this same tongue is not? Are these still God-glorifying words or are they blasphemous words from lying lips?

I am challenged this week to pay attention to my words and the heart behind them.

I suspect it may be a rather quiet week.

MAY 23

Yesterday it was mouth and tongue.

Today it is ears.

This is my beloved Son, in whom I am well pleased; Hear ye Him (Matthew 17:5b).

On the Mt. of Transfiguration, Jesus stood literally and physically in the presence of Peter, James, and John. Yet even in this place, God needed to instruct these disciples to HEAR and to LISTEN. You would think it would be automatic, that

Peter, James and John would listen without even being told to do so because, after all, Jesus was there in their midst.

Not so. Peter was already planning – "Let's build three shelters." He had already assumed certain things and his mind was stirred and rushing ahead.

I come daily to a Mt. of Transfiguration. I open God's Word, and there I find Elijah and Moses and Jesus. And my mind is stirred, and I desire to pitch tents my way and I assume. But, do I listen as I ought? Do I hear Him on this Mt. of Transfiguration? Do I hear Him in my life?

Hearing never happens on accident.

The clock is ticking. My schedule beckons. Demands press in. Such is life.

But still, I can choose to hear Him. I must hear Him! It is He who is to lead. Not the clock. Not the schedule. Not the demands. Not even the needs of those around me. But Him.

This comes neither naturally nor easily to me. Surrender.

There must be, each morning upon my Mt. of Transfiguration, the surrender of my will and my ways to Him. And the surrender must be complete, all the hidden corners, secret places, and vain expectations must be yielded to His expert hands.

Once off the mountain, I am to be about His business, whatever that may be, this day. This He expects. For this He equips.

My ears will soon be flooded with the noise of a loud and busy world. In its midst, Lord, speak and teach me to hear, and may the hearing become obedience and may the obedience become a life lived to your glory, well-pleasing to You.

MAY 24

I felt sad at church yesterday. Part of the service was a confirmation ceremony for four young people. These confirmands had dedicated the last 2 years to studying the Bible and what it means to be a Lutheran. Now they are able to take communion, they are members of our church.

So, why was I sad? These four teenagers stand in such contrast to Sarah. She will never be confirmed as they just were. She will not understand the Eucharist or taste communion. Or intellectually understand the gospel.

I felt selfish, too. I, after all, will not experience what the parents of these confirmands experienced seeing their children standing before the congregation as they mature in their Christian walk.

The sorrow lingered throughout the day yesterday.

This morning, as I took my walk, I took my feelings to Jesus. I told of my sadness and how I feel cheated. As I talked with Jesus, new thoughts came to me. I heard Jesus telling me to feel blessed, not sad. I have heard Jesus tell me this before. It is not an easy thing to do to feel blessed in our circumstances. I must work at this. I heard Jesus tell me that the joy the parents of the confirmands felt, I will feel every time Sarah accomplishes anything. Everything Sarah ever does will be an accomplishment. When she smiles, when she reaches, when she eats, if she waves, if she rolls, if she sits. I will experience joy. Most parents stop appreciating these seemingly small things. I never will, for I know they are not small. These are miracles.

Sorrow has no place here.

MAY 25

It's a hot and humid day. The sun is beating down.

I thank You, Lord, that I am alive, and that on my skin I can feel the rays that originated 499 seconds ago in our star 93 million miles away.

Thank You that electromagnetic radiation can travel through the "vacuum" of space and reach this planet, a planet with an atmosphere transparent to the radiation we need and oblique to that which would harm.

Thank You that the sun's radiation falls within that narrow range of the electromagnetic spectrum that we call visible light. You have made us beings with physical eyes to see. And then, You gave us things to see.

Our bodies are fine-tuned. Our planet is fine-tuned. Our universe is fine-tuned. And You, dear Father, are the best explanation for such profound and specific precision. It is, despite the secular objections, reasonable to believe in You when we are confronted with such accuracy.

Life.

It is good. Yes, there are hard moments.   But they cannot negate that life is sacred, a gift from You to us for as many days as You, Sovereign Lord, determine.

Before the foundation of the earth, You knew my name. You saw my face. You designed a plan.

Your creative power is as big as the universe and as specific as my little life within the vastness of space and time.

How am I to understand a God such as this?

I cannot adequately wrap my mind around You.

If I could, then that would diminish Your greatness.

And Your greatness cannot be diminished.

I strive to understand You.   But ultimately, some mystery shall and should remain…thus I walk by faith.

And I worship You, God of the details.

I praise You for the details of my life…

Thank You, Lord, that I grew up on Partridge Road within a family that knew how to love one another. Thank You for memories of working side by side on the farm, for laughing and learning and growing and becoming.   You gave me a beautiful childhood, for which I am forever grateful.

Thank You, Lord, for that day long ago when my Mom placed a Bible in my hands. My seventh birthday. It is a Bible I still have. It is torn and tattered and held together now with duct tape. Her gift to me that day so long ago has made all the difference.

Thank You, Lord, for that day long ago when my Dad reminded me in a simple, but life-changing way, that You are sovereign. Worry is unnecessary if You, God, are who You say You are.

Thank You, Lord, for Your longsuffering toward me as I maneuvered through my 20s…they are tumultuous years of self-promotion…Thank You for bringing me low and for refusing to give me over to my own desires.

Thank You, Lord, that I am a wife to my Mark and that we together have traveled a path of joy and sorrow…and have made it. Thank You that my husband loves You.

Thank You, Lord, for the sweet daughter You blessed us with…for challenges and memories and beautiful years…forever we are grateful to You for her.

Thank You, Lord, for my kids at CBCS. They mean the world to me. I have no greater joy in this season of life than to share the journey they are on for the short time that they are under my watch and in my classroom.

Thank You for the family of God to which I belong.

Thank You that You call me "beloved" and I call You "Savior, Redeemer, Father."

MAY 26

Rejoice evermore. Pray without ceasing. In everything give thanks: for this is the will of God in Christ Jesus concerning you (I Thessalonians 5:16-18).

The LORD is good, a stronghold in the day of trouble; and He knoweth them that trust in Him (Nahum 1:7).

Looking back, I see clearly three very special moments. Were these moments of divine intervention? Aren't all moments, truly, moments of divine intervention? After all, I cannot even draw a breath of air into my lungs if God does not will and allow it. Yet most of the time I live my life ignorant, distracted, or simply inconsiderate toward His life-giving intervention.

Yes, all moments require His intervention.

And from time to time there will be that moment in which the power of His presence is undeniable. These are moments I want to share with you. These were moments that changed me. Prepared me. These were moments that jolted me awake and shaped me to become His vessel, ready and useful.

Woven into these moments is His ever great salvation….Jesus Christ invading not just history and humanity, but me. Apart from this, the moments of which I will soon refer would be without value or meaning.

The great Creator God breathed the breath of life into me and then poured the blood of His life eternal upon me. This is the foundation upon which all the rest of the moments of my life become meaningful.

Let me share with you my great and lonely moments….

I can still see myself in our barn, the part we called the "new barn" because it was the newest even if no longer new. I, a teenager, shovel in hand, scraping the floor between the two rows of Holsteins. Other than the cows and skinny barn cats, I was alone. Thinking, as I am prone to do. And into my thoughts came this question: *"What type of person will you choose to be and to be known as? Will you choose to be a person of joy or a person of grit and gravel? Will others know you for your smile or for your toughness?"*

In that moment of stillness, I said "yes" to joy.

I was changed, a path had been determined, and with ease I walked it. I have been known as a person of joy and smiles over the years, and it has not been hard for me. God has gifted me with joy. He has also taught me that joy does not exclude grit and toughness and depth. Joy simply frames the day…

I can still see myself struggling. Exhausted. Alone. Yes, Mark was in the house and Sarah was in the bathtub, but I was still alone. Mark was in bed sleeping, for he had to wake at 2:30 am to go to work. And Sarah, in the tub, me kneeling next to the tub, bathing Sarah and caring for her. But so tired was I that I felt alone in my struggles. Sarah, nearly a teenager, depending on me for all things. There we were, mother and disabled daughter well into the evening hours, bath almost done.

Then it started. Sarah, still in the tub, had diarrhea. It was a mess to deal with. But we dealt with it, and then started the bath all over again. Clean. Ready to get out of the tub. Diarrhea in the tub again. Begin process again.

Finally, Sarah clean and in wheelchair.

Diarrhea again.

As I stood there in the bathroom with my beautiful daughter in her wheelchair and another mess to clean up, I feeling overwhelmed and exhausted and completely alone, God's word filled my head…*Be not weary in well-doing, for in due season ye shall reap if ye faint not.* And in the most ordinary and tedious of moments, I was not just reminded, but most certainly assured, that God knows and He sees. The all-powerful omnipotent God who spoke ex nihilo the universe into being is also the all-knowing omniscient God who is intimately aware of the details of mother and daughter and diarrhea in a small, quiet bathroom in a little town in Delevan, NY. He cares about my small life in the same way He cares about the vast universe. Because of this, and His manifest presence in that moment, an ordinary struggle became an extraordinary encouragement and memory…

I can still see myself standing at the top of our cellar steps, the fingers of my right hand pressed against the switch that operated the lift for Sarah's wheelchair. Sarah and her wheelchair were on the lift, moving downward, and I, pressing the switch, prayed, asking God again, to help Sarah hold her head up, to strengthen the muscles of her neck. As I prayed, grumbling arose in my spirit, and silently in the recesses of my human heart, I railed against God. I wondered why He didn't answer this simplest of prayers?

And again, there He was. A moment I will forever carry with me. In His graciousness and long suffering with me, He gently responded to my hidden complaint against Him. With words clear and precise, He spoke to my heart and mind: *"I have heard your prayer, and I have already answered it, and my answer is a resounding YES! Sarah's neck is straight and her muscles are strong! She is restored and healed even now. The problem, dear child, is that you are stuck in time. I have answered Yes and I have healed and I can see already your daughter whole because I am outside of time. You are not. So you continue to see with eyes of flesh a daughter still weak. But, I ask you to see through My eyes with eyes of faith that are not bound by time…your daughter healed with neck strong and head lifted and your prayer answered."*

I will forever remember that quiet lonely moment at the top of my stairs. From that moment on, I no longer prayed for the Lord to strengthen Sarah's neck muscles. Instead I praised Him that He already had, and understood fully that on this earth and in this time and place I would not see it. But that no longer mattered. God Himself, the One who exists outside of time and always has been and always will be, opened my eyes of faith and I knew Sarah was already well. The need to continually plead was gone, and the need to continually praise had come…

MAY 27

Yes, God has blessed me with three great and lonely moments…moments which prepared me and culminated in my loneliest, yet greatest, broken moment, collapsed in sorrow upon the floor of my daughter's bedroom, a daughter who had just hours ago drawn her last breath and died. I fell to my knees, struggling to breath. Alone in her room.

And I praised God.

With joy and gratitude and tears running down my face, I gave Him thanks for who He is and what He does. And I knew, broken on that floor that God deserved nothing but praise and worship from my lips and life.

Somewhere along the line, there came a moment, the exact time of which I am unaware, when I realized that God owes me no explanation. He is not obligated to explain Himself to me or to make clear all the mysteries of life and death and suffering. At some unknown, and yet glorious moment, God's sovereignty and goodness became real to me. His sovereignty and goodness coexist in harmony even in those moments when they seem to us, the small-minded, to be incompatible. God's sovereignty and goodness are rooted in the very essence of His character and we must hold tightly to that truth as the flood of life experiences wash over, and sometimes pound upon, us.

There is mystery in all of this. Yet, I know that He is in control. And, I know that He is good. And, I knew that, perhaps most of all, on the floor in Sarah's room, just hours after her death.

My God is worthy and awesome in power.

That they may know from the rising of the sun, and from the west, that there is none beside me. I am the LORD, and there is none else. I form the light and create darkness: I make peace, and create evil: I the LORD do all these things…Woe unto him that striveth with this Maker! Let the potsherd strive with the potsherds of the earth. Shall the clay say to him that fashioneth it, What makest Thou? Or thy work, he hath no hands?...I have made the earth, and created man upon it: I, even my hands, have stretched out the heavens, and all their host have I commanded (Isaiah 45: 6,7,9, 12).

MAY 28

What we were used to and comfortable with is over. Life with Sarah. This life together is gone…

The book of Nehemiah is about walls. The people returning from captivity were to build walls to protect their city. These were good walls. Protective. These were walls built and maintained to keep enemies out.

It was in the weeks and months following Sarah's death in which spiritual walls in my life were the strongest. In those most awful of moments, Jehovah Nissi was protecting me. When the enemy came in like a flood, He set me up upon a rock. He sheltered me. In my time of sorrow and loss, He was my strong tower, the one to whom I ran and in whose presence I rested. It was oddly in the depth of pain and sorrow and loneliness that I experienced God's power and presence in a way that my human words will fail to express. His walls were strong and safe and real. Nothing else mattered but God's presence in my life. All the lesser things were finally where they were supposed to be – outside the gate.

But here I am three years later living within weakened walls and once again magnifying lesser things to exalted positions. There are cracks and gaps in the wall, and those cracks are of my own making. I'm too busy pursuing my agenda or someone else's much of the time. I've stopped depending on God for my very next breath. I spend a lot of time leaning on my own understanding. My schedule is often more important than people. God gets my scraps rather than the first fruits of this life he has given me.

There is something profoundly precious about our hard times.

I hate to admit it, but so it is.

Sometimes I long for those long days of raw heartache, because they were days of intimacy with God. And really, what else matters?

MAY 29

Truth be told, there is very little, if anything, that I can fix. Yet I, like many women, run around in a self-imposed pressure cooker of "I should be able to fix this" stew.

I can't.

There is freedom in finally understanding that. And, oddly enough, increased usefulness. You see, I cannot be useful in the Kingdom of God if I am driven by the flawed idea that I have the ability to fix the broken lives that cross mine on the rough and tumble highway of life. It's a religious form of humanism, an inflated view of self. And it's useless.

I will only be useful to God when I am small, completely aware of my utter and overwhelming dependence upon Him.

A life well lived is not about doing great things. It's about doing small and ordinary things in a faithful way with eyes ever upon the Savior. Great are the lives of those who daily and deliberately walk in love and obedience to our great God. It's about doing the mundane as well as the spectacular unto God and to His glory. It's about taking the smallest and least noticed task and doing it well. Doing the small things greatly, with joy, with gratitude, with perspective. This becomes a life of character. A life well-lived. A great life.

It is God alone who fixes what or who is broken. He may use us in His plan, but it's His plan and certainly He does not depend on us. I am to point others toward Him. Not fix them.

MAY 30

From <u>The Problem of Pain</u> by C.S. Lewis [21]

"*My own experience is something like this. I am progressing along the path of life in my ordinary contentedly fallen and godless condition, absorbed in a merry meeting with my friends for the morrow or a bit of work that tickles my vanity today, a holiday or a new book, when suddenly a stab of abdominal pain that threatens serious disease, or a headline in the newspapers that threatens us all with destruction, sends this whole pack of cards tumbling down. At first I am overwhelmed, and all my little happinesses look like broken toys. Then, slowly and reluctantly, bit by bit, I try to bring myself into the frame of mind that I should be in at all times. I remind myself that all these toys were never intended to possess my heart, that my true good is in another world and my only real treasure is Christ. And perhaps, by God's grace, I succeed, and for a day or two become a creature consciously dependent on God and drawing its strength from the right sources. But the moment the threat is withdrawn, my whole nature leaps back to the toys: I am even anxious, God forgive me, to banish from my mind the only thing that supported me under the threat because it is now associated with the misery of those few days. Thus the terrible necessity of tribulation is only too clear. God has had me for but forty-eight hours and then only by dint of taking everything else away from me. Let Him but sheathe that sword for a moment and I behave like a puppy when the hated bath is over – I shake myself as dry as I can and race off to reacquire my comfortable dirtiness, if not in the nearest manure heap, at least in the nearest flower bed. And that is why tribulations cannot cease until God either sees us remade or sees that our remaking is now hopeless...*

"*I have seen great beauty of spirit in some who were great sufferers.*"

From <u>The Problem of Pain</u> by C.S. Lewis [21]

MAY 31

The end of the school year. A chapter closing. A time to rest...and then a new chapter opens, and we press on. As your school year ends, as your new chapter begins, remember. Remember what you have learned. Remember who God is. Meditate upon what God does. Hide His Word in your hearts and in your minds. Seek Him early and often.

At CBCS, you were blessed with a wise Bible teacher. Here are some of the words he shared with you in Bible class. Carry them with you. Remember.

"Let us rise with principle and conviction. Let us pledge allegiance to the creeds upon which we base our lives."

"God has a claim on our lives."

"There are no limits over the claim that God has upon our lives. His claim is absolute."

"We are not saved by works but for works."

"We are not saved to do nothing."

"There is no security in sin or apathy."

"We are totally dependent on God in a wilderness world."

"It is God Who saves!"

"We are under wrath apart from the great work of God."

"In God's presence, we will either be consecrated or consumed."

"We are in the shadow of the last days."

"It is good for us to rehearse the deep things of God."

"Discipline is good, not bad."

"Surround yourselves with people that will take you in the spiritual direction you want to go."

"Meet with God."

"God is good and God is great."

"There are blessings in obeying God."

"In the commandments of God there is life."

"It is not a little thing to worship God."

"God is always with us in the person of Jesus Christ."

"The world teaches that there is liberation in going away from God. That is a lie."

"Our God is a God of truth, and in truth there is freedom."

"We love God by loving truth and refusing to be comfortable in a world that calls good evil and evil good."

"All of us were created for a purpose."

"Labor for things above."

"Strive."

"Pray big prayers. Pray hard prayers."

"Arise, O church of God! Have done with lesser things!"

May's Apologetic Moment…Contend for the Faith

Origins Matter…From Whence Came Life?

The popular website **livescience.com** makes the sweeping claim that "*evolution is among the most substantiated concepts in science and is the unifying theory of biological science.*" This same sweeping claim is made repeatedly in science textbooks across our nation's classrooms.

Yet, evolutionary theory has a problem. For if it is truly a "substantiated concept" and "the unifying theory of biological science," then it must answer the foundational question "where did life come from in the first place?" Failure to do so is a fatal weakness to such a sweeping claim.

So, what does **livescience.com** have to say about the origin of life? Their words are printed below. My comments and thoughts are found in parenthesis following each paragraph.

"*Life on Earth began more than 3 billion years ago, evolving from the most basic of microbes into a dazzling array of complexity over time. But how did the first organisms on the only known home to life in the universe develop from the primordial soup? Inside you'll learn just how mysterious this all is, as we reveal the different scientific theories on the origins of life on Earth.*"

{Notice the assumptions built in: the earth is billions of years old, the early earth was "primordial soup." Notice the admission that this is "mysterious." It is mysterious to a secular scientists because they simply do not have a naturalistic explanation that adequately explains the origin of life.}

"*Lightning may have provided the spark needed for life to begin. Electric sparks can generate amino acids and sugars from an atmosphere loaded with water, methane, ammonia and hydrogen, as was shown in the famous Miller-Urey experiment reported in 1953, suggesting that lightning might have helped create the key building blocks of life on Earth in its early days. Over millions of years, volcanic clouds in the early atmosphere might have held methane, ammonia and hydrogen and been filled with lightning as well. Or could simple clay have fueled life's beginning? Read on to find out.*"

{Notice the vague terms: "lightening MAY have provided the spark"; "lightening MIGHT have helped create the key building blocks"; "volcanic clouds in the early atmosphere MIGHT have held methane, ammonia and hydrogen. As for the "famous Miller-Urey experiment," it successfully created a variety of left handed and right handed amino acids. Please note that amino acids are not life. They are nowhere near life, for the amino acids must line up in a specific sequence and then fold in a very specific way in order to function. And, only left handed amino acids are found in living cells. So, a right handed amino acid cannot be allowed into the sequencing order, for it will prevent proper folding and proper function. But, how can right handed amino acids be excluded when equal amounts of each are made and all of the sequencing and folding must be random and undirected? Also, realize that Miller and Urey were intelligent beings, creating in a laboratory. None of their experiment was random and none of the observations resulted accidentally by chance and time...for there were intelligent beings (i.e. Miller and Urey) overseeing and directing the drama. Also, even if a protein were to be created this way, that is not life. The proteins must then congregate in such a way that a cell membrane can encapsulate them, and then these proteins must become self-replicating – able to copy themselves. The probability of all of this happening by random chance is statistically impossible.}

"The first molecules of life might have met on clay, according to an idea elaborated by organic chemist Alexander Graham Cairns-Smith at the University of Glasgow in Scotland. These surfaces might not only have concentrated these organic compounds together, but also helped organize them into patterns much like our genes do now.

"The main role of DNA is to store information on how other molecules should be arranged. Genetic sequences in DNA are essentially instructions on how amino acids should be arranged in proteins. Cairns-Smith suggests that mineral crystals in clay could have arranged organic molecules into organized patterns. After a while, organic molecules took over this job and organized themselves. Or maybe life began at the bottom of the sea. Keep going to learn how."

{Notice the vague terms: "the first molecules of life MIGHT have met on clay"; "these surfaces MIGHT not only have concentrated these organic compounds together"; "mineral crystals in clay COULD HAVE arranged organic molecules into organized patterns"; "after A WHILE, organic molecules took of this job"; "or MAYBE life began at the bottom of the sea." Notice that there is NO EXPLANATION offered or even suggested at HOW organic molecules could have taken over the job of organizing themselves – which is necessary if life is to arise. Notice that there is no comment on where the highly complex DNA came from, nor is there comment on where the information which is stored in the DNA came from.}

"The deep-sea vent theory suggests that life may have begun at submarine hydrothermal vents spewing key hydrogen-rich molecules. Their rocky nooks could then have concentrated these molecules together and provided mineral catalysts for critical reactions. Even now, these vents, rich in chemical and thermal energy, sustain vibrant ecosystems. The next idea is a chilling thought. Read on!"

{Notice the vague terms: "life MAY have begun at submarine hydrothermal vents"; "their rocky nook COULD then have concentrated these molecules." Notice that it is suggested that since these vents are rich in energy, they could be used to explain the origin of life. However, there is NO EXPLANATION offered at HOW the energy could actually organize random molecules and particles into complex proteins and even more complex cells. Just an FYI, even the most basic of living cells is a mini-universe of complexity: cell membrane, cytoplasm, cytoskeleton, microtubules, nucleus, DNA and RNA, ribosomes, endoplasmic reticulum, Golgi complex, mitochondria…
Suggestion: check out "Inner life of a cell" - a video produced at Harvard University. This video can be found on You Tube.}

"Ice might have covered the oceans 3 billion years ago, as the sun was about a third less luminous than it is now, scientists say. This layer of ice, possibly hundreds of feet thick, might have protected fragile organic compounds in the water below from ultraviolet light and destruction from cosmic impacts. The cold might have also helped these molecules to survive longer, allowing key reactions to happen. Understanding life's origin may involve unravelling the mystery of DNA's formation, as we explain next."

{Notice the vague terms: "ice MIGHT have covered the oceans"; "this layer of ice, POSSIBLY hundreds of feet thick MIGHT have protected fragile organic compounds"; "the cold MIGHT have also helped these molecules survive longer." Notice that this theory focuses on how "fragile organic compounds" might have been protected. It does NOT explain where the organic molecules originated from in the first place. Also, consider how this idea ("life originated in the cold") is opposite of the idea proposed immediately before it ("life originated in the hot thermal vents").}

"Nowadays DNA needs proteins in order to form, and proteins require DNA to form, so how could these have formed without each other? The answer may be RNA, which can store information like DNA, serve as an enzyme like proteins, and help create both DNA and proteins. Later DNA and proteins succeeded this 'RNA world,' because they are more efficient. RNA still exists and performs several functions in organisms, including acting as an on-off switch for some genes. The question still remains how RNA got here in the first place. And while some scientists think the molecule could have spontaneously arisen on Earth, others say that was very unlikely to have happened. Other nucleic acids other than RNA have been suggested as well, such as the more esoteric PNA or TNA. We have two last ideas to throw at you."

{Notice the vague terms: "the answer MAY be RNA." Following this vague assertion, there is the admission that "the question still remains HOW RNA GOT HERE IN THE FIRST PLACE." In other words, "we don't know, but since we are here it must have happened." Notice that this line of reasoning involves the starting assumption of naturalism and an exclusion of an intelligent designer.}

"Instead of developing from complex molecules such as RNA, life might have begun with smaller molecules interacting with each other in cycles of reactions. These might have been contained in simple capsules akin to cell membranes, and over time more complex molecules that performed these reactions better than the smaller ones could have evolved,

scenarios dubbed "metabolism-first" models, as opposed to the 'gene-first' model of the 'RNA world' hypothesis. The final theory is truly out of this world."

{Notice the vague terms: "life MIGHT have begun with smaller molecules interacting with each other in cycles of reactions. These MIGHT have been contained in simple capsules....more complex molecules...COULD HAVE evolved." Notice the admission that this idea is a "metabolism first" model as opposed to a "gene-first" model. In other words, "we don't know." This idea is really wishful thinking. If it did occur, from where came the "simple capsules akin to cell membranes?" We know a great deal about cell membranes these days. We know that they are very complex, composed of a bi-lipid layer with channel proteins that act as gates for allowing certain materials in and certain materials out. This is called "semi-permeability" and it is a very organized biological process required for life. Let's now consider the "metabolism first" model. Why would metabolism have arisen prior to genes? What would be the functional purpose in metabolism developing and being preserved? And, how could information directing metabolism be preserved and passed down if there was no mechanism (i.e. DNA) for doing so yet in existence? To believe the idea of "metabolism first" requires a great deal of faith.}

"Perhaps life did not begin on Earth at all, but was brought here from elsewhere in space, a notion known as panspermia. For instance, rocks regularly get blasted off Mars by cosmic impacts, and a number of Martian meteorites have been found on Earth that some researchers have controversially suggested brought microbes over here, potentially making us all Martians originally. Other scientists have even suggested that life might have hitchhiked on comets from other star systems. However, even if this concept were true, the question of how life began on Earth would then only change to how life began elsewhere in space."

{This idea speaks for itself. All I will point out is that it does require faith to believe in panspermia.}

"Oh, and if you thought all that was mysterious, consider this: Scientists admit they don't even have a good definition of life! [55]

Livescience.com offers 7 "theories" of how life originated. High school and college textbooks also offer a multiplicity of ideas. Truth be told, they do not know how life began. Most secular scientists actually admit this, followed by a sigh and statement that, "whatever it was, it was natural." All they can do is guess. All they can do is hope that, however life originated, it was a naturalistic origin. Belief in evolutionary theory is, indeed, a religion...requiring great faith and accepting many unanswered questions and vague possibilities dressed up in pseudo-scientific jargon.

The more I study science, the more the creation model makes sense. It fits what we observe. Yes, faith is required. But, the fit is good. As for me, I will serve the Lord. As for me, I believe that I – and you and all mankind – are made in the image of God.

This is God's creation. And we, among the creatures, are most precious to Him.

The LORD preserveth the simple:
I was brought low, and He helped me.
Psalm 116:6

June

"Hold everything in your hands lightly,
otherwise it hurts when God pries your fingers open."
— Corrie ten Boom

JUNE 1

Who am I, Lord, that Thou has dealt so sweetly with me? I am a profoundly selfish being. I am a wreck. I repeatedly, consistently, and often intentionally fall short.

But God.

What great compassion You have shown me. Your mercy is steady and dependable, new every morning.

The red blood of Your grace has saved me.

Why? Why me?

You…You are WHY, and You alone!

My salvation isn't actually about me, is it?

It's about You.

I manage to miss the depth of that truth frequently. Daily.

Who am I, Lord, to ever treat another person with contempt? Who am I to ever think of myself higher than another? Not only do I think such haughty thoughts. Sometimes I act upon them.

Did it please God yesterday when I grew annoyed with my students and my annoyance soon became the atmosphere of my classroom, an atmosphere that spoke ugliness to my students? Words never came from my mouth (thankfully), but the message was delivered loudly and clearly.

Who am I to ever come across in an ugly way to students in my charge and under my leadership? After all that God has done, how ungrateful my selfish response to a challenging classroom situation must seem to the great God who has redeemed an unworthy me.

Truth is, my kids were wrong to be so unprepared and unconcerned about class. Their lack of preparation, their apathy, yes, these are problems and may even be heart issues. As a teacher, I do need to act to overcome the dangerous waters of youthful indifference. I do need to deal with the selfishness and stubbornness of teenage learners.

But, I need to do so as a godly leader who loves my God and loves my students. The weapons I use to fight apathy and indifference need to be from God's arsenal, not mine.

Yesterday I expressed annoyance, exasperation, and a belief that I am better and smarter. I made my students feel as if they were wasting my time.

Did I exalt God with my attitude yesterday?

Did I teach my students anything of value yesterday?

No.

I, saved so completely and blessed so greatly, gave so little yesterday.

How did Jesus, greatest teacher of all, treat students who were slow to learn and easily distracted? How did He engage those who, after hearing His words, somehow missed the point?

He met them where they were. He led them. He persevered. He reinforced. He was patient and gentle. He had high standards, and He used effective methods, not selfish methods. He knew there were times to press on and push further. And, He knew there were times to wait. He individualized His approach, without compromising the truth, until those with whom He was working could understand.

It was for the learned, haughty Pharisees that Christ reserved His harshest words. It was for those who relied upon their traditions and ways of doing things that Christ proclaimed His greatest warnings.

May I never again be like a Pharisee when I teach.

JUNE 2

More than once the question has crossed my mind, "When was my life easier, when I was walking as an unsaved person or now, living as a saved person?"

Honestly, it seemed easier as an unsaved person.

How can this be? Should such an honest – and unspiritual answer – disturb me? It certainly seems like the wrong answer for a saved person to speak. Never-the-less, life seemed easier before I was saved. True, I was younger and maybe life naturally seems easier for the youthful. But, there's more to it than youth…

Pressure and conflict.

The Christian life, when lived seriously, is a life of pressure and conflict. The hands of the Master Potter is upon we, the clay, molding and making vessels fit for His use. He applies pressure for the purpose of fitting us for His great plan. God is a refining fire, and in His presence with the flame of His Word and Spirit, He will relentlessly, yet sweetly, drive the dross from the metal of who we are until we become who He would have us to be. Until we come forth as gold, valuable and useful.

Here we are, His children in a fallen world, and we are being molded, chiseled, purified. How painful! Yet, how necessary and blessed and beautiful!

The serious Christian life is one of constant conflict. A battle between good and evil rages, without and within. As an unbeliever, there was no conflict. I did what I wanted, when and how I wanted. I listened to what I wanted to listen to and looked upon what I wanted to look upon. There was not war against the lust of the flesh, the lust of the eyes, and the pride of life. Rather, there was an indulgence of these things.

And that, at least for a season, was the path of least resistance.

But the easy path is not a satisfying path. It's not ease our hearts desire.

Our hearts long for purpose and meaning and something bigger than ourselves.

Purpose requires deep roots, roots sown and growing in the soil of the truth of who God is and what God does. Here we become strong oaks in God's great Kingdom. Roots grow deep in a thirsty quest for nourishing waters. Trees grow strong in tempest and storm. It is moments of brilliant sun combined with moments of soaking rain that produce leaves and flowers and fruit.

Lean in! Recognize the excellent value of the pressure of the hand of God and the conflict with which He blesses us. Fight the good fight, fully clothed in His armor and upheld by His righteous right hand. Strive toward the finish line, engaged in the battle, quenching the fiery darts of the enemy and pouring refreshing cups of water for the least of His, remembering that if the yoke is from Him, He will with you bear it. And never – no never – are you alone.

<u>JUNE 3</u>

Guarding our hearts…from what?

I know already the typical answers, and they are good…We should guard our hearts against sin, worldliness, idols. We should guard our hearts from hate. We should be careful what we look at, listen to, think about because if we look at, listen to, and think about things that are wrong, sinful, worldly, then our hearts are at risk of becoming those things, too. We should guard our hearts by choosing wisely who we spend our time with.

This is all true and good.

But incomplete.

One of the greatest things from which we must guard our hearts is having a small view of God. We need to guard our hearts from lies about who God is and what God has the right to do. Our hearts want God to answer our prayers our way. When we want something, maybe a particular gift at Christmas, we pray to get it. And if we get it, we believe God has answered our prayer. Or, maybe we want a certain person to be our friend. So, we pray, asking God to make that happen. If that person becomes our friend, we believe God has answered our prayer. Or maybe when Mom and Dad are not getting along, we pray for them to start getting along and be nice to each other. If that happens, then we believe God has answered our prayers. Or maybe you don't feel well, and you pray asking God to help you feel better, and if you do then you believe God has answered your prayer. Perhaps someone you really love gets sick, and you ask God to make that person better. If God does, then you believe God has answered your prayer.

Guard your heart! Be careful not to limit God in your thinking by believing that the only way He is blessing you is if He is answering prayers your way.

Guard your heart! Believe that God is good even when you don't get what you want, even when things don't work out your way. Believe that God knows best. Believe He is working things out.

Believe He is great.

Come to a place where you understand it doesn't have to be your way. God does not have to explain it all to you. He is worthy of your trust and love and praise. No matter what.

Guard your heart! Don't let the things you go through become bigger to you than the God who has created and redeemed you.

JUNE 4

But He said to me, 'My grace is sufficient for you, for my power is made perfect in weakness. Therefore I will boast all the more gladly about my weaknesses, so that Christ's power may rest on me. That is why, for Christ's sake, I delight in weaknesses, in insults, in hardships, in persecution, in difficulties. For when I am weak, then I am strong (II Corinthian 12:9-10).

God's priorities and His revelation of what is valuable and what is not, what is worthy of pursuit and what is not, seem radical to us only because of our reference point. We tend to be our own reference point...it is ourselves, our personal experiences and humanity upon which we measure "reasonableness." Such a small and limited standard will always cause God's ways to seem radical.

Radical or not, God's ways are the best ways. His ways at times may be the hardest, yet always they are the best. The safest place to be is in God's will, no matter what happens to the flesh.

"Delight" in weakness. "Delight" in hardships. "Delight" in persecutions.

Really? Radical.

God clothed Himself in flesh and walked among us. He emptied Himself, set aside His glory, and grew within the womb of an unknown woman. He was born in a barn, manure and all. He walked dusty roads, worked with calloused hands, exhausted Himself amongst the multitudes of the lost and needy. Like a lamb, He the Great Shepherd, was led to the slaughter. He did not defend Himself. Instead He willingly stretched out His arms, the arms of the Creator, toward lost mankind, and allowed a man created by Him to impale Him upon a cross. And He bled. And He died.

The Creator on a cross. Lamb of God, perfect and without blemish experiencing the wrath of God. The wrath that we deserve. He took it.

Radical.

Me, being asked by Him to delight in weakness and hardship and persecutions is not radical when the reference point is Creator God on the cross.

Lord, may all You say and what You ask me to do become the delight of my heart and life. May I begin to understand that what you ask of me is not radical, but reasonable, in the shadow of the cross which You bore. The time has come to embrace the radical reality that sharing in the fellowship of Your sufferings is a privilege.

It is a high call.

JUNE 5

I stood at Sarah's grave and all I could see in my mind was bones…her bones just feet away from me, separated from me by some dirt. The heaviness of the reality of death full-force rolled over me.

This is the end for all mankind, regardless of status and position and possessions on earth: *death*.

Struggling to catch my breath in the vacuum of this reality, I cried out, "Praise God! I know that my Redeemer lives!" The physical death of these bodies is not the end of the story. For the saved, the ultimate end is glorious victory. For the lost, the ultimate end is willful tragedy.

Sarah is absent from the body and present with the Lord. What that exactly means is unclear to me. I walk by faith that God's promises are good and true, even if the details are unknown. It is not details that I need to know. It is God I must know.

I know God!

Do you understand how absolutely miraculous it is that man can even know God?

Do not take for granted this indescribable gift!

Do not neglect the great mystery of our God who loves us with an unending love.

Lift your eyes. Look. He knows You.

He pours living water into our lives of drought, and He satisfies the hungriest of souls.

And when we walk through valleys of the shadow of death, He walks with us.

JUNE 6

He hath showed thee, O man, what is good, and what doth the LORD require of thee but to do justly, to love mercy, and to walk humbly with thy God (Micah 6:8).

What does obedience to You, Lord, look like? It's more than a list of things to do and things not to do, isn't it?

Obedience isn't a checklist or a skirt length, is it?

Do the many lists we keep deepen our love for You?

Lists are not love.

And they can even be dangerous. Inherent in list keeping and ticking each task or rule off one by one are the seeds of pride and self-righteousness. Failure to perform leads to guilt, but not necessarily to the godly sorrow that leads to repentance, but rather guilt that leads to self-loathing....and self-loathing is just the flip side of the pride coin....it's still about self.

Mere list keeping as an obedience technique is small living based on small thinking and will result in either great self-exaltation or great self-deprecation....either way the self is magnified and distance from the very one we think we are obeying grows. Idols can do just that, and list keeping (or failing) can easily become an idol.

I'm tired of keeping lists and straining at gnats…

Lord, I want to love you. I want to obey You. For the right reasons. Honestly, I'm not sure I know how to do that. I don't know how to love. I don't know how to obey. Lord, how I need you. Every minute. Of every day. I need You.

Help me!

Teach me how to love you with passion and abandon and depth! Teach me how to love you with all my heart, soul, mind, and strength.   Overwhelm me with Your greatness.

<u>JUNE 7</u>

Yesterday, while we were at Mom and Dad's, we watched a few minutes of video tape filmed before Sarah had her stroke. This was the first time I watched this video since the stroke. I had forgotten how different Sarah was before the stroke, how easy life seemed to her, how happy she always was, how she enjoyed music and could clap her hands, how she could wave and use her arms, how she could sit in a high chair and feed herself.

It would be a lie for me to say that it didn't make me feel sad watching this video. But, it didn't make me feel as badly as I thought it would.

I've learned that emotions are something you can think about, sometimes rationalize, and even make conscious decisions about. I studied my feelings after watching the video, and more importantly, I took those feelings to the Lord. I asked Jesus to show me what to do with my feelings, how to make sense out of my emotions and the reality of my life.

With Jesus' help, I decided to not feel overwhelmed with sorrow at all Sarah has lost. I felt sad, but not hopeless and anguished. *"Thank You, Lord Jesus that Sarah used to be able to sit and roll and wave and clap and dance. Thank You that we have memory and even video of this. Thank You that Sarah and we experienced these beautiful moments. Lord, You know Sarah and You know us. You know our lives. You know what we need and what is best. You are Lord of this situation. For some reason, Sarah had a stroke. I don't know why. But, You do and I'll trust in You, the best I can, to lead us through this."*

When there is sadness and loss in our lives (and there will be) we can choose how to respond. That might be the only control we have. We can make decisions about how to handle our emotions and our anger and our emptiness. We choose whether to take it to God or walk it alone. And, believe me, it is much easier to endure if you take it to the Lord Jesus and throw yourself in His arms with all the honest heartbreak with which you are aching. Surrender.

In time you will feel better, even normal, and you will think differently about your loss.

<u>JUNE 8</u>

Quite unexpectedly, I just relived a precious memory.

Mark is at church and Sarah's body is in the ground…so I am home all alone.

I'm recovering from surgery earlier this week. The surgery was no big deal, but I need to take it easy for a few days. So, here I am this Sunday morning. Alone.

I decided to put in one of my Gaither Southern Gospel DVDs. I used to watch them all the time with Sarah, but haven't too much since her death. She and I would watch these DVDs on Sunday mornings if she wasn't well enough to go to church, or we'd watch them on quiet afternoons when it was just she and I and the television.

I would put the DVD in, press "play," and then hold Sarah in my arms. She'd lean her full weight against me, and I'd snuggle her and sing, always off-key.

She didn't care that I was off-key.

Sarah was the person in this world that I felt the most comfortable with. If I wanted to raise my hands high and praise the Lord while tears streamed down my face, I could do that with her. These precious songs to which I would sing and cry opened doors…I would proclaim to my beloved daughter the great truths that Jesus is God, Jesus saves, He forgives, He makes us whole, and best of all He's coming again!

One of the songs was "The King is Coming." I'd belt it out, Sarah leaning on me, tears running down my face, hands held high…and then I would hug her tightly and talk about the beauty of our Savior and His promises and how these promises were for her, how she could look forward to beholding our Lord and praising Him with her very own voice.

These were precious moments, just the two of us sitting on our living room floor, worshiping the Lord together.

I was far from a perfect mom. There was so much I could have done better, so many times I could have been more patient and less selfish. But, the one thing I will NEVER regret is sharing the love of God and the truth of who God is with my daughter. I will never regret opening His Word with her, praying with her, singing songs of praise, and looking forward to the day when He will come again! I will never regret covering her with the great, amazing promises of our great God and assuring her that all her trials were temporary and purposeful.

What a privilege and what a joy to declare to the next generation that God is great!

This morning, I sat alone on the living room floor and listened to songs I hadn't listened to for many moons. I sang them off key, I raised my hands high, and tears streamed down my face as I remembered the little girl who used to lean her full weight on me.

Yes, the King is Coming! Praise God He is coming!

JUNE 9

One way streets…

"Oh, come on!" I thought as I drove down Olmstead Avenue between the school and the bus garage after picking up our daughter, Sarah, at the end of the school day. The "Oh, come on" thought was in response to the police officer who was driving the wrong way down the one-way only Olmstead Avenue. I, heading the right direction, was nearing the end of Olmstead when I saw the patrol car. The vehicle hesitated briefly right in front of the "Do Not Enter" signs. Then, continued onward. The officer passed me, keeping his eyes straight forward…..but, I knew he knew that he was breaking the law…..I had seen the hesitation at the foot of the "Do Not Enter" signs.

You know what? It wouldn't have been so noticeable had it been anybody other than a police officer. Those are the guys who are supposed to set the example, follow the rules. These are the folks we are to look up to as men and women upholding the law. And yet, as small of an issue as it may seem, this was a disregard of a law.

It's the same for Christians. We are supposed to be the example, aren't we, of God's love and His holiness. But, don't we sometimes go down the one way streets of life in the wrong direction? If the truth be told, don't we Christians often hesitate before the "Do Not Enter" signs that God's Word places along the paths of our lives, and then decide, for the sake of convenience or reputation or image or pleasure, to go down that path anyway? And, don't we so often make this decision in front of the very people of the world we are to be witnessing to and sowing seeds among? Maybe we make the decision to use vulgar language because we think it will make us a big shot in the group we are hanging out with. Maybe we give in to peer pressure and drink some of the alcohol that's offered to us at a party. Or, maybe we go with some friends to a movie we know doesn't please the Lord. Or, maybe the cashier makes a mistake when giving us change and gives us too much. Do we give it back to her or do we put it in our pocket? What about the times we overlook the outcast and the underdog at our school, and let him sit alone in the cafeteria instead of reaching out to him. What about the gossip that easily flows from our lips?

It's not always convenient to go the right way on one way streets. But, in the strength of the Lord, it is possible. One decision at a time, it is possible...it is possible to bite one's tongue to hold back vulgarity or gossip...it is possible to say "no" to the alcohol being offered or "no" to the R-rated movie. It is possible to choose purity and virtue. It is possible to reach out to the hurting person in need of help shouldering the load. The Holy Spirit will guide us and the Lord will strengthen us, and when we do go the wrong way (which we surely will do sometimes), the blood of Christ will wash us clean again and get us back on track.

Praise the Lord!

JUNE 10

From <u>Where is God When It Hurts?</u> by Philip Yancey [22]

"What can God use to get our attention? What will convince human beings, we who started the rebellion, that creation is not running the way God intended?

"C.S. Lewis introduced the phrase, 'pain, the megaphone of God.' 'God whispers to us in our pleasures, speaks in our conscience, but shouts in our pains,' he said; 'it is His megaphone to rouse a deaf world.' The word 'megaphone' is apropos, because by its nature pain shouts. When I stub my toe or twist an ankle, pain loudly announces to my brain that something is wrong. Similarly, the existence of suffering on this earth is, I believe, a scream to all of us that something is wrong. It halts us in our tracks and forces us to consider other values....

"Sometimes murmuring, sometimes shouting, suffering is a 'rumor of transcendence' that the entire human condition is out of whack. Something is wrong with a life of war and violence and human tragedy. He who wants to be satisfied with this world, who wants to believe the only purpose of life is enjoyment, must go around with cotton in his ears, for the megaphone of pain is a loud one...

"The megaphone of pain sometimes, of course, produces the opposite effect: I can turn against God for allowing such misery. On the other hand, pain can, as it did with G.K. Chesterton, drive me to God. I can believe God when He says this world is not all there is, and take the chance that He is making a perfect place for those who follow him on pain-racked earth.

"It is hard to be a creature. We think we are big enough to run our own world without such messy matters as pain and suffering to remind us of our dependence. We think we are wise enough to make our own decisions about morality, to live rightly without the megaphone of pain blaring in our ears. We are wrong as the Garden of Eden story proves. Man and woman, in a world without suffering, chose against God.

"And so we who have come after Adam and Eve have a choice. We can trust God. Or we can blame Him, not ourselves, for the world."
From <u>Where is God When It Hurts?</u> by Philip Yancey [22]

JUNE 11

I praise You, Lord, for who You are! I pray for myself, my husband, our family and church. I pray for a spirit of wisdom and revelation to know You better, for our eyes to be enlightened to know the hope to which You call us.

Thank You, Lord, that those of us who are in You will partake of the riches of Your inheritance and Your incomparably great power. Help us to believe.

Stir the hearts and minds and circumstances of those who don't believe. Trouble them with the purpose of seeking and finding You. Your power is the working of Your mighty strength, which you exerted in Christ when You raised Him from the dead. You seated Him at Your right hand and placed Him above all rule and authority, power and dominion and every title in all ages. You placed all things under His feet and made Him to be the head over everything for the church, His body, of which I am part.

May we, Lord, be of Your body, in the place that You would have, faithful to serve any role to which You call us. May Your purpose and perfect peace guide our lives. May our hearts beat passionately for You. You are worthy, beautiful Name above all Names!

In the Precious Name of Jesus…

JUNE 12

Lord, You tell me to be still and know that You are God.

I will be still.

I will stand still while You raise Your banner of love over me, and I will experience Your great salvation as You tear out my heart of stone and replace it with a heart of flesh that beats for You.

But, God…

This operation on my stony heart must find completion in You alone. You must smash rock hard granite heart of self, and You must plow up the fallow ground of stubbornness that so frequently defines me. You must breathe love into me, for I do not know how to love apart from You.

And I must be still.

Lean in. Lean into God.

God, I plead for You to do a mighty work in me. Change me. Renew my mind. Give me a new heart. Pour Your spirit into me to overflowing. And teach me to really love You. It is love that leads me to obey. What a privilege!

JUNE 13

Obedience to God is a way of life.

Obedience to God is a way of thinking.

Obedience to God is a heart beating for Him.

Obedience to God is not the same as meeting the needs – real or perceived – of the people around me.

Obedience to God does not mean doing everything that everyone around me expects me to do.

Obedience to God doesn't even mean I'll always get it right. I won't.

Maybe obedience is less about what I do and more about who I am.

I am less. He is more. He is great. I am not.

I am unable. He is able. There is nothing He cannot do.

I am unworthy. He is the Lamb of God who takes away the sins of the world, who is worthy to open the scroll.

I am weak. He is strong.

I am filthy rags. He is righteous robes.

I am broken.

Yet, in Him…I am accepted in the Beloved.

I am a treasure in an earthen vessel.

I am a new creation.

I am clean.

I am free from bondage to sin.

I am free from the penalty of sin.

I no longer need to fear death, for this enemy will be put under the feet of Christ. Death will be and indeed is now defeated in Him.

I am His slave.

I am His workmanship created in Christ Jesus before the foundation of the world unto good works.

I am more than His creation. I am His child.

I am His.

He is mine.

JUNE 14

I pray for those in our family who are dead in their trespasses and sins.

I, too, was once dead in transgression.

Lord, may those who are dead in sin feel the weight of that sin, may they smell the rottenness and feel the flames…before it is too late.

May they come to know the danger they face while there is still time to escape the danger.

May they come to You with repentance. In brokenness.

Lord, rescue them. Redeem them. Regenerate them, making them alive in You.

May those who are now objects awaiting Your righteous wrath not foolishly believe the world's lies. For while we are all Your creation, we are not all Your children!

God, Your love is great. You are rich in mercy. You made me alive in Christ even when I was dead in transgression. By grace am I saved.

By grace, Lord, save any yet lost in our family.

In the Perfect Name of Jesus…

JUNE 15

From Foxe: Voices of the Martyrs [23]

Lizzie Atwater (1900)

"In June 1900, a fierce nationalist reaction in China against Christian missionaries and churches claimed more than 32,000 lives. The worst massacres occurred in the northern province of Shanxi. The pregnant Lizzie Atwater wrote a memorable letter home before she and six others were martyred:

" 'Dear ones, I long for a sight of your dear faces, but I fear we shall not meet on Earth. I am preparing for the end very quietly and calmly. The Lord is wonderfully near, and He will not fail me. I was very restless and excited while there seemed a chance of life, but God has taken away that feeling, and now I just pray for grace to meet the terrible end bravely. The pain will soon be over, and oh the sweetness of the welcome above! My little baby will go with me. I think God will give it to me in heaven and my dear mother will be so glad to see us. I cannot imagine the Savior's welcome. Oh, that will compensate for all these days of suspense. Dear ones, live near to God and cling less closely to Earth. There is no other way by which we can receive that peace from God which passeth understanding. I must keep calm and still these hours. I do not regret coming to China.'

"On August 15, 1900, soldiers took Lizzie and ten others away from the relative safety of a nearby town and hacked them to death with their swords, tossing the bodies into a pit." From Foxe: Voices of the Martyrs [23]

JUNE 16

God knitting Sarah together just as she was, extra chromosome and all the medical diagnoses with which that involved, was an act of love.

God giving Sarah to us and asking us to suffer with her, was an act of love.

God taking her to Him on the day He determined, was an act of His great love.

There is mystery.

Words cannot explain. Words fall far short. Words create a picture that is incomplete.

But this Mother's heart KNOWS that God is good and great.

Through all these things, He has loved me and my child.

I thank Him and praise Him for who He is and what He does, always and in all things.

JUNE 17

Life.

Stand in awe of the God who gives it and who sustains it.

There was a moment in time when YOU consisted of ONE CELL.

One fertilized egg.

Within that cell was YOU.

Within that cell was all the information needed for you to grow.

Soon, that one cell was two, and then those two were four, and then those four were eight and those eight sixteen...

Soon, those cells began to differentiate into cells with specific jobs. Some cells specialized into cardiac tissue. Some cells specialized into bone and some into nerve and some into epithelial and some into connective tissue. How did the cells know to do this?

Soon, those specialized tissues began to organize into organs and then into systems...nervous, digestive, cardiovascular, skeletal, muscular, endocrine, integumentary, excretory, lymph, reproductive, respiratory. How did the cells know to do this?

How did one fertilized egg become you?

Life truly is a miracle.

And then, you were born...and your lungs drew in air for the first time...and capillaries and alveoli experienced the first great exchange of oxygen and carbon dioxide. Your autonomic nervous system instructed your diaphragm to contract and relax, changing the volume and thus the pressure of your lungs so that you would inhale and exhale...all without having to think about it. Oxygenated blood flowed from capillaries in the lungs back to the heart and then through the aorta and into the body. In the cells of the body, carbon dioxide was picked up and oxygen was delivered...Life...This is amazing. Amazing. Absolutely.

Fearfully and wonderfully made are we.

For by Him were all things created, that are in heaven and in earth, visible and invisible, whether they be thrones or principalities or powers, all things were made by Him and for Him. And He is before all things and by Him all things consist (Colossians 1).

JUNE 18

WHAT MY DAUGHTER MEANS TO ME.

On a beautiful day in June, 1996, our daughter, Sarah, came into the world "fearfully and wonderfully made."

Born with Down Syndrome, a congenital heart defect, hydrocephalus, Sarah had her struggles from the beginning. She spent her first three months of life in the intensive care nursery at our Children's Hospital. She underwent a lengthy heart operation when she was one month old, had a shunt placed to relieve the hydrocephalus when she was one and a half months old, and, after developing a problem with her vocal folds, had a feeding tube placed into her abdomen to provide safe nourishment. Finally, the big day came. We were able to bring our beautiful little girl home! And what fun we had. Sarah learned to smile and laugh and coo and clap her hands and to roll and to sit and to crawl. The problem with her vocal folds resolved, and she was able to eat, and even learned how to feed herself finger foods. The feeding tube was removed. She was standing independently at furniture, and was very close to taking those precious first steps that all parents dream about. But, she never took those first steps. A horrible, rare neurological disease called "moyamoya syndrome" invaded Sarah's body and our lives. Moyamoya causes strokes. In February, 1998, Sarah had a stroke. She was 20 months old.

The stroke took all independence from Sarah. She is no longer able to sit independently, to crawl, to roll. She cannot efficiently use her arms because she has very spastic muscles and movement disorders. She has poor head and trunk control, and has to work very hard just to pick her head up. She has braces for her legs and feet, braces for her hands, braces for her neck. A feeding tube again became necessary. Sarah is non-verbal. Occasionally she will have a seizure. And, then came more. In November, 2003, Sarah was diagnosed with acute lymphocytic leukemia...three years of chemotherapy, and all the side-effects, followed. Sarah's last dose of chemo was given in August, 2006. So far so good!

Despite this long list of medical problems, Sarah is happy all the time. Sometimes, I will ask her, "Do you have the joy, joy, joy of the Lord down in your heart?" She smiles a big smile to let me know that, indeed, the joy of the Lord is hers. She, in her completely dependent and sick body, is the happiest person I know. Some people might think, "What does she have to be happy about?" I guess Sarah doesn't need health and "stuff" to be happy. She knows the truth: real joy is knowing the Lord who Himself suffered and can sympathize and give meaning and purpose to the pains, the losses, the tragedies that we all face.

The Lord has used Sarah to teach me lessons about life and values and priorities that I would have learned no other way than in the crucible of adversity and hardship.

Some of the things that I have learned are...

You can know joy even when you are facing sorrow.

You can find happiness and purpose in pain.

God loves us even when, and perhaps especially when, the days are long and hard. He walked this earth, and He knows much about long, hard days.

God never abandons us. Even when He seems silent, He is there.

Smiles are valuable.

There is no such thing as "good luck" and "bad luck". There is just life, and in life good things and bad things happen to all of us, and what counts is our response.

Little things are important. Life is not about the next big trip you take or the next big car you buy, but about how much you enjoy that first cup of coffee in the morning or the sunset in the evening or the smell of the crisp autumn air or the stranger who held the door open for you.

You affect people, for better or worse, by your attitude.

Strength is not about muscles or muscle tone.

I can do things I never would have thought I could do. The Bible says I can do "all things through Christ which strengtheneth me."

Life is a great gift from a great Creator who numbers every hair on our heads and who knows the number of days of our lives.

Life is not just about the comfort and health of the physical body, but about the maturing of a generous soul, capable of contributing to the world in a special and unique way through the gifts that the Lord gives to each.

Life is not about avoiding difficulties and pain. It's about gratitude to the Giver of life.

Life is about doing the right things, not necessarily the easy and comfortable things.

We are all capable of touching the lives of other people. Sarah, mute and small, can touch the lives of others.

God is in control of all things at all times.

God picks us up in our broken condition, and gives us hope and purpose. Not always ease, but hope and purpose. He walked the paths we walk, He suffered the pains we suffer. My niece, Emily, once said that when Sarah goes to heaven, she will speak with a voice she has not yet heard. I have no doubt that the first words she will speak with that voice yet unheard are words of praise to our heavenly Father for the life she lived and the hope she has in His Son.

JUNE 19

Written years ago on this, Sarah's birthday…my heart to hers…and now to yours…

To my dear daughter, Sarah,

How precious to me you are! You are twelve years old now, and you are a delightful, beautiful young lady who has faced many difficult days with courage and hope. How many lessons about truth and priorities you, my child, have taught me.

When your Dad and I found out that you would be born with Down syndrome, we cried some tears and felt some fear, but then, as is so often the case, joy and purpose followed the initial news.

Honey, there are distortions and lies in this world. I have tried so hard over the years to protect you from them, but the deceptions are very powerful. Even nice people, who live quiet, decent, responsible lives often buy into the deceptions just simply by being silent on the issue. Or, neglecting to think about it at all. Lies such as referring to abortion with non-threatening language and neutral terms as "choice" and "right." The idea that an unborn child has worth and value only if the mother decides to choose life. Have you, my child, only value because I decided to give you birth? Were you without value and worth until I somehow determined you were valuable because I wanted you? Honey, the idea that a child is entitled to life only because a mother makes that choice is a lie. The truth is, you, my dear, are fearfully and wonderfully made. God knit you together in my womb, and He saw your substance as you were developing. He knew you before I knew you. He saw you before I saw you. You are no surprise to Him, and in the Lord's eyes, you are, indeed, fearfully and wonderfully created (Psalm 139). Even if the world denies that truth. Even if the world throws around words such as "choice" and "reproductive rights." Even as the world seeks earlier and earlier ways to test for Down syndrome.

There is truth and there are lies. I want you to know the truth. You are valuable because God gave life to you.

I remember when you were first born. Often, other people would make comments such as, "God only gives special children to special parents." I guess these comments were well-intended, but as I have considered these words over the years, I have come to a different conclusion. I am not a special parent with some sort of extra special skills that have equipped me to be your mother. Not at all. I am simply a mother who was willing to say, "Yes" to God when He sent you to me. God didn't ask me to be anything special. Just willing. And, that's all He asks of any mother and father who find out that their child will be born with a birth defect. "Are you willing? If you are, you will be capable. And, you will be blessed."

You, dear Sarah, are a brave soldier in the war for truth. You are a joyful child who loves life and expresses the truth that, even in a disabled body with a disabled mind, you have a purpose and a God-given reason for being here. You have faced challenges with courage. You have endured medical struggles with hope. I praise God because you are fearfully and wonderfully made, and I praise God that He has blessed you, us, and the world around you...often through that very extra chromosome that the world is fighting to eliminate as an error of nature.

You, my dear, are no error. Never forget how valuable and precious you are. Never forget that you were born with a purpose. And, keep being the sweet soldier of truth that you are in a dark and dangerous world.

Love, Mom

JUNE 20

From Where Is God When It Hurts? by Philip Yancey [24]

" 'Rejoice!' 'Be glad!' How do these suggestions differ from the insensitive hospital visitor who brings a smile and a 'Look on the bright side!' pep talk? Read further in each biblical passage, for every such admonition leads to a discussion of productive results. Suffering **produces** something. It has value; it changes us.

"By using words like 'Rejoice!' the apostles were not advocating a spirit of grin-and-bear-it or act-tough-like-nothing-happened. No trace of those attitudes can be found in Christ's response to suffering, or in Paul's. If those attitudes were desirable, self-sufficiency would be the goal, not childlike trust in God.

"Nor is there any masochistic hint of enjoying pain. 'Rejoicing in suffering' does not mean Christians should act happy about tragedy and pain when they feel like crying. Rather, the Bible aims the spotlight on the end result, the productive use God can make of suffering in our lives. To achieve that result, however, he first needs our commitment of trust, and the process of giving Him that commitment can be described as rejoicing....

"Seen in this light, the apostles' command to 'Rejoice!' makes sense. James does not say, 'Rejoice in the trials you are facing,' but rather 'Count it pure joy when you face trials.' The difference in wording is significant. One celebrates the fact of pain; the other celebrates the opportunity for growth introduced by pain. We rejoice not in the fact that we are suffering, but in our confidence that the pain can be transformed. The value lies not in the pain itself, but in what we can make of it. The pain need not be meaningless, and therefore we rejoice in the object of our faith, a God who can effect this transformation....

"Does God introduce suffering into our lives so that these good results will come about?...Questions about cause lie within God's domain; we cannot expect to understand those answers. We have no right to speculate...Instead, **response** is our assignment....

"Where is God when it hurts? He is in us."
From Where Is God When It Hurts? by Philip Yancey [24]

JUNE 21

> Restrain your voice from weeping and your eyes from tears,
> for your work will be rewarded, declares the Lord.
> They will return from the land of the enemy.
> So there is hope for your future, declares the Lord.

Your children will return to their own land.
-Jeremiah 31:16, 17

Scripture. Blessed, beautiful words of truth.

Scripture that gives perspective.

Scripture that corrects.

Scripture that instructs.

Scripture that reminds.

Scripture that encourages.

Sarah will always depend on us. Most of the time, I think that's ok. But, sometimes, it is daunting. She will always need us to feed her, dress her, bathe her, change her diapers, position her, entertain her. Most kids grow up and get on about the business of their own lives, and many ultimately end up taking care of their parents when the parents age and near the end of life. That is not the case for us. We do not have a normal situation, and sometimes that can be frightening. Will my life always be this same stuff, over and over, even when Sarah is an adult? Most of the time, I'm ok with that idea. I rejoice in it even…but there are moments of exhaustion and discouragement.

Today was one of those days.

I stopped at school. Sarah was in her wheelchair and having lunch. She was not able to pick her head up.   She just looked so weak and weary. Her face has a terrible rash on it that we can't seem to cure despite many doctors' appointments and lots of home remedies. It has been over 2 ½ years since the stroke, and here we are…still working on head control. It has been 6 months since this rash started, and here we are…still trying to pinpoint the cause, not to mention discover the cure.

"Will life always be like this?" I thought to myself as I left the school.

I stopped for a cup of coffee.   Then I went home and opened my Bible. And, there it was…beautiful Scripture, words of encouragement, hope and truth: *"Restrain your voice from weeping and your eyes from tears, for your work will be rewarded,"* declares the Lord.

Words I needed to hear.

The effort we put into Sarah's day to day care and the work that she herself puts into her own recovery is not wasted, as it sometimes may seem. Even if the head control never comes, even if those arms continue to disobey her brain's commands, even if the struggles continue or even increase, we are rewarded...by becoming stronger people, by sensing God's ever-present love over us, and ultimately by realizing that there is a day coming when Sarah's healing will be complete, when her arms will work and she will hold her head up, when she will no longer be trapped in a body that fails to work the way it is supposed to.

"Your children will return to their own land." Perfect land, a land of milk and honey and health and wholeness and promises fulfilled. In God's time, in God's way. Perfect. The enemy and the stroke will not win because perfect health and wholeness in the presence of God awaits.

Scripture. It's a wonderful thing.

JUNE 22

I was washing dishes a few nights ago when the phone rang. With sudsy hands, I picked up the phone and said, "Hello," and was greeted in return by Pete. He was calling to invite Mark and Sarah and I to the next CYC project at Alleghany State Park. He said he would make sure we would have a cabin that would work for Sarah if we wanted to join the group.

It's hard for us to be able to do these things. Sarah was born nearly 12 years ago with quite a handful of significant medical diagnosis'. Hers is a life in a disabled and broken body. Hers is a life of frequent pain. And yet joy.

Life with a totally disabled child seems normal to us now.

Daily, I remind Sarah of her identity...Psalm 139...that she is "fearfully and wonderfully made" and that God "knit her together" and "saw her substance" even before she was born. He knew her before I did! I tell her what Jesus said to His disciples in Matthew 10 and Luke 12...that every hair on her head is numbered. Think about that for a moment...the great true and living God who created the entire universe is aware of every hair on Sarah's head...and on mine...and on yours...

How can this be? We speak often, don't we, of the mystery of suffering. But, what about the mystery of God's willingness to stoop down and love us?

Unexpected and sudden tragedies happen to each one of us on life's journey.

For me, the jolting life-changing twists included hearing the words, "Your baby will be born with Down Syndrome" and "Sarah has leukemia" and my sister's voice on the other end of the phone telling me our Dad was dying. And I know more will come as time goes on because this is real life in a fallen world where pain and loss touch each of us. Yet, somehow when you know the Lord, these heartaches can also be precious. For these are the moments in which faith becomes action. These are the real "rubber hits the road" moments in which we get to work out our spiritual muscles and trust God, to believe – really believe – that God is who He says He is and will do what He has promised to do. These painful moments can become opportunities to grow in the Lord's grace and goodness. And to "rejoice! This is the day that the LORD has made!" I would dare say that Satan is beaten back in our lives the moment when we choose to rejoice even in the face of sorrow.

I don't know what unexpected and sudden life events you may have already experienced or will experience in your future. I don't know all the ways your hearts have been broken. I have not seen all the tears you have cried. Or the temptations you have faced in your young lives.

But God knows.

Even though our circumstances or surroundings will change as time goes by, our God won't. He is the living God who is "the same yesterday, today, and tomorrow." In our unstable world and in our unstable flesh, we yet have the assurance that God is the same. What He has said is what He means and will always mean. What He has promised He will continue to promise and to provide. Remember....you are fearfully and wonderfully made...every hair on your head is numbered. God's grace is sufficient.

Choose this day whom you will serve.

Choose this day to honor the Lord.

Choose this day to cry out to Christ for salvation if He's not yet your Savior and for your every need if He is.

Choose this day to reflect the light of Jesus Christ in this dark world.

Choose to rejoice this day - the day the Lord has made!

Praise His name!

God bless you and the work of your hands and the thoughts of your mind this day and always!

JUNE 23

Dear Father,

Praise You for the Son! Thank You that in times past You spoke through the prophets. But now, in these last days, You speak to us by Your Son – the One whom You appointed heir of all things, the One through whom You have made the universe. Jesus, You are the radiance of the Father's glory, the exact representation of His being. You are sustaining all things by Your powerful Word. You provided purification for sins, and then sat down at the right hand of Majesty in heaven. You are superior to angels. Your throne will last forever.

Forever!

Lord, may my family and my students worship and adore you. May those whom I have known in years gone by worship and adore you. May leaders and people of influence in this nation and the nations of the words worship and adore you. May they and we and I know You and know You well.

Be exalted!

You are the radiance of the Father's glory, the sustainer of the universe, greater and more powerful than any enemy we face. May we know You as You really are, not the small version of this world or of our own minds, but may we know the power of Your might and the beauty of Your holiness.

May we know the truth.

And may the truth – You – set us free.

Praise Your holy name!

In Jesus' Sustaining and Purifying Name…

JUNE 24

Dear Father,

By grace are we saved. By grace alone. Through faith. Not by works. Not by our own effort or goodness. Redemption, salvation, heaven – gifts from You that we do not deserve. Your kindness, Your incomparable riches to us lead us to repentance. Father, strip us of our tendency to rely on our own attempts to reach You. Feeble and ineffective are our efforts, and yet we strive so hard, foolishly and proudly strutting our own attempts at goodness. Yet, Your Word clearly teaches that our efforts are mere filthy rags when held to the light of Your perfection. How foolish and proud we are to think we can somehow earn Your approval. No, for we come as blind beggars and Your grace saves and Your light gives vision.

And victory. I am Your workmanship. I am a new creation in Christ. I am saved freely. Now what?

Saved to serve, saved to now do good works, prepared by You, in advance for me to do. Lord, help our family to know and to grasp this proper order. Salvation first. Then, works. Until there is salvation, works are without eternal value. Not until we are saved do any of our sacrificial and perceived good works accomplish anything lasting. Once saved, each one is priceless and will be duly rewarded.

Lord, You are my peace. You have destroyed the barrier of separation and the dividing wall of hostility. I was a foreigner, without hope and without You in this world. But now, Christ has brought me near. Through His blood, I who was once far away, am now near, now with hope, now with God.

May those who are still separated, still hiding behind that dividing wall of hostility, have no peace. May they sense how lost they are and how they are far from You. Christ's blood is needed. It is the only way, the only hope.

This, may they know.

This, may we remember.

JUNE 25

I feel anger.

It is not anger at God. It is anger at the enemy – the enemy who has come to seek, kill, steal, and destroy. This enemy is a devouring lion, a murderer come to devour whom he can through sheer force or subtle deception.

I am angry that things are not what they are supposed to be. Sin. Sickness. Suffering. Death. Despair. Destruction. Divorce. Depression. Disease. Hatred. Famine. Apathy. Confusion. Ruin. Tragedy…these are not God's intention or original design. These are consequences of man's pride. These are fruits of an enemy that stalks and seeks to reduce man to mere loaves of bread.

The enemy viciously pursues destruction of all things good and pure and holy. He twists truth into lies and dims light in his love for darkness. How angry we should be against this enemy! We should be hostile toward him and engaged warriors in God's battle at every turn. And above all, we are called to be alert and aware of the reality of spiritual warfare and battles raged in heavenly realms and high places.

God is NOT the enemy! Yet, how often do we blame Him and rail against Him, wasting energy that should be spent defeating the foe. Satan must be laid low in our thoughts and our lives. Whenever he gains a foothold, his foot must be cut off and buried. Quickly. May the deceiver rot and decompose in the soil of truth.

The enemy does not need our help in his on-going quest to kill, steal, and destroy. Yet how often we participate in his dirty plans and promote his wicked cause! Knowingly and unknowingly we become willing actors in his ugly play. Every time we gossip or lie or flatter or covet or steal or look with lust or think with hate or blame another or promote self or speak in anger or look upon what is impure or grumble or disrespect parents or become drunk with alcohol, drugs, success or self, or are led by fear and doubt and unbelief...each time we neglect God's Word, His Spirit, His people...when we worship the idols of this world and spend more time in front of the television than time with Him...as we fail to raise our children in the fear and admonition of the Lord...the times we compromise when we should stand...when we hide the light of the gospel under a bushel...This is us colluding with the enemy and advancing the kingdom of darkness.

We are willing participants more than we care to admit.

Be angry at this foolishness! And begin recognizing alliances with Satan that need and must be dismantled...take control from the enemy and give it to God...and do so on purpose. Today.

The day is coming when the Redeemer Messiah will return and judge in truth and righteousness. The Lamb of God is coming again, as Mighty King and Conqueror and He will completely restore to the utmost those who are His.

Are you His?

JUNE 26

WORDS THAT HAVE SEEN ME THROUGH...

God overwhelms me.

What an unspeakable privilege is access to God's Word. It never ceases to amaze and sadden me when I hear people, either in word or deed, claim that the Word of the Lord is outdated or irrelevant, scoffing that it is old-fashioned and not adequate for the problems of our day. Have they ever really read and studied this gift? Have they ever asked God to help them understand His Word and reveal Himself to them? Or, are they merely repeating the words of the world, the world that mocks God?

As for me and my house, we will serve the LORD, and with gladness of heart we will embrace truth, eternal truth that saves the lost and breathes hope into hopeless situations. All I know is that God overwhelms me with His Word.

*God is our refuge and strength, an ever-present help in trouble......'**Be still, and know that I am God**; I will be exalted among the nations, I will be exalted in the earth (Psalm 46:1, 10).*

I remember February, 1998. It was the worst month of my life. Sarah, born in June, 1996 with multiple birth defects, suffered a stroke. Our little girl who had been able to sit and feed herself and clap her hands and crawl stopped being that little girl. Our little girl who had smiled so much and laughed so freely stopped smiling and laughing. Our little girl who had been such a good sleeper now slept fitfully and rarely. Sarah could no longer sit, roll, crawl, or use her hands and arms. It was difficult for her to hold her head up. Her arms and legs were stiff.

Our lives changed. I quit work. Mark, who had been a stay-at-home dad, returned to work. My life became medical appointments, physical therapy, and watching Nick-at-Night while waiting for Sarah to finally fall asleep. Day after day. Night after night.

Nights were the worst. Sarah couldn't sleep. And she was so unhappy and irritable, a consequence of the swelling of her brain following the stroke. Doctors couldn't guarantee that the irritability would get better, although they hoped it would, and eventually it did.

My life felt like a lonely fog. I would think to myself, "This feels like a nightmare, only there is no waking up from this one." I was tired all the time.

A few months into all this, I started laying Sarah in bed in the middle of the night, even if she was still fussy. I would let her fuss for a half an hour or so. While she fussed, I would lay down in the other room, drained. I remember lying in bed one night. I could hear Sarah whining, and I knew that soon I would need to go get her. Lying there, exhausted and scared, I heard God's Word in my head. **"Be still and know that I am God."**

God reminding me that He was in control of even this.

I needed to know that. There is power in His Word. There is hope in His truth. There is peace in His presence. He helped me, supported me, and showed me the way during a very frightening time. The problems didn't go away. Sarah continued to struggle with sleep. Sarah's physical recovery from the stroke was minimal. God never promised us that He would fix our physical and worldly problems, although sometimes He does - that's His decision to make. But, He did do what He promised He would, for He gave me His strength to get through. He carried me. One day at a time. One night at a time.

JUNE 27

WORDS THAT HAVE SEEN ME THROUGH...

God overwhelms me.

As He (Jesus) went along, He saw a man blind from birth. His disciples asked Him 'Rabbi, who sinned, this man or his parents, that he was born blind?' 'Neither this man nor his parents sinned,' said Jesus, 'but this happened so that the work of God might be displayed in his life (John 9:1-3).

As time went on, Sarah did experience some recovery. She started to sleep through the night about 8 months after the stroke. Her smile slowly returned. The constant irritability ceased. Physically, the recovery was minimal. Sarah continued to depend on us for every need. No words formed in her mouth, although many came from her eyes. Joy and sweetness returned to our little girl.

We grew used to the new life into which Sarah's stroke plunged us. But ever lingering in the dust of busy days was "why?" Why did Sarah have a stroke? Medically I knew the answer. Sarah had moyamoya syndrome, a rare vascular condition that led to strokes.

But mere medical answers did not satisfy the ever-nagging "why?" that troubled my mind. Had I done something wrong? Was I being punished? Was my faith too small and weak?

God's Word is more than black ink on white pages.

God's Word is an experience.

He crashes into my life with His Words. He interrupts my small thoughts with great truth.

He speaks to me.

The story of the blind man in John 9. It changed everything.

Perspective framing truth and extending hope...

I had read the book of John many times. The story of the blind man in chapter 9 was not new to me. I had read these words. I knew the story. But, I hadn't experienced the story and the words had not taken root.

But God.

He interrupted the lies I was kicking around in my head. He spoke truth. Powerfully. With His Word.

In the story of the blind man, the disciples were asking Jesus the same questions I was. "Why?" "Why was this man born blind? Why was he suffering? Was it his sin or the sin of his parents?"

In response, Jesus drew a bigger picture. He indicated that there was purpose in the pain. *Neither this man nor his parents sinned but this happened so that the work of God might be displayed in his life.* With purpose comes hope. We can endure when there is a bigger picture being painted, a picture of which we have the privilege of being part because of the suffering. Sarah's struggles and the difficulties thrust upon her and us were not without meaning. The trials were not in vain for they could be used to display the work of God in our lives.

Ultimately, I know the end of the story. Jesus Christ wins.

That is the big picture. My life, a life bought back by His blood, is lived within the framework of His victory.

And thus, I endure. I persevere. I press on.

For there is purpose, even in the mysterious moments of pain and suffering.

Truth is, we have a Savior who suffered just as we do. He can understand pain and fear and loneliness. He gets it because He got it. And He can and will and does weave purpose into all of it.

JUNE 28

WORDS THAT HAVE SEEN ME THROUGH...

God overwhelms me.

Jesus said, "Therefore I tell you, do not worry about your life, what you will eat or drink; or about your body, what you will wear. Is not life more important than food, and the body more important than clothes? Look at the birds of the air; they do not sow or reap or store away in barns, and yet your heavenly Father feeds them. Are you not much more valuable than they? Who of you by worrying can add a single hour to his life? And why do you worry about clothes? See how the lilies of the field grow. They do not labor or spin. Yet I tell you that not even Solomon in all his splendor was dressed like one of these. If that is how God clothes the grass of the field, which is here today and tomorrow is thrown into the fire, will He not much more clothe you, O you of little faith? So do not worry, saying, 'What shall we eat?' or 'What shall we drink?' or 'What shall we wear?' **For the pagans run after all these things, and your heavenly Father knows that you need them.** *But seek first His kingdom and His righteousness, and all these things will be given to you as well" (Matthew 6:25-33).*

Spiritual awakening does not automatically guarantee spiritual growth. This world, it is just so distracting! I'll tell you, it is so easy for me to get caught up in "stuff:" *material stuff, financial stuff, day-to-day stuff, relationship stuff, bad hair day stuff.*

It's one thing to read God's words and it's another to live them. For many years, I went through the common syndrome of keeping God separate. You know, He's just one more task to complete on a long list of tasks. Compartmentalizing God is a sin, yes, but it's also stupid because it prevents God's power in our lives. God does not want to be just another fragment in a fragmented life. He wants to be the glue that gets all the pieces together. He cannot glue if He is segregated away.

The glue needs to be the most important thing, not the pieces.

I was getting pretty used to our life. We had a routine, my husband, Sarah and I. And, it was a nice routine. We enjoyed things again. But there I went, when things were going well, I was forgetting about God. Being busy. And, you know what happened? What will always happen when we keep God in some little cubby hole of our lives. I started to feel overwhelmed. Little things seemed bigger than they were. Worries about health insurance. Worries about jobs. Worries about, "what if Sarah has another stroke?" Worries about getting along with other people. Worries about stuff. You know what I am talking about.

One day it struck me that I was being a pagan. *For the pagans run after all these things, and your heavenly Father knows that you need them.* Children of God are not supposed to be worrying. Sure, we are supposed to be planning (with God's guidance) and preparing and being responsible and wise. But, we are not to be anxious. God will provide. No need to be a pagan. Not to mention worry does no good. It is not practical and it cannot help, so why worry? No good will come from worry. Trust God. Good will come from that.

We need perspective that is grander than our selves and greater than our temporal lives. We need "Joseph-like" perspective: *When Joseph's brothers saw that their father was dead, they said, 'What if Joseph holds a grudge against us and pays us back for all the wrongs we did to him?' So they sent word to Joseph, saying, 'Your father left these instructions before he died: 'This is what you are to say to Joseph: I ask you to forgive your brothers the sins and the wrongs they committed in treating you so badly.' Now please forgive the sins of the servants of the God of your father.' When their message came to him, Joseph wept. His brothers then came and threw themselves down before him. 'We are your slaves,' they said. But Joseph said to them, 'Don't be afraid. Am I in the place of God?* **You intended to harm me, but God intended it for good to accomplish what is now being done, the saving of many lives'** *(Genesis 50:15-20).*

So there I was, a pagan, not at all "Joseph-like," - worrying about stuff and forgetting God in the busyness of life and my assumed importance.

And so God blessed us. With cancer.

Sarah was diagnosed with acute lymphocytic leukemia on November 22, 2003. I don't pretend to understand all of God's ways. But, I do believe and Scripture teaches that God is all-powerful and nothing happens in our world and lives that He does not permit. So, as much as we may resent and question the tough situations that come our way, the fact remains that God permits these things to come.

There are events and battles being raged in the spiritual world of which we are unaware. God has purposes that are beyond our ability to grasp. What matters, really, is how we respond to the tough things of life. We can hate God. We can be mad at God. We can ignore God. We can spend years wondering, "why."

Or, we can walk in faith.

That is why I can now say that God blessed us. No, Sarah's cancer was not the blessing. God's presence was. The truth is, anything we encounter in life that draws us to God is a blessing, and anything that takes us away from Him is a curse. And, being the humans that we are with the free-will that we have, so often the very things that God intended as blessings end up becoming our curses because we, in our God-given freedom, choose to desire the stuff more than the God who gave us the stuff. We become idolaters who covet what other people have, and we grow lukewarm or hostile to our God before we decide we will simply forget about Him while we pursue what we want when we want it. And the very things that we humans would label "bad" (such as cancer and disease, torture, persecution, abandonment, rejection, failures, accidents, loss, bankruptcy) can end up becoming the blessing that drives us to our Lord.

I stand in awe of the One who drew me to Himself.

Joseph was a great man of faith. He suffered. And yet his response was, *You intended to harm me, but God intended it for good.* And, I have no doubt that God intended Sarah's struggle with cancer to bring good into my life and into the world. I believe that with all my heart.

And, I thank God for the story of Joseph in the Bible. It helps me to bear up on the bad days and walk in faith when the path is unclear and the purpose is unknown.

JUNE 29

WORDS THAT HAVE SEEN ME THROUGH...

God overwhelms me.

Rejoice in the Lord always. I will say it again: Rejoice! Let your gentleness be evident to all. The Lord is near. Do not be anxious about anything, but in everything, by prayer and petition, with thanksgiving, present your requests to God. And the peace of God, which transcends all understanding, will guard your hearts and your minds in Christ Jesus (Philippians 4:4-7).

Take every thought captive.

But how?

I have found in my walk that the very best and most effective way to take every thought captive and bring it into obedience to Christ is to REJOICE!

If I am in the middle of a really rotten day or stinky situation, my natural self wants to turn inward toward self-pity and bad habits. I have learned, and am slowly applying the Biblical principal of praise. I don't always want to, but if I find something to say, "thank you, Lord" about in every single circumstance, the load is lightened. Priorities slowly start to align themselves with the will of God.

It takes time.

A rejoicing spirit that seeks to praise God in all circumstances does not come naturally. It is a spirit that must be developed until it becomes the habit, the first response.

It also requires proper definitions. When I first saw the word, "rejoice" in Scripture, what came to my mind was some sort of childish giddiness. I thought of "rejoice" as synonymous with "happy" and "happy" as including laughter and even some silliness. This is a worldly definition of "rejoice." It is shallow. And, it is impossible to apply when the going gets tough.

I didn't have the energy or the desire to be giddy about my child's life-threatening illness that left her with a swollen brain and lots of neurologically based irritability. I couldn't "rejoice" in cancer as long as I thought of "rejoice" as "worldly happiness and worldly expression of that happiness."

Simply stated, I didn't understand the Biblical concept of "rejoice." I did, though, understand, how to complain. God patiently received my complaints. God rejoiced because I drew near to Him, even if my motives were to grumble and cry bitterly against the apparent injustice of the circumstances. I cried out to the Lord, and He joined me in my wilderness walk. Over the years, He taught me - through the Body of Christ, the Word, and the Holy Spirit - how to "rejoice."

Now I understand that I rejoice not because of my circumstances. I rejoice because of my God, the God of Creation and Redemption who is sovereign and unchanging even in the midst of ever-changing situations.

I rejoice because I know Him and the power of His resurrection. I rejoice because sharing in the fellowship of His sufferings is a beautiful privilege. The pain is temporary. The rewards eternal.

And, yes, sometimes giddiness does come upon me as I stand in absolute awe of God and His love, His holiness, His design, and His blessed control over all.

Rejoice. Always.

JUNE 30

From *Where Is God When It Hurts?* by Philip Yancey [25]

"Because of Jesus, I need never cry into the abyss, 'Hey, you up there – do you even care?' The presence of suffering does not mean that God has forsaken me. To the contrary, by joining us on earth God gave solid, historical proof that He hears our

groans, and even groans them with us. When we endure trials, He stands beside us, like the fourth man in the fiery furnace.

"Why did Jesus have to suffer and die? The question deserves an entire book, and has prompted many books, but among the answers the Bible gives is this most mysterious answer: Suffering served as a kind of 'learning experience' for God. Such words may seem faintly heretical, but I am merely following phraseology from the book of Hebrews.

"Hebrews was written to a Jewish audience saturated in the Old Testament. The author strives to show that Jesus is 'better' – a key word throughout the book. How is He better than the religious system they were used to? More powerful? More impressive? No, Hebrews emphasizes that Jesus is better because He has spanned the chasm between God and us. 'Although He was a son, He learned obedience from what He suffered' (Hebrews 5:8). Elsewhere, that book tells us that the author of our salvation was made perfect through suffering (Hebrews 2:10).

"These words, full of fathomless mystery, surely mean at least this: the Incarnation had meaning for God as well as for us...In some incomprehensible way, because of Jesus, God hears our cries differently. The author of Hebrews marvels that whatever we are going through, God has Himself gone through. 'For we do not have a high priest who is unable to sympathize with our weaknesses, but we have one who has been tempted in every way, just as we are – yet was without sin' (Hebrews 4:15).

"We have a high priest who, having graduated from the school of suffering, 'is able to deal gently with those who ignorant and are going astray, since He Himself is subject to weakness' (Hebrews 5:2). Because of Jesus, God understands, truly understands, our pain. Our tears become His tears. We are not abandoned. The farmhand with the sick child, the swollen eight year-old with leukemia, the grieving relatives in Yuba City, the leprosy patients in Louisiana – none has to suffer alone....The surgery of life hurts. It helps me, though, to know that the surgeon Himself, the Wounded Surgeon, has felt every stab of pain and every sorrow."
From _Where Is God When It Hurts?_ by Philip Yancey [25]

June's Apologetic Moment...Contend for the faith

Origins Matter...From Whence Came Information?

What is *information*?

Information can mean "facts provided or learned by someone about someone or something." Information can also mean "what is conveyed or represented by a particular arrangement or sequence of things."

I guess you could say that one recognizes information when one sees it, for information is characterized by specificity, pattern, logic, and organization.

When drawings were found on the walls of caves, everyone knew that a person (i.e. intelligent being) carved them. No one suggested that natural processes, such as erosion over time, had drawn them.

When we are walking on the beach, and we see words spelled out in the sand, we know that a person (i.e. an intelligent being) spelled them. No one believes that natural processes, such as the movement of water, spelled out meaningful words in the sand of a beach.

When we look at Mount Rushmore, we recognize the faces of Washington, Jefferson, Lincoln, Roosevelt. We know that a person (i.e. intelligent being) spent years chiseling and sculpting to create these profiles in granite. No one suggests that natural processes, such as the exfoliation of rock, drew these recognizable faces.

The SETI program spent decades and millions of dollars "listening" for extraterrestrial life. What were they listening for? Patterns...radiation with a sequence because if that occurred, they knew the only explanation would be intelligence.

When we see sentences written on a page of paper, we know that a person (i.e. intelligent being) crafted those sentences. This is because when words and shapes are sequenced into patterns to convey a message, we KNOW intelligence is behind it.

We have learned a lot about DNA. We know that DNA is composed of a series of nucleotide bases linked together by a sugar-phosphate backbone and coiled into a double-helix. We understand the chemistry of this amazing self-replicating material. But realize that what we understand about the chemistry and structure of DNA is merely an understanding of the STORAGE SYSTEM.

DNA is a storage system…it stores and communicates and copies INFORMATION.

But, from where did the information come from in the first place?

When scientists and textbooks speak about DNA, *they assume the information and explain only the storage system.*

This whole topic can get complicated very quickly. On both sides, there are extremely technical arguments with big words. Those of us on the outside are often left intimidated, unable to understand what is being said, much less advance our own arguments persuasively. Information science and information scientists can be overwhelmingly technical and excessively boring if you don't love the topic.

Since most people don't love the topic, let's keep it simple and useful in this brief essay.

I did a google search using the following words: *naturalistic explanation for the origin of information?* The results yielded were lots of websites that mentioned "naturalism" and lots of websites that mentioned "information," but nary one that mentioned both together in a concise straight-forward way.

Paul Davies, a theoretical physicist and astrobiologist at Arizona State University, has spent his life studying the topics of the origin of life, the evolution of life, and the possibility of life beyond earth. Davies stated in an article published in the *Journal of the Royal Society* Interface (12/11/12) that the traditional science approach of trying to recreate chemical building blocks that "gave rise to life 3.7 billion years ago" is an approach that is "failing to capture the essence of what life is about." Davies recognizes that life and the cells that make up living creatures contain information. He also acknowledges that we do not have a naturalistic explanation for the origin of that information. His honesty is refreshing.

Think about yourself for a moment. Go backward in time. At some point in time YOU consisted of a single fertilized cell. Inside that fertilized cell was DNA. Stored in that DNA was information, blueprints that would direct the development of that single fertilized egg into a baby with complex, interdependent body systems which would grow into a toddler, then a teenager, and then an adult. How did that one fertilized egg KNOW, as it divided, that some cells should become muscle cells and some cells should become nerve cells, and some cells should become bone cells, and some cells should become epithelial cells…you get the picture…how did the single fertilized egg KNOW how to DIFFERENTIATE into specialized tissues?

INFORMATION was present that guided this process. There is no naturalistic explanation for this reality. Logically, whenever we observe sequential, specified phenomena, we know there is intelligence behind it…think of Mt. Rushmore and cave drawings and words written in the sand. We know they were put there by an intelligent source.

DNA – and more importantly the information stored in DNA – is way more detailed and complex than are Mt. Rushmore and cave drawings and words written in the sand. Why is it so controversial, then, to claim that maybe, just maybe DNA is the result of an intelligent mind, the result of the Creator God?

The LORD is good to all:
and His tender mercies are over all His works.
Psalm 145:9

July

"Cheap grace is the grace we bestow on ourselves.
Cheap grace is the preaching of forgiveness
without requiring repentance,
baptism without church discipline,
communion without confession...
Cheap grace is grace without discipleship,
grace without the cross,
grace without Jesus Christ, living and incarnate."
— Dietrich Bonhoeffer

JULY 1

One of the things that bothers me about Sarah's disabilities is her inability to learn about Jesus the way other children do. Her language skills have developed to only the 6-9 month level. Cognitively, her IQ tests well below 50. In other words, Sarah may never understand "Jesus Loves Me, This I Know….." or memorize Bible verses or recognize the Apostles' Creed. It's not that I question God's love for Sarah. But it does bother me that she will never comprehend the intellectual reality of God during her lifetime.

I read the Bible to Sarah. I pray with her. We listen to gospel music together.

And sometimes I do goofy things...I have an 8 x 10 framed drawing of Jesus praying in the garden before the crucifixion...sometimes I prop this picture up near Sarah...as though that will have some sort of spiritual effect...since He probably didn't even look like the man in the drawing, I'm not sure what I'm actually trying to accomplish...

Anyhow, the other day I had this picture propped up at a bit of a distance from Sarah. I was completing range of motion therapy exercises with her. When I finished, I said to Sarah, "Roll toward Jesus (obviously meaning the picture...which isn't Jesus at all...but I guess you know what I mean...). Rolling is a lot of work for Sarah. She cannot roll independently and sometimes she gives me a hard time when I try to assist her and make her roll...for rolling can be physically painful to her.

This day was no exception. I encouraged her on, telling her again to, "Roll toward Jesus." As she whined and complained, the truth hit me. In my own attempts in life to "roll toward Jesus" I do the same. I complain. I struggle. Sometimes I just want to quit.

It is hard to be a good servant, willing to exercise spiritual muscles. Sometimes, it is uncomfortable. Sometimes I'm distracted or confused or simply weary. More times than I care to admit, I like to do things my own way in my own time – I like to set the agenda and be in control and decide how to solve my problems (or even if to solve them at all). So, when it seems that Jesus is saying, "Hey, I want you to roll in this direction" and I am trying to go in another, I complain and struggle, just like Sarah.

I am grateful that the Lord is patient with me. As I have been rolling toward Him over these past couple years, I have been brutal in my complaints and questions. In the past, I have blamed him for allowing Sarah's stroke. I have bitterly asked him, "Where are you, where are you??!!!" He has been gentle with me when I have been angry at Him. I understand now that when I was accusingly shouting, "Where are you, where are you?" He was right there with us. He gave Himself. It just took me time to see.

When Sarah finally reached the picture, she smiled. It seemed as though she had forgotten the hard work and was experiencing the rewards of doing good work. It seemed to symbolize to me that, once all of our "rolling toward Jesus" is finally complete and the work is done, that we, too, will be able to smile and rest. May we learn to smile on the way. May we learn to rest even in the pain. Because of Him.

JULY 2

Yesterday, I had an eye opener. I was rebuked for a bad attitude and an exalted view of self. I was challenged to repent of small thoughts of God. I was challenged to embrace a greater and grander perspective.

Here's the story…

After Sarah had her stroke, I questioned God. "Why, why, and why!?" I cried in my head and heart…sometimes with anger, sometimes with despair, sometimes with disappointment, sometimes with exhaustion.

In our culture, convenience and pain-free living are expected. We think we are entitled to health and relief from pain. As a people we question suffering and God's role in it more than most people in the world (who actually suffer more than we do). It is one of those universal questions, isn't it? "Suffering…Why?"

I was speaking with my Pastor yesterday. As it often does, the topic of suffering came up. Eventually, the conversation arrived at the idea that God Himself is not exempt from suffering. Perfect Jesus, God Himself, was betrayed, denied, mocked, beaten, hung on a cross for our sins. Thus, God understands pain and suffering in a unique and real way.

But…

There has always been something about the suffering of the Savior that has bothered me. It's nibbled at my mind that Jesus had an advantage. He is, after all, God. And He had the advantage of foreknowledge. He knew how it would all end. He knew that the suffering on the cross would lead to a resurrection and ultimately the glory of God (not to mention salvation for all of us who believe). In my mind, that complete knowledge somehow diminished the suffering He experienced.

Oh, how small my mind!

Oh, how little I actually comprehend what my Savior went through for me!

In all my self-focused smallness, I blurted out to Pastor, "Yes, I know Jesus suffered. But, let's remember He is God, after all. And, don't forget, He knew how the story was going to end!" The tone of my spewed words was bitter.

Pastor listened patiently.

And then he spoke simple – yet profound words - which gently rebuked me and reframed my circumstances with a much needed eternal perspective…

Pastor simply said to me, *"Well, don't you know how it's going to end, too?"*

I stopped. I shut up.

How obvious.

YES! I, too, know the end of the story.

It's true, I do know how suffering will end for believers in Christ. The suffering will end in VICTORY. Jesus Christ rose from the dead. He rose victorious over sin, death, and hell. He rose victorious over suffering. I share in His victory. Jesus will lead me beside the still waters. I will behold His face. His glory. Him.

I DO know how it will end!

Beautifully.

God owes me no explanations.

JULY 3

Sometimes, I feel far away from God.

Sometimes, I even wonder if there is a God.

This usually happens when I become busy - too busy for God.

Can you believe how foolish this is?

How can any of us ever be too busy for our Creator?

God has given us life. He meets our needs. He promises us salvation through Jesus. He is the solution to our problems. He loves us unconditionally. And, yet, sometimes, I get too busy for him!

He becomes another task on my "to do" list.

I am a fool if I don't try to change this about myself.

What is even worse is that my "too busy" isn't even life changing stuff. It's about changing diapers, cleaning the house, taking Sarah to MD appointments, laundry, dinner, dishes.

You get the point.

Obviously, these things need to be done.

So, why don't I invite God to join and lead me while I tend to the tasks of daily living?

Why do I think God is separate from the mundane grime of life?

Why do I recognize my foolishness and yet persist in it?

Satan has a foothold in my life when I get so busy that I even question God's very existence (or if not His existence, at least His presence in my life).

Satan is sneaky and we must beware of this sort of stuff.

Lord, forgive me for doubting. Forgive me for being so busy that I drift from your love.

Yes, I am prone to wander.

Idiot am I.

Forgive me that I try to be so self-sufficient and independent that I lose my dependence on you.

I am returning to You.

Lead me. You decide what should be on my plate.

And as I labor through the tasks of the day, be ever near…speaking Your wisdom into my ignorance.

JULY 4

God is, thankfully, longsuffering with the hard-hearted.

From the moment Sarah became sick, the "why" question rubbed my brain raw. Mine was a "why" of anger and of resentment and of despair toward God.

As is common to mankind when facing a trial, my emotions cried out *"WHY? Why is this happening? I don't understand? I am afraid. I am confused."*

It got ugly at times.

But God. He was so good to me, even when I was ugly.

He loved me while I was yet a sinner.

His longsuffering. His tenderness. His constant presence…

He changed me.

He taught me that "why" doesn't matter. But the "how" does.

"How to get through this?"

"How to respond to this?"

"How to trust God in even this?"

"How to find the good and the beautiful in the midst of the difficult and the sad?"

"How to give glory and thanks to the Lord in all situations?"

"How to focus on the Lord in the face of painful life events that change everything?

From time to time, that old nagging "why" sneaks in...but never with the duration and intensity that it used to.   For God has changed me.   And, He has equipped me and strengthened spiritual muscles so that I can better fight the good fight and run the race with endurance.

That's what God does. He makes a way when there seems to be no way, for He is a God of vision and deliverance.

In the midst of a world that can at times be ugly, He is beauty.

Leap into His plan for your life. Even if you don't understand it. Even if there are painful moments.

Embrace His vision for your life.

God is real. His power is real. His promise that "all things work together for good to those who love God and are called according to His purpose" is true.

Leap.

JULY 5

I praise You, Father, that You are the All-mighty Eternal God. I praise You for Your wisdom, grace, and mercy toward us. I am grateful that I can approach You. Because of Christ, I can come near to You and pour out my heart to You in full assurance that You will hear me.

So Lord I draw near to You and cry out on behalf of my Uncle Darrill. Father, You know all things. You are the blessed controller. You know the day of birth as well as the day of death for each of us. My Uncle Darrill lies on an operating table, leg being amputated as diabetes ravages his body. He is so sick. This surgery is necessary but dangerous. I plead with You, Lord, to have mercy on my Uncle. Give him Your strength. Strengthen his body and his heart. Lord, You know best. I pray for Your will to be done. We trust You.

Help Uncle Darrill to feel Your presence and to know Your peace. Protect him from pain. Be close to him. Help him to know You. Help him to remember the things he learned about you as a boy…that we are all sinners who need the Savior. May he hold this truth tightly.

Later in the day…the phone rings…

Lord, I am at Grandma Becker's house. The phone just rang…it was my Mom with the beautiful news that Uncle Darrill survived the surgery! I am crying tears of joy, joy that he is still with us and joy in Your kindness and mercy, Lord.

Thank You for giving Uncle Darrill more time. Difficult days are ahead. But I know You have a plan, Lord.

Help Uncle Darrill to know so, too. Protect his body, his mind, his spirit going forward.

Whether we are in healthy bodies or broken bodies, Lord You are ever worthy of all our praise and adoration. Your body, too, was broken. You are the great High Priest who can sympathize with us in all our distress. As Uncle Darrill faces life without legs, protect his mind from the lies of the enemy and remind him day by day of your great sympathy for those broken in this world.

JULY 6

> *Who shall separate us from the love of Christ?*
> *Shall trouble or hardship or persecution or famine or nakedness or danger of sword?…*
> *For I am convinced that neither death nor life, neither angels nor demons,*
> *neither the present nor the future, nor any powers, neither height nor depth,*
> *nor anything else in all creation, will be able to separate us from the*
> *love of God that is in Christ Jesus our Lord.*
> *-Romans 8:35,38,39*

There is no problem or tragedy that is greater than the beautiful promises of our Lord. When you compare His love, His character, His vision to our problems, the problems pale and we can endure.

I know from experience that it doesn't always seem like that.

Learning, and then believing, and, finally trusting that God loves me did not make my problems go away. Rather, such great truth sustained me. Even as the problems yawned seemingly unending before me.

Keep your eyes on Jesus. He is our gift from a God who loves us.

Who is Jesus? Jesus is the assurance that we can live our eternity with God in a heaven where there is perfect peace, perfect love, perfect health, and answers to the questions that now trouble us. Jesus is the reason we can forever be in the very presence of the Lord where there is no sorrow, no pain, no suffering, no hunger, no loneliness, no violence, no fear. Jesus came to earth and became flesh and blood for a reason – to die. And to live again.

Jesus didn't just die. He suffered.

Crucifixion.

God in the flesh was tortured. God in the flesh was humiliated.

God understands pain. God feels our sadness and our tears. He hurts when we hurt. I don't really understand as much as I would like to. But, it is not about understanding. It is about believing in God's love even when the world and our painful experiences tempt us to doubt.

The solution to our problems and the way to endure tragedy is less about immediate temporal deliverance and more about eternal focus. The problem may remain. The tragedies of life are real. But there is victory even in the mournful moments of life when we keep our eyes on Jesus. For we know that the sorrows and the losses do not matter as much as Jesus matters.

We can choose to recognize that our problems are temporary. They really are.

What lasts forever is Jesus Christ and the love of our Father in heaven.

JULY 7

"What if Sarah has another stroke?"

"What if Sarah doesn't recover from the stroke she has already had?"

"What if Sarah never eats and has to be tube fed for the rest of her life?"

"What if Sarah's shunt malfunctions?"

"What if Sarah gets an ulcer from taking aspirin daily?"

Burdened.

Scared.

The future appeared so daunting. Daily, my list of fearful "what if" questions grew. They pounded in my head. They pounded in my heart. I was rendered exhausted.

I asked God to show me how to deal with these questions.

"Cast your cares upon Me," He said.

Ok, but how?

The first thing I tried when the "what ifs" attacked me was to force them out of my thoughts. Simply ignore them. I would tell myself that the Lord loves me, and that I can give Him my problems and my worries – that doing so actually pleases Him. I thought that to trust in the Lord meant to never think about these things.

It didn't work. I couldn't just ignore the fears away. I ended up feeling not just worried about the above things, but also feeling a failure in the faith.

Turns out the solution was simple honesty. Take the "what ifs" and walk them out, extinguishing their power…

"OK, well, what if Sarah has another stroke?" I thought about this. If Sarah has another stroke, the worst that could happen would be death. And then I started thinking about this. *"What's so terrible about death? Death, if we know Jesus as Lord and Savior, takes us to Him where we live forever in His mansion and all our wounds and illnesses are healed."* OK. What else could happen if Sarah has another stroke? Well, she could lose the little function and independence that she has. I would honestly identify the worst that could happen and then the Lord would assure me that I could endure – because of Him - the worst.

In Him. With Him. Through Him.

He assured me that even if I was asked to walk through deep waters, I would not walk alone.

For my God has promised to never leave me nor forsake me.

I began to think more and more about what eternal life with Jesus means. It means no matter what happens to us as humans on earth, no matter which "what ifs" befall us, ultimately, we will stand in the presence of the Lord surrounded by His love and peace. We will be eternally healthy – physically, emotionally, and spiritually. Our needs will be met – completely. Simply put, He is bigger than the biggest trial. He is greater than the deepest loss. Life is hard. But, He is greater even than life. For He is the giver of life, the author of our days, the One who spoke the universe into existence.

He is greater than any "what if."

And I am His and He is mine.

JULY 8

I was thinking about how I read the Bible.

I am prone to read the Bible through the filter of my experiences.

I am prone to read the Bible assuming my experiences and feelings are more real than God's truth.

If Biblical truth appears to contradict an experience or a feeling, I easily believe my emotion over the Word.

This is not good.

This is a man-centered reading of the Word.

Do I really have to understand everything all the time?

If you have faith the size of a mustard seed, you can tell that mountain to be moved into the sea and it will move.

I had faith the size of a mustard seed when I prayed asking God to bring healing to Sarah's body after her stroke.

Her body was not healed.

My prayers, it felt, were not answered.

Is the Bible lying?

I could never say something as horrible as "The Bible is lying."

I can say, however, that I am riddled with questions about how to make sense of the Bible in the midst of the specific life that I am experiencing.

I think it may be simply that I don't understand everything all the time.

Because of the inability to have perfect and complete understanding, I wonder about the validity and the love of the Lord.

And herein enters faith.

Yes, faith is required.

For some questions are not readily answered.

Yes, some of the painful and tragic things we suffer do not make sense.

But this is because we are limited.

Not because God is lying.

The Bible says that God loves us.

The Bible tells me about the crucifixion of Jesus.

He suffered for me.

He rose victorious.

Truth is not dependent upon my feelings.

My starting assumption must be that God's Word is true.

Regardless of emotions.

Have I been thinking backwards?

Yes, I have been…my thinking has been flawed because my emotions have been given more credence than God's words.

The Bible tells the truth even when it may not feel like it.

Even when a loved one for whom you have been praying for remains sick.

Even when tragedy strikes.

When these things happen, the only thing that seems to be true is that you are lonely and afraid and in pain.

When you feel that way, it can be difficult to read Scriptures that talk about how much God loves you. That's because we just don't feel loved by Him at that particular moment.

But He does.

I can't make it always make sense.

It won't always make sense.

But, it doesn't have to.

We must strive to walk by faith and not by sight.

Even when it's hard.

Especially when it's hard.

JULY 9

I'm sitting across the table from my husband in a restaurant in Cooperstown, NY. It's a Wednesday evening on a warm summer in July. We are celebrating our 20th wedding anniversary.

As I sit here looking at the man to whom I am married, I remember 20 years ago…we at our wedding reception, convinced that we had everything figured out. But, we didn't.

We had no idea that night 20 years ago of all the joys and sorrows we, together, would face.

Since that warm summer night, so much has happened…Sarah was born, she lived, she died. My Dad died. The house I grew up in burned down. Mark's oldest grandson grew up and is now days away from becoming a marine. Mark's grandchildren Kaygan, Ruby, and Ryder have all been born. Who would have thought 20 years ago that I'd be teaching science at Central Baptist?

So much has happened, much of it, maybe even most of it, unexpected and unforeseen.

Twenty years ago, we were optimistically clueless! Now, I sit across the table from my husband, and I am optimistically grateful and ever aware of both the precious and the fleeting nature of life. I know now that we are not guaranteed the next twenty years, or even tomorrow. I know now that all the things I think I control, I do not. I know now that God is real and good and all-powerful and sovereign and merciful and holy and eternal. I know now that God's plans are greater than my own. I know now that God is worthy of all my praise....always. In every circumstance.

I have no idea what the next twenty years of my life will look like. And, it's good and humbling to know that I don't know. But, God does. And, I know Him. Thanks be to Jesus Christ, Lord of lords and King of kings!

JULY 10

From <u>Bonhoeffer: Pastor, Martyr, Prophet, Spy</u> by Eric Metaxas [26]

[Bonhoeffer wrote]: "First of all I will confess quite simply – I believe that the Bible alone is the answer to all our questions, and that we need only to ask repeatedly and a little humbly, in order to receive this answer. One cannot simply read the Bible, like other books. One must be prepared really to enquire of it. Only thus will it reveal itself. Only if we expect from it the ultimate answer, shall we receive it. That is because in the Bible God speaks to us. And one cannot simply think about God in one's own strength, one has to enquire of Him. Only if we seek Him, will He answer us....Only if we will venture to enter into the words of the Bible, as though in them this God were speaking to us who loves us and does not will to leave us along with our questions, only so shall we learn to rejoice in the Bible....

"If it is I who determine where God is to be found, then I shall always find a God who corresponds to me in some way, who is obliging, who is connected with my own nature. But if God determines where He is to be found, then it will be in a place which is not immediately pleasing to my nature and which is not at all congenial to me. This place is the Cross of Christ. And whoever would find Him must go to the foot of the Cross, as the Sermon on the Mount commands. This is not according to our nature at all, it is entirely contrary to it. But this is the message of the Bible, not only in the New but also in the Old Testament...

"And I would like to tell you now quite personally: since I have learnt to read the bible in this way – and this has not been for so very long – it becomes every day more wonderful to me. I read it in the morning and the evening, often during the day as well, and every day I consider a text which I have chosen for the whole week, and try to sink deeply into it, so as really to hear what it is saying. I know that without this I could not live properly any longer.

"The church has only one altar, the altar of the Almighty...before which all creatures must kneel. Whoever seeks something other than this must keep away; he cannot

join us in the house of God...The church has only one pulpit, and from that pulpit,
faith in God will be preached, and no other faith, and no other will than the will of
God, however well-intentioned...."
From <u>Bonhoeffer: Pastor, Martyr, Prophet, Spy</u> by Eric Metaxas [26]

<u>JULY 11</u>

*And the daughter of Zion is left as a cottage in a vineyard, as a lodge in a garden of
cucumbers, as a besieged city. Except the LORD of Hosts had left unto us a small
remnant, we should have been as Sodom, and we should have been like unto Gomorrah
(Isaiah 1:8-9).*

I am part of the remnant! It is a heavy charge.

My life can NO LONGER be about me. Because of who HE IS, I must yield all
unto Him. Because I love Him, I must yield all unto Him. More than that,
because He loves me, I must yield all unto Him. Nothing can be mine any longer.
It must all be His, to do with as He sees best. I need to learn to hear Him in the
midst of life, in times of confusion. I must cultivate stillness in His presence. I
must be taught the art and skill of listening to and for Him, of discerning His
voice in a loud world.

This does not come easily to me.

*Thy silver is become dross, thy wine mixed with water(Isaiah 1:22)....*Is this me now?
Am I diluted, my life a mixture of truth and deception? I need to be refined and
purified. Lord, purge the dross, take away the tin. Help me to understand better
who You are and the depth of Your love as You hold me lovingly in the refining
fire....whatever that may mean.

May you find me ready, faithfully Yours, and Yours alone.

Remnant of the Lord.

<u>JULY 12</u>

May my family be free…

Free from the penalty of sin.

Free from the bondage to sin.

May we be aware of the penalty.

May we recognize the bondage.

May we walk the narrow road that leads to You, Lord, and be safe and free and clean, nigh unto You, Father, by the blood of Christ.

May we seek You, Lord, while You can still be found.

May today be the day of salvation for any who are not yet saved!

Bless my family with hungry hearts, dry and thirsty souls, driven to You, drawn to You by You, Lord.

Praise Your Name! You are Elohim, Mighty Creator, All-Powerful God!

You are righteous.

We have sinned against You; we have been unfaithful to You.

We have rebelled and demanded our own way.

Lord, in mercy, pour troubled waters upon our lives until we give our attention to Your truth and to You.

You are righteous, in everything You do.

You bring Your people out of Egypt with a mighty hand.

Bring my family out of Egypt with Your mighty hand and Your precious blood.

In Jesus' Supreme Name…

JULY 13

Truth matters.

We live in dangerous times.

In no small part that danger resides in the tone of relativism that has gripped truth in a stranglehold these recent years…

For even in the church, there is a tendency to think in shades of relative truth and personal experience.

We are prone to be uncomfortable with absolute truth…for absolute truth demands a response. It demands obedience. It demands sober mindedness and alertness.

It may require sacrifice.

Part of fighting the good fight is demanding truth and standing for truth.

Do not be comfortable with the half-truths and relativism of the world.

Do not be one of those who decides ahead of time what you want to believe and then go seeking the narrative that fits your desired reality. It is easy – too easy – these days to simply decide what you want to believe and then google ideas to justify it…

But that kind of living is living with the cart before the horse. And that is ineffective at the best and damning at the worst.

There is absolute truth.

And it matters.

Demand it.

Seek it.

Stand for it.

JULY 14

And why do you worry about clothes? See how the lilies of the field grow. They do not labor or spin. Yet I tell you that not even Solomon in all his splendor was dressed like one of these. If that is how God clothes the grass of the field, which is here today and tomorrow is thrown into the fire, will he not much more clothe you, O you of little faith? So do not worry, saying, 'What shall we eat?' or 'What shall we drink?' or 'What shall we wear?' For the pagans run after all these things, and your heavenly Father knows that you need them. But seek first his kingdom and his righteousness, and all these things will be given to you as well. Therefore do not worry about tomorrow, for tomorrow will worry about itself. Each day has enough trouble of its own (Matthew 6:28-34).

I read these words this morning over a cup of coffee. And to me, these words spoke.

Pagan. Could it be that I, a professing Christian, am at times a pagan?

So do not worry, saying, 'What shall we eat?' or 'What shall we drink?' or 'What shall we wear?' For the <u>pagans</u> run after all these things, and your heavenly Father knows that you need them.

I may not be all that concerned about my next meal or having clothes to wear. But I sure spend enough time worrying about the modern day equivalent. I worry about health insurance. I worry about retirement (and I just turned 30). I worry about planning for Sarah's future. I worry about the price of gas. I worry about finding time to do all that I want to do (note the emphasis on "I").

I am definitely a pagan.

Perhaps I am even worse. My basic needs (food, clothing, shelter) have been met from the moment I was born. I have never had to worry about where my next meal is coming from or where I will sleep tonight or how to stay warm. Instead of being thankful and walking by faith, I devote time to worrying about stuff that matters even less than food, clothing and shelter.

God must shake His head in wonder and sadness at we human beings. He meets needs, and yet we just want more and more all the time. We trust his sovereignty in our lives when it is convenient or when everything else has failed.

I really felt badly as I read this Scripture this morning. I am sorry for this "pagan" attitude I have carried with me most of my life.

I don't know what our health insurance situation will be ten years from now. I don't know how I will "fund" my retirement. I have no idea how the high gas prices will affect my family.   But, when I really stop and think about it, I do know that the Lord has met my needs every single day all of my life. Why, then, do I worry like a pagan? Why do I waste time and energy trying to solve problems independently of my loving Father?

Forgive me, Lord, for my pagan attitude and approach to life.

Forgive me, Lord, that I have compartmentalized my walk with You.

All of my life is to be Yours.

Help me to think differently, to approach life with perspective, and to become a person of faith, deep and strong and joyfully grounded in You.

<u>JULY 15</u>

From <u>Foxe: Voices of the Martyrs</u> [27]

Maximilian Kolbe (1894 – 1941)

" 'Ten Polish pigs will die for the one who escaped.' A normal day at the Auschwitz extermination camp in 1941, and a normal punishment announced by the SS commandant, 'Butcher' Frisch. He then called the ten names of the condemned. All the prisoners were weak and dehydrated, having stood in the sun without food or water all day, waiting for the escapee to be caught. None wanted to die. One of them, Polish sergeant Francis Gajowniczek, cried out for mercy for his young wife and child, and for himself – just the sort of weakness the SS relished. Then in the line of prisoners someone stirred, moved, spoke up. It was forbidden.

" 'Who are you?' demanded Frisch.

" 'I am a Catholic priest. I wish to die for that man.'

"Frisch hesitated. A hero in the camp? No matter. Better to rid the place of such heroes. Better for the hopelessness that breaks the spirit. In any case, none of these prisoners would likely live long anyhow. Frisch accepted the fool's offer. The ten, including Father Maximilian Kolbe, were marched to the camp's starvation cells.

"Raymond Kolbe was born to hard-working Polish nationalists near Pabianice on January 8, 1894. His father died later, executed by the Russians for fighting for the independence of a partitioned Poland. His mother, a pious Catholic, saw her prayers for her son answered when Raymond was only twelve. In that year, his 'wild youth' gave way to lifelong Christian devotion. In a vision, he had seen two crowns from which to choose. The first was white for purity, the second red for martyrdom. Young Raymond asked for both. From that day, his life was given to study, missionary work, evangelism, and care for the oppressed. Everything he attempted prospered.

"At age thirteen Raymond and his brother Franciszek, illegally crossed the Russian-Austro-Hungary border to join the Franciscans at Lwow. At seventeen he professed first vows, and took his final vows at twenty, when he also took the name Maximilian...He aimed high and he received a doctorate of philosophy at the Gregorian University at age twenty-one, and a doctorate of theology at twenty-four. His other accomplishments include missionary service in Japan; the opening of a seminary near Warsaw; a start-up of a radio station, newspapers, and magazines; and the founding of an Order, the Militia of the Immaculata, which grew from 650 friars under Maximilian's leadership, making it the largest Catholic religious house in the world.

"Kolbe was a vibrant leader, but to be a Polish leader in 1939 was neither safe nor prudent. He could see the storm gathering. Indeed, Kolbe's media outreach began to assail the dangers of Germany's militarism, and his monastery took in Jewish refugees. Before his arrest by the Gestapo, Kolbe kept nearly 1,500 Jews under cover.

"On February 17, 1941, the German war machine caught him. Kolbe knew what he believed. In a well-known statement he said, 'No one can change the Truth. What we can do is to seek truth and serve it when we have found it...There are two irreconcilable enemies in the depth of every soul: good and evil, sin and love. And what use are victories on the battlefield if we are defeated in our innermost personal selves?' When Kolbe was sent to Auschwitz in May, he was prepared for his innermost battle.

"During Kolbe's two weeks in the starvation cellblock, a Nazi guard in charge of the prisoner log made note that Kolbe led in prayers and hymns. When he grew too weak to speak, he whispered. Kolbe and three others survived those two weeks, but the Nazis needed their cells for other miscreants. So the end came by a lethal injection of carbolic acid on August 14, 1941. The body of the 'escaped prisoner' was later discovered drowned in an Auschwitz latrine. Francis Gajowniczek lived to an old age, dying in Poland in 1997.

"Maximilian Kolbe had the kind of devotion to Christ that stands up to evil and takes a condemned man's place. He wrote about his relationship with Christ: 'You come to me and unite Yourself intimately to me under the form of nourishment. Your Blood now runs in mine; Your Soul, Incarnate God, penetrates mine, giving courage and support. What miracles! Who would have ever imagined such!' "
From Foxe: Voices of the Martyrs [27]

JULY 16

The darkness of my world was all cleared away
The flowers are blooming, it's a beautiful day
There's a girl with a heart as big as the sky
She's sunshine and I know why
All for the love of sunshine
All for the love of sunshine
The Lord smiled down on this life of mine
And sent me the love of sunshine

The words of this song, sung by Hank Williams, Jr., remind me of Sarah, my sunshine.

Sarah is a blessing.

Some may look at her and see only a burden. But she's not. The world values independence, self-sufficiency, and high I.Q.s. Sarah will never be independent. She will never know self-sufficiency. Her I.Q. is very low.

Yet, without ever speaking a sentence, this little girl has taught me volumes about some other qualities. Sarah is dependent on others for her every need. Sarah trusts without question or fear. In our society, Sarah is considered weak. In God's society, though, I think Sarah sets a beautiful example of qualities which God values. I think God is overjoyed when we trust him. I think He longs for us to depend on Him.

Sarah is a blessing for so many reasons.

But, the reason that really matters is that Sarah, weak, dependent Sarah, has led me to Jesus. She inspires me. If Sarah can be used in God's Kingdom, just think what we walking, talking, "normal" Christians can accomplish!

Sometimes I wonder if we, the healthy and average to above average I.Q. Christians, are in some ways the ones who are handicapped in the Kingdom of God. We have to struggle against our tendency to be too busy for God. We have to battle our independent will, our too full calendar, our hunger for wealth and recognition. We have to work on trusting God. And I don't know about you, but I fail miserably on a daily basis to trust and love God with all my heart. It is I who am handicapped in God's Kingdom. It is I who daily needs His life support to keep me going. The minute I think I can breathe on my own without the respirator of Jesus' forgiveness, I am in trouble. I need to learn how to depend on God always.

I am just so thankful for the sunshine that God has blessed me with.

JULY 17

Sometimes we struggle against a nameless enemy that we do not understand. The enemy is slippery and we grow weary as we flail about, trying to land blows upon a nameless adversary, an elusive foe who constantly weaves and bobs in the shadows. So we fight, and we don't even know what the fight is for or against. All we know is that we are wore out. Exhausted. Defeated. Confused. Alone. We cannot even explain to ourselves, much less someone else, what we are fighting.

This is oppression.

Spiritual oppression.

And the adversary is the greatest liar of all. Satan. The father of all lies. A murderer who has come to steal, kill, and destroy. He wants to crush our joy in the bitter waters of confusion.

And he is smart.

He knows that if he gives me an obvious enemy to fight, I am more likely to rally the troops into a focused knock-out punch.

So with great and quiet civility and subtlety, he gives me attractive adversaries. They draw me in. They look good and seem safe. Yet, they are masqueraders of angels of light and I am easy prey to these powerful predators.

Suddenly, or slowly, I find myself in a spiritual conflict with an enemy I cannot identify, and know not how to engage, much less defeat.

This is spiritual oppression, and it is insidious and ubiquitous and uniquely designed by a roaring adversary who doesn't always roar as loudly as I wish he would, but always seeks to devour in me what is good and righteous and pure and noble. He wants to take the best of what I have to offer to God, and masticate it, rendering me useless. Confused. Tired. Busy.

Of such has been my recent past.

But the enemy, who can be very smart, is also very proud. As a proud devouring lion so self-impressed and self-absorbed, he forgets.

He forgets that God can take what he, the devouring lion, has intended for harm and turn it to good.

He forgets that God gives beauty for ashes, and the oil of joy for mourning.

He forgets that Jesus Christ has come to set the prisoner free.

He forgets that God has promised that ALL things work together for good to them who love God and who are the called according to God's purposes.

And he, the devouring lion, forgets that it is in the very moments of brokenness in which he renders me useless, that God can actually speak the clearest to me. In the quiet, awful moments of brokenness, God's still, small voice is at its loudest.

And he who has ears to hear will hear. And he who has eyes to see will see. And he who has a heart that seeks God will know that God is in his corner (or rather he in God's) and thus the battle has been already won and the enemy defeated.

Even if I must live my life with a gaping wound, I know that a lake of fire awaits the devouring lion.

But above all I know there is another gaping wound, a wound from which precious blood has flowed, that will close the gap of my own brokenness and will give me life eternal and whole and useful. Even here, starting now, in this body of flesh in which I live.

His blood for mine.

The blood of Christ shed for me.

He, great Creator God bleeding upon the cross in my place.

The penalty of my sin upon the perfect Lamb of God.

I need to remember....

I fight from victory!

JULY 18

Christian service. Yes, there are many needs. Yes, God expects us to serve. Yet, we must approach this reality less determined to meet all needs and more determined to discover His will.

He has designed us in His image for the purpose of glorifying Him. One of the ways in which we glorify Him is to become humble servants. He has gifted each of His children with talents, abilities, and tendencies which are to be yielded to Him for glory and service.

Beware. For we have become a Christian culture steeped in programs and conferences and long lists of good things to do. In my experience, I have found that an overflowing schedule – even one that overflows with Christian ministry tasks – causes me to become less concerned with God's glory and more concerned with keeping up. And then I am prone to drift and become worldly in my approach even in the midst of Christian activity.

It is God's will I must discover. It is His priorities that must fill my plate...not the will and priorities of even the godly people around me. I can be overwhelmed with the idea that I must keep up with the expectations of people. This is the fear of man. This becomes an idol.

Am I not obligated to make careful and prayerful decisions about commitments so that my schedule does not grow into a golden calf?

I think Christians make the well-intended error of being led by the needs – real or perceived – of others rather than being led by the Spirit of God that dwells within.

Satan can use good and honorable activities to make us so busy that we stop listening for God's still, small voice. I need to be led by the Holy Spirit. God's Word instructs me that the Holy Spirit is a guide and a teacher, One to whom I have access at all times and in all places. Do I believe this? Or do I make hasty commitments based on needs and pressure? If there is an unmet need, doesn't God expect me to meet it if I can? Maybe yes, maybe no…but it is He who must lead me to know the answer…a need of which I become aware is not always a need of which I am to strive to meet.

I am to be obedient and faithful to God's purpose for my life, my time, my schedule. I am to surrender to Him. Sometimes what He expects of me is different from what others expect of me – even Christian others.

Beware of underlying assumptions that can usurp the role of the Holy Spirit in our thinking. Be aware of what drives your commitments. We tend to assume – especially we females – that we are to try to meet all needs that cross our paths. Sometimes we rescue people when we're not supposed to. Does this sound harsh and unreasonable? Sometimes God is in the process of bringing a person low for the glorious purpose of revealing to that very person pride and sin and spiritual need. And we, with our assumptions, step in and interfere with the very work God may be doing.

We simply need to be thoughtful about what drives our decisions. We need to be led, as individuals and institutions, by God's Spirit. Not by programs, conferences, and traditions. We need to actually slow down, listen, and seek God's wisdom and counsel despite the fact that everywhere we look there are needs. We need to cultivate quietness in a loud world. And, we need to be honest. If God is not telling us to say "yes" to the commitment, the program, the need…then say "no" despite the pressure from without and the false guilt from within.

But then…whatever and wherever God is leading…go and that do and that become. Work at it with all diligence and duty, striving for excellence in service to God and others in the area in which He, and He alone, has called you. Our service must be unto Him, for His glory, and we must pour ourselves fully into it.

No excuses.

<u>*JULY 19*</u>

I thank You, Lord, my God, every time I think of my family, my students, the church. May I always be thankful and not a grumbler. Help me to be grateful even for the difficult people, knowing that You use them for Your purposes, for teaching us how to love when it's not easy to love, how to love like You do.

Lord, I pray for my family. I pray for my students. I pray for the church. Help us to have knowledge of You and depth and insight, the kind that changes darkness into light. Help us to discern Your holiness and pureness, to the glory and praise of God!

Father, may Sarah's life, struggles, and death be a ministry in this family that serves to advance the gospel. Equip Mark and I for such a task. For those who are already saved in our family, Lord, encourage them to speak Your Word courageously and wisely. Be preached in this family, Lord! May Christ be proclaimed! Teach us how to live for You, to love You, to share You. The struggles we face, our loss of Sarah, these will be turned into good in ways only You can accomplish.

May Christ be exalted, whether by life or death.

Thank You that I believe.

Thank You that I have been granted the opportunity to suffer.

May I suffer for You.

In Jesus' Sovereign Name…

<u>*JULY 20*</u>

From <u>**Bonhoeffer: Pastor, Martyr, Prophet, Spy**</u> *by Eric Metaxas* [28]

…Bonhoeffer was thinking about God's highest call, about the call of discipleship and its cost. He was thinking about Jeremiah and about God's call to partake in suffering, even unto death. Bonhoeffer was working it out in his head at the same time that he was thinking about what the next move should be….He was thinking about the deep call of Christ, which was not about winning, but about submission to God, wherever that might lead.

In the letter to Sutz, he said, "Simply suffering – that is what will be needed then – not parries, blows, or thrusts such as may still be possible or admissible in the preliminary fight; the real struggle that perhaps lies ahead must simply be to suffer faithfully...[F]or sometime [the church struggle] hasn't even been about what it appears to be about; the lines have been drawn somewhere else entirely."

It's hard to escape the conclusion that Bonhoeffer was somehow thinking prophetically, that somehow he could see what was ahead of him, that at some point he would be able to do nothing more than "suffer faithfully" in his cell, praising God as he did so, thanking him for the high privilege of being counted worthy to do so....

During this tense time of waiting, Bonhoeffer preached his now rather famous sermon on the prophet Jeremiah. It was Sunday, January 21. Preaching on a Jewish Old Testament prophet was quite out of the ordinary and provocative, but that was the least of the sermon's difficulties. The opening words were typically intriguing: "Jeremiah was not eager to become a prophet of God. When the call came to him all of a sudden, he shrank back, he resisted, he tried to get away."

The sermon reflected Bonhoeffer's own difficult situation. It is extremely doubtful whether anyone in his congregations could understand what he was talking about, much less accept that it was God's word to them that Sunday. If they had ever been puzzled by their brilliant young preacher's (messages), they must have been puzzled now.

The picture that Bonhoeffer painted of Jeremiah was one of unrelieved gloom and drama. God was after him, and he could not escape. Bonhoeffer referred to the "arrow of the Almighty" striking down its "hunted game." But who was the "hunted game"? It was Jeremiah! But why was God shooting at the hero of the story? Before they found out, Bonhoeffer switched from arrow imagery to noose imagery. "The noose is drawn tighter and more painfully," he continued, "reminding Jeremiah that he is a prisoner. He is a prisoner and he has to follow. His path is prescribed. It is the path of the man whom God will not let go, who will never be rid of God." The sermon began to get seriously depressing. What was the young preacher getting at? ....[The congregation] continued listening, hoping for an upturn in Jeremiah's fortunes.

But alas, Pastor Bonhoeffer delivered an unrelenting homiletic bummer. He marched farther downhill: "This path will lead right down into the deepest situation of human powerlessness. The follower becomes a laughingstock, scorned and taken for a fool, but a fool who is extremely dangerous to people's peace and comfort, so that he or she must be beaten, locked up, tortured, if not put to death right away. That is exactly what became of this man Jeremiah, because he could not get away from God....And Jeremiah was just as much flesh and blood as we are, a human being like ourselves. He felt the pain of being continually humiliated and mocked, of the violence and brutality others used against him. After one episode of agonizing torture that had lasted a whole night, he burst out in prayer: 'O Lord, you have enticed me and I was enticed; you have overpowered me, and you have prevailed.'"

Bonhoeffer's congregation was lost. God maneuvered his beloved servant and prophet into imprisonment and agony? Somewhere along the line they must have missed a crucial sentence! But they hadn't.

And what none of them could know was that Pastor Bonhoeffer was talking, in some large part, about himself and about his future, the future that God was showing him. He was beginning to understand that he was God's prisoner, that like the prophets of old, he was called to suffer and to be oppressed – and in that defeat and the acceptance of that defeat, there was victory.
From <u>**Bonhoeffer: Pastor, Martyr, Prophet, Spy**</u> by Eric Metaxas [28]

JULY 21

Lord,

Thank You that I am united with Christ. Help each one in my family and in my classroom be also united with Christ. May each one experience salvation, comfort from Your love, fellowship with the Spirit, tenderness, compassion, and joy complete. May Your purpose, dearest Father, be our goal. Help us to set our hearts and minds on You. Help us to each esteem others better than ourselves.

Lord, thank You for Jesus' attitude…Love, humility, a servant's heart, willing to make Himself nothing, willing to become flesh, obedient even to the point of death on a cross. Lord, may we strive to have such an attitude as the Savior had, even though the world laughs and scoffs at such thoughts.

Jesus, You now are exalted to the highest place with the Father. Be exalted in my life and the lives of each in my family and in my classroom. Jesus, You have the name that is above all names. At Your name, every knee shall bow and every tongue confess that You are Lord to the glory of God the Father! May You find us ready and willing to bow and confess. Help us, Lord, to work out the salvation You freely offer. May we desperately seize and tightly embrace Your great salvation, working it out and growing in it with fear and trembling before You, Holy God.

Help us to become and persevere as children of God in a crooked and depraved generation. Save the lost in my family and in my classroom, making them Your children. May we shine like stars as we reflect Your brilliance and hold out the Word of Life. Be magnified above all circumstances, trials and fears.

In Jesus' Strong and Mighty Name…

JULY 22

There we were...sitting in the grandstand of the Cattaraugus County Fair in Little Valley, NY. My husband and I were looking forward to an evening of loud, obnoxious truck pulling....not the loud and obnoxious people sitting directly behind us. But there they were, directly behind us, their 10 year old son kicking the back of the seats, the father with his feet pushed up against the back of my chair and through the slats of my seat's back, the daughter with her feet on the back of the chair next to me (i.e. feet in my face), their refusal to stand and their on-going talk during the National Anthem. At one point, my husband turned around and asked them to stop kicking the seats. I won't lie, I myself sunk into the pit of obnoxious and inconsiderate when I, after being kicked in the behind 20 times or so by the father, decided to get up, and as I stood I grabbed the bottom of my seat (it was an "auditorium" chair where the seat folds up against the back) and flipped it backward in one swift motion. In other words, I pinched his feet in the chair when I stood up. True, after this he did not put his feet up against my body any longer. Truer still, I felt pretty good about giving him a taste of his own medicine.

I don't really know how to handle people like this. I am pretty certain that God would have preferred I didn't intentionally pinch a stranger's feet in my chair, and I am pretty certain that I was taking the risk of escalating the problem even further.

Always pray. I didn't. I didn't seek God's counsel on dealing with my situation. I was irritated and I reacted without praying. Perhaps God had a different plan of action than I had. I will never know because I didn't give Him the chance to participate.

It seems to me that people often respond to rudeness in an extreme way...either the extreme of letting the rude person get his way or the extreme of being rude in return. I wonder, though, is there a "peculiar" response that we Christians should be cultivating?

Is it possible to stand our ground, but to do it politely?

Is it possible to be strong and gentle at the same time?

Is it possible to stop taking everything personally and start responding Biblically?

This takes effort. And insight. And practice. And prayer.

Reflect on your own behavior. When somebody is rude to you, does it ever remind you of yourself and how you have treated another? When someone tailgates you, do you just get irritated, or do you remember it the next time you are tailgating somebody?

JULY 23

Lord,

Help me. Help my husband. Help our family. Help us to be holy and faithful. May we understand Your grace in all its truth. Lord, fill us with knowledge of Your will through all spiritual wisdom, of which You are the source. May we be saved. Then, may we reflect Your glory by living lives worthy of You, yielded to You, seeking to please You in every way, with every thought, bearing fruit in every good work, and growing in knowledge of You, being strengthened with all power according to Your glorious might and giving thanks to You always.

Lord, it is You, alone, who qualifies us to share in Your inheritance, to be part of Your Kingdom of Light. Father, You alone can rescue us from the dominion of darkness and bring us into the Kingdom of the Son You love. Through Him, there is redemption and the forgiveness of sins. For all in our family who are still stumbling in the darkness, help them to know it, may it press in heavily upon them and lead them to a place of distress and despair where they will seek truth and knowledge and find Your free, sweet, amazing redemption.

May every unsaved person in our family know that they are in a dangerous place with a devastating condition. The carnal man and mind is at enmity with You, Lord. May they make no mistake in grasping this. If they are trying to establish their own righteousness, teach them, Father, how impossible this is. Draw them to You and empower them by Your intervention and the working of the Holy Spirit to submit to You. It's not about church attendance or membership or baptism or good works. It's about relationship with the only One who can supply the righteousness we lack.

We stand before You clothed in the filthy rags of our own vain attempts to be good enough. Our clothes will never be clean from trying to wash them with our own dirty hands. We can only stand clean before You when clad in the white robe of Christ's righteousness. We must discard our filthy rags and put on Christ.

Help!

In Jesus' Beautiful Name...

JULY 24

If I complain about Christians who complain does that make me a Christian who is complaining, and am I, like they, become an Israelite in the wilderness, wandering in unbelief?

Probably.

Mark and I went to McDonalds today after church. The drive-through and the restaurant were both packed. The staff was unprepared for the rush. The service was excessively slow and highly inefficient. The crowd, waiting for their value fries and Big Macs, was grumbling. Moods were not good.

I noticed a man wearing a Voice of the Martyrs tee-shirt. He was, like the rest of the well-fed crowd, discontent as he waited for his greasy food. The contrast was stark…Voice of the Martyrs tee-shirt and a sea of over-fed grumbling humanity. I wondered how any of the actual martyrs of the Christian faith would look upon this situation.

Why do we Christians in our comfortable country live such small lives? Can it get any smaller than standing in line in an air-conditioned McDonalds on a hot day waiting a couple extra minutes for the food you really don't even need? People die in the world every day, and many go to hell because they do not know the Savior. People suffer persecution and some even die because of true devotion to Jesus Christ.

Do we have the right to expect efficient service and tasty food at a fast food restaurant? I guess we probably do. But can't we also lay this right down and chose instead to be humble and grateful? Perhaps I am not being very humble by suggesting this in the first place? Perhaps my criticism is itself a proud complaint against my fellow Christians. Just seems we should be living bigger lives, ever aware of God's presence, alert to the fiery darts of Satan, and alive to the truth that there is a bigger picture than what we want or even what we need.

God forgive us, forgive me for small and selfish thoughts that shrink You into practical meaninglessness. Forgive me when I act like an atheist.

JULY 25

Dear Father, I am so grateful for You. I am so glad that You are all-knowing. You see and know all things. You see us when we sin. You see us when we celebrate. You see us when we hurt. Before You, Lord, may we tremble, ever aware that Your all-knowing eye is upon us.

Lord, may You matter to us more than our sin, our celebrations, and our hurts. May we, with Your holy help, put You first always and no matter what.

As I think of my beloved Uncle Darrill today, I wonder how he must feel as he lies in his hospital room. I know how life in a hospital room is, how the whole world shrinks and nothing outside that small room seems to matter anymore. Everything other than that room seems distant. Hospital rooms can be very isolating, no matter how many doctors, nurses, and visitors come through the door.

Lord, keep my Uncle Darrill from being lonely and isolated. Hold him near You. Give him vision to see You in his suffering. Help him to see beyond the pain and to believe You really do have a plan for him even now in all of this. As he mourns the loss of his legs, help him to gain an eternal perspective that will give him strength for the day and the fight to come, a fight that will be both physical and mental. When he doesn't understand why this is happening, help him to trust You. Help him to know how deeply loved he is.

In his brokenness, reveal Your wholeness.

In his grief, teach him that his identity can be in You.

In his suffering, remind him that You suffered for him.

In his sorrow, pour the joy of victory. For You, Jesus, are the Risen Savior who is set at the right hand of the throne of God and intercedes for us in prayer. You are the Conqueror. The grave and hell have been defeated for all who belong to You.

My Uncle Darrill can be more than a conqueror in You, no matter what happens to his body! Make this possibility his reality, and this day speak to him in a way that he can hear.

Thank You, Lord, that You are our refuge and strength and an ever-present help in the storm.

JULY 26

Be exalted, O Lord, in all things, including Sarah's death. Use her life, her joys, her sorrows, her memory, and her death for Your glory and purposes. Be lifted up and magnified in the thoughts and hearts of every person in our family. Lay eternity upon each heart. May the lost tremble in awareness of their need and in response to Your overwhelming holiness. May they come to the waters of salvation and freely drink. May the saved grow and see You and proclaim You.

Thank You, God and Father of my Lord Jesus, that You have blessed me in the heavenly realms with every spiritual blessing in Christ. Thank You for choosing me before the creation of the world. Thank You for adopting me. This was Your pleasure and will. Praise You for such glorious grace, freely given to me in Christ, the One You love. In Christ I am redeemed. Through His blood, redemption is mine. Thank You, Father, for the riches of Your grace. Thank You for making known to me the mystery of Your will according to Your good pleasure purposed in Christ.

I thank You. All praise and glory are due You, Lord. I pray for our families. May they hear the word of truth, the gospel of salvation. Adopt them. Choose them. Seek them. Cover them in Your blood and Your grace. May they each respond to the Word of truth. Help us to seize the truth and embrace the One and only Savior. Seal us, Lord, with the promised Holy Spirit. Thank You that I am sealed. Thank You that I am Your possession. May each person in my family be Your possession, a sealed possession eternally safe.

Yours. Saved. Safe. In the Powerful Name of Jesus…

JULY 27

What I wish I had known when I was 17 years old…

I am created in God's image.

I am a jewel to the Lord, and in Him I possess exceptional potential.

He values and treasures me.

My purity matters to Him.

I am created for a purpose, a purpose that far surpasses any that I could design for myself. It is, thus, of the utmost importance that I guard my heart, my mind, my body…for when a woman gives away her body, her heart goes with it.

God thinks that I am beautiful. Even acne cannot diminish the beauty He sees when he looks upon me, His child. I may look in the mirror and see imperfections. I may look in the mirror and the image that looks back is merely average in the eyes of the world, and sometimes even less than that. But God thinks of me as beautiful. And thus, I am so. He knit me together to look exactly as I look.

I am bought with a price. I am not my own. I belong to the Creator Redeemer God who calls me "His" and I call Him "Mine."

Lust is not funny.

Lust is not harmless.

Crude jokes and course talk do not advance God's light in a dark world.

Short skirts and low-cut blouses revealing flesh do not advance God's kingdom on earth.

Waiting will be worth it.

Wait.

But if you haven't waited…then start today.

Failing to remain pure is a tragedy. But, it is one that our God, the great Redeemer, can redeem.

Loss of purity does not preclude you from this day, this moment, being washed clean and pure before a Holy God.

He waits for you.

Find your beauty, your identity, your essence in Him.

JULY 28

Yesterday at ladies' Bible study, the issue of suffering came up. Particularly, why is healing not given to a sweet sister in Christ, a sister who has been prayed over fervently, a sister who has faithfully expressed love for the Lord in the midst of the trial?

We cry.

We feel confused.

We don't understand this.

We expect healing because we know that God can heal.

And if we are honest, we think He should heal our sister.

After all, we have labored in prayer. We have lifted our sister up in faith. And truth be told, we believe her usefulness and fruitfulness in advancing the Kingdom of God would only be enhanced and extended should healing be experienced.

So I pose a question: Would we be more fruitful if our broken situations and the trials of our lives were overcome through deliverance rather than endurance? It is hard for us to think otherwise. It is not natural for us to see past the pain and into the purpose. I argue that we must think bigger about these things. I argue that we must not limit God by assuming that He is only doing a great work if there is healing or physical protection.

Many children get sick with pneumonia. Most, at least in our country, survive the disease. But my daughter didn't. Was she any less blessed than the children who live? Were we, her parents, any less blessed because she died?

No.

God's blessing has been abundant and sufficient even though my beloved daughter was laid in the ground. God has not blessed me less than the parent whose child came home from the hospital. He has just blessed me differently.

"God is good." I always told Sarah this, day after day. He is good when He heals. He is good when He doesn't. Do I always understand His ways? I do not. But must I understand His ways to trust His character? No, I need not. Instead, I lean hard into the God who has revealed Himself to me to be the all-powerful, sovereign, eternal, holy, loving, merciful, gracious shepherd of my soul. Of my daughter's soul. Of our lives.

The unifying thread that runs through all cultures at all times and in all places is suffering. It is a language we all speak. The planet groans. Cultures groan. Families groan. Pain. Suffering. Death. These are real and these are everywhere. Rail not against God, for humanity is the author of this groaning. It was our pride and disobedience – despite God's warning and His presence – that caused the fall and led to the groaning. No, rail not against God, for He could have abandoned this rebellious and broken place. But He did not.

I give up rather easily on things that don't work like they are supposed to.

But not God. He does not give up. Rather, He partook of the brokenness and walked among us, sharing in humanity and experiencing its suffering at a level we can know nothing about. He, too, has groaned.

This is my God! Creator. Redeemer. Lover of my soul. Living hope. Eternal truth.

For this groaning planet and the people upon it, He is the only hope. And He allows us the privilege of being a part of His redemptive plan. He needs His Holy Spirit filled people to be in all places. He needs us to be in hospitals. In prisons. In labor camps. In dysfunctional homes and families. In workplaces hostile to truth. We are called to be light and salt in all of the world, including the dark and difficult places.

And not only does He call us. He equips us. Whatever HIS plan is for us, He will make a way. He will provide what we need. He will strengthen us to endure. But remember, His ways and His provision and His strength in our lives sometimes looks different than we expect or what we want...nonetheless, His ways are the best ways and His plans are the best plans.

Sometimes His prosperity come to us in poverty.

Sometimes His nourishment comes to us in hunger.

Sometimes His peace comes to us in persecution.

Sometimes His healing comes to us in sickness.

There is something rare and exceptional to this groaning world when it beholds a suffering child of God yet praising His name, proclaiming His truth, and with a grateful heart giving glory to the One always worthy.

We are called to be a peculiar people. What could be more peculiar than this?

There is power in praising God in the midst of the trial. This is an offering of eternal value. This is beautiful beyond words to the One Who is beauty beyond words.

This is a response that delivers a blow to the enemy and shines light in dark places.

So I pose the difficult question: can God use us as much in our suffering and pain as He can in our comfort and health?

JULY 29

Lord, You are just. Your Word tells us that You will again be revealed from heaven, that You will come again, LORD Jesus, not as a baby, but as a mighty warrior in blazing fire with powerful angels. We are told that You will punish those who do not know God and do not obey the gospel of the Lord Jesus. With everlasting destruction, the lost will be forever shut out from Your presence and from the majesty of Your glory.

Truly, Lord, You are pure, and You have every right, as Creator, Sustainer, the Source of all, to judge and condemn those who reject Your Son.

I pray for my family and for my students. God, count them worthy of Your calling, fulfill every good purpose in their lives, and may the Name of the Lord Jesus be glorified in them, according to Your mercy and grace. Save all in my family and in my classroom, Lord, through the sanctifying work of the Holy Spirit, through belief in the truth, and a seizing of Jesus Christ as Lord, Savior, Master, and soon and coming King!

I thank You, Lord, for my family and my students. I stand in the gap and continually remember them before You and pray for the salvation of each. Choose them, Lord! May the gospel reach their ears, their minds, their hearts, their consciences, their lives...not simply with words but with power, with the Holy Spirit, and with deep conviction. Lord, show them what sin is, what it cost You, and how deeply You hate sin. Reveal idols, things that are more important to them than You are and ways that they may think about You that do not really reflect the truth of who You have revealed Yourself to be in Your Word. Keep them, Father, from making a god to suit their own tastes. Give them a taste for truth. Make all else bitter.

Turn us, Lord, from serving idols to serve the living and true God and to wait for His Son from heaven, whom You raised from the dead, who rescues us from the coming wrath, who will again be revealed and descend as conquering King!

In the Name of Jesus, Alpha and Omega, the True and Living God...

JULY 30

From **_Bonhoeffer: Pastor, Martyr, Prophet, Spy_** *by Eric Metaxas* [29]

For Bonhoeffer, there is no reality apart from God and no goodness apart from Him. All pretense to that effect is....a scheme to subvert God altogether and make a fallen humanistic path to heaven alone. It is (a) tower of Babel, and it is the fig leaf that tries to fool God, but fails.

"All things appear as in a distorted mirror," Bonhoeffer wrote, "if they are not seen and recognized in God." So God is not merely a religious concept or religious reality. God is the one who invented reality, and reality can only be seen truly as it exists in God. Nothing that exists is outside His realm. So there are no ethics apart from doing God's will, and God – indeed, Jesus Christ – is the nonnegotiable given in the equation of human ethics:

(Bonhoeffer wrote): "In Jesus Christ the reality of God has entered into the reality of this world. The place where the questions about the reality of God and about the reality of the world are answered at the same time is characterized solely by the name: Jesus Christ. God and the world are enclosed in this name...we cannot speak rightly of either God or the world without speaking of Jesus Christ. All concepts of reality that ignore Jesus Christ are abstractions.

"As long as Christ and the world are conceived as two realms bumping against and repelling each other, we are left with only the following options. Giving up on reality as a whole, either we place ourselves in one of the two realms, wanting Christ without the world or the world without Christ – and in both cases we deceive ourselves...There are not two realities, but only one reality, and that is God's reality revealed in Christ in the reality of the world. Partaking in Christ, we stand at the same time in the reality of God and in the reality of the world. The reality of Christ embraces the reality of the world in itself. The world has no reality of its own independent of God's revelation in Christ...(T)he theme of two realms, which has dominated the history of the church again and again, is foreign to the New Testament"

Bonhoeffer believed that, historically speaking, it was time for everyone to see these things. The evilness of the Nazis could not be defeated via old-fashioned "ethics," "rules," and "principles." God alone could combat it....

The solution is to do the will of God, to do it radically and courageously and joyfully. To try to explain "right" and "wrong" – to talk about ethics – outside of God and obedience to His will is impossible. "Principles are only tools in the hands of God; they will soon be thrown away when they are no longer useful. We must look only at God, and in Him we are reconciled to our situation in the world. If we look only to principles and rules, we are in a fallen realm where our reality is divided from God...

(A)part from Jesus Christ, we cannot know what is right or do right. We must look to Him in every situation. Only in Him can the fathomless evil of the world be dealt a death blow.

From <u>Bonhoeffer: Pastor, Martyr, Prophet, Spy</u> by Eric Metaxas [29]

J*ULY 31*

We human beings, so proud in our hearts and small in our thinking, need God to resist us!

Oh, we Christian types tend to blame Satan when we come up against opposition. Yet, I propose that more often than we suspect, the opposition may just be the grace of God. Don't get me wrong. I know Satan is real. I know He is hurling fiery darts and whispering subtle lies. I know he seeks to rot the fruit we strive to bear for the Kingdom of God. I understand that spiritual warfare is real.

But, let's watch out for faulty assumptions that always give credit (and thus power) to Satan. Let's not give the enemy more power by carelessly attributing every closed door or every difficult person or every challenging situation to him. For our God can use these to direct, to protect, and to prevent us from becoming too comfortable in our own proud plans and priorities.

God can break up the fallow ground of apathy within by using the blessed sharp edges of opposition. We need resistance in our lives. Without it, we become spiritually atrophied and dull. Without resistance, our inertia will propel us into ever accelerating self-focus, self-interest, self-importance, and deadly self-righteousness. Without resistance, self grows dangerously monstrous.

Whether the resistance comes from Satan or God, the Christian response is to be the same: **More of God and less of self.**

July's Apologetic Moment...Contend for the faith

Illusion of Design?

*"Natural selection is the blind watchmaker, blind because it does not see ahead, does not plan consequences, has no purpose in view. Yet the living results of natural selection overwhelmingly impress us with the **appearance of design** as if by a master watchmaker, impress us with the **illusion of design and planning**. The purpose of this book is to resolve the paradox to the satisfaction of the reader, and the purpose of this chapter is further to impress the reader with the **power of the illusion of design**."*

*"Biology is the study of complex things that **appear to have been designed for a purpose**. Physics books may be complicated, but ...The objects and phenomena that a physics book describes are simpler than a single cell in the body of its author. And the author consists of trillions of those cells, many of them different from each other, organized with intricate architecture and precision-engineering into a working machine capable of writing a book."*

"All appearances to the contrary, the only watchmaker in nature is the blind forces of physics, albeit deployed in a very special way. *A true watchmaker has foresight: he designs his cogs and springs and plans their interconnections, with a future purpose in his mind's eye. Natural selection, the blind, unconscious, automatic process which Darwin discovered, and which we now know is the explanation for the existence and apparently purposeful form of all life, has no purpose in mind. It has no vision, no foresight, no sight at all. If it can be said to play the role of watchmaker in nature, it is the blind watchmaker."* **{From Richard Dawkin's book <u>The Blind Watchmaker</u> [56]}**

Richard Dawkins...atheist...a man disgusted by God's people wrote the words above in his book, <u>The Blind Watchmaker</u>[56]. Let's consider the historical context and legitimacy of his claims...

In the later 1700s, theologian and naturalist William Paley authored <u>Natural Theology or Evidences of the Existence and Attributes of the Deity</u>. It was in this book that Paley crafted the classic apologetic "watchmaker argument" In a nutshell, the "watchmaker argument" posits that if one were walking through the woods and came upon a watch, one would assume that the watch had been created by an intelligent source, for it has specificity, complexity, and function. Since objects in nature – from plants to bugs to people – are even more complex than a watch, is not their very existence evidence of design? Is not such complexity best explained, even if not formally proven, by the existence of an intelligent Creator?

And thus the title of Dawkin's book: <u>The Blind Watchmaker</u>...a reaction to Paley's argument. Underpinning all of Dawkin's work and held as a starting assumption is the idea that faith in God is irrational and anti-science.

Is this so?

Is it not rational to believe that an intelligent Designer exists if design is observed? And even Richard Dawkins admits that design is observed. The difference between Paley and Dawkins is in interpretation. Paley interprets design to suggest a Designer. Dawkins interprets that design as illusion; he admits there is design, but argues that it is mere appearance of design while not actually being designed.

Which argument is most rational and reasonable? Which argument requires more faith?

In 1996, Michael Behe, an accomplished biochemist, published <u>Darwin's Black Box</u> in which he presented his pro-designer argument of "irreducible complexity." While dogmatic evolutionists resort to ad hominin methods of mocking Behe and referring to his work as "pseudoscience," others with a more thoughtful approach acknowledge that Behe has a legitimate scientific claim. You see, what has happened since Darwin's days is that we have learned more and more about the complexity of life, including individual cells. When Darwin was penning <u>On the Origin of the Species</u> (in which, by the way, he never actually explained the *origin*) it was believed that cells were simple little boxes containing protoplasm (i.e. "goo"). There was no understanding of the fact that cells, even the most basic, contain a microscopic universe of organelles and systems and machinery.

Darwin didn't know about the bi-lipid cell membrane with channel proteins. He was not familiar with the cytoskeleton and microtubules. He did not know that proteins were coded for by DNA and constructed in a seriously sequential way by ribosomes and later packaged and refined by endoplasmic reticulum and Golgi apparatus. He did not realize the complex nature of energy production in a cell by mitochondria. The necessity of protein-based enzymes was also unknown at the time. And this, my friends, is a mere scratching of the surface of the complexity of a cell. If any of these parts are missing, the cell will not survive. There will not be any reproduction and the passing along of genetic information...which is required if Darwinian evolution is to be true. The more we have actually learned about cells and their operation, the more unlikely the Darwinian evolution model fits what is observed.

In <u>Darwin's Black Box</u>, Behe highlights what was always believed to be a simple structure: the flagellum. Under a microscope, the flagellum appears as a whiplike "tail" attached to some cells. Is it a simple structure? As Behe studied the description of the flagellum in even secular texts, he was astonished to see that it was a machine – designed much like an outboard motor on a boat. The flagellum is capable of self-assembly and repair. It possesses a water-cooled rotary engine and proton motive force driving system. It has forward and reverse gears. It can operate up to 100,000 rpm and is capable of reversing direction within ¼ of a turn. Should any part of this molecular motor be removed, it would no longer function. If it no longer functions, it no longer offers a survival advantage and thus should not even exist. The flagellum requires a minimum of

40 protein components all organized in a specific manner to function. Darwinian evolution cannot explain this level of complexity at the molecular level.

Behe also discusses the eye. He references the Darwinian argument that the eye evolved from slight, successive modifications beginning with a "simple" light-sensitive spot. Behe zeroes in on that "simple" light-sensitive spot that Darwinian evolutionists start with, and he shows how it could not be "simple" after all:

"When light first strikes the retina a photon interacts with a molecule called 11-cis-retinal, which rearranges within picoseconds to trans-retinal. (A picosecond [10^{-12} sec] is about the time it takes light to travel the breadth of a single human hair.) The change in the shape of the retinal molecule forces a change in the shape of the protein, rhodopsin, to which the retinal is tightly bound. The protein's metamorphosis alters its behavior. Now called metarhodopsin II, the protein sticks to another protein, called transducin. Before bumping into metarhodopsin II, transducin had tightly bound a small molecule called GDP. But when transducin interacts with metarhodopsin II, the GDP falls off, and a molecule called GTP binds to transducin. (GTP is closely related to, but different from, GDP.) GTP-transducin-metarhodopsin II now binds to a protein called phosphodiesterase, located in the inner membrane of the cell. When attached to metarhodopsin II and its entourage, the phosphodiesterase acquires the chemical ability to 'cut' a molecule called cGMP (a chemical relative of both GDP and GTP). Initially there are a lot of cGMP molecules in the cell, but the phosphodiesterase lowers its concentration, just as a pulled plug lowers the water level in a bathtub." [57]

If you just read that paragraph and wondered what it all means because it seems so complicated…that is the point. Even a simple light-sensitive spot is complicated. Something this complicated cannot be reasonably explained by slight successive modifications over long periods of time.

And this is only the beginning. Hundreds, thousands, yea hundreds of thousands of pages could be written describing the complex nature of the most microscopic organisms and the molecules, organelles, machinery, and processes that make life possible. You need not take my word for it, for there are volumes and volumes already written, by secular and naturalistic scientists, detailing the complex nature of life and the functions that support life.

Appearance of design or simply design?

Which model most reasonably fits?

If it be so, our God whom we serve is able to deliver us
from the burning fiery furnace,
and He will deliver us out of thine hand, O king.
But if not, be it known unto thee, O king,
that we will not serve thy gods,
nor worship the golden image which thou hast set up.
Daniel 3:17-18

August

"When Christ calls a man, He bids him come and die."
— Dietrich Bonhoeffer, The Cost of Discipleship

AUGUST 1

Lord,

I pray for all those in positions of authority and influence, especially in the homes of this land.

May we be a people rejoicing in You!   Trusting in You.

For You, Lord, and You alone, save.

In You is the only true, eternal hope.

Government cannot save.

Entertainment, electronics, technology cannot save.

Success cannot save.

Medical advances may prolong life, but ultimately are powerless to save.

Tradition cannot save.

Neither can church attendance or baptism or good works.

But God.

God alone, His great grace and mercy, buys us back…the blood of Jesus Christ is the price He paid for a wandering proud and sinful people.

Salvation is, indeed, a great work of God, of God alone.

May we worship You in spirit and truth, rejoicing in Christ Jesus and having no confidence in our own flesh!

Father, may we, like the apostle Paul, count ALL things but loss for the excellency of the knowledge of Christ Jesus.

May I, may we, be willing to suffer the loss of all things and win Christ.

May we be found in Him, not having our own righteousness, but that which is through faith of Christ, the righteousness which is of God by faith.

May we know Him and the power of His resurrection and the fellowship of His sufferings.

May we press toward the mark for the prize of the high calling in Christ Jesus!

In Jesus' Wonderful Name…

AUGUST 2

God speaks to my undeserving heart, and I hear the words, "Let Me."

"Let Me help you."

"Let Me guide and teach you."

"Let Me give you the words to speak."

"Let Me deliver you from fear."

"Let Me transform you into a godly wife."

"Let Me grow you into a bold witness with a powerful testimony."

"Let Me establish your plans and priorities."

"Let Me direct your steps."

"Let Me guard your heart and mind."

"Let Me forgive you."

"Let Me crush your pride and self-sufficiency."

"Let Me interrupt your plans."

"Let Me use your failures."

"Let Me give you rest."

"Let Me…" God speaks this to my heart, and I know…

I know I am exhausted and overwhelmed and fearful all because I have not "let Him." Pride and self-promotion are alive and well in this human heart.

I need Him, and I know I need Him, and yet how foolishly and frequently I fail to "let Him." I hold tightly the reins of my life. I say I want to live "palms up" but when confronted with a challenge or a conflict or a joy or anything really, I curl my fists vicelike around "mine."

After all these years, it's still all about me, isn't it?

And, Lord, I'm tired of it. I'm tired of me.

Take the reins of this life I call mine, and make it a life that belongs entirely, Lord, to You.

AUGUST 3

So I'm thinking about Stevie's Facebook post that I listened to yesterday. She shared her testimony, a beautiful testimony of how God has worked and continues to work in her young life. It is hard and confusing to be a teenager and a 20-something…there is no way I would ever go back to those years of inner turmoil. Protect Stevie, Lord, and help her to truly know the depth of your love for her.

Self-image. Seems like this is something that just about every woman struggles with. Each one of us looks in the mirror and tends to see the flaws rather than the beauty. For each one of us, there exists the temptation to make destructive choices in our attempts to overcome the ugly we think we see in ourselves.

I've always been plain to look at. My hair is flat and straight as straight can be. My face is round and my cheeks chubby. And from age 12 until now, decades later, I've battled an acne-prone complexion, still relying on Clearasil in this 5th decade of my life! To this day, I avoid looking in a mirror if I pass by one in a public place.

This is not right.

As I think about this, I truly do understand that this is not right thinking. Oh, I cover up my insecurities quite well now as an adult with a lot of things to do. But, those same old insecurities linger and whisper lies.

I want victory.

And, Lord, Your Word teaches that I can have victory.

I need to repent of wrong thinking.

I need to choose to walk in the truth…

The truth is…

I am made in God's image.

I am a treasure to the great Creator and Redeemer God.

He knit me together.

He has plans for me.

I am not my own.

I was bought with a price.

Jesus, a man of sorrows and acquainted with grief…a man in whom was no beauty that He should be desired…a man beaten and bloodied and marred…This Man, God Himself emptied His veins.

The truth is, I am beautiful because I am His.

I am accepted in the Beloved..

He knows my name.

He knows my frame.

He loves me with a love high and deep and wide and long and everlasting.

This is truth.

This is beauty.

AUGUST 4

God, I pray for You do great and mighty things in me. I pray for great and mighty thoughts, thoughts that exalt You and that cause my mouth to speak words of truth, my lips to praise You, and my hands to serve You.

You are both the source and the reason for all things great and mighty.

You are God, and there is no other!

The world, and sometimes even the church defines "greatness" one way, and God defines it another.

How often we think of greatness as quantity: the size of the accomplishment, the value of the bank account, the number of people in the pews, and the number of likes and shares on Facebook.

But God considers quality, not quantity.

God wants depth!

Quantity should never be our goal. Quality should.

Quality first. And should God bless with quantity, praise His name! And should God bless not with quantity, praise His name! Numbers are always to be secondary. Pursue quality. Guard quality. Value quality.

God will determine the numbers.

And Jesus sat over against the treasury, and beheld how the people cast money into the treasury: and many that were rich cast in much. And there came a certain poor widow, and she threw in two mites, which make a farthing.   And He called unto Him His disciples, and saith unto them, Verily I say unto you, That this poor widow hath cast more in, than all they which have cast into the treasury: For all they did cast in of their abundance; but she of her want did cast in all that she had, even all her living {Mark 12:41 – 44}.

There was great quality in the widow and her two mites. Perhaps she thought not. Yet even today, two thousand years later, I think of this nameless widow and pray for God to help me be great like she was. She was unknown in the moment, but remembered through the ages because her act was an act of obedience and her life one that glorified God through her faith. She gave to God obediently out of her need, not out of her abundance. That is quality. That is greatness. The value of the mites was slight. But, the value of the faith of this nameless widow was great.

AUGUST 5

Dear Father, a short time ago we didn't know if Uncle Darrill would live to the end of the day. He did! And now he is healing and growing stronger. It will be a difficult journey. But God, You have given him more time. Help him to rejoice in this, not just on the good days, but on the bad ones, too.

Father, may this crisis cause our family to cleave one to another and to love one another in a way that is deeper. In all things may we set aside what is unimportant and grab a hold of what is. May You be the center of our relationships with one another.

I pray for Uncle Darrill's wife, my Aunt Kathy. Help her to be strong. Help her to get the rest she needs. Keep her healthy. Provide all that Uncle Darrill and Aunt Kathy need financially, practically, and spiritually. Put good, wise, qualified people along the path they are now on. Give them patience as they face and struggle to overcome any barriers in this new chapter of their lives.

May Your truth, presence, and peace be so powerful to them that any fears they may have will be dashed and replaced with sweet anticipation of what only You, God, can accomplish through even this.

I kneel before You, Lord, and I pray that out of Your glorious riches You would strengthen Uncle Darrill and Aunt Kathy. May Christ dwell in their hearts and minds through faith. Establish and build up with Your truth. Help them to truly grasp the width and length and height and depth of Your enduring love. Fill them to the measure of all fullness in Christ.

This is a new season in life for my Uncle and my Aunt. In this season, I pray that you would show them the depth of your ways and give them eyes to see what you are doing. May this difficult season become beautiful to them because of You.

Lord, You are able to do immeasurably more than all we ask or imagine.

To You, Lord, be the glory now and forever.

AUGUST 6

It has been almost a year since 8 year old Jeffrey drown. It was a tragic death that turned the lives of many people upside down. I sat down this morning to write a card to Jeffrey's parents to let them know I am thinking about them and praying still for them. All my words seemed inadequate and awkward. I wanted to be able to write something unique and meaningful and perfect. Something that would remove the pain. Something that would make everything seem normal again.

I mentioned Sarah briefly, but it felt uncomfortable doing so, and guilty too. After all, despite everything she has been through, Sarah is still with us. She is still here, and while we know we may someday loose her, we have time…time to "come to grips," so to speak, with such a possibility. Jeffrey's parents didn't have that opportunity. It just happened so suddenly and with such enormous finality.

I am learning that all that really matters is that God offers us a home in heaven if we accept His gift of salvation and believe ("seize and embrace") Him. God loves us. That doesn't mean it comes easily or naturally to accept pain and loss. It hurts just as much. The difference now is that I know it is temporary.

Can you imagine being with God? It must be incredible!

Since Sarah's stroke, I have had a year and a half to think about this and learn to believe it. How do I take what I have learned and share it with someone else? Jeffrey's parents didn't get the opportunity to adjust and prepare for his death. There were loose ends and no peaceful good byes.

I can't transfer what I have learned to feel. I can't even know for sure that I would, should it happen, handle Sarah's death in a dignified and faith-filled way. It is a lonely process that we all have to go through – each in our own unique way and time.

The most powerful gift I can give to these hurting parents is my time in prayer on their behalf.

I pray they find peace.

I pray they feel God's presence and his comfort.

I pray they learn to love and trust God.

I pray that they will eventually smile and laugh when talking and thinking about their son.

I pray their family remains strong.

I pray they find and give forgiveness.

I pray that something beautiful comes out of all this.

I pray they find answers to their unanswerable questions.

Where was God? Where was he when Jeffrey died? Where was he when Sarah had her stroke? God is with us now and He was with us and those children then...even in the struggle and suffering.

It doesn't always make sense. But, I believe.

AUGUST 7

Shout for joy to the LORD, all the earth. Worship the LORD with gladness; come before Him with joyful songs. Know that the LORD is God. It is He who made us, and we are His; we are His people, the sheep of His pasture. Enter His gates with thanksgiving and His courts with praise; give thanks to Him and praise His name. For the LORD is good and His love endures forever; His faithfulness continues through all generations (Psalm 100).

Been thinking about how prone we are to praise God when the burden is eased, and prone to forget to praise Him when it is not.

Is it possible that our praises to Him are sweeter yet when raised while we are in the fire of affliction and the tragedy of loss? Is He any less worthy of our praises when the storm is still raging?

The God who felt the bitter sting of rejection, the tearing of His flesh, and who shed His blood for me is worthy of my praise. Always.

He deserved praise from my lips and from my heart on the day Sarah drew her last breath as much as on the day she drew her first. I choose to praise Him for who He is and for what He does. I choose to praise Him because of His very nature and character...all-powerful, mighty Creator and Redeemer God, perfect in holiness and unending in love. I praise Him because He is, and was, and is to come. I praise Him because He is greater than any circumstance, greater than any fiery trial, greater than any tragedy or failure or disappointment.

Therefore, *I will rejoice always, pray continually, give thanks in all circumstances...I will bow down in worship and kneel before the LORD our Maker; for He is God and we are the people of His pasture, the flock under His care.*

AUGUST 8

Father,

Help me to pray big prayers to You, God of all creation! You are Elohim, El Shaddai, Jehovah Jireh, Jehovah Rophe! May all in my family experience Your great healing of the grievous sin wound. I pray for sound doctrine in my mind, heart, my inmost being, and the words I speak. I pray for sound doctrine in my husband and our family. May our beliefs conform to the glorious gospel of You, blessed God and Savior.

No matter where we have been, or what we have done, You are mighty to save and rescue. May we know our need of You, Lord. This is a trustworthy saying and deserves full acceptance, Christ Jesus came into the world to save sinners. I, so full of pride and self-will and determination to do it my way, was a sinner destined for Your righteous judgment and wrath. But You saved me.

Jesus Christ in His great love saved me!

Lord, save each lost and wandering soul in our families. Call them each by name. Seek them, Lord, so that they may seek You. You, Lord, are the King eternal, immortal, invisible, the only God. Honor and glory forever and ever to You.

In Jesus' Worthy Name…

AUGUST 9

Early Sunday morning, walking down the hill alone toward Betterton Beach in Maryland, the whole town sleeping.

Traces of pink scattering through the eastern sky above the waters of the Chesapeake Bay; yellow light peaking around the edges of the horizon slowly warming the air around me. The sound of waves meeting the sand of the shore and the smooth rocks of the pier, and I, listening with ears and breathing with lungs that God has given me...ears that hear and lungs that breathe without any conscious effort on my part, complex processes constantly occurring and sustaining.

As I walk, drawing closer to the beautiful scene stretching out before me, changing moment by moment, a song begins singing in my head and in my heart..."*How great is our God, sing with me, how great is our God...name above all names, He is worthy of all praise, and my heart shall sing how great is our God...*"

…The same song that played at Sarah's funeral.

Two very different scenes. Yet the same Great God…unchanging, all powerful, sovereign…the One who determines the number of days we will live, the One who spoke and the sun and the stars and man himself came to be.

Always, no matter what, Good and Great Name above all names!

AUGUST 10

From <u>The Hiding Place</u> by Corrie Ten Boom [30]

Suddenly I sat up, striking my head on the cross-slats above. Something had pinched my leg.

"Fleas!" I cried. "Betsie, the place is swarming with them!"

We scrambled across the intervening platforms, heads low to avoid another bump, dropped down to the aisle, and edged our way to a patch of light.

"Here! And here another one!" I wailed. "Betsie, how can we live in such a place!"

"Show us. Show us how." It was said so matter of factly it took me a second to realize Betsie was praying. More and more, the distinction between prayer and the rest of life seemed to be vanishing for her.

"Corrie!" she said excitedly. "He's given us the answer! Before we asked, as He always does! In the Bible this morning. Where was it? Read that part again!"

I glanced down the long dim aisle to make sure no guard was in sight, then drew the Bible from its (hidden) pouch. "It was in First Thessalonians," I said. We were on our third complete reading of the New Testament since leaving Scheveningen. In the feeble light, I turned the pages. "Here it is: 'Comfort the frightened, help the weak, be patient with everyone. See that none of you repays evil for evil, but always seek to do good to one another and to all….' It seemed written expressly for Ravensbruck.

"Go on," said Betsie. "That wasn't all."

"Oh yes: '…to one another and to all. Rejoice always, pray constantly, give thanks in all circumstances; for this is the will of God in Christ Jesus-'"

"That's it Corrie! That's His answer. 'Give thanks in all circumstances!' That's what we can do. We can start right now to thank god for Every single thing about this new barracks!"

I stared at her, then around me at the dark, foul-aired room.

"Such as?" I said.

"Such as being assigned here together."

I bit my lip. "Oh, yes, Lord Jesus!"

"Such as what you're holding in your hands."

I looked down at the Bible. "Yes! Thank You, dear Lord, that there was no inspection when we entered here! Thank You for all the women, here in this room, who will meet You in these pages."

"Yes," said Betsie. "Thank You for the very crowding here. Since we're packed so close, that many more will hear!" She looked at me expectantly. "Corrie!" she prodded.

"Oh, all right. Thank You for the jammed, crammed, stuffed, packed, suffocating crowds."

"Thank You," Betsie went on serenely, "for the fleas and for –"

The fleas! This was too much. "Betsie, there's no way even God can make me grateful for a flea."

*" ' Give thanks in **all** circumstances.' Fleas are part of this place where God has put us."*

And so we stood between piers of bunks and gave thanks for fleas.
From The Hiding Place by Corrie Ten Boom [30]

AUGUST 11

So often our first response to loss and suffering is anger.

Often anger at God.

I know it was one of my first responses after Sarah had her stroke. I think God is kind and patient when we are angry and begging to understand "why". I don't think His longsuffering toward us is because we have the right to be angry. Rather it is because He loves us, and He knows we are created beings with limited vision.

Every day is a gift. Not an entitlement. I don't deserve this day. That was lost in the Garden of Eden. Despite our disobedience, God loves us so much that He continues to give us the gift of days. Death and suffering became a part of our lives because of us, not Him.

I look back to the days before Sarah had her stroke. Spiritually, I was so backwards back then. Rarely, if ever, did I thank the Lord for the generous gift of each day. It was more than just taking days for granted. I actually felt that I deserved each day and every breath I took. I believed Sarah had the right to each day. Such entitlement feelings caused a shift in focus from God to self and from God to this world. Such assumptions caused me to be downright steaming mad at God when the stroke happened.

But the truth is, we are not entitled to life or health. These are gifts that God defines and determines.

I am not suggesting that when we experience loss or pain or hate that we should just passively accept it or jump for joy. Anger and deep sorrow have a place in the process of maturing and worshiping. We should aggressively and honestly seek God's guidance. We should boldly take all our feelings and confusions to Him.

This is time to be broken before the throne of God.

That is a rich place to be.

AUGUST 12

Jesus answered, 'Everyone who drinks this water will be thirsty again, but whoever drinks the water I give him will never thirst. Indeed, the water I give him will become in him a spring of water welling up to eternal life' (John 4:13 – 14).

The phone rang. It was the pharmacy. One of Sarah's medications needed to be pre-authorized by our new insurance company because it wasn't on the company's "formulary".

What is a formulary? I never even heard of it.

While I scrambled to try and figure out what a formulary was, Sarah's seizure medicine was running low. From the pharmacist, I learned that I would need to contact Sarah's neurologist and ask her to contact the insurance company with the appropriate form requesting that this medication be dispensed per contract rules. I called the neurologist. I spoke to a secretary who took my message and promised that a nurse would call right back.

I waited.

Then I waited some more.

And more.

I called the pharmacy in the long-shot hope that the nurse had just somehow taken care of the situation and had forgotten to call me back. The pharmacy had not heard from anyone. I called the neurologist again. I left a firmer and more frantic message. Someone did call me back. The paperwork was on the neurologist's desk. But, the neurologist was on vacation until Thursday, and she'd sign it as soon as she returned.

Thursday came. I called the pharmacist. No news.

Friday. I called the neurologist. She had signed the form. But, then it had to be faxed to the insurance company for approval.

Saturday. I called the pharmacist. No news.

I explained I was almost out of Sarah's seizure medicine. The pharmacist said she would call the insurance company directly. She called me back. The medicine was pre-authorized, and she would fill the prescription right away.

I picked it up later that day.

It was exhausting trying to track down all the needed people so that Sarah could get one small bottle of pills. Would it be like this every month? I sat down at the kitchen table, and I flipped open my Bible. By chance, I turned to the Gospel of John chapter 4: *Jesus answered, 'Everyone who drinks this water will be thirsty again, but whoever drinks the water I give him will never thirst. Indeed, the water I give him will become in him a spring of water welling up to eternal life.'*

Earthly accomplishments are only temporarily satisfying. Sure, I accomplished the feat of getting Sarah's medication pre-authorized prior to her running out of the stuff this month. What about the next time? This whole routine could start all over again - scrambling, phone calls, waiting, worrying. I might feel comfortable today because the pill bottle is full, but by next week it will be noticeably less full, and by the week after it would only be half full, and shortly thereafter, it will be time to return to the well of the pharmacy and possibly the deep dark well of the neurologist and insurance company to beg for the refill.

There is only one water that satisfies completely and eternally. It is the water of Christ found in His forgiveness and His gift of grace given to us as He suffered on the cross.

He pre-authorized salvation for all who believe in His life, death, and resurrection, and it does not need to be pre-authorized on a monthly or semi-annual basis. The prescription needs filling only once, and the cure is guaranteed. The cure…sin forgiven. Life eternal. Home in heaven.

I wrote the words from John 4 on a yellow post-it note and stuck it on the front of the insurance contract. The next time the shadow of worry created by drug formularies and neurologists threatens to consume the light of faith, I will read that little post-it, take a deep breath, and calmly start making the necessary phone calls. Hopefully with bigger and better perspective.

AUGUST 13

Where there is "good news" there exists "bad news" right? How would we recognize "good news" if the "bad" were not also made known?

We Christians like to talk a lot about the "good news." The gospel of Jesus Christ…

Jesus – God in the flesh come willingly to earth.

Jesus – God in the flesh gone willingly to the cross as the propitiation (satisfactory payment) for sin.

Jesus – God in the flesh raised from the dead.

Jesus – God in the flesh victorious over sin, death, suffering, and hell.

Jesus – alive and at the right hand of the throne of God.

Jesus – preparing a mansion for all the repentant who die in Him.

The Holy Spirit living within all believers who have turned from the old way of life and received Christ as Savior.

This is, indeed, good news!

But, this good news cannot stand alone, for it is merely one leg of a two legged truth. The good news, apart from the bad news, is incomplete – perhaps even inaccurate – and shallow.

The good news is only good because the bad news is so bad.

Built within the good news of Christ's atonement for sin is a warning...

(Jesus said,) For God sent not His Son into the world to condemn the world; but that the world through Him might be saved. He that believeth on Him is not condemned: **but he that believeth not is condemned already**, *because he hath not believed in the name of the only begotten Son of God. And this is the condemnation, that light is come into the world, and men loved darkness rather than light, because their deeds were evil. For every one that doeth evil hateth the light, neither cometh to the light, lest his deeds should be reproved'...'The Father loveth the Son, and hath given all things into His hand. He that believeth on the Son hath everlasting life:* **and he that believeth not the Son shall not see life; but the wrath of God abideth on him** *(John 3:17-20 and John 3:35).*

After His resurrection, Jesus instructs the disciples, *"Go into all the world and preach the good news to all creation. Whoever believes and is baptized will be saved,* **but whoever does not believe will be condemned"** *(Mark 16:15, 16).*

If you do not have the Son, then *the wrath of God abideth on you.* The bad news is: **He that believeth not is condemned already.**

The bad news is as bad as the good news is good. God's salvation is a gift that is sufficient to cover the sin of all men of all times and places. But, this gift must be opened by individual repentant sinners. If a person ignores the gift or rejects the gift, thus failing to open the gift, this person will experience God's wrath.

Here I am! I stand at the door and knock. If anyone hears my voice and opens the door, I will come in and eat with him, and he with me (Revelation 3:20).

Come, all you who are thirsty, come to the waters; and you who have no money, come, buy and eat! Come, buy wine and milk without money and without cost....Listen, listen to me, and eat what is good, and your soul will delight in the richest of fare. Give ear and come to me; hear me, that your soul may live (Isaiah 55:1,2b,3a).

For he who ignores the Holy Spirit's pleadings to open the freely given gift of salvation, God's righteous and deserved judgment falls upon him. He alone will bear the penalty of sin before a holy God.

This is frightening!

No human being is sinless *(For all have sinned, and come short of the glory of God; Romans 3:23).*

No human being has ever met God's perfect standards in thought, word and deed *(The heart is deceitful above all things, and desperately wicked: who can know it? I the Lord search the heart, I try the reins, even to give every man according to his ways, and according to the fruit of his doings; Jeremiah 17:9,10).*

God is holy. He warned Adam in the Garden of Eden that sin leads to death. God had blessed Adam and Eve with a perfect home and one rule: *You are free to eat from any tree in the garden; but you must not eat from the tree of the knowledge of good and evil, for when you eat of it you will surely die (Genesis 2:17).* Adam and Eve disobeyed that one rule, unleashing sin and its consequences into the world.

Die they did, and die we will. God cannot lie. There are consequences.

The penalty for sin is steep because God is Holy. Holiness is part of His very essence and character.   A blood sacrifice is required to atone for sins.

Adam and Eve, prior to the fall, had existed in a perfect creation. They were naked and unashamed before God and each other in purity. Enter sin, and with it distortion of all things pure. No more could they be naked before God or one another.   God clothed them with the skin of an animal (Genesis 3:21).   The first blood sacrifice.

Jesus Christ is the final and sufficient blood sacrifice.

Are you aware that you stand – apart from Christ - condemned before a Holy God?

AUGUST 14

Do you understand that sin is real and so too are its consequences?

Or, have you fallen prey to the world's denial of sin and its shallow definitions of evil?

Apart from frequent walks in the Word of the Lord and conversations with Him in prayer, we live in the danger of clothing ourselves in the world's "wisdom". The world would have us believe that "wickedness" is relative and that "tolerance" is supreme.   "Do what you want! Do what works for you!" Moral absolutes and God's standards? No! For moral absolutes and God's standards are "intolerant" and thus must be slain on the world's alter.

But the world is lying to you. *....for Satan himself masquerades as an angel of light. It is not surprising, then, if his servants masquerade as servants of righteousness..... (II Corinthians 11:14,15)....Be self-controlled and alert. Your enemy the devil prows around like a roaring lion looking for someone to devour"* (I Peter 5:8).

The world and its ever metastasizing sense of political correctness, announces there is no hell. But there is! The world proclaims that the concept of sin is old fashioned. But it is not! The world wrongly believes that it offers redemption. It does not.

All of us have become like one who is unclean, and all our righteous acts are like filthy rags; we all shrivel up like a leaf, and like the wind our sins sweep us away (Isaiah 64:6).

Oh, what objections the world has to the truth of wickedness. "How dare God consider me wicked! I am special! I am important! I do good things and these good things outweigh the bad. I **am** good enough to get myself into heaven. God is a god of love, and He will not judge me." These are lies. These are dangerous.

Holy God has not just the right to judge guilty man. He has the duty to do so.

God forgive the Christian who proclaims only the Good News...who speaks only of God's love and ignores the truth of God's holiness.

Why would a Christian fail to mention God's holiness when sharing, either in word or deed, the gospel? Fear and pride. The world's message has sunk its claws into us, and we fear offending even though it is sometimes offending that is most needed. We fear rejection even though we should expect rejection when truth confronts error. We fear other people's opinions even though God has clearly told us that praise from God is to be sought more than praise from men. We fear being overwhelmed. "What if I don't have all the right answers?" But God promises us that the Holy Spirit will give us the words to say (Mark 13:10,11 and Luke 12:11,12).

And sometimes, we are simply lazy. It takes more time and investment to share God's holiness. It is easy to tell someone that he is loved by the great Creator of the universe. Who doesn't want to hear that? But to share God's holiness, that is time consuming and takes great effort to prepare and to perform.

Shame on us if we share only the good news.

AUGUST 15

From <u>Foxe: Voices of the Martyrs</u> [31]

Jim Elliot, Pete Fleming, Ed McCully, Nate Saint, Roger Youderian (1956)

"A news flash alerted the world: 'Five Men Missing in Auca Territory.' The date was Monday, January 9, 1956. A team of missionary pioneers trying to make peaceful contact with an infamous tribe of Indians in Ecuador had failed to make a scheduled radio call. For almost a full day no word had come from their camp on the Curaray River, which they named 'Palm Beach.' Then a hovering pilot reported the badly damaged plane at the camp. This was followed by a gruesome confirmation on Wednesday, January 11, when the first body was spotted in the river. Though a search and rescue team was quickly formed, the discovery of more bodies quickly changed the mission from rescue to retrieval and burial.

"By Friday of that week the team reached the missionaries' campsite and hurriedly buried four of the bodies. The men had died violently from repeated spear wounds and machete cuts. The fifth body (Ed McCully) was never located after being identified on the beach but then washed away by the river. Five widows and eight orphans mourned the deaths and looked to God for comfort and direction. The world witnessed in stunned amazement.

"Shockwaves from the tragedy traveled around the globe. Eventually, thousands of Christians identified the news of the deaths of five young men as the turning point in their lives. In her book, Through the Gates of Splendor, written a year after the deaths, Jim Elliot's widow Elisabeth described some of the remarkable early results from what seemed like a tragic waste of life. The places of service vacated by those men were filled many times over by young men and women moved and motivated by their selfless sacrifice. Fifty years later, the effects continue to be felt.

"Within two years of their deaths, Jim Elliot's widow and Nate Saint's sister made a friendly and lasting contact with the Waodanis. Bible translation into the Waodani language began. One by one, the men who committed the murder became believers in the One who sent the missionaries to reach them. Steve Saint spent much of his childhood among the Waodanis. Despite the fact that they had killed his father, Steve became an adopted son of the tribe and eventually took his own family to live for a time among them. The painful arrival of the gospel among that violent people worked a miracle of transformation.

"While martyrdom has always been part of the great battle between good and evil in the spiritual realms, the death of believers has not always resulted directly from those seeking to silence their witness. Violence has often been an expression of fear, suspicion, ignorance or timing rather than a conscious rejection of the message. The five men who died in Ecuador had spent months contacting the Waodanis through over-flights and gifts exchanged via an ingenious bucket drop devised by the team's pilot, Nate Saint. Though the tribe had a history of violent encounters with outsiders, the men had decided they had established some degree of mutual trust that would support a direct contact. At first, their cautious optimism had been rewarded by a *visit from three Waodanis. That had occurred without incident. They had expected further contact. Little did the missionaries know that they had stepped into an intra-tribe squabble.*

"When the attack party killed the five men, their actions weren't personal or even driven by what or who the white men represented. The violence was almost a diversion from internal issues the Waodanis couldn't handle. Two of the three who had visited the camp at Palm Beach reported that the missionaries had mistreated them; the third person argued otherwise. Though others in the group recognized the false accusations, it seemed easier to eliminate the cause (the missionaries) than to address the internal issues. Once the possibility of killing was raised, the general tone in the tribal group shifted to well-established patterns of preparation for battle. They knew the white men had guns; they didn't know they wouldn't use them. Several of the Waodanis reported hearing strange supernatural voices and seeing moving lights in the sky during the attack, as if God sent an angelic choir to celebrate the faithfulness and the homecoming of His loyal servants.

"Steeped in generations of horrific hand-to-hand combat, combined with the heightened memory that tends to characterize verbal cultures, the Waodani display an amazing capacity for remembering the details of battles. Lengthy conversations among the Waodani often consist of show-and-tell descriptions of spear and machete scars and gruesome minutiae of the deaths of enemies. But it wasn't until years later, after the death of Rachel Saint, Nate's sister who had come to live among the Waodani and bring God's Word to them, when Steve Saint heard the full story of the raid. Reminiscing by a fire late at night, the aging warriors gave an account of the event, still amazed that the white men had done nothing to defend themselves. Steve learned that Mincaye, who had since become a father to him, had actually been the one who had dealt the deathblow to his father. As soon as he knew, Steve realized it didn't really matter. What mattered was that God had used an amazing mixture of spiritual weapons, including the deaths of five servants, to defeat the power of fear and violence that had kept the Waodani captive as far back as they could remember.

"In his book, The End of the Spear, Steve reports that he has been frequently asked over the years about the struggle he must have experienced to forgive those who had taken his father from him. He has always responded that it was never a struggle for him. Even to his grieving five-year-old mind, the death of his father and friends had been a part of God's plan. You don't have to forgive someone whom you have never held responsible for an act. True to the Maker and Mover behind the scenes, the story of the Waodani displays God's ways. Those who were once the impossible-to-reach are now taking their place among those who reach out. Believers among the Waodani have suffered for Christ and at least one has experienced martyrdom. Their long history with violence makes them keen observes of the state of the 'modern' world, where the increasing fascination and practice of hatred, violence, and killing appear all too familiar for those recently freed from that life of despair. God's deeper

purposes take time to come to light. Occasionally, those who are paying attention get to see those purposes shine and are amazed."
From *Foxe: Voices of the Martyrs* [31]

AUGUST 16

Everything seems so complicated and complex to me. God bless those people who can look at life and see black and white and right and wrong. God bless those people who can read the Bible and see clearly how the Bible directs their lives. I am not one of those "black and white, this all makes sense to me," sort of person. Everywhere I look, the Bible included, I see complexity. Sometimes things are complicated simply because I am resisting truth and seeking loopholes to fit sin comfortably into my life. And sometimes things are complex just because things are complex.

Sharing Biblical truth with others seems complicated to me.

Sometimes I feel like a coward.

Words about God flow freely from my pen, and I do frequently share with nonbelievers via written words. But, speaking about God to nonbelievers feels very awkward and daunting to me.

To a certain extent, that is ok. After all, it is no small thing to discuss God. It should not be done lightly. There should be a sense of my own inability so that it will be upon the Holy Spirit which I lean, rather than my own understanding.

Yet, I know my heart. It's not wisdom holding me back. It's fear.

Why am I hesitant, inhibited, cautious?

Do I doubt His existence, His promises, His power?

Am I afraid of rejection?

Am I anxious that I will not have answers to questions?

Is my fear really fear, or is my fear embarrassment?

Or, am I just making myself too important in this whole equation?

That would indicate pride...and aren't all sins – including fear – ultimately rooted in pride?

Here I am, God.

I struggle.

Forgive my unbelief.

Forgive my pride.

Deliver me from fear and confusion.

Equip me with boldness.

Confidence.

Not in myself, but in You.

AUGUST 17

It all started when I decided I would exercise on our treadmill down in our basement. I was all set: music playing, treadmill plugged in and ready to use. Just one thing missing.

Socks.

I'd forgotten to bring a pair with me. I thought, "Well, I should run upstairs and grab a pair." But, I didn't. Instead, I slipped into my sneakers and stepped onto the treadmill.

It was a mistake.

About half way through my workout, I could feel the blister begin, a slight but manageable throb on my ankle. I'd reached my target heart rate, and I was on a schedule so I kept going.

I spent days afterward limping around. It was indicative of the entire weekend to come...

Let me share a few of the details...

Mark and I went to the races at Holland Speedway. It was Bank of Holland night there. As patrons of the bank, we could go to the races on a reasonable buck. Like the old people we are becoming, we were the first to arrive so that we wouldn't miss out on the free hot dogs. Even though it was June, there was a chill in the air, and I hunkered down in a big, warm sweatshirt.

The races bore me. But, my family was there, and I enjoyed their company - and fried dough - with an occasional glance at the track. I endured the cold and the noise. I enjoyed the family and the food. Soon enough, it was time to go. Mark and I jumped into our little car, Mark in the passenger side and me behind the wheel. We waited in a line of traffic at the red light in Holland. I turned right when I finally reached the intersection and headed home toward Delevan.

I saw the deer, a previous victim of another person's car, dead already in the road, huge and intimidating, lying in the middle of my lane. I had nary a second to determine a course. Should I swerve left or right around the deer, risking collision with cars around me? Should I slam on the brakes? I squeezed shut my eyes. I gripped the steering wheel tighter. And I drove over top of the deer...much to my husband's horror and disbelief.

Next morning, with the blood and hair of the deer cleaned off the grill of the car, I headed to church. At church, I ran into a friend. We were visiting in the parking lot before church, when we realized we had visited slightly too long. For the service had begun. We snuck quietly into the sanctuary. The congregation was mid-prayer when we found a pew within which to sink...and as I sat, I really thought I heard Pastor say something about someone's death...the death, so I thought, of a relative of one of my fellow church members. Later that morning, as the service ended, I found this fellow church member, gave her a hug, and told her how sorry I was for the passing of her relative.

As I'm sure you already know, I had it wrong. Guess I didn't hear everything in the right order when I arrived mid-prayer, for there was no dead relative of whom to express my sympathy. I fumbled for the right words to speak once I realized my error. But, my dignity had already been dismantled, and there I stood. Embarrassed.

And now a new day and a new week begins.

How grateful I am for second chances. And third...and fourth...and fifth chances...I dreadfully require them! How frequently I miss the mark and fumble the football of life. And just as frequently God forgives me, and at times even makes useful my failures...and my blisters...and my idiot words...

Oh, how I need Jesus!

And on we go...beginning yet again...rejoicing...in Him.

<u>*AUGUST 18*</u>

I remember (barely) being in middle school.

I remember a girl sitting behind me. I didn't like her very much. I felt intimidated by her. One day, for no reason at all, she twanged me in the back of my head.

I guess she and her friends thought it was funny.

Back in middle school days, our enemies were obvious.

Now I'm all grown up, and my enemies do not always announce themselves so obviously.

The Bible tells us, *Put on the full armor of God so that you can take your stand against the devil's schemes. For our struggle is not against flesh and blood, but against the rulers, against the authorities, against the powers of this dark world and against the spiritual forces of evil in the heavenly realms (Ephesians 6:11, 12).*

The Bible teaches that there is a literal Satan, and that he and his gang want to mess with our lives and render us useless to the Kingdom of God. Sometimes Satan tries to seduce us with his lies and with our weaknesses when facing temptation. Sometimes he beats on us and makes our lives almost unbearable.

And sometimes, just like the middle school girl behind me, he just gives us a twang in the back of our heads in a bitter attempt to intimidate us.

I wonder sometimes whether Satan's outright punches are easier to maneuver than his sneaky annoying twangs? At least the punches are recognizable. This enemy is a liar, a liar who does not necessarily want to be recognized by we, the wandering sea of humanity. He wants guards down and vulnerable underbellies exposed. With this in mind, He is a master masquerader of an angel of light. He knows the value of mixing just enough truth with his lies to deceive us.

"Are you really out there, God?" Sometimes I wonder. I don't like to admit this. For decades, I have read the Bible just about every day. I pray. I go to church. I fellowship with other Christians. But, I still catch myself sometimes wondering if He is really real. Is there really a heaven to look forward to when I die? Of all the apostles, doubting Thomas is my friend. I can hear my voice in his questions in John 14: *Lord, we don't know where you are going, so how can we know the way?* And, after the resurrection, *Unless I see the nail marks in His hands and put my finger where the nails were, and put my hand into His side, I will not believe it.*

Just like Thomas, I long for proof of God. He has given His Word. He has revealed Himself by weaving design into all of creation. He has provided the Holy Spirit. And yet I still long for proof? I am, of all sinners, the most miserable.

God is longsuffering. One day, He responded gently to my doubt. Sarah only had a half day at school today. The end of June, the school year almost over, lots to do. I was busy. I wasn't particularly reflecting on anything spiritual as I prepared lunch for Sarah after school. Since I'm not much of a cook, it wasn't much of a lunch…An apple with a big soft bruise on one side. A banana. A bowl of homemade chili.

I was sitting at the kitchen table, Sarah was in her wheelchair beside me. I peeled the banana. Suddenly, with banana and peel in my hand, a half-eaten apple next to the bowl of chili, and my beautiful daughter next to me, I was overcome with a sense of awe. I stared at that banana in wonder. I moved my gaze to the apple sitting next to the chili and then to my daughter sitting next to me. Yellow bananas and red apples and children simply cannot be explained by mere natural processes and evolution. The origin of life and living cells and complexity…nature alone is insufficient to explain the wonder of it all.

These are God designed gifts in a God designed moment.

I sit in awe of the Creator in an unexpected rush of belief in a quiet, ordinary moment of life. I realize I am breathing…and that, too, becomes suddenly miraculous to me. God has showed up in this minute of my life, clock ticking in the background, to assure me He is real. He has created. He does redeem. He sees my doubt, and He gently gives me eyes to see Him in everyday things that truly cannot be explained apart from Him.

This is His grace to one of His children.

Satan prowls around like a roaring lion looking for someone to devour (I Peter 5:8).

But God silences Satan's roar…with a banana, an apple, and a girl with an extra chromosome…and the roaring lion retreats.

AUGUST 19

And, then there is marriage.

Marriage is work, and on the bad days of marriage, it can be so bad that you can't think about anything else and the last thing you really want to do is pick up your Bible and pray and spend time with the Lord.

It is just so much easier to be consumed with anger or irritation against your spouse.

Do you think Satan is unaware of that? He can use problems in marriage to estrange us from our Father in heaven.

Even as I write these words, I am having one of those bad days of marriage. And, I don't feel like writing. The details of this bad day of marriage are unimportant. We all have them and the specific story is less relevant than the bottom line: Satan loves it when we are out of sorts with our spouses. He loves the sin and consequences that freely flow from these ugly moments.

Ephesians 5 teaches, *Husbands, love your wives, just as Christ loved the church and gave Himself up for her to make her holy, cleansing her by the washing with water through the word, and to present her to Himself as a radiant church, without stain or wrinkle or any other blemish, but holy and blameless. In this same way, husbands ought to love their wives as their own bodies...*

My thoughts...

"Well, well, guess what? I don't feel like my husband is loving me like Christ loves the church! Not at all! I don't even care right now what the Bible tells wives about how they are supposed to behave. What does that matter if my husband isn't bearing his end of the load? Why should I be expected to carry mine? I want to stew and brew over his, his, his 'personality' and the way he acts and talks. And, I'd really like to call a friend and get some sympathy and pats on the back right now. I'm so much better than my husband after all, so wouldn't it be great to call a friend and go over his vices a few times while emphasizing my superior qualities?"

And the enemy is smiling. For he has me right where he wants me...

Flooded with negative thoughts about the guy to whom I am wed. Ready to gush gossip to the next available set of listening ears. Focused on my rights. Desiring to bear a grudge. Wallowing in self.

Estranged from God.

I have been forgiven. Yet, I bear a quality of unforgiveness and a stubborn unwillingness to move away from my tightly held belief that I have the right to withhold forgiveness.

I have no such a right.

Upon a crossroad I stand. Upon what shall I choose to fix my mind? What shall rule my mind: feelings or truth?

Get rid of all bitterness, rage and anger, brawling and slander, along with every form of malice. Be kind and compassionate to one another, forgiving each other, just as in Christ God forgave you (Ephesians 4:31, 32).

He who covers over an offense promotes love, but whoever repeats the matter separates close friends (Proverbs 17:9).

This is love: not that we loved God, but that He loved us and sent His Son as an atoning sacrifice for our sins. Dear friends, since God so loved us, we also ought to love one another. No one has ever seen God; but if we love one another, God lives in us and His love is made complete in us....God is love. Whoever lives in love lives in God, and God in him...We love because He first loved us. If anyone says, 'I love God,' yet hates his brother, he is a liar. For anyone who does not love his brother, whom he has seen, cannot love God, whom he has not seen. And he has given us this command: Whoever loves God must also love his brother (I John 4:10, 11, 16b, 19-21).

With the tongue we praise our Lord and Father, and with it we curse men, who have been made in God's likeness. Out of the same mouth come praise and cursing. My brothers, this should not be. Can both fresh water and salt water flow from the same spring? (James 3:9-12).

Jesus said, 'And when you stand praying, if you hold anything against anyone, forgive him, so that your Father in heaven may forgive you your sins' (Mark 11:25).

Love is patient, love is kind. It does not envy, it does not boast, it is not proud. It is not rude, it is not self-seeking, it is not easily angered, it keeps no record of wrongs. Love does not delight in evil but rejoices with the truth. It always protects, always trusts, always hopes, always perseveres (I Corinthians 13:4-7).

Choose truth.

It takes effort.

But it's worth it.

And, it's the right thing to do.

My husband is at work. I'm going to call him.

And tell him I love him...and wipe the smile off Satan's face.

<u>**August 20**</u>

From <u>The Hiding Place</u> by Corrie Ten Boom [32]

"Schneller!" a guard screamed at (Betsie). "Can't you go faster?'

Why must they scream, I wondered as I sank my shovel into the black muck. Why couldn't they speak like ordinary human beings? I straightened slowly, the sweat drying on my back. I was remembering where we had first heard this maniac sound. The Beje (home). In Tante Jans's room. A voice coming from the shell-shaped speaker, a scream lingering in the air even after Betsie had leapt to shut it off.

"Loafer! Lazy swine!"

The guard snatched Betsie's shovel from her hands and ran from group to group of the digging crew exhibiting the handful of dirt that was all Betsie had been able to lift...

The other guards and even some of the prisoners laughed. Encouraged, the guard threw herself into a parody of Betsie's faltering walk. A male guard was with our detail today and in the presence of a man, the women guards were always animated.

As the laughter grew, I felt a murderous anger rise. The guard was young and well fed – was it Betsie's fault that she was old and starving? But to my astonishment, Betsie too was laughing.

"That's me all right," she admitted. "But you'd better let me totter along with my little spoonful, or I'll have to stop altogether."

The guard's plump cheeks went crimson. "I'll decide who's to stop!" And snatching the leather crop from her belt she slashed Betsie across the chest and neck.

Without knowing I was doing it, I had seized my shovel and rushed at her.

Betsie stopped in front of me before anyone had seen.

"Corrie!" she pleaded, dragging my arm to my side. "Corrie, keep working!" She tugged the shovel from my hand and dug it into the mud. Contemptuously, the guard tossed Betsie's shovel toward us. I picked it up, still in a daze. A red stain appeared on Betsie's collar; a welt began to swell on her neck.

Betsie saw where I was looking and laid a bird-thin hand over the whip mark. *"Don't look at it, Corrie. Look at Jesus only."* She drew away her hand: it was sticky with blood.
From **The Hiding Place** by Corrie Ten Boom [32]

AUGUST 21

Yesterday afternoon, I arrived home with Sarah. She'd had a great day at school. As always, those minutes and hours between arriving home from school and bedtime are crazy, and this day was no exception. I hefted (really, this the right word) Sarah out of her wheelchair, up the basement steps, into the living room, and onto her blankets and pillows on the floor so she could watch TV. I gave her some fluid in her feeding tube, flushed her PICC line, and catheterized her. Then, I carried her back to her room so she could take a nap.

I also put some eggs on the stove to hard boil.

Next on the list of things to do: computer time. I needed to check e-mail and research a few things...looking for a clarinet for me and a bath chair for Sarah.

Our computer is in the basement. So, I headed down the stairs...

We still have dial-up internet here, and today good old dial up wasn't in the mood to dial up. I restarted the computer twice. I attempted to connect four times. Error message...*this page cannot be displayed*...the joys of computers...

I gave up.

Went upstairs.

Just in time to discover a forgotten about pan on the stove... water evaporated and the bottom of the pan black and burned...eggs definitely hard boiled.

I went on-line later that night without any problems.

God in the details, protecting my home from my forgetfulness.

Psalm 91 tells us: *He who dwells in the shelter of the Most High will rest in the shadow of the Almighty....He will cover you with His feathers and under His wings you will find refuge; His faithfulness will be your shield and rampart....If you make the Most High your dwelling - even the Lord, who is my refuge - then no harm will befall you, no disaster will come near your tent. For He will command His angels concerning you to guard you in all your ways; they will lift you up in their hands, so that you will not strike your foot against a stone.*

AUGUST 22

Dear Lord,

In Acts 12, we are told how Peter was sleeping even though he was in prison, bound by chains and under the eyes of guards.

Yet, he slept.

He rested.

May my walk with You be such that when I am in a prison, still I rest in You.

May I be right with You, so that my faith will endure and peace will abound even as storms rage.

I pray this for my husband. For my family. For my students.

May we be a praying people, wise to recognize your unique answers to those prayers, and humble enough to praise You always…whether in freedom or fetters.

In Jesus' Comforting and Calming Name…

AUGUST 23

Even though we are having beautiful summer-like weather here in Western New York, I decided yesterday to start the process of "winterizing" my garden.

Throughout the summer season, I had been reluctant to cut my roses and bring the blooms into the house to enjoy. We have not-the-best soil here, so the rose blooms certainly are not voluminous. But, the few that I get are ok enough. Because I like how they look outside, I usually do not cut the blooms for in-door enjoyment.

Yesterday was different, though. I decided to cut them all (a total of five) and bring them in the house. Weather forecasts are calling for cold and rain later this week.

So, I snipped the rose blooms from the bushes and gave them a temporary home in a maroon cut glass vase in our kitchen. Two of the roses are peach on the outside with a slow fading change to cream at the center of the bloom. Three of them are perfectly all-girl pink. All of them are fragrant.

Each time I walk by my vase of five pastel colored roses, I feel the need to stop, look, and smell. I can hardly believe how beautiful in appearance and aroma these roses are. I am in awe of their design and their smell and their colors...

The heart of the attraction I have for these flowers is how exquisitely they proclaim the existence of God. I behold these little roses and I wonder, "How can anybody doubt that the world was created by a loving and imaginative Designer?"

How can evolution explain a rose?

Many believe Darwinian evolution can explain a rose simply because they have been told repeatedly that Darwinian evolution can explain a rose.

But it can't.

No matter how many times a lie is told, and no matter how prone you may be to begin to believe it, it is still a lie.

And Darwinian evolution and naturalism are lies that seek to cut the Creator out of His creation. The secular Darwinian evolutionary worldview does more than attempt to exclude God. It is an attempt to mock God.

But be not deceived. God is not mocked.

AUGUST 24

I remember my younger years. I have changed from the person I was those decades ago.

Back then, I was the most important thing to me. It was all about "me." Even when I read the Bible, I would read through selfish eyes. I perceived the Bible as basically existing for me and my conveniences. Thus, when Jesus stated in John 14 that He "is the way, the truth, and the life" He must mean merely "a way, a truth, a life." After all, if Jesus exists for man, then he must make many ways, right? In other words, aren't all religions kind of the same? Aren't there multiple ways to heaven?

Reading is not the same as comprehending.

Back then, I read. I didn't always comprehend.

Back then, I wanted to believe what I wanted to believe even as I read God's Word.

I wanted to believe all religions led to heaven. I wanted to believe there were multiple ways to God. I did not want to believe that Christ is the ONLY way...after all if that is true...then I must share that truth with others...and that, my friends, is a heavy load that I cared not to bear at the time.

I even used Scripture to convince myself that there were multiple ways to God. In other words, I did not properly handle and divide the Word of truth...and the only reason I didn't was because I didn't want to. Here is the Scripture I used to purposefully deceive myself: *Jesus said, 'I am the good shepherd. The good shepherd lays down His life for the sheep. The hired hand is not the shepherd who owns the sheep. so when he sees the wolf coming, he abandons the sheep and runs away. Then the wolf attacks the flock and scatters it. The man runs away because he is a hired hand and cares nothing for the sheep. I am the good shepherd; I know my sheep and my sheep know me - just as the Father knows me and I know the Father - and I lay down my life for the sheep.* **I have other sheep that are not of this sheep pen. I must bring them also.** *They too will listen to my voice, and there shall be one flock and one shepherd'* (John 10:11-16).

"Other sheep from other sheep pens!" Perfect! I could use this singular passage to pretend that there were multiple ways to God. And so I did throughout my college years.

I used this passage as an excuse to keep my mouth shut in a cellular biology class led by a professor who denied the Creator.

I used this passage as an excuse to party.

I used this passage as an excuse to follow my own wisdom, understanding, and desires.

I justified my sin because I believed there were many ways to heaven.

Then it happened.

The rocking of my world.

Slowly at first.

It started with a Bible study at Redeemer Lutheran Church in Colden. It was a great group with an exceptional leader, Pastor James Murr. I will be always thankful for his patient and honest teaching of scripture.

One Thursday afternoon, when I was feeling particularly smart, I asked a question about John 10. I, in my haughtiness, wanted to point out how that passage must refer to Jesus somehow manifesting and revealing Himself to people in ways other than the cross and resurrection. Slam dunk, I thought!

Except, my theory was way full of lots of holes, and Pastor Murr confronted my thinking by pointing out the leaks. I, bachelor of arts summa cum laude history/government graduate in the great year 1994, did not know my history.

So, what's the history lesson? Jesus was born a Jew. He was an Israelite. God had made a covenant with Abraham, patriarch of the Jewish people. The Old Testament is all about that covenant and the prophesy of the Christ-child to come through that contract. God promised Abraham that his descendants would become a great nation. As a result of this promise, Israel came to be. Eventually, the long anticipated Messiah (Jesus) came to earth through the Israelites. He came to save.

Lots of folks at the time thought that Jesus was going to save and redeem **only the Israelites**.

In John 10, when Jesus talks about saving sheep from other pens, He is talking about expanding HIMSELF. The new covenant (that would be established when Jesus sacrificed Himself for the sins of the world) would be available not only to the Jews, but also to the Gentiles (i.e. everyone who was not a Jew).

However, to be included in the covenant, one would still need to enter through Jesus. Accessibility to God would be extended beyond Israel. The original sheep were the Israelites. The "other sheep that are not of this sheep pen" was the rest of the world, the Gentiles. But, whether Israelite or Gentile, the door through which entry must be made was the same: Jesus Christ. Jesus said *'I tell you the truth, I am the gate for the sheep....I am the gate; whoever enters through me will be saved'* (John 10:7, 9).

I left Bible study that day no longer comfortable with my personal interpretation of Scripture, an interpretation designed to give my itching ears what they wanted to hear.

And thus began a journey.

I began to seek...

And what I discovered humbled me and changed my life.

Lee Strobel's book <u>The Case for Christ</u> and Josh McDowell's book <u>More than a Carpenter</u> exam the historical, archeological, scientific, and prophetic evidence to support Biblical reliability and accuracy regarding the claims of Christ's divinity. These authors do an outstanding job of examining evidence. Both of them were skeptics when they began their own searches.

Ultimately I was confronted with the question of, "Why?"

Why, if there are a plurality of paths to heaven, would Jesus hang on a cross? Why would He suffer so if there were any other way, any way in which mankind could earn heaven on his own?

One day, I was reading Galatians. I read a verse I had read before. But this time, light shined and I comprehended: *I do not treat the grace of God as meaningless. For if keeping the law could make us right with God, then there was no need for Christ to die (Galatians 2:21).* In other words, if there were any other way that we could be good enough to stand before God, then Christ's death on the cross was unnecessary.

His death on the cross was necessary.

Therefore, there is no other way.

Jesus Christ is the only way, the only truth, the only life.

I believe. Praise God, I believe!

AUGUST 25

Lord, what a wonderful reality it is that I am allowed to approach Your throne and share my heart and cast my cares upon You.

I pray for my Uncle Darrill and Aunt Kathy as they face the scary and uncertain days ahead. Protect them Lord from being consumed by the circumstances. May You, Father, be bigger to them than the stormy sea of this trial. May they fix their eyes steadily and constantly upon You. May they seek You with all their heart and soul and mind and strength.

Protect them, Lord, from the lies of Satan. That enemy will want to discourage them. He will want to cause doubt about You in their weary minds. He will try to convince them to question Your goodness. He will try to cause division between them as a couple. The enemy wants them to fight with one another. He will try to convince my Uncle Darrill to doubt his own value as a man. He will try to make them think like victims. Satan is a liar, a thief and a murderer. Protect my Uncle Darrill and Aunt Kathy from this wicked foe. Clothe them, Lord, in Your complete armor so that the fiery darts of this enemy will be deflected.

Your Word tells us that You have overcome the enemy! He is defeated because of Christ's death and resurrection. The power of the resurrection is available to Uncle Darrill and Aunt Kathy and all of us. Help us all to be strong in the power of Your might.

Truth comforts. This day, comfort my Uncle Darrill's heart and mind with Your truth and presence. Help him to seek first You and Your Kingdom and Your righteousness. May he know and believe that Your grace really is sufficient and that Your power is made perfect in our weakness. Bless Uncle Darrill and Aunt Kathy with Your perfect peace that passes all understanding, peace that is bought by the blood of Jesus Christ.

Give them rest when they are weary.

Give them knowledge of how to carry this load.

Give them hearts of gratitude to You for who You are and what You do.

May they go forward, trusting You, washed in Your blood, ever hopeful because of the resurrection power that You appropriate to us, made new in You and daily renewed and ready.

Help Uncle Darrill to remember that he doesn't need legs to stand for You.

AUGUST 26

I often counsel my students to "strive for excellence."

Yet, I wonder, am I forgetting something? Is there a subtle danger of incompleteness in my counsel?

What I have left out I assume is known intrinsically by my audience. But perhaps that is a flawed assumption.

For whom are we striving?

Is a drive for excellence about God or self?

As I think about it, I realize that in "striving for excellence" we must purpose to glorify God. It will not haphazardly happen, for our natural tendency is to glorify self. Our natural inclination is to enjoy the fruit of our striving ourselves rather than reap fruit for the Kingdom.

I wonder, when I speak of "striving for excellence" in the ears of my teenage listeners what they envision will be the end result of such effort on their part? Do they look forward and see a large, comfortable home undergirded by a large, comfortable bank account and lives decorated by the best the world has to offer? Do they peer into the basket of the fruits of excellence and see happy relationships and self-fulfillment and self-advancement and personal success, reputation, and recognition?

While these things are not, in and of themselves wrong, they must not be the ultimate goal. The goal must be higher and loftier....the goal must be God's goal, God's will for His glory. Forever.

Striving for excellence motivated only by a desire to enjoy the good life for one's self is not at all excellent. It is shallow and worldly and corrupt.

We must strive for excellence for the right reasons, for His reasons...advancing the Kingdom, shining His light, planting His seeds, sharing His truth, living His way, knowing Him and the power of His resurrection, and walking in the fellowship of His sufferings fully surrendered to His will.

It is more than merely "doing our best."

It is "doing our best for Him and by Him and in Him."

And if in the process material blessings and happy homes occur, praise Him....but may these not be our final goal.

Seek first His Kingdom! And live excellently.

AUGUST 27

Will I be brave enough to share my words, my thoughts, my heart with you?

You are enduring a hardship right now that I can't even imagine. I guess that's the nature of suffering...it's completely unique to each of us. We all suffer. Yet the extent and type of suffering is different for each.

Suffering is a lonely place to be.

In my own journey through suffering, I have learned that the greatest battle is the battle in the mind. There is a war that goes on in our heads when we suffer. Will we see the suffering as a strange gift from the hand of a loving God within a greater plan? Or will we fall prey to the fiery darts of Satan who desires to consume us in self-pity and anger at God? Satan loves to whisper lies into the minds of hurting people. He loves to make us feel like we are victims. He is pleased when we doubt the very God who gave us life and who Himself was well acquainted with grief and sorrows.

You and I, our circumstances are different. But I, too, have been in the valley of despair and vulnerable to the temptation to believe I am a victim.

This battle is fought in the mind. Fight it! Do not give in to the discouraging lies of the enemy, an enemy that wants you to be lost and defeated. This enemy is a liar and a thief and he wants to kill steal, and destroy…and what he especially wants to destroy is your faith in God.

We must speak what we know to be true about God in our own minds. That God is good, all the time. He is mighty to save. He is shelter in the storm. He has a great purpose in each of our lives and He can take the painful and ugly things we go through and give them meaning, purpose, and beauty.

The truth is Jesus – God Himself – knows suffering and pain. He emptied Himself of all that He was entitled and became a man. He put on flesh…flesh that would get sick…flesh that would ache…flesh that would bleed…flesh that would die. The suffering He endured, He did not deserve. But the truth is, He endured it anyway. His life for ours. Our debt paid by His blood. The truth is, up from the grave He arose! He is alive and victorious over sin, death, and hell. He is the mighty conqueror and glorious hope who liberates us from bondage to sin and delivers us from chains of defeat. No matter what awful suffering we may experience in our lives on earth, if Jesus Messiah is our Savior, we too are conquerors! We are not victims.

The truth is our suffering on earth may continue for as long as we are alive. But if we know Him, intimately know Him, everything will be ok. God can make our suffering valuable. He can breathe purpose into the pain. He can conform us into the image of His Son.

Satan wants us to live low, defeated lives. He wants us to doubt God's goodness. Often Satan has a willing participant in us, for our default position often bends his way. The world taunts us to believe we are victims to be pitied. Our own flesh deceives us and we easily sink into self-pity.

But God!

He holds out nail scarred hands and proclaims that a new identity awaits. We can be acceptable in the Beloved. We can be stripped of our filthy rags. We can be clothed in His white robes of righteousness. We can be whole, even in our brokenness, if we are His. He gives beauty for ashes and the oil of joy for mourning. He sets prisoners free…and he whom the Son sets free is free indeed!

Earlier today I was reading the story of the paralytic whose friends carried him to Jesus and asked Jesus to heal him. Jesus, looking at the broken man unable to move, lovingly said, "Son, thy sins be forgiven thee."

How strange this must have sounded to this man's ears. How strange it may sound to ours. Here is a man paralyzed. We look at him and see physical needs. Jesus looked at him and saw spiritual need. Ultimately Jesus met both the spiritual and physical needs of this man. But He did not give in to the pressure to be concerned first or only about the physical. He focused on the spiritual first – the need to be forgiven – and the physical need was secondary.

We're not like this. We tend to amplify the physical because it is the physical that is so real and present to us. It is easy for us to neglect the spiritual when the physical hurts.

As the paralytic was helpless before the Savior, so too are we. We cannot earn his healing. We receive. He pours grace and mercy into lives devastated by sin and sickness. He binds up the sin wound. He cuts out the infection. He gives us new life.

Will He heal us physically, too? Ultimately, yes! A resurrection day is coming, a day in which our bodies will be new. A day of leaping and rejoicing. And praising God. Forever. Yes, there is a day of physical wholeness coming. Until then, we must continue on. Until then, we must examine ourselves and make sure we know Jesus Messiah. Until then, we must reach out to others with truth and compassion. Until then we must endure, remembering that we are not alone no matter how lonely we may feel. For our God has promised never will He leave us nor will He forsake those who are His children.

Maybe I've used too many words to share a simple message. Jesus Christ is our only hope. He is the way, the truth, and the life. And He has great plans for you. Today. Right where you are. He is greater than your pain, greater than your loss, and greater than the enemy seeking to devour you.

It's all about surrender.

Give it all to Him.

Live palms up.

He will wipe dry your tears.

He will pour His Spirit upon you.

He will heal your hurting heart.

He will forgive your sins.

He will give you everlasting life in a whole and resurrected body.

He will be with you.

He will reveal to you love that is deep and high and wide and long.

He will bear you up on eagle's wings and underneath you will be His everlasting arms.

He will call you His.

Fight the lies of the enemy with the truth of the risen Savior, the soon and coming King.

AUGUST 28

This is both crushing and freeing.

Dots are being connected.

What I have always sensed is becoming belief.

There is more going on behind the scenes of the world stage than I ever could have imagined. There is a spiritual enemy at work and his most powerful generals operate secretly and obscurely, nameless agents as far as the masses of humanity are concerned.

Did every teacher I ever had in school and college lie to me? Have I been a sheep misled by teachers and professors with good intentions but bad doctrine and evil worldviews?

I have a history/government degree. The crowd applauded as I walked across the stage and accepted my diploma, as though I had accomplished something. But now I'm not so sure I accomplished anything, at least not anything of value.

I am realizing that despite a history/government degree, I know next to nothing about real history and real government. Instead, I know what "they" want me to know.

It's hard to believe people who are patting you on the back are lying to you. Their praise tickles the ears, stirs the pride, ends the questions...and dumbly and dully and dutifully I have marched over the decades to the beating repetitious drum of progressive education.

But God.

There's more to the story of history than what I have been told, isn't there? Help me, Jehovah, I want to know the truth. I want to glorify You. And that includes glorifying You in my mind by demanding truth from those who teach me.

I'm sorry for all the moments wasted...all the small moments when the world and its ways have distracted me. I've spent more time thinking about how to have a clear complexion, less gray hair, whiter teeth, and a better shaped body than I have thinking about truth. I want to be done with the smaller stuff and the lesser things.

Lead me, Lord, on a plain and clear path. Help me to see and walk in truth. Help me to think and discover and sort through the confusion and distractions. Help me to find and fulfil Your purpose for this brief life.

And as I learn hard truths, let me not become hard. May I always be pliable in Your great hands. Give me thick skin, a tender heart, and a strong mind.

I feel fear fading. Fear has been a lifelong companion. Yet as I gain a glimpse of the huge size of the real war that wages between powers and principalities often unseen, I realize I cannot fight this. It's too big. I must depend on You, God. This is Your battle. And I am Yours. And fear is fading.

AUGUST 29

Dear Father,

Thank You for putting up with me. You are longsuffering, and Your mercy is abundant toward me even though Your mercy is undeserved. I deserve to be consumed in Your righteous judgment. But instead, You made a way. Instead of consuming me, You are purifying me.

How we deserve Your punishment! Oh, Lord, we bitterly complain and declare emphatically that our complaints are justified. We proclaim our innocence and goodness and chafe against the idea of You as the final authority and perfect judge. But we are fools to do so, and our grumbling against this truth is merely announcing that we have failed to recognize that You are greater than we.

You are not a "big guy in the sky" or the "man upstairs."

You are GOD ALMIGHTY, the author of life and truth, the creator of all. So, shame on us for making a god, an idol in our minds that merely suits our tastes and makes us comfortable. We have limited You in our minds. But, You are unlimited in reality. You will judge whether we like it or not. You need not our permission to judge us righteously.

Almighty Lord, You are perfectly holy and perfectly just. Any who are unclean cannot be in Your presence. And who amongst us is not unclean? Yes, we clean up the outside some of the time. But, that just makes us whitewashed tombs. We try hard to clean ourselves, but with the dirty water we are using apart from You, all we accomplish is covering up the filth that remains within. We attempt to be righteous, but our own righteousness leads only to pride, not to cleanness.

And it is clean that we must be.

What can we do? To Whom can we go?

For it is a dreadful thing to fall into the hands of the living God, the God Who knows all our thoughts and sees clearly our motivations and the intentions of our hearts.

You KNOW us!

And it is dreadful to be known.

Your light exposes what is really within us, and it is not pretty.

But God. There is Christ. There is His righteousness. He is the Clean One. He is clean within and without. We can be, and must be, clothed in His righteous garments. Our scarlet sins can be forgiven. The debt can be paid, but not by us, it must be paid by You or it will not be settled. We who are dirty and stained can be clean.

All because of Christ. He is the only way, the only truth, the only life.

We are without hope if we are without Christ.

AUGUST 30

From <u>The Hiding Place</u> by Corrie ten Boom [33]

It was at a church service in Munich that I saw him, the former S.S. man who had stood guard at the shower room door in the processing center at Ravensbruck concentration camp.

He was the first of our actual jailers that I had seen since that time.

And suddenly it was all there - the roomful of mocking men, the heaps of clothing, Betsie's pain-blanched face.

He came up to me as the church was emptying, beaming and bowing. "How grateful I am for your message, Fraulein." He said. "To think that, as you say, Jesus has washed my sins away!" His hand was thrust out to shake mine. And I, who had preached so often to the people in Bloemendaal (a home in Holland opened to help holocaust victims shortly after the war ended) the need to forgive, kept my hand at my side.

Even as the angry, vengeful thoughts boiled through me, I saw the sin of them. Jesus Christ had died for this man; was I going to ask for more? Lord Jesus, I prayed, forgive me and help me to forgive him. I tried to smile, I struggled to raise my hand. I could not. I felt nothing, not the slightest spark of warmth or charity. and so again, I breathed a silent prayer. Jesus, I cannot forgive him. Give me Your forgiveness.

As I took his hand, the most incredible thing happened. From my shoulder, along my arm and through my hand, a current seemed to pass from me to him, while into my heart sprang a love for this stranger that almost overwhelmed me. And so I discovered that it is not on our forgiveness any more than on our goodness that the world's healing hinges, but on His.

When He tells us to love our enemies, He gives, along with the command, the love itself. **From <u>The Hiding Place</u> by Corrie ten Boom [33]**

AUGUST 31

Dear Father, Light of the world,

I shout for joy to You, LORD! May all the earth shout for joy! I worship You, LORD, in gladness, and I come before You with joyful songs.

I know that You, LORD, are God. It is You who created, powerfully and beautifully. You made me, LORD, and I am Yours. I am a sheep in Your pasture. May my heart be ever seeking to enter Your gates with thanksgiving and Your courts with praise. There is, in Your presence the fullness of joy. I give thanks to You, LORD. I praise Your Name. For You are good and Your love endures forever. Your faithfulness continues through all generations.

Reach into the lives and the very hearts and minds of my family and shine. I pray for Your light to disclose and reveal and purify. Apart from You, Father, there is only lost-ness, hopelessness, and the wrath of a righteous God. Call my family, each and every one in all places where they may be, and equip them to find their way to You, to arrive at the foot of the cross and to cleave to the Savior. May they hear hints of rejoicing in the presence of angels over a sinner repenting, and may that sinner be them! May it be their names sung out in the heavenly rejoicing! May they go forward new creations in Christ heading in a new direction and shouting for joy.

In the Name of Jesus, Light of the world...

August's Apologetic Moment...Contend for the faith

Natural Selection and Mutations?

If the model of Darwinian evolution is true and all of life originated and evolved through only natural processes, then the model is obligated to provide an explanation for HOW this happened. Officially, the HOW is referred to as the "mechanisms of evolution."

Let's get some words straight from the mouths (or the website) of naturalists. The quotes below are taken from the University of California at Berkeley's website (**www.evolution.berkeley.edu/evolibrary/article/evo_16**):

"Each of these four processes is a basic mechanism of evolutionary change.

"Mutation. A mutation could cause parents with genes for bright green coloration to have offspring with a gene for brown coloration. That would make genes for brown coloration more frequent in the population than they were before the mutation.

"Migration. Some individuals from a population of brown beetles might have joined a population of green beetles. That would make genes for brown coloration more frequent in the green beetle population than they were before the brown beetles migrated into it.

"Genetic drift. Imagine that in one generation, two brown beetles happened to have four offspring survive to reproduce. Several green beetles were killed when someone stepped on them and had no offspring. The next generation would have a few more brown beetles than the previous generation – but just by chance. These chance changes from generation to generation are known as genetic drift.

"Natural selection. Imagine that green beetles are easier for birds to spot (and hence, eat). Brown beetles are a little more likely to survive to produce offspring. They pass their genes for brown coloration on to their offspring. So in the next generation, brown beetles are more common than in the previous generation.

"All of these mechanisms can cause changes in frequencies of genes in population, and so all of them are mechanisms of evolutionary change. However, natural selection and genetic drift cannot operate unless there is genetic variation – that is, unless some individuals are genetically different from others. If populations of beetles were 100%

green, selection and drift would not have any effect because their genetic make-up could not change."

Reading deeper into articles on the Berkeley website, one comes upon fancy sounding words...*advantageous intermediates, co-opting, adaptive radiation, differential reproduction, co-speciation...*

None of the mechanisms suggested or the fancy language used by the evolutionary model provide sufficient explanation for macroevolution (change from one kind to another kind). All of the suggested mechanisms explain only microevolution (change within a kind). Microevolution is simply speciation or adaptation or variation. Speciation is not macroevolution...thus mechanisms that explain speciation are not sufficient to explain macroevolution. Macroevolution would be a fish evolving into a bird. Microevolution is a bird evolving (through natural selection) a longer beak in order to better access the food sources of the area. We do not observe macroevolution. We do observe microevolution.

The naturalistic Darwinian evolutionary model claims MACROEVOLUTION, but offers mechanisms that prove only MICROEVOLUTION (speciation). Bait and switch...for green beetles and brown beetles are still beetles, after all.

Like Darwinian evolutionists, I too, recognize the power of mutations, migration, genetic drift, and natural selection to lead to great diversity. However, I also recognize the limits...for these mechanisms lead to beautiful diversity within a kind. These mechanisms perfectly fit the Biblical model; there is no contradiction and tension between the reality of these mechanisms and the claims of creation scientists. The tension comes when these mechanisms are stretched beyond viability for the purpose of building up the Darwinian – natural processes only – model. And there should be tension under these circumstances, not only because of the denial of Biblical tenets, but because these mechanisms are insufficient to explain how macroevolution could have happened.

The Darwinian evolutionary model makes sweeping claims. The model claims that all life originated and experienced variation and diversity as the result of natural processes ONLY. When one considers the complexity of life...when one considers even the complexity of a single cell...when one considers the fact that information is coded in a complex DNA system...one must admit that the claims of Darwinists are bold. And, bold claims require evidence. Evidence for microevolution (speciation) is simply not evidence for macroevolution. A leap of faith is indeed required if one is going to proclaim macroevolution while clinging to the only available evidence – evidence for microevolution.

If there were mechanisms that demonstrated macroevolution, would not they be offered up?

Where are these needed mechanisms?

I suggest they do not exist.

There is much more to say about all of these. There are technical arguments that could be unwrapped and dissected. But, for now, I'll leave it at this…Let's at least agree to be honest.

I support the creation science model of origins and diversity of life. Faith is required to do so. But, I believe this model is logical, rational, and fits well what we observe.

Supporters of the Darwinian evolutionary model, too, must have faith. Their faith lies in their starting assumptions about naturalism, age of the earth, origin of life, and mechanisms of macroevolution.

If you support the Darwinian evolutionary model, at least honestly admit that mechanisms that explain speciation are insufficient to explain macroevolution.

EXTRA: I have reluctantly included the terms "macroevolution" and "microevolution" in this section. These are not the best terms to use. However, I included them because I think they help draw a clearer preliminary picture of the scientific flaws in Darwinian evolution. Below is an excerpt from Creation Ministries International's website (www.creation.com) that describes why the terms macro- and micro- evolution are not the best vocabulary:

These terms, which focus on 'small' v. 'large' changes, distract from the key issue of information. That is, particles-to-people evolution requires changes that increase genetic information (e.g., specifications for manufacturing nerves, muscle, bone, etc.), but all we observe is sorting and, overwhelmingly, loss of information. We are hard pressed to find examples of even 'micro' increases in information, although such changes should be frequent if evolution were true. Conversely, we do observe quite 'macro' changes that involve no new information, e.g. when a control gene is switched on or off. Importantly, the term microevolution will be seen by many as just a 'little bit' of the process that they think turned bacteria to people. In other words, it implies that simply given enough time (millions of years), such 'micro' changes will accumulate to amount to 'macro' changes. But this is not so.

Behold, I send you forth as sheep in the midst of wolves:
be ye therefore wise as serpents and harmless as doves.
Matthew 10:16

September

"Forgive me for being so ordinary
while claiming to know so extraordinary a God."
— Jim Elliot

SEPTEMBER 1

A great life is made up of many small moments, moments in which we act in obedience to the Word and Ways of God.

Strive for excellence…do things well…even when no one is looking.

A little folly, a little sin, a little indulging of the flesh are big enough to wreck a great life.

"If Satan can't make you sin, he'll try to make you busy." (Adrian Rogers)

"If the thing is worth doing at all, it is worth doing well." (G.K. Chesterton)

"If you run with skunks you are going to end up smelling like one." (author unknown)

The fear of man is a snare. Beware of peer pressure.

Don't be like a city with broken down walls. Discipline yourself and be self-controlled. You are not an animal – you can restrain yourself from going after everything your flesh desires in the moment.

Don't worry about being part of the majority.

But make sure you are part of the remnant.

Be ready before you need to be ready.

Be a person of your word.

Failing is not the same as being a failure.

Remember, when you fail, there is a God who can take those failures and make them useful.

Cultivate quietness in a very noisy world.

SEPTEMBER 2

"Most people, sometime in their lives, stumble across the truth. Most jump up, brush themselves off and hurry on about their business as if nothing had happened." *(Winston Churchill)*

Truth matters.

Absolute truth exists, and there is a war going on against it.

Demand truth…from others…and within your own mind.

Ideas have consequences.

God's Word is truth…not your feelings…not your experiences.

Think about what you are thinking about.

Think in complete thoughts.

Think before you speak.

Don't think like a victim.

Don't be functionally illiterate when it comes to God's Word. Know, really know, His Word.

If you do not know God's Word…if it's not hidden in your heart and tucked in the corners of your mind…you will be deceived in this world and you will compromise what should not be compromised.

Work hard.

Be humble.

Sometimes less is more and sometimes more is more. Be wise to know which one is needed in any given moment.

If you don't know what you are talking about, don't talk.

SEPTEMBER 3

Be like Abel: offer your best even if it costs you your life.

Be like Noah: build an ark and bring your family into it.

Be like Abraham: when called to leave all that you know and are comfortable with, go. Sojourn into the land of promise.

Be like Joseph: when you are tempted don't just stand there looking for loopholes and ways to justify sinful behavior. Rather, FLEE!

Be like the Israelites: come out of Egypt.

Be like Moses: stand in the gap.

Be like Joshua: Fear not, be of good courage! Seek God and trust Him.

Be like David: when you sin, repent. Be a man after God's own heart.

Be like David: face Goliath with your small, smooth stones, your simple slingshot, and your Great God.

Be like Ezra and Nehemiah: reinforce foundations and rebuild broken down walls.

Be like Mary: live palms up with a heart that cries out, "Behold the handmaid of the Lord; be it unto me according to thy word."

Be like John the Baptist: decrease so that Jesus Christ can increase.

Be like Peter: step out of the boat.

Be like Zacchaeus: do whatever you must to get near to Christ. Climb a tree.

Be like Stephen: lift your eyes and behold Jesus, standing at the right hand of the throne of God, interceding for you.

Be like Paul: rejoice even when bound in prison, held between guards, suffering for the faith.

Don't be like Lot: don't pitch your tent toward Sodom.

Don't be like Lot's wife: don't look back and long for the old life.

Don't be like Esau: don't sell your birthright just because your flesh is hungry.

Don't be like the Israelites: don't grumble and complain and end up wandering in the wilderness.

Don't be like Aaron: build not a golden calf, a useless idol, the work of a man's hands.

Don't be like Judas: wear not a mask, pretending to be something you are not. Betray not the Savior.

Don't be stubborn and hard-hearted.

Be a vessel fit for the Master's use, a vessel designed and crafted by Him.

Be pliable in His capable hands, and let Him have His way with your life.

SEPTEMBER 4

Home. We arrived home from a short trip to St. Augustine on Friday. We needed this time away and this time together.

But always it's good to get home.

We drove our black Elantra 1100 miles down and back. We stayed at the Casablanca Inn on San Marcos Drive overlooking the bay in the heart of the city. Each morning, we enjoyed breakfast on a charming veranda, our waitress a sweet girl named Rose. Every morning, we watched the sun rise over the water of the bay. One morning, we got up really early and drove the darkened streets of the city and over the Bridge of Lions to the beaches of Anastasia Island. We watched the sun rise over the ocean, waves crashing, sand between our toes...eyes and ears beholding the glory and power of our great Creator God.

We rode the trolley through town. Toured the Presbyterian Church built by Henry Flagler after his daughter died while giving birth to his grandchild. Walked St. George Street. Visited the Fort. Ate at the White Lion and at Sonny's B-B-Q. Walked over the Bridge of Lions and witnessed a minor accident between a car and a motorcycle while on the bridge. Got sunburned on our first day there.

Everything had a feel of uniqueness about it, as though this could be our last time here. While this may sound sad, it's not. Recognition of mortality can cause moments to grow sweeter still.

On Wednesday night, we went to a worship service at the Anastasia Baptist Church on the Island. The church complex was huge, but the congregation meeting in the sanctuary for Wednesday night pray was small and intimate. Songs were sung. Prayers were lifted up. Praise was shared. The Word was read and discussed. These were strangers, people with names I no longer remember. Yet, there was familiarity and comfort one with another because we are of the same family, the family of God. We share what matters most of all – salvation through Christ. This is beautiful. Far away from home, yet family near.

On our last morning in St. Augustine, I walked one last time down to the Fort. I was captivated as I walked – for the first time – into the dry mote of the Fort. Many times I have been in the Fort and have explored its rooms and heard its history. I have stood on top of the Fort, next to the cast iron and bronze cannons, looking over and into the mote far below. But this time, as the sun was coming over the horizon, I ventured down into the mote. It was unlike what I expected…a completely different perspective. The walls of the Fort were suddenly huge. Much of the city disappeared from view, leaving only roof peaks in the line of my vision. I could no longer see the bay, but could still hear waves crescendo in rhythm. Traffic noise diminished. I was sheltered by the wall of the Fort on one side and the wall of the mote on the other. It felt very safe. I was fascinated. This was a new perspective. The busyness of a waking city was replaced with a beautiful calm.

Beauty exists in even this, our fallen and groaning earth. The ocean – looking over it and seeing no end to it, knowing that it is wide and deep and teeming with life. Feeling the chill of its water as it flows over my toes and carries sand from beneath my feet as it returns to the boundaries set by God. Me jumping into the waves as they rushed to shore. Me, lifted up by waves and carried along by the power and energy of water moving. Loving it, yet slightly fearful of the great power of God's Atlantic Ocean. I was the only middle aged woman in the water that morning. I, in an unflattering and outdated bathing suit, in the waters of the Atlantic…worshiping the Lord…Creator, Redeemer, Giver of Life.

SEPTEMBER 5

How creative God is!

Yesterday, I stood on the shore of the Atlantic Ocean, sand under my feet, waves crashing, sea gulls crying above.

Today, I am surrounded by the mountains of West Virginia.

The stark contrast of ocean and mountains speaks of the creativity of the God who formed both. Each uniquely reflects the power of God. Here in West Virginia, rock and strata rise high and stand strong, flanking both sides of us as we, in our little car and our little lives, move among the grandeur of God's handiwork. Like the ocean, the mountains are beautiful. Like the ocean, somewhat frightening. We drive by faith, not certain of what is around the next twist and bend of the mountainous highway. We speed over Route 77, through Big Walker Mountain Tunnel and East River Tunnel – tunnels sliced through mountains by the hand of man.

Driving under the mountain through the tunnel, we have faith the mountain will not crush the path upon which we drive. We exit the tunnel, other side of the mountain, safe and sound. We must live by faith in the God who raised up these mountains, in the God who gifted men with the ability to tunnel through mountains, in the God who sets the boundaries of the seas. He is the God who sees us driving our Elantra and He cares about who we are and where we are going.

Journeying through the Appalachians of West Virginia, we missed our exit from Route 77 onto Route 19. We drove miles before realizing our error. The mountains were steeper and taller on our unexpected detour. The road was unfamiliar. We were in coal country. Unlike my husband, I loved our detour. I enjoyed our detour quietly, not wanting to increase Mark's anxiety by rubbing his face in my joy. It is good to be sensitive to the struggles of those near us.

This is an interesting season of life. But aren't they all?

I'll end my reminiscences with this…as I lingered long in the waves of the ocean, my husband remained patiently on the beach. He was enjoying me enjoying the ocean. He found an ivory colored shell. He picked it up and brought it home. At home, he gave it to me and told me how he took it to remember our time together.

This is worship! Finding God in all things and recognizing His goodness in the details that whisper in our lives.

Memories.

Thank you, Lord, for memories.

SEPTEMBER 6

Lord,

For all my family near and far, I pray.

I pray for those in my family who are facing trials. May such difficulties drive them to You. And, Lord, if trials are necessary to humble the proud to the point of repentance, then I pray for the blessing of trials and the gift of repentance.

As for my brethren in the faith, help us, Lord, to glorify You in our trials, temptations, disappointments, and even our failures.

May we, by Your mercy, count it all joy when troubles come. Develop within us hearts and minds of trust. Cultivate perseverance in us, Lord. In the days of ease and plenty, perseverance is not needed. But, in days of trouble, perseverance is both necessary and rare. May we be a strong people, the rare type who not only persevere in a trial, but grow.

Thank You, Lord, that You do not change like shifting shadows.

Thank You for the good and perfect gifts given by You.

Help us, Lord, to be a people quick to listen, slow to speak, slow to anger.

May we desire the righteous life that You only can bestow.

May the Word be planted in each heart in my family, and may the seed grow deep roots, aromatic flowers, and nourishing fruit.

May we look into Your righteous law and never, ever forget our desperate need for You.

In Christ's Immutable Name…

SEPTEMBER 7

Today, I had a war with a wheelchair. It's our daughter's wheelchair.

After that I had a war with my attitude.

I lost both.

Today is Sarah's first day back to school. I should have adjusted the wheelchair days ago. Actually, I should not have been adjusting it at all. Who am I to move and change and rearrange parts (some of them very small by the way)? Sarah's wheelchair is complicated. I am not competent to be taking it apart and putting it back together.

I failed to acknowledge my limitations and decided I would, qualified or not, adjust this chair. Now. Right before we were supposed to be out the door for day one at school.

I didn't think the adjustments would take too long. I just wanted to raise the back of the chair a little bit. Raising the back would move the lateral supports up (these are under Sarah's arms) and would move the head support up, too. Seemed like a necessary adjustment and a good idea.

Necessary, perhaps, but not necessarily necessary on the first day of school.

Old habits – such as foolishness – die hard. So, I foolishly jumped into a project for which I was, literally, ill-equipped. I made the adjustments. I cleaned the chair. I was just about done when I noticed something I had never noticed before. The back of the wheelchair could be adjusted to allow a little bit of recline. Just a couple of nuts and bolts on each side to remove. Might as well try it, huh?

I grabbed a wrench (at least I think that's what it was), don't ask me what size, but it seemed to fit the nut on the end of the bolt pretty well, and I removed bolt number one. Then, I removed bolt number two. Then number three. Finally, number four. Nothing to it! I was quite impressed with myself! Bolts removed, adjustments could be made, and then bolts could be returned.

Except, each bolt needed to fit through 4 aligned holes. It was easy to remove bolts from 4 aligned holes. Replacing them was not. I tugged and pushed and pulled. Suddenly some little part that had been tucked between a couple pieces of metal fell to the ground. I'd never seen a part quite like this. It wasn't a washer...too fat for that, and it was misshapen, clearly needing to fit exactly one way and one way only against the pieces of metal from which it fell. I learned later, when I actually pulled out the owner's manual, that this little part is called a "coved spacer." At that point, though, I could care less what it was called, and I was wondering if I could just throw it away?

Tick, tick, tock, tick, tock, tick...The clock was ticking away...school was soon to begin and Sarah was still in bed...

With eyes swelling with tears of frustration, I persisted.

Suddenly the back of the wheelchair crashed with a loud thud onto the concrete floor. Panic set in. The tears that had balanced on my eyes began to slide down my face. They were not sad sobs. They were mad sobs. I started to pray. *"Please*

God, help me put together my mess. I don't know what I was thinking! I shouldn't have started this project. It was dumb. Help me, please help me get all these parts back together!"

What a silly little child I must have looked at that moment as I sat on the cold concrete basement floor, late for the day, disheveled, crying.

It was time to apologize. *"God, I'm sorry. I rushed foolishly into this. I created this mess. I have no one to blame but myself. Please help me."* And He did. He calmed my heart and He steadied my hands. As my breathing returned to normal and my eyes dried, I gently, slowly slipped each bolt into its place.

War with the wheelchair was now over.

Wheelchair had won.

How often the small stuff becomes the big stuff!

It's all about perspective. What matters? Stuff and schedules? If stuff and schedules matter most, then prepare to live a stressed out life. Prepare to become overwhelmed when little things go wrong. Something as small as a "coved spacer" threatened to wreck this God-given day for me. Are my thoughts so small that a piece of plastic can cause such despair?

My life is truly abundant only when my eyes are on God. Abundance, joy, and success have much less to do with circumstances than they have to do with perspective, and to whom I place my trust and faith. The ever present and always available Word of God is medicine to tired souls if we will only open up, consume the medicine, and make Him the biggest part of who we are and how we think. Our days may be brighter and our loads may be lighter if we actually do put Him on the throne of our lives.

SEPTEMBER 8

Truth.

Christians are to be all about love, yes. But we are also supposed to be all about truth. And truth, especially truth in love, is willing to confront and challenge, and be courageous.

Christian love is not to be mushy love.

Mushy love is love following the path of least resistance.

We are to be both love and truth.

And that takes work. Prayer. Determination. Persistence. Endurance. Courage.

SEPTEMBER 9

Jehovah-Raah,

There is an enemy, and he hates You and he hates us. We are nothing to him except pawns that he can toy with to try and grieve You. To the adversary, we are sheep to slaughter.

Father, You became flesh and walked among us. You took upon Yourself the pain and brokenness of humanity and allowed Yourself to be led like a sheep to that slaughter. You became the perfect lamb to take away the sins of the world. Sadly, much of the world, then and now, cares nothing about having their sins taken away. They love their sin and despise Your right to judge. They despise and reject Your sacrifice, Your formal and full payment. Between lust and pride, they refuse You.

But, thanks be to God! Not all refuse.

Thanks be to You, Lord, that in You I am more than a conqueror through Him, my Mighty Savior, who loved us. Through Him sin, death, and hell are defeated, and I stand in Him a victor!

He, my Savior, is a sweet smelling aroma of life renewed and hope restored. His cross is sweet to me, the blood is beautiful!

To those perishing, the cross is a gory stinking mess and mere foolishness.

What is foolishness to the perishing is salvation to me.

May each in my family be a saved conqueror breathing in the fresh, sweet fragrance of Your great salvation!

In the Name of the Lord my Shepherd...

SEPTEMBER 10

From <u>A Shepherd Looks at Psalm 23</u> by W. Phillip Keller [34]

"For the man or woman who recognizes the claim of Christ and gives allegiance to His absolute ownership, there comes the question of bearing His mark. The mark of the cross is that which should identify us with Him for all time. The question is – does it?

"Jesus made it clear when He state emphatically, 'if anyone would come after me, he must deny himself and take up his cross daily and follow me.'

"Basically what it amounts to is this: A person exchanges the fickle fortunes of living life by sheer whimsy for the more productive and satisfying adventure of being guided by God.

"It is a tragic truth that many people who really have never come under His direction or management claim that 'The Lord is my shepherd.' They seem to hope that by merely admitting that He is their Shepherd somehow they will enjoy the benefits of His care and management without paying the price of forfeiting their own fickle and foolish way of life.

"One cannot have it both ways. Either we belong or we don't. Jesus Himself warned us that there would come a day when many would say, 'Lord, in Your name we did many wonderful things,' but He will retort that He never knew us as His own.

"It is a most serious and sobering thought which should make us search our own hearts and motives and personal relationship to Him.

"Do I really belong to Him?

"Do I really recognize His right to me?

"Do I respond to His authority and acknowledge His ownership?

"Do I find freedom and complete fulfillment in this arrangement?

"Do I sense a purpose and deep contentment because I am under His direction?

"Do I know rest and repose, besides a definite sense of exciting adventure, in belonging to him?

"If so, then with genuine gratitude and exaltation I can exclaim proudly, just as David did, 'The Lord is my shepherd!' and I'm thrilled to belong to Him, for it is thus that I shall flourish and thrive no matter what life may bring to me....

"It is all indicative of the unrelenting energy and industry of an owner who wishes to see his sheep satisfied and well fed. It all denotes my Shepherd's desire to see my best interests served. His concern for my care is beyond my comprehension, really. At best all I can do is to enjoy and revel in what He has brought into effect.

"This life of quiet overcoming, of happy repose, of rest in His presence, of confidence in His management is something few Christians ever fully enjoy.

"Because of our own perverseness we often prefer to feed on the barren ground of the world around us. I used to marvel how some of my sheep actually chose inferior forage at times.

"But the Good Shepherd has supplied green pastures for those who care to move in onto them and there find peace and plenty".
From *A Shepherd Looks at Psalm 23* by W. Phillip Keller [34]

SEPTEMBER 11

Lord,

Help me, my husband, our families to submit to You.

The desires and the battles within us lead to fighting and quarreling, grumbling, gossiping, backbiting.

Sin.

Lord, help us to have right motives. We must have settled accounts with You in order to have right motives. Father, You oppose the proud, but give grace to the humble. Teach us to be humble. To submit to You. To resist the devil. Father, enable us to come near to You. We are double-minded, unclean people. May we grieve, mourn, and cry out for a right relationship with you, Lord. Teach us to humble ourselves so that You can lift us up.

Keep us from boasting. Truly, there is very little that we control. We can plan and prepare, but ultimately, if it's not Your will, it will not be. Our lives appear for a little while. Then they vanish. Like a mist. May we recognize the great frailty of life and our desperate need for You and Your abundant ability and willingness to carry us through, to meet our deepest needs, and to purify us with the sacred blood of Jesus.

In Christ's Gracious Name…

SEPTEMBER 12

Father,

You are the God of Abraham, Isaac and Jacob.

Be the God of my life in every detail and moment. Become and be the God of every person in my family now and in the generations yet to come. Cover, protect and fill each of my students…students from the past, students now, and those in the years yet to be.

Lord, I pray for rest, the rest that comes from being right with You.

Turn our hearts and minds toward You, to walk in Your ways and keep Your commands. Uphold my cause, unless my cause is wicked. And Lord, if there be any wicked way in me, tear it out.

Meet each day's needs. But help me to remember that You, Lord, are the judge of what is needful and what is not.

May all the peoples of the earth know that the LORD is God and there is no other! May each person in my family and classroom know that the LORD is God and there is no other!

Our hearts and minds must be fully committed to You. Help us to understand and to do this. Father, may all the kingdoms on earth and each and every person in this family in which I am a part know that You ALONE, O LORD, are God.

You are light.

You are glory.

May Your light and Your glory blaze in my heart.

Shine brightly in a way that is clear, obvious, and absolutely undeniable in each heart. Save the lost!

In Jesus' Eternal Name…

SEPTEMBER 13

Father,

May we hunger for righteousness, the righteousness that comes from You, the righteousness of which You are the source.

I pray for each person in my family to desire You above all else.

May there be an appetite for Your Word within each.

Help us, Lord, to rightly divide and understand Your Word.

You have given us sound minds.

Now, give us the desire to yield these sound minds back to You and to learn all we can about who You are.

May our hearts and minds burn with longing to be near You and to know You more fully! May our flesh thirst for You in a dry and weary land.

In Christ's Compassionate Name…

SEPTEMBER 14

Dear Lord,

Your Word is full! So wonderful!

Teach us, Lord, to love Your Word and to desire it more than the sweetest dessert. We will be deceived, and easily so, if we do not know You and Your truth etched in the Bible.

Teach us, Lord, to follow Your decrees.

Give us understanding to keep Your law and to obey it with all our hearts.

Lord, direct us in the path of Your commands, for there we will find delight.

Lord, turn our hearts and minds toward Your statutes and not toward selfish gain.

Turn our eyes away from worthless things.

Preserve our lives.

Fulfill Your promises to Your servants.

Equip us to know that if we have not been saved, then we are not Yours and neither, then, are we beneficiaries of Your promises. We cannot claim Your promises if to You we have not yet come.

Your promises are intended for Your children.

You want to save and rescue the lost and pour Your goodness, truth, and promises upon suffering and deceived souls.

May we stand still and experience Your salvation.

Your great deliverance.

Bring us through the waters of the Red Sea, out of Egypt and into Your Kingdom.

Take away the disgrace I dread.

Your laws are good. So much greater and purer than my way.

May I long for Your precepts.

For only in truth, which You are, is there comfort and safety.

Preserve my life in Your righteousness!

In Christ's Merciful Name…

SEPTEMBER 15

From Foxe: Voices of the Martyrs [35]

Janani Luwum (1922 – 1977)

"Janani Luwum was killed by the president of the Republic of Uganda, Idi Amin, on February 16, 1977. That same year the Christian church in Uganda marked 100 years of existence.

"Janani Luwum was born in Northern Uganda and began his career as an ordained minister in the Anglican Church in 1956, in the Northern Uganda diocese. Later he trained in theology at St. Augustine College in Canterbury and at the London College of Divinity in the UK. He rose through the ranks from a priest to become archbishop. An active member of the East African Revival Fellowship since 1948, Janani is remembered as one who always told his congregations, 'God does not have grandchildren. He only has sons and daughters.' He always urged people to have a living personal relationship with God through Jesus and not depend on one's parents' faith. The East African Revival also taught, and Luwum certainly believed, that God is never absent, no matter how difficult life becomes. When Luwum was accused of treason – death sure to follow – he replied to Amin, 'We must see the hand of God in this.'

"Luwum became archbishop of the Anglican Church in Uganda, Rwanda, Burundi, and Boga-Zaire in 1974. Trouble started when he began criticizing the gross human rights abuses perpetrated by the Amin regime, including public executions, disappearances, and expulsions. Property was regularly confiscated without due process. As head of the Church of Uganda, Luwum publicly confronted this lawlessness in the pulpit. Very few critics of Idi Amin who did not flee for their lives survived his eight-year reign of terror.

"After Luwum was killed, his family and some of the bishops of the Anglican Church fled the country, but his death certainly strengthened opposition to Amin's brutality. The church continued under intense persecution until two years later in April 1979, when the regime fell to a combined force of Ugandan rebels and the Tanzanian troops.

"Life was cheap in Idi Amin's Uganda. People lost their lives for small things such as having a nice car or a beautiful wife. These were the ills Janani Luwum had the courage to say were against the will of God. Today he is honored as one voice crying in the wilderness when few dared to speak out." **From <u>Foxe: Voices of the Martyrs</u>** [35]

SEPTEMBER 16

Abiding in Him.

He the vine. I the branch.

Jesus is the true vine, and I am a mere, yet highly valued, branch.

From Him flows living water and life and truth.

I am to receive. I am to abide. In Him.

But, what does this abiding look like?

Abiding means waiting. Quietly. Patiently. Peacefully. God's timing requires waiting, and waiting requires abiding.

Abiding demands humility. I must be low. He must be exalted. I must be small. He must be big. I must be nothing. He must be everything.

Abiding grows in surrender. The funny thing about surrendering to the Lord is that it is the one time in which surrender actually results in victory! I am to surrender my rights, my expectations, my comforts, my schedule, my life. Everything must become His. A palm's up life is a life of abiding.

Abiding is birthed in gratitude, a holy gratitude for all things easy and for all things hard.

Abiding results in perseverance. As we abide, we persevere in times of trials and in times of failure, in times of joy and in times of success.

Abiding believes that God is who He says He is and He will do what He has promised to do.

Abiding nourishes a heart and mind that is calm even when the body is busy, quiet in the midst of noisy, and steady in stormy seas.

Abiding is His strength for my weakness…His beauty for my ashes…His joy for my sorrow…His certainty for my confusion.

Abiding flows from His grace. I cannot make myself abide. But for the fountain of His beautiful grace!

Abiding…eyes on the Throne of God. Knees bent, body bowed. Mouth praising. Mind on You, O God. Seeing You, Lord, in all things. I'm at Your mercy, Father. All I have is You. And You are enough.

Have Your own way, yes, have Your own way.

Abiding…the Son has set me free, and I am free indeed!

SEPTEMBER 17

How do I abide when I am in a hurry?

I am rushing out the basement door, loaded down with my bags of books, on my way to school, on my way to life with my kids. I am late, yet able to see the large snowflakes falling around me as beautiful.

I slow my pace, I lift my face, and fat snowflakes fall on my warm cheeks and melt and slide. This same snow that later will need to be shoveled and plowed, is gently falling now on me. Gratitude wells up within, warming me from the inside out.

This is a glimpse, and God has given me eyes to see beauty in even this, our fallen world, a world that groans. The glory of God's Kingdom is coming. In the chaos of the planet, I sense that God is yet on the throne, always in control. I am gripped in the safety of His sovereignty.

It is here, in this moment of stillness in the busy, that I abide. And I carry the calm with me as I rush into the rest of the day.

SEPTEMBER 18

Abiding is built on the fear of the LORD...standing in awe, absolute speechless awe of who He is and what He does. It is trembling at His presence and perfect knowledge and righteous judgments.

He is a consuming fire! So it is consumed I must be...consumed with thoughts of Him as I live life. Consumed with discovering His purpose for my days. Consumed with casting my cares upon Him. Consumed with casting down idols and vain thoughts and imaginations in high places...crushing anything in my heart or mind that competes with Him for pre-eminence.

The gospel changes everything.

The gospel is about more than personal salvation. It is to influence every relationship, every decision, every conversation that I ever have from this day forward and beyond.

Abiding involves growing in the reality that it's all sacred. There is to be no dichotomy. All that I am and all that I do is His, and He is sacred, thus all of my life, too, is to be sacred and refined in His fires. From doing dishes to teaching teenagers to being a wife to serving in church...it's all His.

And it's all sacred if done to His glory. This is all that matters.

God breathes His truth into me...and I abide.

The joy of the Lord is my strength...and I abide.

In awe I fall before the feet of my Master, at the throne of this Great God in whose image I am made.

SEPTEMBER 19

Abiding...shedding tears at the graduation of my seniors each year...believing that God is doing a great work in them, that He is equipping them and will bring to completion all that He has begun. A strong foundation has been laid. Now they each must build. May their constructions be of gold and silver and precious stones.

Abiding means honesty. As my beloved seniors graduate each year, tears fall from my eyes and sorrow rises in my heart...not only because I will miss these seniors...but because with each step they take toward the stage of graduation, the scab of grief is ripped open and I am reminded that I will never have a child hand me a white rose. I will never hug my child in front of the sanctuary while a diploma is placed in the hands of an excited and nervous teenager ready to begin adult life. I will neither hear the applause nor share the accomplishments of my own child.

This reality is raw and new to me every graduation.

And while nobody else really knows that my tears fall for many reasons, my God knows.

And in Him, I abide.

And in Him, the victory has been already won.

Abiding...by grace alone.

SEPTEMBER 20

From _A Shepherd Looks at Psalm 23_ by W. Phillip Keller [36]

"...(I)n the terminology of the sheepman, 'summertime is fly time.' By this, reference is made to the hordes of insects that emerge with the advent of warm weather. Only those people who have kept livestock or studied wildlife habits are aware of the serious problems for animals presented by insects in the summer....

"Sheep are especially troubled by the nose fly, or nasal fly, as it is sometimes called. These little flies buzz about the sheep's head, attempting to deposit their eggs on the damp mucous membranes of the sheep's nose. If they are successful, the eggs will hatch in a few days to form small, slender, worm-like larvae. They work their way up the nasal passages into the sheep's head; they burrow into the flesh and there set up an intense irritation accompanied by severe inflammation.

"For relief from this agonizing annoyance sheep will deliberately beat their heads against trees, rocks, posts, or brush. They will rub them in the soil and thrash around against woody growth. In extreme cases of intense infestation a sheep may even kill itself in a frenzied endeavor to gain respite from the aggravation...

"All this excitement and distraction has a devastating effect on the entire flock...

"Only the strictest attention to the behavior of the sheep by the shepherd can forestall the difficulties of 'fly time'. At the very first sign of flies among the flock he will apply an antidote to their heads...What an incredible transformation this would make among the sheep. Once the oil had been applied to the sheep's head, there was an immediate change in behavior. Gone was the aggravation, gone the frenzy, gone the irritability and the restlessness. Instead, the sheep would start to feed quietly again, then soon lie down in peaceful contentment.

"This, to me, is the exact picture of irritations in my own life. How easy it is for there to be a fly in the ointment of even my most lofty spiritual experience! So often it is the small, petty annoyances that ruin my repose. It is the niggling distractions that become burning issues that can well-nigh drive me round the bend or up the wall. At times some tiny tantalizing thing torments me to the point where I feel I am just beating my brains out.

"And so my behavior as a child of God degenerates to a most disgraceful sort of frustrated tirade.

"Just as with the sheep, there must be continuous and renewed application of oil to forestall the 'flies' in my life; there must be a continuous anointing of God's gracious Spirit to counteract the ever-present aggravations of personality conflicts....

"It is both a logical and legitimate desire for us to have the daily anointing of God's gracious Spirit upon our minds. God alone can form in us the mind of Christ. The Holy Spirit alone can give to us the attitudes of Christ. He alone makes it possible for us to react to aggravations and annoyances with quietness and calmness...

"It is this daily anointing of God's gracious Spirit upon my mind which produces in my life such personality traits as joy, contentment, love, patience, gentleness, and peace. What a contrast this is to the tempers, frustration, and irritableness which mar the daily conduct of so many of God's children."
From <u>A Shepherd Looks at Psalm 23</u> by W. Phillip Keller [36]

SEPTEMBER 21

Marriage.

One man. One woman. Covenant before a Holy God...this is considered old-fashioned in today's progressive culture...a culture that fails to recognize that the author of marriage is the very God of creation and order...a culture that distorts marriage into a "me-centered" shape and labels it optional.

God has a magnificent and exalted view of marriage.

Do we?

For marriage is not merely a picture of two people. The wedding day is not merely about a bride and a groom. Marriage is a sacred reflection of God's everlasting covenant with His people. It is a picture of His everlasting covenant with you.

My prayer for you is that you will develop and hold tightly God's glorious perspective on marriage. It is a covenant intended to endure through good times and bad, through thick and thin, through happy and sad, through years of plenty and years of leanness.

My own marriage started out very "me" centered. It has taken years of chiseling at the hardness of my heart to carve out a person who now understands that my marriage is not about me. It is not about my happiness. It is about the Lord. It is about His holiness.

There is a word in the Bible that today's culture at best rejects and at worst despises. The naughty word is "submission." Yes, it's true, the Bible does direct wives, shockingly, to submit to their husbands. May I share with you that I am not a wife for whom submission came easily. I remember reading that word in the book of Ephesians and thinking, "No way! That can't be for today!" In the early years of my marriage, I was clueless about Biblical submission. I was married in a church, I stood at an altar, but no one explained to me that Biblical submission is a beautiful gift under which we wives can find shelter and protection from the storms of life.

There is often a shallowness in our understanding of submission. We hear that word and immediately recoil, falsely believing that it means "to be made inferior" or "to be mistreated and taken advantage of." That's not at all what submission means from God's point of view! God knows that a body, such as a marriage, cannot exist and be healthy, with two heads. Thus, husbands are commanded to lead and to love their wives as Christ loved the church. May I suggest, that is no easy task! God has set a high standard for husbands. And, let's admit it, we wives are not always all that loveable. We have our days when we make it very difficult for our husbands to follow God's instructions to love us sacrificially. Nonetheless, God tells husbands to love, and commands wives to follow. Ultimately, both husband and wife are to submit to the Lord's authority in their lives. In a marriage, it is not about who is superior and who is inferior. It is about roles in a home that, when properly filled, lead to satisfying, God-honoring lives. Life is hard. But we often make it harder by ignoring God's practical instructions.

There is also the flawed idea of, "I'll give 50% IF he will." Or, from a Christian point of view, it may sound something like this: "I'll submit to his leadership IF he loves me like he was told to." But, it's not about each spouse giving a mere 50%. It's about each giving 100% even when the other is not.

It's not about demanding your rights. It's about laying down your rights, just as Christ did.

It's not about proudly promoting yourself. It is about humbly dying to self, just as Christ did.

There is something special about marriage that makes it a unique place in which to be conformed more and more into the image of Christ.

These things do not come naturally to these bodies of flesh. But in the Spirit, we can do all things through Christ who strengthens us. So, put on the full armor of God and prepare to press on toward the prize of the high calling of God in Christ Jesus.

Life is frail and fleeting. We have all laughed. And cried. We are each acquainted with joy as well as with sorrow. To each of us have come unique triumphs and unique trials. You will face challenges in life, the details of which are yet unknown. When Mark and I married, we had no idea the valleys we would walk through. None of us do. **Decide now**, before the challenges come, how you will respond to them. Purpose in your heart to cleave to God and to one another as husband and wife no matter what. **Decide now** to be faithful to God and one another no matter what. Be prepared to face the challenges before the challenges come. Be well-grounded in the truth that when the enemy comes in like a flood, the Lord will raise up a banner under which you can find shelter and safety. Go deep in the truth that God's grace is sufficient always and under all circumstances. He and He alone is enough. Be prepared to reflect the glory of God and proclaim His goodness. No matter what.

But from the beginning of the creation God made them male and female. For this cause shall a man leave his father and mother, and cleave to his wife; and they twain shall be one flesh: so then they are no more twain, but one flesh. What therefore God hath joined together, let not man put asunder (Mark 10:6-9).

SEPTEMBER 22

Wives...

Study your husband to know his heart. He's going to make mistakes. He's going to fall short of your expectations. He's not always going to say the right things. But, if you know his heart, you will be able to patiently extend grace.

Be slow to speak, swift to hear, and slow to anger

No matter how busy you are, make time for him. Be a good listener. It's easy to be interested in all that your husband has to say when you are first married. But the tendency is to lose that interest over time. Purposefully strive to always be interested in what your husband has to say. He will know you respect him if you do.

Don't ever lie...even about the supposed "little" things.

Don't try to manipulate your husband with your tears.

Never, ever joke about him at his expense.

Do not share your disagreements on Facebook.

Make sure you have someone in your life who will speak truth to you even when you don't want to hear it.

Don't let little things become big things. I look back at most of the moments when Mark and I have struggled in our marriage, and almost always, the problem started as something very small that became unnecessarily big.

Remember, we do face an enemy. There will be days, believe it or not, when you may be tempted to think the enemy is your husband. But, it's not your husband. The enemy we face is Satan and this adversary would love to destroy your marriage. Satan is a thief and a liar and wants to kill, steal and destroy all that is good. Be prepared to fight the good fight and know that you do not fight it alone.

The same God who created the universe and all that is therein, has promised to never leave you nor forsake you. The same God who sustains this universe and holds it together in His mighty power is the same God who has promised that, in Christ, we are more than conquerors.

And always, trust in the Lord with all your heart and lean not on your own understanding. In all your ways acknowledge Him, and He will direct your paths.

And pray. And pray. And pray some more…every day and fervently…for your home, your marriage, your husband…

In my marriage, Lord, help me…
To esteem my husband better than I.
To respect my husband.
To follow my husband and to encourage him in the difficult task of leading.
To bring my husband good, not harm, all the days of my life.
To be willing to overlook an offense.
To be longsuffering.
To remember that love is patient and love is kind.
To remember that love is not rude nor is it self-seeking.
To remember that love keeps no record of wrongs and it keeps hoping.

Lord…
Guard my heart.
Guard my mind and my thoughts.
Guard my mouth.
Protect me from having an unforgiving heart.
Protect me from having an unrepentant heart.
Protect me from any roots of bitterness taking hold.
Protect me from pride.

And, forgive me, Lord.
I am not a perfect wife.
I am not always even a good wife.
But, I love my husband and I love You, Lord.
And I want to honor You.
I want to be the wife that you expect me to be.
The wife that you will help me to be through the power of the Holy Spirit.
Forgive me when I fall short and help me to press on in Christ.

There may be scars and wounds that exist in our marriages.
But, there is hope and there is healing and it can be found in Your truth, Lord.

In a world that is hostile to You as author of marriage…
Lord equip us to remember…
To remember that You are the source and the reason.
To remember that You are holy.
To remember that marriage is a covenant.

To remember You. Always and in all places.
To hunger and thirst for righteousness.
To seek first the Kingdom of God.
With all our heart, soul, mind, and strength…

SEPTEMBER 23

I remember standing in the spare room across the hall from Sarah's room.

It was dark.

I was holding Sarah.

It was time for her to go to bed, and I had stepped quietly into the spare room.

I was praying.

As I left the room, I realized that's how I pray – I say my words and then I leave.

I don't really listen or wait or sit quietly.

I talk and then I leave. It's like talking with God at my front door. We chat (or I chat) and we share (or I share) and when we (or I) are all done, I close the door and go on about my business in quite an independent way.

I leave God standing outside of my life. He knocks. But I am busy. Or tired. Or irritated.

He waits.

I rush around, full of self.

Idiot…this is a good adjective for me.

Jesus does not want to stand outside my door.

He wants to be in my home, my heart, my mind, my life. All of it, all of me, all the time.

He is willing to be there as I decide what to make for dinner, as I do the laundry and change Sarah's diapers. He is willing to spend time with me when I am quiet and when I am crazy. He wants me to come to Him with everything, the extraordinary to the mundane.

Prayer is intended to be vibrant...not rote and routine. Prayer is intended to change our lives from the inside out. Prayer is intended to be alive.

Prayer is more than a thing we do. It is a way of life.

Prayer is breathing in God's presence throughout the day...in the quiet moments...in the crazy moments...

Prayer...and the God to whom we pray...is not meant to be just another thing on our long list of things to do today. He is our companion and our conscience and our ever present help in a world of trouble.

I don't believe this is what most of us experience.

But it should be. And, it can be.

SEPTEMBER 24

Dear Abortion Provider:

Thank you for taking the time to read this letter.

I am simply writing to let you know that I am praying for you.

You and I are on different sides of the abortion issue.

I am pro-life.

I gave birth to a child that others would have chosen to abort.

Her life was hard.

But valuable.

And so is yours. So, I am praying for you.

My Sarah was made in God's image.

And so are you. So, I am praying for you.

I am praying for you to know the truth, and I am praying that the truth will set you free.

I am praying you will recognize lies you are believing, and come to the realization that the author of life is God, and He only has the right to give and to take life.

I am praying that you will be honest with the medical and scientific evidence that is now readily known...that within the complex strands of DNA exist all the information necessary for life. All that those few cells can become, given time, is present upon conception. This truly is amazing!

What you are dealing with is more than mere cells and tissue. You are dealing with life.

My heart breaks for the babies that are aborted, for the babies that will never be held, that will never see their mother's faces, that will never draw air into their lungs, who will never grasp a finger in tiny hands.

But my heart doesn't break only for them.

It breaks for you.

I pray that the love of Christ, poured out for us upon the cross, will reach you and change you.

I pray that you will cry out for God's truth and forgiveness.

This then is the message which we have heard of Him, and declare unto you, that God is light, and in Him is no darkness at all. If we say that we have fellowship with Him, and walk in darkness, we lie, and do not the truth: But if we walk in the light, as He is in the light, we have fellowship one with another, and the blood of Jesus Christ His Son cleanses us from all sin. If we say that we have no sin, we deceive ourselves, and the truth is not in us. If we confess our sins, He is faithful and just to forgive us our sins, and to cleanse us from all unrighteousness (I John 1:5-9).

I pray that this reality will grow in your heart and mind, and that you will seek truth and forgiveness.

God's love is wide and high and long and deep.

The blood of Christ, poured out for you, is sufficient.

Truth and forgiveness are available to you.

I pray that you will desire them and seek Him with all your heart, soul, mind, and strength.

May God, in His mercy, bless you with a godly sorrow that leads to repentance.

Three days after His death on the cross, Jesus was raised from the dead. He is alive and is victorious over sin and death. He has poured out His blood on your behalf, and He holds out His victory to you.

I pray that you will reach toward Him.

SEPTEMBER 25

As long as I can remember, I've wrestled with how to live an integrated life. I have always wanted my life to be consistent, and for many years – since I've been saved – wanting my life to be consistent within the framework of Christianity.

But, I've struggled.

It has often seemed like I've lived a split life, one part of me spiritual and another part of me secular. In other words, relegating God to certain aspects of my life and ignoring Him in others, believing that God belongs in certain parts of my life but does not belong in others. Ultimately, this is diminishing God's relevance in my life as a whole. Anything that diminishes God should cause pain and conflict in my life. There should be a battle raging.

Ideas have consequences.

The idea that God matters in some parts of my life and matters less in others is no exception. There are consequences.

All of these consequences can be summed up in one ugly word: Compromise.

We compromise because we want the pieces to fit together – even when they really can't – so we smash inconsistencies together with the glue of compromise and end up with half-truths and a small god.

Consider evolution. When I was first introduced to the concept of Darwinian evolution in public high school, I was intrigued. The way the teachers approached it, as an assumption already proven true, and the tools they had to present it were impressive. Thick textbooks with long words and colorful pictures and a captivating timeline convinced me that they MUST know what they are talking about. As a high school student, I was never once challenged to question any of the specific claims made within the Darwinian worldview. I was just told, one way or the other, to believe them. They were presented as "scientific." Science was given god-like status.

Simultaneous with this indoctrination of secular naturalism, I was also a teenager hungry for God's Word. I read the Bible. I wanted to believe the Bible. I found all of this both confusing and intriguing, and ultimately I decided I could believe both the Bible and Darwin...as long as I rejected, ignored, or stretched thin the book of Genesis. I drew the conclusion, as many had before me and many since, that Darwinian evolution occurred and God caused it...thus sloppily and inaccurately and temporarily reconciling irreconcilable ideas. Such reconciliation is only possible as long as one is willing to be intellectually dishonest with the words of Genesis...for the creation account recorded in Genesis does not match the evolution account etched upon the mind of secular humanity...something must give...and generally it is Genesis that is made to suffer. And I dare say that if the creation account suffers, then the understanding of the origin and nature of sin is diminished, thus dangerously diminishing the very gospel upon which we stand.

Well, then came college...and with it the pride of life and the lust of flesh. I thought I was pretty smart. I remember my cellular biology class. I remember the bespectacled, graying professor standing in the front of the lecture hall with words dripping from his lips: *"Evolution is true. I am not interested in arguing about that in this class."* His comment alerted my conscience, and I knew it was a red flag...but I ignored the danger...because all I cared about at that point was my own life and my own fun. I sat in the class, I answered the test questions as expected, and received a good grade without causing any stir.

Some may think, "Does it really matter? Can't a person live a godly and moral life while still believing in Darwinian evolution?" I suppose one can. But, I didn't...for me this compromise was a springboard for other compromises...the details of which are not important to share. Suffice it to say that my relationship with Mark, my testimony in workplaces, my political and social positions on issues such as homosexuality and abortion, all of these were affected by my secular worldview built upon Darwinian evolution and a compromised Genesis.

The God who created the universe....who spoke all things into being, the God who knit me together in the womb and who was familiar with all my ways, the God who sustains all...this BIG, all-powerful, amazing, all-mighty, Lord of lords and King of kings had been reduced in my life to a small god with a small place.

God had become small to me for many reasons. One of them was that no one – even in the church – told me that Christianity is about more than salvation. All my life, I grew up thinking about God and salvation in a sort of "whew, I made it!" kind of way. At least I'd get to heaven, and whatever happened until then, that was just random "whatever."

No one taught me how Christianity is a WORLDVIEW that can speak to ALL areas of life (science, medicine, law, philosophy, politics, education, sexuality, marriage, raising kids, work, handling finances, entertainment, use of time).

HE IS TOTAL TRUTH IN ALL AREAS.

I didn't know this.

My 20s were years of wasted time.

The darkness of my belief system came to a head one day when I was on the phone with my cousin, Jeanne. I can still picture myself on the phone, standing in my living room, around the time I got married. Somehow the topic of God came up, and awful words spewed from of my mouth, *"God exists for us. He's there for our benefit. So, he reaches people in different ways. Some people might call him Jesus, some call him Allah, some call him Buddha. It doesn't matter, they're all the same."*

Praise God...in that very moment in which I spoke these words, the God of Creation and Redemption gripped my heart and fear rose up within me. In my inmost being I knew my words were blasphemous, dangerous lies.

This moment was a turning point. It was one of those rare defining moments to always be remembered, for it began a new chapter in my life, a chapter in which I would earnestly seek and settle for nothing less than total truth.

It is a long story, but ultimately, it was SCIENCE that convinced me that Darwinian evolution is flawed and that the creation account recorded in Genesis is reliable and best explains what we observe.

There is total truth into which all reality fits. It is the Christian worldview built on God's eternal, unchanging character. God created and it was good. Mankind fell and all of creation was affected. God provides redemption in the person and finished work of Jesus Christ. This is total truth and it is intended for more than Sunday morning worship services! It is intended to be the filter through which all of life is understood.

Beware of how you think.

Beware of lies you may be believing.

Seek truth.

Total truth.

SEPTEMBER 26

Dear Lord,

Help me to love my neighbor as myself.

Keep me from being a judge with evil thoughts who shows favoritism and partiality.

Help me to remember that whoever keeps the whole law and yet stumbles at just one point is guilty of breaking all of it.

I am guilty before You, Lord.

We all are.

Yet, Your law gives freedom! It is the safest, most secure way to live. In obedience to You, we find safe harbor and protection.

Your law gives freedom because You, Lord, have fulfilled that law through the blood of Jesus Christ.

It is finished.

It is fulfilled.

I am free because of Christ, and I know I need Him.

I know I need Him because Your LAW gives me knowledge of what sin is and reveals my guilt, my need. That leads me to Christ, and He frees me beneath the fount of His cleansing, forgiving blood.

Lord, I pray for each person in my family to know they are lawbreakers, guilty before You, just as I was. And may they know the way – YOU!

Upon You our guilt can be transferred to Christ the great substitute.

Your law, indeed, is freedom.

In Christ's Holy Name…

SEPTEMBER 27

"My love is warmer than the warmest sunshine, softer than a sigh.
My love is deeper than the deepest ocean, wider than the sky.
My love is brighter than the brightest star that shines every night above.
And, there is nothing in this world that can ever change my love..."
{"My Love" written by Tony Hatch and sung by Petula Clark}

We hurried through dinner. I rushed through the dishes.

I whisked Sarah into her wheelchair, and off we went, on our way to the swimming pool at the middle school in Holland. Sarah, who has such difficulty moving her arms and legs when out of the pool, moves them with vigor when buoyed up by the water.

Sarah and I, all loaded into the van, headed out.

We pulled onto Route 16, north bound and running...

I pushed a tape into the cassette player of the van and enjoyed the 60s music proceeding from the one speaker in the van that actually worked.

Blessings come to us in all places and at unexpected moments. The unanticipated blessings of life are sweet...Petula Clark singing *"My love is warmer than the warmest sunshine, softer than a sigh. My love is deeper than the deepest ocean, wider than the sky. My love is brighter than the brightest star that shines every night above. And, there is nothing in this world that can ever change my love..."*

Sarah on my mind as my ears soaked up the words of this pretty melody. How unknown to me were these feelings until Sarah came along, and now how powerfully my heart pounds for this child. Without hesitation, would I jump in front of any danger that might confront her. Without thought, how joyful it is to sacrifice my needs to meet hers.

How I love this child!

And there was the blessing: the knowledge that no matter how much I love my child, God's love for her is greater still.

Never does He grow weary.

Never does He become distracted.

Never is He too busy. Or grumpy.

Never is he limited.

I love Sarah. But I grow weary and distracted. I get busy. Grumpy. I am limited. My love, which feels so strong for this little girl, is but a tainted and blurred image of the constant love of the Father for His children.

Herein is love, not that we loved God, but that He loved us, and sent His Son to be the propitiation for our sins...And we have known and believed the love that God hath to us. God is love; and he that dwelleth in love dwelleth in God, and God in him (I John 4:10, 16).

You see, at just the right time, when we were still powerless, Christ died for the ungodly. Very rarely will anyone die for a righteous man, though for a good man someone might possibly dare to die. But God demonstrates His own love for us in this: While we were still sinners, Christ died for us (Romans 5:6-8).

SEPTEMBER 28

I am convinced that if we do not deliberately purpose in our hearts and minds to be godly, then we will be worldly. Our natural bent is worldly. True godliness and holiness will come only with an intentional decision to strive and to seek to become that godly person God is calling us to be.

What God is calling us to become, He will equip us to become.

God calls us to become peculiar, different from the world around us. If we are to possess that wonderful quality of peculiarity, we must do so on purpose and with intent. It will not just happen by chance.

All else must be abandoned.

We must let go of all things and hold tightly to Jesus with both hands.

Sometimes I become discouraged. I see worldliness in my students. I know how far they have yet to go to become the people God wants them to be. Suddenly I feel aware of how my response to their worldliness is worldly itself. I can become irritable and proud when responding to their worldliness...these are, indeed, worldly responses, are they not?

As a teacher in the classroom, I am to lead out of worldliness, not react in a worldly way.

I, too, have a long way to go.

SEPTEMBER 29

"Blessed be the name of the Lord. Blessed be Your glorious name!"

Lord,

Your name is a strong tower.

The righteous run to it and are safe!

Bless the Lord, O my soul, and all that is within me.

Father, may I bless You with my words, my thoughts, the cry of my heart, and the work of my hands.

May I labor under Your great and mighty yoke, all while leaning fully on You. When the days are difficult – sometimes too long and sometimes not long enough – make Your presence and purpose powerfully known to me.

On the busiest of days, keep me, Lord, always sensitive to Your presence.

May my family and my students lift high their hands unto You.

May they and we fall before You, adoring You and calling You Elohim and Jehovah Shalom, our Jehovah Nissi and El Shaddai and El Elyon, our El Roi…

May we be speechless before You, my God and my Savior.

How I love and long for m vy Jesus!

In Christ's Ever-Present and Always Purposeful Name.

SEPTEMBER 30

From *A Shepherd Looks at Psalm 23* by W. Phillip Keller [37]

"But summertime for the sheep is more than just fly time. It is also 'scab time.' Scab is an irritating and highly contagious disease common among sheep the world over. Caused by a minute, microscopic parasite that proliferates in warm weather, 'scab' spreads throughout a flock by direct contact between infected and non-infected animals.

"Sheep love to rub heads in an affectionate and friendly manner…When two sheep rub heads together, the infection spreads readily from one to the other.

"In the Old Testament when it was declared that the sacrificial lambs should be without blemish, the thought uppermost in the writer's mind was that the animals should be free of scab. In a very real and direct sense scab is significant of contamination, of sin, of evil

"Only once did my sheep become infected by scab. I had purchased a few extra ewes from another rancher to increase the flock. It so happened they had, unknown to me, a slight infection of scab which quickly began to spread through the entire healthy flock…At great expense, to say nothing of the time and heavy labor involved, I had to put the entire flock, one by one, through the dipping solution to clear them of the disease. It was a tremendous task and one that entailed special attention to their heads. So I know precisely what David meant when he wrote, 'You anoint my head with oil' (Psalm 23)…

"In the Christian life, most of our contamination by the world, by sin, by that which would defile and disease us spiritually comes through our minds. It is a case of mind meeting mind to transmit ideas, concepts, and attitudes that may be damaging.

"Often it is when we 'get our heads together' with someone else who may not necessarily have the mind of Christ that we come away imbued with concepts that are not Christian.

"Our thoughts, our ideas, our emotions, our choices, our impulses, drives, and desires are all shaped and molded through the exposure of our minds to other people's minds. In our modern era of mass communication, the danger of the 'mass mind' grows increasingly grave. Young people in particular, whose minds are so malleable, find themselves being molded under the subtle pressures and impacts made on them by television, radio, magazines, newspapers, and fellow classmates, to say nothing of their parents and teachers.

"Often the mass media that are largely responsible for shaping our minds are in the control of men whose character is not Christ-like, who in some cases are actually anti-Christian.

"One cannot be exposed to such contacts without coming away contaminated. The thought patterns of people are becoming increasingly abhorrent. Today we find more tendency to violence, hatred, prejudice, greed, cynicism, and increasing disrespect for that which is noble, fine, pure, or beautiful….

"Just as by faith we believe and know and accept and thank Christ for coming into our lives, so by simple faith and confidence in the same Christ, we believe and know and *accept with thanks the coming of His gracious Spirit upon our minds. Then having done this, we simply proceed to live and act and think as He directs us.*

"The difficulty is that some of us are not in dead earnest about it. Like a stubborn sheep we will struggle, kick, and protest when the Master puts His hand upon us for this purpose. Even if it is for our own good, we still rebel and refuse to have Him help us when we need it so desperately.

"In a sense we are a stiff-necked lot, and were it not for Christ's continuing compassion and concern for us, most of us would be beyond hope or help."
From _A Shepherd Looks at Psalm 23_ by W. Phillip Keller [37]

September's Apologetic Moment…Contend for the faith

What About the Fossil Record?

Charles Darwin knew it.

He knew there was a problem.

That problem was the fact that there were not intermediate fossils in the geologic record. If Darwinian evolution is true, then yes, there must be transitional forms. Darwin knew it, too. Darwin went so far as to admit that many in the animal kingdom appeared SUDDENLY in the lowest layers of fossiliferous rocks. [58] In other words, he acknowledged that major body forms appear fully formed and functioning in the LOWEST layers of rocks in which we find fossils.

If Darwinian evolution be true, this ought not be the case.

If Darwinian evolution is true, then the model must fit the observations.

"If the biological diversity of life today is the result of nearly 4 billion years of descent with modification through natural selection, the fossil record should provide the ultimate evidence for it. It turns out that one can hardly find a more factual example for the weakness of such a naturalistic view, making the fossil record a true Achilles' heel of evolution. Darwin knew it, and modern paleontologists know it." [59]

Here are some problems that the fossil records poses to those who hold a naturalistic worldview:

Evolutionary stasis. This means that the fossil record does NOT show the continuous change and progression expected if Darwinian evolution were true. Rather, many animal groups are simply the same today as they were in the days when fossils were formed. *"The most stubborn example involves stromatolites: colonies of cyanobacteria that have not changed over allegedly 3.4 billion years."* [60]

Offset fossils. These are also referred to as "derived" or "reworked" fossils. These are fossils that are found "out of order" in the fossil record – they are located where they were not supposed to be (such as finding a flying, fully functioning bird in strata older than the supposed ancestors of birds). "Out of order" fossils have been found in the Salt Range Formation in the Punjab province of Pakistan, the Roraima Formation in Venezuela, the Ediacara vertebrate in South Australia's Flinders Range, Hadrosaurs (duckbilled dinosaurs) found in marine sediments in Montana's Bearpaw Shale, Nodosaurus (armored dinosaurs) found in marine sediments in western Kansas, and new phyla and unique arthropods in the Burgess Shale in British Columbia.

Lack of transitional fossils. *"One can then ask, 'How does one define a transitional fossil?' The evolutionist's answer is rather simple, 'A transitional fossil is an organism that shares common characteristics with both its precursors and its descendants.' The next question will then be, 'How does one know which are the precursors and which are the descendants?' And the answer goes, 'A precursor lived before (is found in layers dated older than the transitional fossil) and had more primitive features. A descendant lived after (in layers dated younger than the transitional fossil) and had or has more advanced features.'…Who establishes where a fossil is placed on the evolutionary ladder? Fossils can be moved up and down according to discoveries and theories."* [61]

Bones don't tell the story. People do. People find the bones and then people interpret the bones. Interpretation is influenced by worldview and starting assumptions. Let's just be honest about that. Sometimes people think, wrongly, that fossils easily prove one thing or another. But fossils alone don't prove anything. The bones always must be interpreted. Science involves models as often as it involves measurements. We cannot observe the bones being buried and fossilized. Those days are gone and will not be repeated. Instead, we discover the bones and we seek to find a model that best explains the forensics of what we now hold in our hands. What was the past for this creature? When was it? What is the story behind these fossils? What model best fits what we are now observing?

When you are reading a secular textbook and difficult to pronounce examples of transitional forms are thrown your way, refuse to be intimidated! Instead, dig deeper (pardon the pun). When you are told that Archaeopteryx is a link between dinosaurs and birds or that Tiktaalkik is a transitional form between fish and tetrapods or that Puijila is a transitional form between land mammals and sea mammals or that Pakicetus, Ambulocetus, and Rodhocetus are all transitional forms of modern day whales…just take the time to dig a little deeper and you will find that all these fossils required interpretation and that there is disagreement amongst paleontologists about the transitional nature of these fossils.

And, remember the bigger picture. Most of the proposed examples of transitional forms focus on one change when multiple changes are actually required. For example: for a dinosaur to evolve into a bird, more than just wings and feathers must evolve. There also needs to be evolution from cold-blooded to warm blooded and from reptile lungs to bird lungs. And, these evolutionary changes must be occurring simultaneously.

Think big picture. And, refuse to be intimidated by long words and confusing details.

And what of man? *"Out of all the major sequences of Darwinian evolution, the evolution of man is the nearest to us in time and should, therefore, be backed by an abundance of* *fossils. It isn't... Even worse, most of the fossil evidence is in the form of teeth, not skeletons or even individual bones.*

Over the last 50 years, the story of the evolution of Homo sapiens has changed drastically, from the classical tree diagram, to a tangled bush, then to an orchard. None of these visual representations offers a clear, even if fragmentary descent of man. Every such representation abounds with uncertainties and many possible alternative evolutionary paths, and representations have shifted radically over the decades. We are left with the impression that any path from multiple candidates can be chosen, according to preference, since they all 'prove' that man evolved from 'ape-like progenitors' as Darwin put it. [62]

This can all get technical...but again, refuse to be intimidated. When reading a secular textbook, and words like Zinjanthropus boisee (Nutcracker Man) or Paranthropus or Ramapithecus or Australopithecines (A. afarensis, A. africanus, A. sediba), or Homo habilius (Handy Man) or Homo erectus (Upright Man) and Neanderthal Genome Project...just take a little time to dig a little deeper. And think big picture.

You will find it takes much more faith to hold to the Darwinian naturalistic worldview than it does to hold to the Biblical creation worldview.

And what of hoaxes? *"Hoaxes have stained the face of anthropology from its inception – the ape men that never were."* [63]

Piltdown Man was a hoax. Turned out to be human skull fragments and the jaw of an orangutan with filed down teeth.

Nebraska Man was a hoax. Nebraska Man was developed from the discovery of a tooth...later it was admitted that the tooth was a pig's tooth.

Tasaday Tribe in the jungles of Mindanao Island, Philippine was a hoax. Turned out that a former head of a government agency, in a quest to protect cultural minorities, perpetrated this hoax.

The research of Professor Rainer Prtosch von Zieten was a hoax. He fabricated and plagiarized data for the purpose of showing a link between humans and Neanderthals. This scandal erupted in 2005 and the Professor was forced into retirement.

"These are just a few of the many cases that could be cited. It makes us wonder why the need for so much fraud if the evolution of humans is certain? The answer is obvious: fossils do not support the evolution of humans and apes from a common ancestor." [64]

And this is life eternal, that they might know Thee
the only true God, and Jesus Christ, whom Thou hast sent.
John 17:3

October

"He is no fool who gives up what he cannot keep
to gain that which he cannot lose."
— Jim Elliot

October 1

We were designed with the desire for significance.

We all want to believe that in some way our lives matter.

The journey of pursuing purpose is unique to each of us. There are moments of loneliness. Frustration. Confusion. There are also moments of confidence and certainty, moments when we glimpse the bigger picture and the purpose comes into focus, even if only briefly.

But ever shadowing our best understanding of life and purpose is the threat of change.

And yes, change is sure to come. Sometimes the change will be slow and plodding and barely perceptible. Sometimes the change will be drastic and sudden, dramatically throwing our lives out of the equilibrium we crave.

Circumstances change. Health changes. Finances change. People change. Seasons change. People come and people go. Jobs come and jobs go. Children arrive and then they grow and soon, they too are gone. Truly, we do not know what one day can bring. Change may excite us or scare us or paralyze us or exhilarate us…but it will indeed come to us.

God never changes.

He is the same yesterday, today and forever…..thus, as the seasons and circumstances of life change, as they surely will and always do, it is God alone who can define and defend our purpose and meaning in each unique season.

Our reason for living, if not based upon Him, will easily be washed away when the realities of life overwhelm us. When tragedy strikes. When bad news comes. When others disappoint or betray us. These changing and often sudden realities can crush our purpose because we define who we are and why we are here based upon a shifting foundation that relies on other people.

And, other people change.

And other people die.

And other people are unable to save or completely satisfy us.

But, a life of purpose built on the unchanging God is a life that can endure and even thrive in those tough times.

God never promises an easy life.

But He promises that all things will work together for good to those who love God and are the called according to His purpose.

He promises that we can find rest even while pulling the yoke designed by Him for us.

He promises peace that passes understanding.

Faith in God's character...faith that He is faithful...no matter what our feelings are...this is the key to unlocking the purpose and peace we all hunger for.

OCTOBER 2

Being a slave to Christ is freedom.

There is nothing the world can offer, and there is nothing the world can do to me to destroy my freedom in Christ.

I, should I take my eyes off Him and gaze instead upon the things of earth, can neglect and endanger my freedom. But in Christ, no mere man can take my freedom from me.

Mere mortal man may have the power to cast into prison...but God with me means I am free even if my body is bound.

The power of man is no power at all in the presence of the power of God.

Mere mortal man cannot destroy an eternal perspective that counts it pure joy and privilege to have been found worthy of sharing in the suffering of Jesus Christ.

Where the Spirit of the Lord is, there is freedom.

Where is the Spirit of the Lord?

Within me.

And there abides freedom…within. For whom the Son sets free is free indeed!

OCTOBER 3

I was listening to someone I love talk about a hurt in her life.

While the details are not important, the essence is. Someone she cared about was not caring back. Someone she loved was ever taking and never giving. Someone wanted what she had to offer, but did not want her.

Rejection.

Painful.

A place we have all been at one time or another.

Do you remember those moments when your love and your gifts were neglected or trampled underfoot by someone you loved?

Do you remember being ignored?

As I was listening to the sad story, God reminded me that He stands at the door and knocks.

Picture it.

Creator God who spoke the entire universe into existence ex nihilo waits for us.

God cares for us. But we do not always care back.

God loves. But we do not always love Him back.

God gives. We take.

We want God's stuff. But we do not always want God.

We reject God.

We ignore God.

With one breath, He could consume us.

But He stands at the door and knocks.

Don't be an idiot.

Open the door.

OCTOBER 4

"Just who do you think you are!?"

I was walking, drinking a cup of hot coffee in the cool stillness of a dark Fall morning. I was praying and struggling in prayer with the details of my life, my decisions, and my words.   How are all the threads of my life to fit into God's grand design?

Excruciating details of a life I claim I want to surrender, but then cling to like a tyrannical owner play in my mind and wander through my prayers.

Specifically on this morning walk, I was struggling with how to surrender an upcoming interaction with a person I don't really like. Something about her just annoys me, but that is no excuse, no matter how much I may want to make it one, to fail in my Christian duty to love and serve others and to obey God's call.

I was walking and praying and asking God how I, a Christian woman, am to interact with her. I was intently focused on my own sense of importance.   I was like the Pharisee…proud…thanking God that I wasn't like that "tax collector" over there…

"Who do you think you are?"

All of a sudden, my mind filled with images of myself – gossiping and slandering, making myself look good by making her look bad all while smiling at her when face to face.

I kneeled on the damp grass in our yard. The Holy Spirit was shouting unsolicited insights about my own attitude and behavior. *"For most of your life, you have thought you are smarter than just about everybody you meet. And, for most of your life, you have taken every opportunity you can to make yourself look good in the eyes of the world whether you are good or not. And you have often, without hesitation, done this at the expense of other people.*

You love praise of men more than praise of God, just like a Pharisee! Sometimes you have been stealth enough to recognize the worldly value of manipulating the circumstances so others are patting your back and you play humble. You know that if you blow your own horn, others see you as arrogant. You don't want to be perceived as arrogant, just superior....so you have developed skills to manipulate others into blowing your horn for you. You have developed these skills well....false humility.... talking about your struggles just loud enough that others can hear but won't think you are bragging about your unending endurance...participating in gossip pretending it's not really gossip but 'concern.'

Just who do you think you are to be walking around in prayer seeking ways that you are to influence this person, whom you barely know beyond surface judgments? The best way you can affect her life is to shut your mouth and remember you are her equal. You are equally a sinner. You are saved by grace. You, just like her, desperately need the blood of Christ shed for you to renew you day by day.

You are no better than her, and after shutting your self-important, prideful mouth, the next thing you can do is get a tight grip on that fact and remember while you are interacting with her that she is your fellow pilgrim on this journey...not your project. She needs your attention. She needs your prayers. She needs Christian love, and, yes, the day may come when you are led to lovingly confront sin in her life. But, that day is not here yet, so get over yourself! Sin is not to be tolerated or promoted or ignored. But, before you start being intolerant of her sin, start being intolerant of your own. Before you start confronting her sin, you need to confront your own!"

I was stunned and reeling.

I was rebuked.

It was beautiful.

The Holy Spirit was not soft-spoken, non-offensive or politically correct as He chastened my heart. He loves me too much to be non-offensive...for I need to be offended...The Holy Spirit sometimes must be a hammer within hearts of stone. Pride will not be gently eroded. It must be hammered out.

Praise God that He doesn't give up on me, but He lovingly uses the hammer of truth through the Holy Spirit to get my attention and bring me to a place of repentance. Salvation without repentance is useless and stagnant. Salvation without repentance may even be dead.

Dear Lord, I am sorry for my arrogance and my sneakiness in promoting my own importance. I am sorry for my willingness, and often eagerness, to gossip and slander and think negative, unloving thoughts about other people. Unless clothed with your righteousness through Jesus' blood on the cross, all my acts are but filthy rags. Thank you for revealing this sin to me, and I ask you to continue revealing such sin to me, and to continue bringing me to your place of repentance and restoration. Reveal to me who I really am and what my sin really is. I cannot grow in you unless I recognize the sin in me, repent of it, and allow you to change and transform me.

Lord, forgive me, help me, and change me. Thank You for hammering me.

OCTOBER 5

Abiding means remembering that Satan is a liar. He can do no more harm to me than the harm that I allow him to do. Abiding means that I recognize the nature of the enemy…He is a liar. A murderer. A thief. He is subtle. He knows how to discourage God's people.

But who is he really? This enemy is a defeated foe! How dare he defy the armies of the Living God!

I am not a pauper. I am not a victim. I am a child of the Most High King. I am precious to the Creator, the Redeemer.

When Satan attacks, I must remember my value in the King.

Abiding means remembering that I dare not live life discouraged, for my God is greater than all. He is greater than the enemy. He is greater than the circumstance. He is greater than the pain. He is greater than the failure. He is greater than the success. He is high above each. Discouragement does not come from the Living Vine in whom I abide.

Abiding means remembering that my identity is in Jesus Christ. I am rooted in the branch, and from Him flows life eternal, nourishment everlasting, power from on high and strength enough for this day.

OCTOBER 6

It is a beautiful day. It's in the 80s in October in Western New York...practically unheard of, and sure to be short lived. So, here I sit in a very old (and somewhat dangerous) lawn chair waiting for the inspiration that will birth words to write.

I thought about my morning. I had made rice pudding. While waiting for it to finish baking, I had tuned our radio to AM. Talk radio. I love it. I was listening to our local WBEN and its conservative (kind of) AM talk show personality, Tom Baehrle. It was a busy news day. President Bush just completed a Rose Garden press conference where he discussed yesterday's nomination of Harriet Myers to replace the retiring Sandra Day O'Connor on the Supreme Court. He answered questions related to this, and about the effects of Hurricanes Katrina and Rita. And Iraq, of course. And, racial tensions. And, energy problems and predictions. Reporters asked questions obviously designed to stir the pot of a somewhat disgruntled conservative base.

As the press conference and Tom B's talk show comments played in the background, and as I continued to wait for the rice pudding to finish baking, I ate an early lunch. Tuna fish sandwich and some baked beans with homemade chili sauce. With the radio and the oven going, and myself pigging out, I opened my Bible to read.

In 1 John chapter 5, I read: *This is love for God: to obey His commands. And His commands are not burdensome, for everyone born of God overcomes the world. This is the victory that has overcome the world, even our faith. Who is it that overcomes the world? Only he who believes that Jesus is the Son of God* (I John 5:3-5).

I think most people agree with these words of Jesus, *In this world you will have trouble (John 16:33).* Most people have either experienced or observed problems. Troubles are everywhere...day after day and year after year...century after century. Troubles can be found within our individual physical bodies, in our individual emotional states, in our families, under the roofs of our homes, within the ledger lines of our check book, between the walls our schools, our churches, within our civil government. We are reminded of them with every natural disaster, with every man-made disaster, and every time we turn on the news. There is no person on the face of the earth, either now, in the ancient past, or in the distant future who has not experienced (or will experience) illness, loss, pain, and eventually physical death.

Yes, there are troubles, many and numerous and frequent, in our lives and in our world.

Quite the optimist, huh?

Christ agrees. We have troubles. We need to get our eyes off this world and the mistaken notion that somehow the world, if rearranged properly, offers the solutions for which we hunger. Is it possible to "rearrange" the political, social, economic, and educational systems in such a way that problems will be ultimately solved eternally? Obviously not. Certainly these systems can be used to alleviate suffering (although that sometimes leads to suffering in other areas and systems). I am by no means advocating that we abdicate our role in all systems to try to help those who are hurting and suffering. We should always seek to do good to ease suffering and persecution where these exist. Our eyes should be always open to see where there is need that we can meet…if led by the Spirit to meet it.

But, ultimately, we humans and our systems and institutions will fail to provide the perfect solution that only Christ offers.

The temporary solutions offered by the world are just that: temporary. The hook of worldly solutions is a deceptive hook upon which to hang your hat. If you are planting your hope in the soil of the temporary solutions offered by the world's social, political, economic or other systems, you are indeed doomed to disappointment.

Trusting in man, the systems of man, and the programs of man to solve your problems is foolishness.

Beware of modern day towers of Babel. They are man's attempts to replace God, and they are wicked to the core regardless of the appearance of beauty and unity they may have.

The true and real problem is SIN, and the only solution is Jesus Christ.

In order to understand that, you need to take your eyes off the things of this world and grab hold of Christ who is always waiting to grab hold of you.

Jesus tells us, in the Gospel of John 16:33, *I have told you these things so that in me you may have peace. In this world you will have trouble.* **But take heart! I have overcome the world**. And, in I John 5:5, we are asked, *Who is it that overcomes the world? Only he who believes that Jesus is the Son of God.*

The world is not something we need to fix. The fixing will be perfectly done when Jesus returns. What we need to do is overcome! We need to overcome the world and the only way that can be accomplished is through faith in Jesus. We, through the Holy Spirit working in our lives and minds and hearts, victoriously overcome the world when we say, "NO" to temptation and physical lust, when we seek and obey God's will in our lives, and when we say, "Yes" to Jesus as Savior.

Politically, I am a conservative, and the main reason I am a conservative is that I do not believe civil government is the answer (although I used to). Deception has spawned the belief that answers to life's problems are best found in civil government and social programs. Culturally, government has become our idol and deity. This is more than sad. This is dangerous. We have moved far away from a God-based understanding of authority both within our families and our civil governments. We are humanists now, convinced that we are capable, without God, of establishing rule and defining social order. We are mistaken. Humanistic tyranny is but around the corner. Man, without God, will only make problems worse. It seems so obvious.....but we have stopped opening our Bibles...so how are we to know?

OCTOBER 7

The Christian life is a life of risk.

At least it's supposed to be.

When the talents were provided, the master expected his servants to invest. There is risk in investment. Does this include recklessness? Perhaps sometimes. But I think more often it involves calculated risk, well-thought out investments, but not so well-thought out that fear settles in and we become like the scared servant who, in trembling, merely hid his talent in a safe place while he waited, with his untainted talent, for the master's return.

Christians can be so afraid of getting it wrong, that we get it wrong by doing nothing (or doing the same thing) and staying in our comfort zones where there is no risk.

We will get it wrong sometimes. Abraham did. Moses did. Elijah did. David did. Peter did. Paul did. Did their failures negate their usefulness in the Kingdom of God? No. They responded to their failures by leaning harder upon God, and that response made them useful.

Perhaps our usefulness is negated when we choose to only travel the safe, well-trodden path.

Once we are ready, we need (with prayer, caution, and alertness) to spend some (just some) time with people who do not think like we do. If we don't, then we are not taking the gospel to the ends of the earth. Is there risk in this? Indeed. We won't always know what to say. We may say the wrong thing. We won't always know what to do. We may do the wrong thing. God doesn't need us to be perfect. He desires that we be out there, taking risks for Him and with Him, believing that He is able to lead and protect us on dangerous paths, believing that He is able to take our imperfect widow's mites and use them mightily in advancing His Kingdom and the message of the gospel. And, remembering that we don't need to save ourselves (nor can we) by getting it always right, remembering that *there is now no condemnation for them which are in Christ Jesus, who walk not after the flesh, but after the spirit.*

We are saved! He has left us here on earth for a purpose. It is no longer about what we are comfortable with or what we want. It is about living life here and now as clay in the hands of the Potter.

Believe me, there is nothing I would prefer more than always being with fellow Christians who think like I do and share my worldview. How absolutely comfortable that would be! But that is an un-invested talent.

I want to abandon my life to the will of God. Paradoxically, the will of God involves risk, and yet is the safest place to be. I want to learn how to live palms up, holding on to nothing in this world, including my comfort zone.

OCTOBER 8

O, God, Thou art my God!

I pray for my family.

I pray for my students.

I pray that early they will seek You.

I pray that their souls will thirst for You and that their flesh will long for You in a dry and thirsty land.

Everything apart from You is a dry and thirsty land. There may be temporary satisfaction and pleasure, but so quickly this wears off. Things of this world rot. Die. Decay. Rust. Grow old.

How can such things ever satisfy eternal souls? They cannot!

You, only, Lord, can! You alone have the power and ability to quench the thirst and nourish the hunger of eternal beings made in Your image.

Lord, Your lovingkindness is better than life!

Praise, Thee, my Lord and my God.

I pray that You, in the glory of Your eternal goodness and lovingkindness will reach into the lives of each person in my family and in my classroom.

Through all things, in all times, at all places, may You, Lord, be recognized and magnified in our lives.

May our souls follow hard after You!

In the Reliable Name of Jesus, the One who ransoms those who are bound.

OCTOBER 9

I knocked on the bedroom door. "Amy, I'll be sitting in the bathroom doing paperwork when you decide you want to talk." Then I walked the few steps down the hall to the bathroom, put the toilet seat down, sat down, and started writing case notes from the day's events. I work with developmentally disabled adults, and Amy is one of our residents in a group home. Amy has good days and bad, much like the rest of us, except her bad days are supervised and scrutinized by staff.

Today was day number four since Amy took a shower, and she was refusing again. Earlier in the day, house staff had called me to ask if I'd come over and see if I could convince Amy to take her much-needed shower. So, there I was, sitting in the bathroom, doing paperwork, waiting for Amy to come and talk with me. Knowing Amy as I did, I knew that telling her the obvious "You will smell and nobody will want to be near you" and then insisting she take a shower would not work. Thus, I waited and did paperwork, in the bathroom. I knew she would think that too bizarre to ignore. It didn't take long before I heard Amy open her door, stomp down the hall, and appear in the bathroom door. She stood leaning against the door frame, eyes swollen and red.

"What's up?" I said barely taking my eyes off my paperwork.

"Bad day," she said.

"Tell me about it." Now I stopped the paperwork and looked into Amy's eyes. She was very sad and lots of mad. She told me how she had trouble at workshop today. She told me how things weren't going well at the group home for her the last couple of days. Then, she rolled up her pant leg to show me that she had fallen and had a brush burn on her knee. She said she was afraid it would hurt if she got it wet in the shower. Her eyes were getting even redder.

I reached out my hand toward Amy, and she walked toward me, crying. She wanted and needed a hug. She hugged me for a minute. Then, she went and told the house staff she would take her shower.

She even brushed her teeth.

She didn't need a lecture about the virtues of hygiene.

She didn't need a reminder that people don't want to be around people who smell.

Calling her refusal to shower a "behavior problem" wasn't helping much.

She needed a listening ear on a person with a closed mouth.

What is it like for God being God to we human beings?

We, like Amy, have bad days.

We, like Amy, don't always comply with the rules.

We, like Amy, sometimes have brush burns that affect our behaviors.

And we, like Amy, need a hug from time to time.

OCTOBER 10

From *Streams in the Desert* by L.B. Cowman [38]

"The hand of the LORD has done this (Job 12:9).

"A number of years ago the most magnificent diamond in the history of the world was found in an African mine. It was then presented to the king of England to embellish his crown of state. The king sent it to Amsterdam to be cut by an expert stonecutter. Can you imagine what he did with it?

"He took this gem of priceless value and cut a notch in it. Then he struck it one hard time with his hammer, and the majestic jewel fell into his hand, broken in two. What recklessness! What wastefulness! What criminal carelessness!

"Actually, that is not the case at all. For you see, that one blow with the hammer had been studied and planned for days, and even weeks. Drawings and models had been made of the gem. Its quality, defects, and possible lines along which it would split had all been studied to the smallest detail. And the man to whom it was entrusted was one of the most skilled stonecutters in the world.

"Now do you believe that blow was a mistake? No, it was the capstone and the culmination of the stonecutter's skill. When he struck that blow, he did the one thing that would bring that gem to its most perfect shape, radiance, and jeweled splendor.

"The blow that seemed to be the ruin of the majestic precious stone was actually its perfect redemption, for from the halves were fashioned two magnificent gems. Only the skilled eye of the expert stonecutter could have seen the beauty of two diamonds hidden in the rough, uncut stone as it came from the mine.

"Sometimes, in the same way, God lets a stinging blow fall on your life. You bleed, feeling the pain, and your soul cries out in agony. At first you think it is an appalling mistake. But it is not, for you are the most precious jewel in the world to God. And He is the most skilled stonecutter in the universe.

"Someday you are to be a jewel adorning the crown of the King. As you lie in His hand now, He knows just how to deal with you. Not one blow will be permitted to fall on your apprehensive soul except what the love of God allows. And you may be assured that from the depths of the experience, you will see untold blessings, and spiritual enrichment you have never before imagined."
From <u>Streams in the Desert</u> by L.B. Cowman [38]

OCTOBER 11

My breaking, broken heart as I watched the other day as my Dad's old truck was hauled onto a flatbed to be carried away...

Dad has been gone for years, and now something that was once his is gone, too.

And the wound of my Dad's death bleeds again as I watch and am reminded how short, how frail is life and how I miss him so and love him still and always.

I am grateful my heart weeps and remembers, and thankful for the man who was my Dad and the Great God who gave him to me.

Been missing my Dad a lot lately.

Since Sarah's death, I haven't thought much about Dad's death and absence. I've been so focused on Sarah's.

Lately, though, I remember Dad and miss him awful. It's almost like I forgot he died, and now I am remembering it and experiencing his death a fresh. It seems new, like he died again. Suddenly, I'm a little girl without her father and at the same time I'm a mother without her child.

So much I don't understand. My heart breaks.

But God.

He is nigh unto the broken hearted, isn't He?

Lord, I know You are worthy of my trust and praise. I understand that You are greater than the sorrow of loss. You are hope. My hope. My comfort.

I mourn for my earthly father. He was so good to me. I rejoice that I have a heavenly Father, a Father from whom I can never be separated.

OCTOBER 12

The word of the Lord came to me: 'Son of man, with one blow I am about to take away from you the delight of your eyes. Yet do not lament or weep or shed any tears. Groan quietly; do not mourn for the dead. Keep your turban fastened and your sandals on your feet; do not cover the lower part of your face or eat the customary food of mourners.' So I spoke to the people in the morning, and in the evening my wife died. The next morning I did as I had been commanded (Ezekiel 24:15-18).

Are we all supposed to respond to loss and sorrow the way Ezekiel did?

I don't think these verse are intended to be instructive regarding grief and the proper expression of it. Rather, I think these verses are all about how God designs purpose for each one of us, and in our individual lives we must follow His will even when it seems odd or unreasonable or unclear.

What did Ezekiel do?

1) Ezekiel **listened** for the word of the Lord.

2) Ezekiel **discerned and recognized** the voice of the Lord.

3) Ezekiel **obeyed** the Lord's instructions.

What would I do if God told me that I was going to lose the "delight of my eyes?"

Would I respond in faith and obedience? Would I despair? Would I doubt?

Would I, as Ezekiel, wake up the next morning and do "as I had been commanded?"

This is life. There will be loss. There will be sorrow. I cannot pretend I know for sure how I would respond in those moments of grief, those moments when the delight of my eyes is taken away. My prayer is that I would respond as Ezekiel did: obediently.

God has a plan. His plan is good. We doubt this sometimes when we stand face to face with awful: cancer, Alzheimer's, car accidents, natural disasters, bankruptcy, rejection. The Bible does not directly answer the oft ask "why" question. It is clear, though, that God is more concerned with our eternal souls than our earthly bodies, and sometimes I think that seems unfair to us with such limited vision. Whether we think it's fair or not, God's ways are not our ways. We have no choice – we must walk by faith in order to walk with God…for God is beyond our ability to comprehend in His entirety.

We do not need to know everything to believe that God does have our eternal best interest in mind.

So we believe.

That doesn't make life easy.

Following God is hard, time-consuming work.

Trusting God is hard, time-consuming work.

Listen. Discern. Obey. God's grace really is sufficient.

OCTOBER 13

The truth is, you can be in the throes of grief…and yet you can experience joy.

The tears may be pouring out your eyes and down your cheeks, but if you can exalt God and magnify Him above your circumstances, that is joy unspeakable. Sobs of grief may be choking you, but if you can cry out "Yes, God. I trust You in even this. I believe You are now and always good. In even this. I am struggling to understand 'why', but ultimately I don't have to understand why. Instead, I must cling to You. I must remember my identity is in You, not this sorrow or this loss. I have You. You have me. I am Yours and You are mine. And Your grace is sufficient. In even this...." If these words become the groan of your broken heart, then even the sorrow itself is beautifully transformed into joy unspeakable.

Joy is bound and wed to our life in and with the Lord. Joy is beyond our circumstances, grounded and rooted in relationship with the Creator Redeemer God who has promised to never leave us nor forsake us. Joy is found in abiding in Him and being upheld by His righteous right hand, praising Him for who He is, and remembering what He has done already and what He has promised He will do.

Yes, weeping may endure for a night. But, joy cometh in the morning. Remember.

In the valleys, remember. In the darkness, remember. In the pain remember. When fear presses in, remember. Remember who God is. Remember what God has done. Remember what God will do. Remember that our light affliction is but for a moment. Remember that though the outward man perish, yet the inward man is renewed day by day. Remember that all His promises are YES in Christ Jesus!

You see, joy matters. Not for ourselves. But in the Kingdom of God. For we fight not against flesh and blood, but against principalities and powers in high places. The war in which we are engaged is spiritual. And in that war, joy is a weapon. A powerful weapon. Joy is not a mere feeling. It is an act of faith and it delivers a blow to the enemy of our soul, the enemy which has come to kill, steal, and destroy. As the pebble in David's sling shot, so is joy in our arsenal. It doesn't have to be big to be powerful - it just has to be surrendered to the mighty God of all creation.

David faced the uncircumcised Philistine with these words, "Who are you to defy the armies of the living God?" Then, in faith, he slung his pebble at the giant. His pebble hit the mark, but it was God who brought down the enemy. And when we, in faith, sling our small pebble of joy and gratitude at the uncircumcised Philistines in our own lives, it is the same as crying out, "Who are you to defy the armies of the living God?" This, my friends, is victory...no matter what happens to our physical bodies or our earthly relationships or our bank accounts...this is spiritual victory.

Joy matters because it is nourishment to a starving world. It is part of the fruit of the Spirit. And, it is part of our testimony and witness. It is one of the ways in which we are light in the darkness and salt in the earth. Jesus has called us to the Great Commission. He has called us to bring His message of total truth and redemption to the lost and dying world around us. We can only properly share this message when we have an exalted and grand view of God, a view in which

He is greater than our circumstances and our enemies. When we express faith in God through humble joy and gratitude even when we are in vice grip of personal pain, the world - or our little piece of it - notices. It is peculiar. Confusing. Strange. And completely full of potential to become - at least to some - the sweet aroma of the truth that Jesus Christ is the Creator God who has stepped into history, and He alone saves and is hope, eternal everlasting unfailing hope.

A joyful response to suffering is a bold response. It is so unusual, that it presents untold possibilities to open otherwise closed doors in our witness to family, friends, strangers, enemies....it will be different for each of us because God has a unique calling for each life...

I don't know the details of how He can take your pain and make it purposeful. I just know He can.

October 14

And men took of their victuals and asked not counsel at the mouth of the Lord (Joshua 9:14).

How could Joshua, God's chosen leader of His people, be so deceived? *He asked not counsel at the mouth of the Lord.* The Bible does not tell us why he failed to seek God. Maybe he was tired. Maybe he assumed what he shouldn't have assumed. Perhaps he was distracted. Busy. Flattered. Or just having a plain lazy day.

He looked at the outward appearance of these men, and Joshua leaned on his own understanding. He trusted his own judgment. Pride.

How restrained is the Lord! If one of my own is posed to make a foolish decision, I would thrust myself upon them, stop them, cry in desperation, pace in anxiety. At the very least, I would offer my opinion.

But God...He is restrained.

I know how capable I and we are of making awful, fleshly, short sighted decisions with long-term consequences. God sees beyond all of this. How gracious He is to keep working with us and loving us even in the midst of our often hasty decisions.

Beware.

Don't ever be deceived into thinking you are big enough, smart enough, experienced enough to make decisions without the counsel of the Lord.

Joshua was as big, smart, and experienced as they come, and he messed up.

Be Ye the Salt of the Earth

Seek God always.

OCTOBER 15

From Foxe: Voices of the Martyrs 39

Chester A. "Chet" Bitterman III (1952 – 1981)

"Chet Bitterman went in with his eyes open. He knew that sharing the gospel could be costly. It would cost everything. But he willingly went to Colombia to bear the Good News. '...I find the recurring thought that perhaps God will call me to be martyred for Him in His service in Colombia. I am willing.' Chet penned those words in his diary before he and his wife, Brenda arrived in Colombia. Chet's devotion to his Savior was evident: 'I am willing.'

"When the gunmen came into the Wycliffe Bible Translators guest house in Bogata, Colombia early the morning of January 19, 1981, they were looking for the mission's leader, a more high-profile hostage whose captivity could somehow help their cause. Who they got instead was Chester A. Bitterman III, 'Chet' to his friends. The next day President Ronald Reagan took the oath of office, and American hostages left Iran after 444 days in captivity. Their ordeal was over, with Chet and Brenda's just beginning.

"Chet and Brenda hadn't been in Colombia long. Their mission career and their translation work lay before them. They had gone to language school and helped in various tasks for Wycliffe, including managing the guest house, serving as buyer for goods needed by mission workers and even as radio operator. Finally, it seemed God was opening the door for them to move into the jungle with the Carijona Indian tribe to begin language study and eventually translation work. In the days before M-19 terrorists kidnapped Chet, he had been scouring hardware and building supply stores, stockpiling materials for their move to the Carijonas.

"The terrorists' demands were twofold. First, they wanted their views printed in several of the world's leading papers. The second demand was that all Wycliffe mission workers be out of Colombia in thirty days, or Chet would die.

"Wycliffe's stand was clear: The work God had called them to in Colombia was not complete, and they could not desert the effort. Chet wouldn't want them to leave with so many people still unable to read God's Word in the language of their heart.

"Negotiations went on in fits and starts. Brenda and her two young daughters – one barely old enough to walk – waited and prayed and hoped. They prayed Chet would remember the Scriptures that he had faithfully memorized. The guerrillas maintained their stance that Wycliffe must leave; Wycliffe agreed to leave when their translation work was done, more than a decade into the future.

"His captors released a letter from Chet. His words carried not discouragement and worry, but an exciting sense of mission and possibility: 'The Lord brought II Corinthians 2:14 to mind: 'But thanks be to God, who always leads us in triumph through the Lord Jesus Christ.' The word for 'triumph' was used for the Roman victory parades, when the soldiers were received back at home by the cheering crowds after a successful battle...I have had a lot of free time to think about such things as Daniel's three friends...and Paul and Silas' experience in the jail at Philippi. In the case of Daniel's friends, God did something very unusual through His power for a specific purpose, so that through everything, all concerned would learn (i.e. have their misconceptions corrected) about Him. The result of the experience was that everyone learned who He was. Remember Paul and the Praetorian Guard. Keep this in your thoughts for me. Wouldn't it be neat if something special like this would happen?'

"Brenda was thrilled to see that her prayers were being answered. Chet was remembering the Scriptures.

"Even as he was held hostage, the Lord's work was being accomplished. Colombian media reports about Wycliffe's work included reference to the gospel message and shed a positive light on Christian workers. Bible verses Chet had mentioned in his letter were printed in Colombian newspapers. The Word was going out.

"On the morning of March 7, 48 days after Chet's abduction, his life was ended by a bullet to the chest. His body was left on a bus. A sedative in his blood suggests he may have felt no pain.

"And still the message went out, even after his death. A radio interview with Chet's parents was broadcast numerous times across the country. 'I'm sorry I won't see Chet again in this life,' Chet's father said, 'But I know I'll see him again in heaven.' He went on to say how much Chet loved the Colombian people. Chet's mother said that even though her son had been killed, she still had love for Colombia and its people. 'We're hoping the guerrillas come to know God,' she said.

"Chet was buried at Lomalinda, the Wycliffe base where he'd lived and worked. His burial, in Colombian soil, carried its own message of his love for that land and its people.

"At memorial services around the world, men and women stepped forward to answer God's call to full-time service, to take Chet's place on the dangerous front-lines of ministry work. Applications to Wycliffe skyrocketed in the months after Chet's death.

" 'Wouldn't it be neat if something special like that would happen?' Chet's words carry the echoes of prophecy. Something special did happen. God's Word went forth;

people's hearts were touched and changed. Through one man laying down his life for his Savior, many lives where changed. The avalanche of blessing and ministry began with three words: 'I am willing.'"
 From *Foxe: Voices of the Martyrs* [39]

OCTOBER 16

Father,

Help us to live for You.

Christ suffered in His body. May we have His attitude and willing obedience within us. As He, may we be willing to suffer. To sacrifice and to be done, literally done, with sin.

May we live the rest of our earthly lives for Your will. Enough time has already been spent doing what pagans do…debauchery, lust, drunkenness, carousing, idolatry. May we recognize this trash as the detestable and rotting sin that it is. May we no longer plunge with the world into this flood of sin. No matter the cost, may we turn to You now and live in the full joy of obedience to You.

The end of all things is near.

May we be clear-minded and self-controlled so that we can pray.

May we love each other deeply.

May we offer hospitality without grumbling.

Whatever gift we have received, may we faithfully administer it.

In all things, may You, Lord, be praised through Jesus Christ.

To Him be the glory and power forever and ever! May these words be on my lips, in my heart, and in my mind.

And upon the lips, hearts and minds of each person in my family.

And my students.

In Christ's Loving Name…

OCTOBER 17

I'm grateful for glimpses of eternal beauty...a lush, green tree-covered mountainside. My eyes drink in this drop of perfection in our fallen world.

My eyes drift slowly downward and I behold, in startling contrast, a gray and sullen cemetery with ashen concrete and slate and marble stones protruding from the cold earth.

Stark reminders that this earth, even with its hints of glory, is not my home. I am heaven bound, thanks to Christ.

How grateful I am for the hints of heaven pressed up against the reality of the Fall of man.

And, I look forward with hope, and I live in joy because of Christ's gift of salvation to me.

I watch the sun rising in the east over the horizon, over the gravestones. These graves where bones lie under dark soil...these are not the end of the story. And that is why I look up more than I look down.

For He is coming again.

In sickness and in health.

In death and in life.

In want and in plenty.

In sorrow and in joy.

In all these, praising Him.

OCTOBER 18

Done with chemo. Sarah is done with chemo. It is now October, 2006, and chemo ended in August, 2006 after 2 years and 9 months. Sarah has been kind of out of sorts the last few days. I haven't thought much about it. I've just figured she is tired from some sinus and allergy stuff or maybe an ear infection. She has an appointment tomorrow with her pediatrician for a physical. Nothing to really be concerned about, just the normal kid stuff.

Hopefully.

But, as I was lifting Sarah out of the bathtub this morning, and she was whining and complaining some, a gloom came over me briefly. I thought, "What if she is relapsing?" I hadn't even given this possibility a thought until that very moment. When she was first diagnosed with acute lymphocytic leukemia, it was Autumn. It is Autumn now. When she was first diagnosed, she was tired and unhappy and uncomfortable, among other more serious symptoms (bruising, fevers, loss of appetite). Now, she is tired, unhappy, uncomfortable...she has been like this for about a week. I've just assumed it's the normal kiddy stuff.

But, I really don't know, do I?

I'm not panicking while thinking about this. I have learned to be still. It is good to be still sometimes. Now was such a time. Enough troubled water has rushed under and over our bridge of life the past few years, that my husband and I know that whatever is going on will be discovered soon enough. Lab work will be done tomorrow before seeing the pediatrician. Until then, we go on our way and our normal routine. I get Sarah ready for school.

I keep thinking.

It's not really worry. Just thinking. All thoughts need to be taken captive. The thought life is powerful...most of our sins start innocently enough in the brain in the shape of a thought. Most of our fears and anxieties start innocently enough in that same brain. All thoughts need to be taken captive. We need to control them, through the help of God and the power of the Holy Spirit, rather than they us.

No one, including our amazing Father in heaven, promised that would be easy.

But, it is possible.

So there I am, wondering if my daughter is possibly relapsing. Is the leukemia making a return? I need to take this thought captive. So, I ponder and I pray.

Suddenly, I think about my niece, Emily. I love Emily just as if she were my own daughter. She and Sarah have grown up together. Em is only 10 months older than my Sarah. What would I say to Emily if Sarah relapsed? That is the thought that takes hold in my head. What would I say to my dear Emily?

You see, a relapse for Sarah would be no small thing. Indeed, it is no small thing for anyone of course, but for Sarah it would be devastating. Due to multiple medical problems, the chances of Sarah surviving a bone marrow transplant would be unlikely. And, bone marrow transplants are the major method of treating someone with acute lymphocytic leukemia who has relapsed.

The doctors always have their reality chat with patients and families at the end of chemo. "Things look good. But, now is a higher time of risk because the protective chemo meds that you have been taking are now being removed..." And in Sarah's case they added, "And if there is a relapse, we can treat with chemo again, but a bone marrow transplant and its side effects would be potentially lethal in Sarah's case."

In other words, relapse = very likely terminal.

What would I say to my dear 11 year old niece who adores Sarah and has grown up at her side? It is this thought that I ended up thinking about. What to say to the innocent regarding the tragedies of life that we all taste and experience.

It was no struggle to know the answer. God made it clear.

"Sometimes, knowing the end of the story needs to be good enough."

The details and the circumstances of life's sorrows may be many and may be devastating, and the reasons may be cloudy or completely unknown to us. But, the end of the story is...Victory...Jesus saves and Jesus heals. Sarah knows Jesus, and so do we. She may not experience His healing touch until she is home in heaven. But, knowing the healer is greater than knowing the healing, and that has to be enough, and thus it is. That is the end of the story for those who know the healer, Jesus.

The events of life, the frailties of the mind, and the failing of the body are not the end of the story. Indeed, for those who are covered by Christ's saving blood on the cross, victory awaits beyond these temporary circumstances common to all.

I know the end of the story. The Bible tells me so.

Jesus saves, and we know Jesus.

I would assure Em...

All things will be well.

OCTOBER 19

Dear Lord,

Why me?

Why have You chosen me?

Why have You made me acceptable in the beloved?

There is nothing worthy in me to cause You to choose me.

It is Your grace, solely Your grace, that rescued me, redeemed me, reconciled me, regenerated me. I stand on the rock of Your righteousness, not my own.

I don't remember the exact moment of my new birth any more than I remember the exact moment of my physical birth.

But, both are real.

Apart from Your direct and constant attention to and intervention in my life, I would be completely absorbed by and consumed in the world and the ways of the world and the lust of the flesh and the pride of life.

But, You stooped down and gave me eyes to see, ears to hear, and a heart ready to receive the truth of the gospel. You plucked me off the wide road leading to destruction and placed me on the narrow road paved with the blood of Jesus Christ.

I praise You for that moment of spiritual birth. I have an anchor for the soul, firm and secure. And, I will rest in You from this day on.

Your child. Your slave. Your beloved.

In the Name of Jesus, Lamb of God…

OCTOBER 20

From *Streams in the Desert* by L.B. Cowman [40]

"As God's chosen people...clothe yourselves with...kindness (Colossians 3:12).

"There is an old story of an elderly man who always carried a little can of oil with him everywhere he went, and when he would go through a door that squeaked, he would squirt a little oil on the hinges. If he encountered a gate that was hard to open, he

would oil the latch. And so he went through life, lubricating all the difficult places, making it easier for all those who came after him. People called the man eccentric, strange, and crazy, but he went steadily on, often refilling his can of oil when it was nearly empty, and oiling all the difficult places he found.

"In this world, there are many lives that painfully creak and grate as they go about their daily work. Often it seems that nothing goes right with them and that they need lubricating with 'the oil of joy' (Psalm 45:7), gentleness, or thoughtfulness.

"Do you carry your own can of oil with you? Are you ready with your oil of helpfulness each morning? If you offer your oil to the person nearest you, it may just lubricate the entire day for someone who is downhearted. Or the oil may be a word of encouragement to a person who is full of despair. Never fail to speak it, for our lives may touch others only once on the road of life, and then our paths may diverge, never to meet again.

"The oil of kindness has worn the sharp, hard edges off many a sin-hardened life and left it soft and pliable, ready to receive the redeeming grace of the Savior. A pleasant word is a bright ray of sunshine on a saddened heart. Therefore give others the sunshine and tell Jesus the rest.

"Be devoted to one another in brotherly love (Romans 12:10)."
From *Streams in the Desert* by L.B. Cowman [40]

OCTOBER 21

Dear Jesus,

Sometimes when I look at Sarah and my life,

I feel so blessed.

And then sometimes when I look at Sarah and my life,

I feel trapped.

Most of the time, Sarah's disabilities seem manageable.

And life feels normal.

But, from time to time, the self-pity and pity for Sarah sneak in.

From time to time, I feel overwhelmed by her delays and her needs.

My prayer, dear Jesus, is to not get stuck in the pity and the exasperation.

My prayer is to hang on tightly to those times when the blessings are obvious.

My prayer is to have clearer vision of Your will when the blessings are not so obvious.

Forgive me when I slip into selfishness and pull me back and protect me.

Help me to remember that all parents experience feelings of being trapped, being exhausted and being alone.

Help us all, Lord, to be better parents.

Help us to be more like you.

Thank you, Jesus, for Sarah and for my life.

OCTOBER 22

The time has come.

I must stop being impressed with myself.

This is an on-going battle of who will be on the throne of my life – me or Him.

He could blow me away with one breath of His mouth. He could consume me in a second. Yet, He does not.

Instead, He fights for me.

I am my greatest idol, and the God of Amazing Grace continually sands down this ugly idol of self, smaller and smaller and smaller. It can be a painful process as rough edges are chipped away. Yet essential. Valuable. Beautiful.

I am not my own. I belong to the One who created me in His image.

I belong to the One who redeemed me by His blood.

I do not have the right to make choices that oppose Him and that mock the absolute moral law He authored when He spoke the universe into being.

There is absolute truth.

And it matters.

And it belongs to Him.

The altars of "self" and "choice" and "my way" are not altars that can save.

Only the blood of Jesus Christ can.

OCTOBER 23

Biking in the cool moist air of a summer morning, pedaling past a corn field, stalks holding silken ears.

I breathe.

And I smell it.

Memories.

Corn, fresh and sweet, with memories in the aroma lingering.

I look back, and I see a farm girl.

Blue baseball cap and knee high rubber barn boots, country music and calloused hands.

And family together pulling the load of life.

I have smelled fresh corn growing on stalks before.

Younger years.

Simpler days.

Long ago.

Beautiful memories.

I remember.

But I do not look back for too long.

Just long enough to be grateful.

For my sweet Savior causes me to look forward.

In hope.

Great hope.

His hope.

Eternal in the heavens, pounding in my heart.

OCTOBER 24

Dear Father,

Praise Your name! Be magnified and exalted above all the distractions and disturbances of life. Give us the strength and spiritual maturity to live in harmony with one another. May we be sympathetic, compassionate, and humble. Prevent us from repaying evil with evil or insult with insult.

Lord, Your Word says that Your face is against those that do evil. May I, my husband, our family cherish that truth and tremble. You are holy, righteous. Our evil is rampant and regular. We need Your help. Even more, we need Your righteousness. Most of all, we need You.

Your eyes are upon the righteous. Your ears are attentive to their prayer. May we long, with the deepest of longings, to have Your eyes upon us, Your ears listening. May we desire You more than the temporary and fleeting vain successes and possessions of this world.

Strip us, Lord of the lust of the flesh, the lust of the eyes, and the pride of life.

And once bare before You, clothe us in Your righteousness. Our only hope!

Jesus, You are at the Father's right hand and angels and authorities and powers are in submission to You. May we willingly and eagerly yield to Your authority and submit our wills to Yours.

Be exalted, be glorified in this family! In Jesus' Glorious Name…

OCTOBER 25

Abiding means that sometimes I must STOP.

I have to stop trying to do what only God can.

I have to stop seeking glory for myself.

I have to stop trying to earn God's approval.

I have to stop grumbling.

I have to stop leaning on my own understanding…

Abiding means that sometimes I must START.

I have to start walking by faith and following God out of an obedient heart.

I have to start giving glory to God.

I have to start serving God from a heart of love.

I have to start praising.

I have to start leaning on His understanding.

Abiding means CONTINUING to do and be what and who God is calling me to do and be…willing to do anything and go anywhere any time He calls.

Abiding means that I am PREPARED, in season and out, always and every day.

OCTOBER 26

My miracle…part one…

Prayer: what a mysterious joy and struggle it can be.

My prayer life has been a roller coaster. There have been times of intimate highs and days of drought and famine. It is not God who is inconsistent. It is I.

I'll start my story in 1998, shortly after Sarah had her stroke. My prayers then were prayers of distress. I was truly distraught. *"Please heal Sarah. Please help us."* Sometimes, my prayers were angry, especially when Sarah would not sleep.

"God, how much do you think I can take! Where are you! What do you think you are doing to me! I don't know what you think you're doing!"

My prayers were often bitter pleas for a change in circumstances. And, they were completely self-centered prayers. There were no reservations, no inhibitions, just an honest outpouring of everything in my heart.

Back then, Sarah was typically peaceful and calm first thing in the morning. I could count on about 30 minutes of quiet time. I remember sitting at the kitchen table, every muscle and bone in my body aching as the result of all-night walking and rocking Sarah. Every nerve in my head pounding with the realization that it would all begin again in a few moments.

It was terrible. Sometimes, I would just sit at the kitchen table, drinking my cup of coffee, and stare straight ahead thinking, *"This can't be happening, this is a nightmare."*

In desperation to have some sort of control over this spinning world we were in, I searched the New Testament for promises, thinking, *"If I figure out the right way to pray, I can get what I want, and Sarah will get better."* I wrote down every passage, every story, every account of healing in the New Testament. I wrote down every verse spoken by Jesus that promised answers to prayers.

Sometimes at night when Sarah wouldn't sleep, I would take a few minutes and find a quiet spot. I would put Sarah in bed or have my husband hold her. She would cry and carry on. But I needed a few minutes apart from the reality that our lives were at that time. I would lay down on the bed in the spare room, and just repeat, over and over, Psalms 46:10: *Be still, and know that I am God...*

This was prayer. And it calmed my very anxious heart.

Eventually, Sarah did start sleeping better. I began taking brief morning walks while she slept. I would walk around our yard, holding my cup of coffee. I would pray, in specific detail, about every part of her body that was not working the right way. *"Please protect Sarah from more strokes, and help her brain to organize and do a more normal and better job of handling information and responding. Help her to use her arms better, to retract her shoulders less. Help the stiffness in her arms and legs decrease and the strength to increase. Help her to hold her head up with less effort. Bless and protect her heart. Bless, protect, and strengthen her muscles, bones, tendons, ligaments, joints..."*

Well, guess what?

Sarah was not healed. She still cannot independently sit, roll, walk, talk, feed herself. She still has a feeding tube. She still has seizures. She is experiencing muscle contractures around her knees. She is diapered. Catheterized. She requires total care for every single need. There is not one thing she can do for herself.

How can Jesus promise *"Ask and it will be given to you, seek and you will find; knock and the door will be opened to you,"* and then not heal Sarah?

Where is the miracle?

When reading the New Testament and the stories of Jesus on earth, clearly his will was for healing. He was not happy when people suffered. He healed people.

I was very confused. I wasn't sure how to make sense of His Word and promises in the light of our circumstances.

I bought and borrowed Christian books about suffering. I labored in Scripture. I struggled. I cried out to God and begged Him to help me make sense of the hard things and to endure. I don't know "why" Sarah had a stroke. It's taken time and tears and prayers, but I have accepted that "why" doesn't matter, or at least doesn't matter as much as I used to think it did. God is more concerned with "how" we respond to suffering than whether or not we figure out "why" the suffering is happening. May we learn to suffer well. May we learn from Christ, the greatest example of faithful obedience in the face of suffering. He experienced excruciating physical, emotional, and spiritual pain.

He suffered for us.

That doesn't make the mystery of suffering any less, but at least we have a God who knows, first hand, the pain of human life.

Obviously, volumes have been written regarding suffering. Greater minds than mine have addressed this topic and come to no resolution, so I doubt that I will.

I have learned we don't need resolution and understanding as much as we need the everlasting arms of God under us.

We need Him.

We need His presence.

We need to become comfortable with questions unanswered, but all needs met by His sufficient grace.

The miracle came…not as physical healing…but the very presence of God.

He never left us.

He never forsook us. He was with us.

God Himself…God with us…that is the miracle.

OCTOBER 27

My miracle…part two…

I had been struggling to make sense of God in the light of our circumstances.

I came to realize that this was backward.

For, it was my circumstances that needed to be understood in the light of God.

And this new way of thinking changed everything.

There have been turning points along the way, moments when familiar Scripture leaped off the page with new life.

II Corinthians 12…In this passage, Paul, God's faithful servant, had some sort of medical condition (which he referred to as "a thorn in my flesh"). Paul prayed three times pleading with God to take this from him. God did not do so. Instead, God told Paul, *My grace is sufficient for you, for my power is made perfect in weakness.*

Wow! There's Paul, doing incredible things for the Kingdom of God and advancing the good news of Jesus, and he suffers. We tend to assume that God can use us best in healthy bodies. It may be a flawed assumption, for God tells his servant, *No – the thorn will not be removed.*

Paul's example demonstrates that "answer to prayer" really means "God giving you what you need for both your good and the good of the Kingdom." And God, rather than us, is the one who decides what is the most profitable.

We really limit God's power in our lives when we bind him with the thought, "answered prayers = getting our way and getting it immediately."

We really limit God's power in our lives when we assume that silence on God's part is the same as unanswered prayers.

Sometimes, the answer may lie within the silence.

Consider Jesus' prayer on the Mount of Olives immediately preceding His arrest in the garden. He went to the garden following the Last Supper. He took Peter, James, and John with him. In the garden, Jesus knows that He will soon be arrested and crucified. Jesus realizes that the crucifixion will be horrible. He understands that He will face physical torture, spiritual and emotional hell, an abandonment.

In distress Jesus prays, '*My Father, if it is possible, may this cup be taken from Me. Yet not as I will, but as you will...My Father, if it is not possible for this cup to be taken away unless I drink it, may Your will be done...Father, if You are willing, take this cup from me; yet not My will but Yours be done.'...And, being in anguish, He prayed more earnestly, and His sweat was like drops of blood falling to the ground.*"

The reason Jesus was on earth in a human body was to sacrifice Himself for the salvation of the sinful human race and glorify God in this accomplishment. The reason Jesus was on earth in a human body was because God LOVES human beings. Jesus came as a sacrifice for our sins so that we could have the opportunity to live forever in God's kingdom. Jesus, in his human form, despite His knowledge and ultimate understanding of what was going on, was terrified. And, He prayed to His Father to find another way, if it be possible, to save the human race.

God's answer was silence.

And, that silence meant, there was no other way. Thus, Jesus prayed honest prayers from His heart in that garden, and His prayers were not answered the way He may have wished them to be. But, He trusted, He had faith, and He walked the path intended for Him.

His prayer and response are good examples for us: His prayer was honest in anguish and His response was faith despite the pain.

Another turning point for me occurred one day during church service.

Sarah was with me. She was fussing. I was tired. I was feeling irritated with her grumpy behavior, and I was struggling to be nice to people sharing the same church pew. My husband and I took turns holding Sarah. But, the fussing continued. I kept thinking, *Is it always going to be this way? NO! It's only going to get worse! She's just going to keep getting bigger, and then all the things that are already so hard will get even harder! What am I going to do?*

I felt overwhelmed. Exhausted. Depressed.

And God spoke.

And I heard His beautiful counsel in the depths of my heart: *Rest. Don't think about the future of caring for Sarah when you are tired or when you are having a bad day. I know you need to think about it, and I know you need to plan, but don't think about it when you are tired. Wait until you are rested to deal with it, make decisions then. Calm down, and just focus on surviving on the bad days, that's all you have to do.*

Ever since that moment, I surrender the negative thoughts when I am tired or overwhelmed. I absolutely cast them upon Him, for He careth for me. That doesn't mean I ignore the obvious things that need attention or the obvious decisions that must be made.

It simply means I wait with my palms held open and up…until I am rested and better able to make decisions with love and wisdom.

Survival mode does have an important place from time to time in our lives. And, now I know, when I am overwhelmed, that the feeling will pass. The next day will begin better. I don't bite off more than I can mentally chew anymore.

Now here we are, five years later, 2003.   And, I don't feel like I have to stretch for reasons to be optimistic about our situation anymore.

I simply feel optimistic.

God did answer prayers.

No, not in the exact way we prayed them. Better.

For He has given us Himself.

He has given us strength and joy and perseverance and peace IN THE TRIAL.

The hard things remain…but God is greater…and the joy is real.

Truly, we do count this all joy.

Truly, we do know there is beauty and purpose in this.

How Great Is Our God, Sing With Me, How Great Is Our God…

OCTOBER 28

My miracle…part three…

Sarah is the delight of my life. She smiles a beautiful smile. She enjoys life. She looks at me with the most appreciative gaze of anyone I've ever met.

You know what? It's a choice.

I could look at Sarah and be angry at God because I do not have a daughter who walks and talks. She could even die any time or get seriously ill again.

Or, I can look for the ways that God has moved, sometimes clearly and sometimes subtly in my life.

He has changed me.

And that, my friends, is a miracle.

I prayed for Sarah to be healed. Instead, God has shown me that I am the one really in need of healing. I am the one who depends, wrongly, more on myself than upon God. I am the one who lets my irritability bubble up into mistreating people whose paths cross mine. I am the one who secretly feels satisfaction when someone I don't like has a bad day.

I, truly, am the one in need of healing.

And He has healed me and cleansed me and made me whole. He has taken my worldly perspective and dashed it upon the rocks of hard times. He has crafted a heavenly perspective and given me a vision greater far than any I could have ever imagined.

He has taken my stubborn stony heart and ripped it from me, replacing it with His heart of flesh.

I was dead in trespasses and sin.

Now I am alive.

His.

Forever.

This is life. Beautiful life.

Eternal.

This is my God.

This is my miracle.

OCTOBER 29

Do I know how to love God's way?

No.

My love is conditional.

My love is inconsistent, changing with my moods.

I love when it's comfortable and convenient and safe to love.

I avoid loving if it requires I be vulnerable.

I love when I am loved back.

I expect something from the object of my love.

My love has limits.

I love like a human.

Shallow.

I need God.

There is no way I can love as I am supposed to and as I am called to, unless He, in me, loves through me.

It is hard to love.

It costs to love God's way.

It can hurt to love God's way.

It hurt Him to love us His way.

How it must still hurt Him when we fail to love one another His way.

Worse yet, when we fail to love Him…the ONE so worthy, the ONE always worthy, the ONE who loves us in our unworthiness.

How merciful to us that His love is not like our love!

October 30

From <u>Streams in the Desert</u> by L.B. Cowman [41]

"*Sorrowful, yet always rejoicing (II Corinthians 6:10).*

"*Sorrow was beautiful, but his beauty was the beauty of the moonlight shining through the leafy branches of the trees in the woods. His gentle light made little pools of silver here and there on the soft green moss of the forest floor. And when he sang, his song was like the low, sweet calls of the nightingale, and in his eyes was the unexpectant gaze of someone who has ceased to look for coming gladness. He could weep in tender sympathy with those who weep, but to rejoice with those who rejoice was unknown to him.*

"*Joy was beautiful, too, but hers was the radiant beauty of a summer morning. Her eyes still held the happy laughter of childhood, and her hair glistened with the sunshine's kiss. When she sang, her voice soared upward like a skylark's, and her steps were the march of a conqueror who has never known defeat. She could rejoice with anyone who rejoices, but to weep with those who weep was unknown to her.*

"*Sorrow longingly said, 'We can never be united as one.' 'No, never,' responded Joy, with eyes misting as she spoke, 'for my path lies through the sunlit meadows, the sweetest roses bloom when I arrive, and songbirds await my coming to sing their most joyous melodies.'*

"'*Yes, and my path,' said Sorrow, turning slowly away, 'leads through the dark forest, and moonflowers, which open only at night, will fill my hands. Yet the sweetest of all earthly songs – the love song of the night – will be mine. So farewell, dear Joy, farewell.'*

"*Yet even as Sorrow spoke, he and Joy became aware of someone standing beside them. In spite of the dim light, they sensed a kingly Presence, and suddenly a great and holy awe overwhelmed them. They then sank to their knees before Him.*

"'*I see Him as the King of Joy,' whispered Sorrow, 'for on His head are many crowns, and the nail prints in His hands and feet are the scars of a great victory. And before*

Him all my sorrow is melting away into deathless love and gladness. I now give myself to Him forever.'

" 'No, Sorrow,' said Joy softly, 'for I see Him as the King of Sorrow, and the crown on His head is a crown of thorns, and the nail prints in His hands and feet are the scars of terrible agony. I also give myself to Him forever, for sorrow with Him must be sweeter than any joy I have ever known.'

" 'Then we are one in Him,' they cried in gladness, 'for no one but He could unite Joy and Sorrow.'   Therefore they walked hand in hand into the world, to follow Him through storms and sunshine, through winter's severe cold and the warmth of summer's gladness, and to be 'sorrowful, yet always rejoicing.'"
From <u>*Streams in the Desert*</u> *by L.B. Cowman* [41]

OCTOBER 31

Masks and costumes.

That's what we do on Halloween.

But let's make sure that's not what we do the rest of the days of the year.

It's very easy in the Christian community to adorn ourselves with masks and costumes.

We want to project the expected image to those around us in the community.

Sometimes the community expects that and even rewards that….

It's easier that way, after all.

But may I suggest that masks and costumes can become walls behind which we and our sin can hide.

Let's be honest.

Let's be sincere.

Let's be transparent.

Let's be vulnerable one with another.

I know it's sloppy and messy and not everyone wants it that way, but….

We cannot be victorious behind masks and costumes.

Don't live your life as if every day is Halloween.

Tear off the mask and be stripped of the costume.

God has clothes for you to wear.

Struggle to find them.

Strive to put them on.

Wear them well.

October's Apologetic Moment...Contend for the faith

When someone claims there is no such thing as absolute truth...
Ask him, "Are you absolutely sure about that?"

From I Don't Have Enough Faith To Be An Atheist [65]
by Norman Geisler and Frank Turek
(selected quotes from chapter one, "Can We Handle the Truth?")

"Contrary to what is being taught in many public schools, truth is not relative but absolute. If something is true, it's true for all people, at all times, in all places. All truth claims are absolute, narrow, and exclusive. Just think about the claim, "everything is true." That's an absolute, narrow, and exclusive claim. It excludes its opposite (i.e., it claims that the statement 'everything is not true' is wrong). In fact, all truths exclude their opposites...

"There are many truths about truth. Here are some of them:

"**Truth is discovered, not invented.** It exists independent of anyone's knowledge of it. (Gravity existed prior to Newton.)

"**Truth is transcultural**; if something is true, it is true for all people, in all places, at all times. (2+2=4 for everyone, everywhere, at every time.)

"**Truth is unchanging** even though our beliefs about truth change. (When we began to believe the earth was round instead of flat, the truth about the earth didn't change, only our belief about the earth changed.)

"**Beliefs cannot change a fact, no matter how sincerely they are held.** (Someone can sincerely believe the world is flat, but that only makes that person sincerely mistaken.)

"**Truth is not affected by the attitude of the one professing it.** (An arrogant person does not make the truth he professes false. A humble person does not make the error he professes true.)...

"*In short, contrary beliefs are possible, but contrary truths are not possible.* We can believe everything is true, but we cannot make everything true...

"A self-defeating statement is one that fails to meet its own standard. 'There is no truth' is a self-defeating statement because it claims to be true and thus defeats itself. It's like saying, 'I can't speak a word in English.' If someone ever said that, you obviously would respond, 'Wait a minute! Your statement must be false because you just uttered it in English!'

"Can all religions be true? No, religious beliefs cannot all be true, because many religious beliefs are contradictory – they teach opposites. For example, conservative Christians believe that those who haven't accepted Christ as their Savior have chosen hell as their ultimate destination. It's often overlooked, but many Muslims believe the same about non-Muslims – they're headed for hell as well. And Hindus generally believe that everyone, regardless of beliefs, is caught in an indefinite cycle of reincarnation based on works. These contradictory beliefs can't all be true.

"In fact, world religions have more contradictory beliefs than complementary ones. The notion that all religions teach basically the same thing – that we ought to love one another – demonstrates a serious misunderstanding of world religions. While most religions have some kind of similar moral code because God has implanted right and wrong on our consciences, they disagree on virtually every major issue, including the nature of God, the nature of man, sin, salvation, heaven, hell, and creation!...

"While we should respect the rights of others to believe what they want, we are foolish, and maybe even unloving, to tacitly accept every religious belief as true. Why is this unloving? Because if Christianity is true, then it would be unloving to suggest to anyone that their opposing religious beliefs are true as well. Affirming such error might keep them on the road to damnation. Instead, if Christianity is true, we ought to kindly tell them the truth because only the truth can set them free.

"What does the vast plurality of religious beliefs tell us about truth in religion? At first glance, it might appear that the existence of so many contradictory beliefs just reinforces the elephant parable we mentioned in the introduction – namely, that truth in religion cannot be known. But exactly the opposite is the case.

"To refresh your memory, in this parable an elephant is being examined by six blind men. Each man feels a different part of the elephant and thus reaches a different conclusion about the object in front of him. One grabs the tusk and says, 'This is a spear!' Another holds the trunk and says, 'This is a snake!' The one hugging the leg claims, 'This is a tree!' The blind man holding the tail thinks, 'I have a rope!' The one feeling the ear believes, 'This is a fan!' And the one leaning on the elephant's side is certain, 'This is a wall!' These blind men are said to represent world religions, because they each come to a different conclusion about what they are sensing. Like each blind man, we are told, no one religion has THE truth. Religious truth is relative to the individual. It is subjective, not objective.

"This may seem persuasive until you ask yourself one question: 'What's the perspective of the one telling the parable?' Hmmmm, let's see, the one telling the parable...He appears to have an OBJECTIVE perspective of the entire proceeding because he can see that the blind men are mistaken. Exactly! In fact, he wouldn't know that the blind me were wrong unless he had an objective perspective of what was right!

"So if the person telling the parable can have an objective perspective, why can't the blind men? They could – if the blind men suddenly could see, they too would realize that they were originally mistaken. That's really an elephant in front of them and not a wall, fan, or rope.

"We too can see the truth in religion. Unfortunately, many of us who deny there's truth in religion are not actually blind but only willfully blind. We may not want to admit that there's truth in religion because that truth will convict us. But if we open our eyes and stop hiding behind the self-defeating nonsense that truth cannot be known, then we'll be able to see the truth as well."

*From **I Don't Have Enough Faith To Be An Atheist** [65]*
by Norman Geisler and Frank Turek
(selected quotes from chapter one, "Can We Handle the Truth?")

For in Him we live, and move, and have our being.
Acts 17:28a

November

"Can we follow the Savior far, who have no wound or scar? "
— Amy Carmichael, God's Missionary

NOVEMBER 1

Dear Lord,

You, despised and rejected by men...You, a man of sorrows, familiar with suffering...

The great, all-powerful God...forgive us.

Save us.

Rescue us.

Restore us.

You, who took our infirmities and carried our sorrows, and was pierced for our transgressions and crushed for our iniquities, forgive us.

Forgive us that, despite this gift freely held out to us, we live our lives overlooking You.

Neglecting You.

Rejecting You.

Father, You sent the Son, and He was pierced for us. Now, pierce us with Your truth, the truth that we are lost apart from Your forgiveness and cleansing. The truth that hell is a real destination for those who try to reach You in their own strength and supposed goodness.

Jesus, the punishment that brought us peace was upon You. We stray and go our own way. And this straying caused You suffering.

Thank You that You allowed the Father to lay my iniquity upon You. Pierce me with the truth of Your suffering and bless me with godly sorrow that leads to true repentance.

By Your wounds am I healed.

May all in my family who yet have the grievous sin wound oozing upon their lives, fall before You in brokenness and be healed and be saved.

Holy is Your name!

And beautiful are Your wounds.

In the Healing Name of Jesus…

NOVEMBER 2

Despite the cold air of this morning (or perhaps because of it), I decided to take a bike ride.

As I was slicing through the brisk air, I prayed.

Today is Sunday. Soon I will be in church. *Offend me this day, Lord. May I hear a message at church today that interrupts my comfort and one that bothers me and shakes me up.*

Offend me, today, dear Lord.

Make me to hear things this day that will cause me to struggle and have to work out my spiritual muscles in deep spiritual truths. May I be uncomfortable in church today, hearing things that I need to hear even if I don't want to hear them. For that is where growth occurs.

For gardens to grow fruitful, fallow ground must be ploughed up. Weeds must be hacked out and pulled up by the roots. And so it is, for spiritual fruitfulness in the life of God's children…fallow ground must be ploughed up. Lies believed must be hacked out. Apathy taken root must be pulled up and out.

So this day I pray, dear Lord, that you would plough up any fallow ground you find in my heart and in my mind, and that You would pull out, by the roots, any deception that is obscuring my understanding of You, Lord, and the life You have given me.

If it requires offending me, then Lord, offend me. Deeply. But do not leave me in a place of stagnating comfort where heart and mind grow apathetic and eyes and ears dull to spiritual truth.

NOVEMBER 3

Psalm 126:4-6: Turn again our captivity, O LORD, as the streams in the south. They that sow in tears shall reap in joy. He that goeth forth and weepeth, bearing precious seed, shall doubtless come again with rejoicing, bringing his sheaves with him.

I read these beautiful words from Scripture, and I am assured that there is goodness and meaning and hope in even our moments of captivity. When we are held captive to tragedy or pain, when we are sowing tears of sorrow, God is at work. Delivering us through the waters of the Red Sea. Bringing us forth refined as gold. Preparing us to be stones in His Glorious Temple. Fashioning us to be vessels fit for His use. God doesn't simply give us joy. He is our joy. Once we awake to this reality, we go forth, yes weeping, but also bearing precious seed, and we labor in the harvest. This is joy unspeakable and full of glory.

Joy matters because it is a proper response to WHO GOD IS and WHAT GOD DOES. God is the Creator. He spoke our universe, all matter and energy, sun, moon, and stars into being. He sustains the world. He literally holds it and us together. Joy is a proper response to this reality. God is also the Redeemer. God of all Creation humbly stepped into flesh, and that flesh bled and that flesh died and that flesh experienced the wrath of Holy God in our place. And that flesh, as the day of crucifixion ended, was laid in a cold, dark tomb. But, guess what? Morning came! And up from the grave He arose! Our Redeemer is ALIVE! And the proper response to this reality is joy unspeakable.

Let's run this race well. Let's look unto Jesus, and as He did, may we, too, endure hardships well. For there is joy set before us.

Joy isn't a "what" or a "where" or a "when." Joy is a "WHO." And the WHO is the GREAT I AM who always has been and always will be, the One who inhabits eternity. The One who spoke and all matter and energy and time and space came to be. He is the One who hung the stars in place and calls them each by name and not one is missing. He is the One who created mankind in His image. He is the One who draws us out of deep water and sets us on the firm and solid ground of His holy, unchangeable truth and character. He is the great High Priest who sympathizes with us in all our infirmities because He, too, suffered. For us. He has bought us with a price. His blood. And the who of joy is the One who is victory. He is victory over sin, suffering, death, and hell. He is our victory. He is alive, and we will one day behold His glory and forever worship He who is Holy, Holy, Holy.

For we are the redeemed of the Lord. And this, yes this, is joy unspeakable.

Go, my friends, in the strength you have. The joy of the Lord is our strength.

Jude 24-25: Now unto Him that is able to keep you from falling, and to present you faultless before the presence of His glory with exceeding joy, to the only wise God our Saviour, be glory and majesty, dominion and power, both now and ever. Amen.

NOVEMBER 4

Comparing. We do it frequently.

We compare ourselves to others.

This leads to sin…

Either the sin of discouragement because the other is better than I or the sin of haughtiness because I am better than the other.

In each case, comparing self to others makes it all about self.

And this is pride.

And pride is sin.

Abiding in the Savior means I choose humility…and stop comparing myself to others.

Others are not the standard. The Lord Jesus Christ is the standard. As I abide in Him, I should tremble at this reality and both cling to His side and rest in His arms…the side pierced for me and the arms opened wide for me.

The place of hope.

NOVEMBER 5

Abiding is perspective.

Abiding…standing next to the ocean. I small, it big, and the God who created both bigger yet. Sun rising over the horizon, casting colors onto crashing waves. My heart, my mind, my being in awe of Creator God! Fully aware that the heavens truly do declare the glory of God!

Abiding...driving through the beauty of the Appalachian Mountains in West Virginia. This is a completely different scene from the smooth and sandy beach. Yet, it is the same all-powerful creative God who gave rise to these mighty mountains. And my heart, my mind, my being bow before His Great Majesty. Fully aware am I that the earth is the Lord's and the fullness thereof!

Abiding...walking in the dry mote that surrounds the Fort in St. Augustine and gaining a new perspective on an old scene. The Fort appears huge as I stand at its base. The town appears distant as parts of it vanish from view at this angle in the depth of the mote. I hear the water of the bay, but can no longer see it from where I stand. Many times have I been to this Fort, yet this view I missed until this moment. I am fascinated.

Abiding...making memories with my husband in St. Augustine, sensing our mortality and the brevity of life as we do so. Savoring the moments, recognizing the uniqueness of the day and the goodness of God who gives us life.

NOVEMBER 6

Are not two sparrows sold for a penny? Yet not one of them will fall to the ground apart from the will of your Father. And even the very hairs of your head are all numbered. So don't be afraid; you are worth more than many sparrows (Matthew 10: 29-31).

Our daughter, Sarah, just finished 2 years and 9 months of chemotherapy. She was seven years old in November, 2003 when she was diagnosed with acute lymphocytic leukemia. Chemotherapy led to clumps of hair falling out all over our house. It was hard to believe that such a little head could hold so much hair - it was everywhere - it would fall out in my hands when washing her hair. Fistfuls of blonde hair stuck to my wet hands. It was simply everywhere. A constant reminder of the suffering my child was going through.

But, there were blessings along the way of that rough and dismal journey through cancer. Jesus became real to me. What He had to say about eternal life and life here and now became real to me. What a blessing! In Matthew 10, Jesus tells us how the details of our lives are known to God the Father. And, how God, ultimately, is in control of these details.

Jesus told me in these very special verses, that every hair on Sarah's head was, and is indeed still, numbered. He knows them all. He loves her deeply. Because I believe in the absolute truth of the Bible, I believe in the truth of God's awareness of Sarah...and her needs, and her illness, and who she is. We've never had to go through this alone. God has been there every time a hair fell out. Every time platelets were low. Every time Sarah threw up blood. Every time the sheets were stained with blood from an overnight nose-bleed. Every fever. Every mouth sore. Every hospitalization. God is aware, and nothing comes to Sarah or to us that has not first been sifted through God's great mighty hands.

And why? Why was Sarah diagnosed with cancer? I used to wonder the things that many wonder when the sad things strike. What did I do wrong? What is God trying to teach me? Am I being punished? Is my faith weak? I no longer wonder "why." Instead, I cling to another lesson from the Bible, recorded in John 9. Jesus was spending time with His disciples one day. They happened to notice a blind man, and they questioned Jesus, "Why is that man blind? Is it because of his sin or the sins of his parents?" Jesus told them, "Neither. He is blind to bring glory to God."

Somehow, some way, Sarah's cancer and our response to it can bring glory to God.

She, and we, have an important job to do. We are to seek how we can glorify God in the circumstances that we experience. I praise God that He has been so patient with me.

Getting past the "why" is never something that we can do successfully separate from God. A person cannot, of his own strength, ever step beyond the "why". Human beings need bigger vision in order to do that, and such bigger vision comes only from the eternal God, the God of the big picture.

God tells the truth in the Bible.

And one of those truths is that every hair is numbered.

And, God is more than aware. He is near. God promises us that *Never will I leave you; never will I forsake you (Hebrews 13:5 and Deuteronomy 31:6) and ...surely I am with you always, to the very end of the age (Matthew 28:20b).*

NOVEMBER 7

Be not shocked by the evil in the world.

Yet somehow remain shocked by its reality.

Evil must be faced. We must be able to look at it without becoming desensitized to it.

We must never allow evil to feel normal in our lives.

We must be sensitive to the truth that evil exists. We must recognize evil and its many tentacles. But, we must not become so sensitive that we fear and hide. They who have embraced the evil agenda that is present in the world want to shock us so that in shock we fall silent and hide in our caves.

Don't hide.

But do anguish.

Anguish over the lost-ness of the world.

Anguish over the hardness hearts.

Anguish when God is blasphemed by the world, but even more anguish when God is blasphemed among His own people and within my own self.

Anguish when eyes are blind and ears are dull.

Anguish before the throne of God.

Anguish when God's Word and God's ways are mocked in the world, in the church, and in our own minds and hearts.

Anguish when Your people live in defeat and bondage.

Lord, the evil in this world is real. Show me the way to walk with You in the midst of a crooked and depraved generation. Teach me how to think in a day of deception. Protect truth. Shine light. Into the darkness, send the remnant, and may they be prepared to stand for You amongst the lost. May we be prepared to live for You. To die for You. You have work for each of Your children. May we be faithful to discover Your work for us. Faithful to obey.

NOVEMBER 8

Dear Lord,

Praise Your name!

You are the God who creates.

You are the God who saves.

You are Jehovah and there is no other.

Praise You for opening a way for us to the Most Holy Place.

The way is open through the blood of Christ.

We can run to You with confidence.

And Your body is the curtain through which we must enter.

May every person in my family know that You are the Great High Priest.

May the unsaved be terribly burdened with the weight of the guilt which sin is.

May consciences be alert and sorrowing.

You have been grieved, Holy Lord!

Grant that our sin may grieve us as well.

And then, crying out to You, may the burden of sin be removed and consciences washed clean, and lives made new through Your saving power.

Lord, You are absolutely faithful. And righteous.

It is a dreadful thing to fall into Your hands, the hands of a living God.

Your hands, all powerful, could crush us.

Yet, You instead allowed those hands to bleed for us.

God have mercy upon us if we allow that blood, the blood that saves, the blood shed for us, to come to naught in our lives.

Raise up godly men and women in the generation now and the ones to come.

May there be no shrinking back!

In the Name of Jesus the Great High Priest...

<u>**NOVEMBER 9**</u>

Do not limit God to your personal salvation.

God is woven into the cosmology and fabric of the entire universe, each life, and all things.

Yes, He is personal salvation. But, He is not only personal salvation. He is more…He is a worldview, a way of life, a way to understand all that we experience and observe.

It is this worldview, as well as His salvation, that must be embraced…For God intends to impact cultures as well as individuals. God's redemption is intended to be both personal and societal. We, the redeemed, are to impact the culture with the message of redemption – in whatever way the Spirit of God moves each one of us.

God's message of redemption is greater than the depravity of culture.

Do not shrink back!

Do not be discouraged!

For discouragement is simply unbelief…for if God is who He has revealed Himself to be, then we do not have the luxury or excuse of discouragement.

NOVEMBER 10

From *Total Truth: Liberating Christianity from its Cultural Captivity* by Nancy Pearcey [42]

Divided Minds

" 'Thinking Christianly' means understanding that Christianity gives the truth about the whole of reality, a perspective for interpreting every subject matter. Genesis tells us that God spoke the entire universe into being with His Word or what John 1:1 calls the 'Logos'. The Greek word means not only 'Word' but also 'reason or rationality,' and the ancient Stoics used it to mean the rational structure of the universe. Thus the underlying structure of the entire universe reflects the mind of the Creator. There is no fact/value dichotomy in the scriptural account. Nothing has an autonomous or independent identity, separate from the will of the Creator. As a result, all creation must be interpreted in light of its relationship to God. In any subject area we study, we are discovering the laws or creation ordinances by which God structured the world….

"What is the antidote to the secular/sacred divide? How do we make sure our toolbox contains biblically based conceptual tools for every issue we encounter? We must begin by being utterly convinced that there **is** a biblical perspective on everything – not just on spiritual matters. The Old Testament tells us repeatedly that 'The fear of the LORD is the beginning of wisdom' (Psalm 111:10; Proverbs 1:7, 9:10, 15:33). Similarly, the New Testament teaches that in Christ are 'all the treasures of wisdom and knowledge' (Colossians 2:3). We often interpret these verses to mean spiritual wisdom only, but the text places no limitation on the term. 'Most people have a tendency to read these passages as though they say that the fear of the Lord is the foundation of religious knowledge,' writes Clouser. 'But the fact is that they make a very radical claim – the claim that somehow all knowledge depends upon religious truth.'....

"The Christian message does not begin with 'accept Christ as your Savior'; it begins with 'in the beginning God created the heavens and the earth.' The Bible teaches that God is the sole source of the entire created order. No other gods compete with Him; no natural forces exist on their own; nothing receives its nature or existence from another source. Thus His Word, or laws, or creation ordinances give the world its order and structure. God's creative Word is the source of the laws of **physical** nature, which we study in the natural sciences. It is also the source of the laws of **human** nature – the principles of morality (ethics), of justice (politics), of creative enterprise (economics), of aesthetics (the arts), and even of clear thinking (logic). That's why Psalm 119:91 says, 'all things are Your servants.' There is no philosophically or spiritually neutral subject matter."**
From <u>Total Truth: Liberating Christianity from its Cultural Captivity</u> by Nancy Pearcey [42]

<u>NOVEMBER 11</u>

Do we even get it anymore?

Do we understand what SIN is and what it means to God?

God's commandments are found in Exodus 20. We are instructed that God is to be first in our lives - no idols, nothing more important than God to us. We are told not to take His name in vain. To remember the Sabbath. Honor our parents. Do not murder or commit adultery or steal or lie. Do not covet, do not desire what belongs to someone else. Jesus, in His Sermon on the Mount, expands these commandments. Looking with lust is just as bad as adultery. Hating is just as bad a murder.

God knows the condition of our hearts and sees the secret sin that exists there.

The world does NOT encourage us to recognize and deal humbly with sin. The world talks about **self**-esteem and **self**-actualization and **self**-confidence and **self**-reliance.

But the world rejects the truth that real "esteem" and "actualization" and "confidence" come from walking in a right relationship with the Creator who gives us every breath we take and who is the One who allows our hearts to beat.

*You are worthy, our Lord and God, to receive glory and honor and power, for You created all things, and by **YOUR WILL** they were created and have their being (Revelation 4:11).*

*He (Christ) is the image of the invisible God, the firstborn over all creation. For by Him all things were created: things in heaven and on earth, visible and invisible, whether thrones or powers or rulers or authorities; all things were created by **HIM AND FOR HIM**. He is before all things, and in Him all things hold together (Colossians 1:15-18).*

I have an inadequate view of sin.

The world tries to convince me, and more than I like to admit succeeds in its convincing, that it's not a sin if *"it doesn't hurt someone else. Whatever works for you."* But this is a flawed argument. For sin always hurts someone else.

There is a "someone else" for whom sin is always painful. God.

In I Peter 2, we are reminded of what Jesus did for us as a result of our sin: *When they hurled their insults at Him, He (Jesus) did not retaliate; when He suffered, He made no threats. Instead, He entrusted Himself to Him (God the Father) who judges justly. **He (Jesus) Himself bore our sins in His body on the tree (cross), so that we might die to sins and live for righteousness; by His wounds you have been healed.** For you were like sheep going astray, but now you have returned to the Shepherd and Overseer of your souls (I Peter 2:23-25).*

Jesus willingly SUFFERED and DIED as the sacrifice for OUR SINS.

Yes, sin actually is serious to God who suffered because of it.

I'm weary of our society's general attitude toward God.

Sin is real.

It is serious.

God is not the "big guy in the sky."

He is the Holy, Eternal Creator and Redeemer.

He is my holy Father expecting me to take His commandments seriously, even though I cannot live these holy commandments perfectly.

If I think only of His love, I will eventually be convinced that He will overlook my sin. If I think God will overlook my sin, then it's ok for me to overlook my sin, and if I overlook my sin, eventually my life will be a mess of self.

God gave us His commandments out of His holiness and **for our benefit**. They deal with our relationship with God, our relationships with each other, our actions, and the condition of our hearts. God's commandments reflect His holiness and they are paths of abundance and health. I cannot live a safe, abundant, and healthy life apart from God's commandments.

There is danger inherent in trying to live life outside of God's gracious commandments.

Recently, I read a story that illustrates the danger. Pretend you live in a beautiful high rise apartment. It has an elaborate balcony. But, there are no rails on the balcony, and a fall from the balcony would bring death. No way would you let your children play on that balcony! Now, pretend that railings are installed. All of a sudden, it becomes ok to let your children play on that balcony. What those railings are to the balcony is what God's commandments are to our lives. Within those railings, we can go freely out onto the balcony of life and enjoy the view and the fresh air. We can live free.

Ignoring God's commandments leads to bondage. Paul counsels us, in the book of Romans, that, like it or not, we will be a slave to something...either sin or obedience: *Don't you know that when you offer yourselves to someone to obey him as slaves, you are slaves to the one whom you obey - whether you are slaves to sin, which leads to death, or to obedience, which leads to righteousness?* (Romans 6:16-17).

Sin is inadequately defined, if it is defined at all, in the world. Sadly, this is often also true in our churches today. *For the time will come when men will not put up with sound doctrine. Instead, to suit their own desires, they will gather around them a great number of teachers to say what their itching ears want to hear* (2 Timothy 4:3).

We are quickly losing the courage to honestly acknowledge "sin." We are quickly losing our ability to recognize sin in our own lives and in our own thinking. We are quickly losing the willingness and ability to repent. Repentance is necessary for salvation. The Bible teaches us that we are saved by **confessing** with our mouths that *Jesus is Lord* and **believing** in our hearts that *God raised Him from the dead...and everyone who **calls** on the name of the Lord will be saved (Romans 10:13).*

If we are unable to recognize our sin and what it means to God, if we don't think that our sin is all that bad, if we believe in the world's standards as supreme, then we won't see our need to "confess, believe, and call" will we?

NOVEMBER 12

Salvation message...the simplicity.

Me...always complicating what is simple.

I get wrapped up feeling I need to solve other people's problems, and then the salvation message becomes tangled up in life's stuff and problems.

Salvation is simple once one sees the need. We complicate the seeing because we look so much at circumstances and possessions and our own understanding of these lives we live. We are told that government is our salvation. We are told that education is our salvation. We are told that science is our salvation. We are told that the environment is our salvation. We are told that medicine is our salvation. We are told that success is our salvation. We are told that enjoyment is our salvation. We are told that self-fulfillment is our salvation.

These are lies.

Jesus Christ – His life, death, and resurrection – are both salvation and solution. He is the solution to all problems we humans face. He does not always solve the problem by fixing the circumstances. Mostly He has to just fix us and teach us to fix our eyes upon Him.

How does it all get worked out in our lives? How are we to know the unique solutions we each need for the many problems we face day by day?

It gets worked out in relationship...we with Him...step by step, moment by moment. The relationship we have with the God of creation and redemption is the solution to the problem we face and the battle we fight.

This takes work. It's hard. It's a drawn out process. There are ups and downs and highs and lows. But this is where we find beauty for ashes and the oil of joy for mourning. It is in this place of striving that we find perfect rest.

In Him. Relationship.

But seek ye first the kingdom of God, and His righteousness; and all these things shall be added unto you (Matthew 6:33).

NOVEMBER 13

Dear Father,

Praise You!

The sermon this morning was a glorious reminder of Your love, mercy, grace, holiness, and righteousness.

Your Son is the Only Way to heaven. Anything that diminishes this truth, anything that dethrones Jesus as the Only Way is evil.

Even if it looks good.

Even if it is religious

Good works and religion do NOT save!

And, actually, they are evil if they exalt any other way to enter the Kingdom.

We can sacrifice our lives to care for others, and if we are trusting in this to save us instead of Jesus, all our sacrifice, suffering, service are filthy rags.

Hell awaits those who trust any other way than Jesus Christ and His blood shed for you.

Offensive?

I guess if you are trusting any other way, then yes.

May you be offended enough to seek!

May you be offended enough to think about this.

May you be offended enough to be born again, into spiritual life eternal.

Father, please, offend anyone in my family and in my classroom who is not saved!

Offend them.

Interrupt their day.

Trouble the waters of their lives.

Wake them from spiritual slumber.

Pursue them.

With Your truth.

Your holiness.

Your righteous white robes.

Your love.

Tear down idols.

Destroy darkness with light.

Rip out lies with truth.

Dismantle strongholds and consume the high places.

Humble the proud.

Save the lost.

Bring each to a place of brokenness before Your exalted throne.

May we be terribly offended…and completely saved.

In the Name of Jesus, the High and Exalted One…

NOVEMBER 14

"Big guy in the sky" theology.

Secular Christianity with a small view of a pure and holy God.

The social gospel.

It sounds good. It is comfortable.

It doesn't bother with sin and hell.

Thus it falls short of true redemption…

For meeting needs without sharing truth is no gospel at all.

It is a temporary reprieve.

It is putting a Band-Aid on gangrene.

The rot remains.

And spreads.

God is not the "big guy in the sky."

God is not the "man upstairs."

God is a consuming fire.

He is eternal in the heavens.

He is Righteous Judge.

He is soon and coming King…

At whom every knee will bow and tongue confess.

Throw off the secular!

For it seeks to diminish God.

And God cannot be diminished!

<u>**NOVEMBER 15**</u>

From <u>Foxe: Voices of the Martyrs</u> [43]

Theresia, Alfita, and Yarni (October 29, 2005)

"The four high school girls walked down the path leading to Poso Christian High School. The sun was shining in a cloudless sky and the girls looked forward to another day of school. It was a holiday for the Islamic schools in the area, celebrating the holy month of Ramadan. But Christian schools like the one the four girls went to were still in session. Their friendship and fellowship brought smiles across their young faces as they enjoyed the peacefulness of the early Saturday morning.

"The stillness of the air was broken as six men dressed in black and with veils covering their faces jumped out of the bushes and ran toward them. Before the girls could move, the men surrounded their young victims and viciously began swinging machetes. *Screaming for help, the girls fought for their lives. Only Noviana Malewa was able to escape. Covered in blood from cuts mostly on her face, she ran to find help. The bodies of Theresia Morangkir (fifteen years old) Alfita Poliwo (seventeen), and Yarni Sambue (fifteen) were left on the ground, their heads severed from their bodies and missing.*

"A couple of women walking to the nearby market had heard the girls screaming for help. Filled with fear, the women ran toward the military post, reporting what they heard. The Indonesian soldiers began looking for the source of the screams but instead discovered the three decapitated teenagers.

"The attackers had put the girls' heads in a sack and dumped them in different areas around the county. Two of the heads were found near a police post, while the third was discovered outside a local church.

"It wasn't enough for the radicals to attack churches or Christian leaders. They purposely targeted young Christian girls – girls who refused to recognize the Islamic holiday of Ramadan. Girls who would never be able to be forced into marriage with a Muslim man. They also made a deliberate statement by taking their heads and leaving them by a police station and a church. The message was clear: Neither the church nor the government could stop their cowardly attacks on young girls in the area.

"These teenagers knew of the dangers to Christians in the area, but with confidence and joy they made their daily trek to the Christian school. They chose to rise above fear and trepidation. Though their lives were mercilessly taken that Saturday morning, their faith lives on. Word of their testimony traveled worldwide, giving encouragement and hope to others to possess lives full of youthful joy in Christ, and a sober reminder that we are all just visitors in this corrupt world."
From _Foxe: Voices of the Martyrs_ [43]

NOVEMBER 16

It is a very personal journey, isn't it? The journey through pain and sickness and suffering and death is lonely and unique for each wandering soul.

I've been there. Praise God, the wandering and suffering led me into the arms of the Savior. The suffering Savior who knows pain and death first hand.

Yes, pain is personal. While suffering and death are indeed common threads of all humanity, they are also very unique experiences for each person. Suffering is loud. When we are on its path, it's all we can hear. It's all we can think about. For as C.S. Lewis said, it shouts at us. It gets our attention.

Life is short. And it is precious. And it is often painful.

I am inadequate to the task of understanding another person's pain. I can share and I can empathize and I can walk alongside another, but ultimately, I am ill-equipped to completely know what it is like to go through what you are going through.

Pain, personal as it is, needs a personal Savior to overcome it

Yes, I am inadequate to solve the problem of pain in your life.

But, Christ is not.

He knows the end of the story.

He is the end of the story.

Victory is His and can be ours.

Right now, we are living in bodies that are mere earthly tents vulnerable to pain and sickness and subject to death.

But, we are more than earthly tents.

God breathed the breath of life into all of us, and we have souls that will live on.

Forever.

And, God more than breathed the breath of life into us. He knows our frames intimately and completely inside and out. Psalm 139 tells us, *O Lord You have searched me and You know me. You know when I sit and when I rise; You perceive my thoughts from afar. You discern my going out and my lying down; You are familiar with all my ways. Before a word is on my tongue, You know it completely, O Lord. You hem me in - behind and before; You have laid Your hand upon me....For You created my inmost being; You knit me together in my mother's womb. I praise You because I am fearfully and wonderfully made; Your works are wonderful, I know that full well. My frame was not hidden from You when I was made in the secret place. When I was woven together in the depths of the earth, Your eyes saw my unformed body. All the days ordained for me were written in your book before one of them came to be. How precious to me are Your thoughts, O God! How vast is the sum of them! Were I to count them, they would outnumber the grains of sand.*

Like it or not, God knows us. He knows every single thought and decision and flaw and sin.

And God knows our pain.

Personally.

He's walked that lonely path of pain. The Bible tells us in Hebrews, *For we do not have a high priest who is unable to sympathize with our weaknesses, but we have one who has been tempted in every way, just as we are - yet was without sin. Let us then approach the throne of grace with confidence, so that we may receive mercy and find grace to help us in our time of need....Let us fix our eyes on Jesus, the author and perfecter of our faith, who for the joy set before Him endured the cross, scorning its shame, and sat down at the right hand of the throne of God. Consider Him who endured such opposition from sinful men, so that you will not grow weary and lose heart.*

Peter tells us, in I Peter 2:21-24, *To this you were called, because Christ suffered for you, leaving you an example, that you should follow in His steps. He committed no sin, and no deceit was found in His mouth. When they hurled their insults at Him, He did not retaliate; when He suffered, He made no threats. Instead, He entrusted Himself to Him who judges justly. He Himself bore our sins in His body on the tree, so that we might die to sins and live for righteousness; by His wounds you have been healed.*

We all need healing.

We all need Jesus.

The way of healing is through the blood of Christ shed for us for the forgiveness of sins. He is the fount of healing. He is living waters. Bread of life. The great physician.

Dear Lord, I am sick without you. I am so lost without you. I get caught up in things of this world. I am a sinner. I am so flawed and full of myself. Father, thank you for making a way home to you through the blood of your Son. Forgive me and help me to turn to You and turn away from the things of this world.   I need You every day. I pray for You to wash me clean. I can't do it myself. I've tried. I've failed. I need the gift of Christ that You offer freely to all who call and confess.

And, I thank you, dearest Father, that once rescued and saved by Your precious Son, that I am assured that nothing will separate me from You...*And we know that in all things God works for the good of those who love Him, who have been called according to His purpose...If God is for us, who can be against us? He who did not spare His own Son, but gave Him up for us all - how will He not also, along with Him, graciously give us all things?....Who shall separate us from the love of Christ? Shall trouble or hardship or persecution or famine or nakedness or danger or sword?....No, in all these things we are more than conquerors through Him who loved us. For I am convinced that neither death nor life, neither angels nor demons, neither the present nor the future,* nor any powers, neither height nor depth, nor anything else in all creation, will be able to separate us from the love of God that is in Christ Jesus our Lord *(from Romans 8).*

Alleluia!

NOVEMBER 17

My soul sings a new song to You, Lord!

Worthy are You, Lord.

Overwhelm my life with the truth of who You are.

Overwhelm my students, my husband, my family, his family.

Lord, at one time I was foolish, disobedient, deceived, and enslaved by all kinds of passions and pleasures.

I lived in malice and envy.

I hated and was hated.

Then, the kindness and love of the Savior appeared.

And overwhelmed me.

Saved me.

Not because of righteous things I had done, but because, Lord, of Your mercy.

You washed me through the washing of rebirth and renewal by the Holy Spirit.

New birth.

New life.

A new creature in Christ am I.

Overwhelmed, praise God, overwhelmed!

You poured Yourself out for me.

And You poured the Holy Spirit out...upon me, into me...filled to overflowing.

Generous are Your portions, generously did You pour Yourself out, completely have You overwhelmed me.

I have been justified by Your grace.

I am now an heir having the hope of eternal life.

Alive.

I am alive, and eternal life is mine.

You continuously overwhelm me, Lord, with who You are, with what You do.

Through the blood of Christ and the power of the Holy Spirit, save the lost in my family and those in my classroom.

Overwhelm them.

Make them heirs having the hope of eternal life.

May this be the Day of Salvation!

I believe in the power of Your might to accomplish such a great miracle.

In Jesus' Overwhelming Name…

NOVEMBER 18

I have a story to tell…we all do.

I was born in 1969 just days before the first man walked on the moon. I was the oldest of three children, born to a Mom and Dad who were married only ever to each other. I grew up on a dairy farm and spent my days at Holland Central school and my evenings in the barn, side by side with my parents and siblings. My Grandmother (Dad's Mom) lived with us. Or, rather we lived with her. She'd had a stroke when I was six years old, and we moved into the big old farm house with her after that. We were all very well behaved children who grew into well behaved teenagers who managed, thanks to strong family expectations and commitment, to avoid the dangerous pitfalls of the teenage years. There was no fornication, drug use, or disrespect of authority spewing forth from my brother, sister or myself as we maneuvered through those growing up years.

Once, I did stick my tongue out at my Mom on the school bus (she was our bus driver). Later that day, my Dad looked me straight in the eye and sternly reminded me that only snakes stick out their tongues. It was all he needed to say. I never stuck my tongue out at Mom again.

Now, I am a thirty-seven year old wife with a husband and a daughter. My husband, Mark, is within seven years of being able to draw Social Security. Yes, there is an age difference between he and I. Twenty years to be exact. I am Mark's second wife. He and his first wife, Marge, were married for nearly twenty-four years and have three children (all grown up by the time I met Mark). I met Mark after he and Marge had split up. From the day she met me, she was kind to me. I consider her a friend. Together, Mark and Marge had three children: Diane, Karen, and Chris. They, too, are my friends. It is unusual, I suppose, but I praise God for the good relationships I have with all of Mark's first family.

Mark and I have one child. Our little Sarah, will be ten years old this June. Dear Sarah is severely physically and mentally disabled. Sarah was born with Down Syndrome, a heart defect, and hydrocephalus. Since then, she has experienced a stroke from a rare vascular disease called "moyamoya syndrome." This stroke left Sarah a spastic quadriplegic. In 2003, she was diagnosed with acute lymphocytic leukemia. As I write, we are two and a half years into chemotherapy treatment. Sarah is in remission and her prognosis for "cure" of the leukemia is pretty good. To top it all off, Sarah is as cute as a button! She has the most spectacular, beautiful smile and personality of anyone in this whole wide wonderful world. She is the jewel of our lives and a most precious blessing daily showering joy upon us. God has been good to us.

Here I am, farmer's daughter, wife to an almost senior citizen, mother to a disabled child, and college graduate. I graduated Summa Cum Laude from Daemen College in Amherst, NY in 1994. I have a Bachelor of Arts degree in history/government. Let's just say that the degree is collecting dust while I fulfill, with joy, the traditional role of wife and mother.

After graduating from college, I began a much hated job at the Department of Social Services in Cattaraugus County, NY. For three years, I worked with families that were falling apart and with children who had been placed into foster care. The ultimate goal was always to reunify the family. If we couldn't safely reunify, then we pursued termination of parental rights. Almost from the day I started working at DSS to the day I left, I wanted out. I loved the children, and most of the time I loved their parents, too. But, the depth of the family problems, the frequent failures of the system to succeed, and the weight of decision making upon my relatively young and inexperienced shoulders was a heavy load.

Then Sarah arrived. Between Mark and me, I was the one with the better job and health insurance. It made economic sense for me to be the working parent. After four months of maternity leave, I returned to my despised job at DSS, and my husband became a stay-at-home Dad. He did great, too. Well made plans these may have been, but even well made plans could not then, and cannot now, prevent disaster when disaster's mind is made up to invade lives.

And, invade our lives disaster did.

It was February, 1998. Sarah developed a fever and cough. She was admitted to Children's Hospital of Buffalo. It looked like RSV, so she ended up spending a few days in an oxygen tent at the hospital. She seemed to be doing better when, all of a sudden, she started having some really weird symptoms. A droopy smile. Difficulty swallowing. For days, the doctors just figured she was wiped out from the RSV stuff. Then, she woke up one morning and couldn't use the right side of her body. MRIs and CT scans followed. "Cerebral vascular accident"...stroke...maybe from a carotid artery dissection of idiopathic nature...later diagnosed as moyamoya syndrome...lots of awful blood draws on very tiny veins...neurosurgery at Boston Children's Hospital...arteries repositioned to supply collateral blood flow to Sarah's brain, now so horribly damaged.

Sarah was a different person.

Her physical skills were wiped out completely. She could no longer sit up by herself. She could no longer use her arms and hands. Her limbs became spastic and stiff. Her trunk and neck became weak. She could no longer crawl. She could no longer feed herself.

It wasn't just her physical body that changed. So, too, did her personality. She hardly ever smiled. She looked sad most of the time. She cried frequently and had extreme difficulty sleeping.

Simply put, everything was a mess.

With Mark's unending support, I quit work. I didn't just take family medical leave. I quit. We knew we were in for the long haul. We had no idea what Mark was going to do to make a living for us. But, we knew I had to be home.

Mark went to school to earn his CDL license. For a short time, he drove over the road. Having him gone from home for a week or so at a time was more than he or I could bear. We really didn't even know if Sarah was going to live. Mark quit the big truck and drove a local dump truck until a good job with Cattaraugus County Department of Public Works came along his way.

As time went by, life became more normal for us. While Sarah's physical skills and strength only improved slightly, her happy and contented personality slowly returned.

Mark was nearly three years at his county job, and I over five years as a stay-at-home mom when I stumbled upon an employment ad in our local Penny Saver for a "Medicaid Service Coordinator" with a local nonprofit organization that served adults with developmental disabilities. Sarah's health was relatively stable at that point. I applied for and was hired to fill that Medicaid Service Coordinator position. Mark was granted an approved leave of absence from his job.

Medicaid Service Coordinator. It was a good job for me. The office was close to home and health insurance was available. I had experience, as a parent, with the disabled. I enjoyed the work.

Mark settled into life, again, as stay-at-home Dad. As previously, he did a great job with Sarah. We thought we had it all worked out!

Two months into our new routine, Sarah started having some problems. Low grade fevers. Bruising. Lethargy. Hip pain.

Friday, the week before Thanksgiving, 2003, Mark called me at work.

He had picked Sarah up from school, and she was very upset and not at all herself. I left work and went home. Mark was doing everything he could to console Sarah, but she was just in misery. I held her in the rocking chair, and she fell asleep. When it was dinner time, I woke her, and she started crying all over again. We decided to let Sarah rest and hope that she would be more herself by the next day.

Wishful thinking.

Deep down, we knew that bad news was just around the corner for us. We could feel it in the air.

The next morning, Sarah seemed more calm. She didn't cry like the day before. But, the calmness was eerie. She was too calm. All she wanted to do was sleep. I gave her a bath and even in her bath chair, she fell asleep.

Mark and I took Sarah to the pediatrician's office. The pediatrician examined Sarah. Then he called the neurosurgeons at Children's Hospital. The neurosurgery resident instructed us to bring Sarah to the emergency room at

Children's Hospital.   As much as we abhor (and I mean that word wholeheartedly) the emergency room, we knew the time had come.

We drove Sarah to Children's Hospital from Springville. I still remember being on Route 219, listening to the radio.   It was the 40th anniversary of JFK's assassination.

At the ER, Sarah was taken back to one of the drafty cubicles. Blood was drawn. We waited.   We were in the middle of a consult with a young neurosurgery resident. A nurse came in and handed him a paper with lab results.   I remember his face. I remember his words. Sarah had leukemia blasts in her blood. Her platelets were only 7000 (normal is 150,000 or more).

She needed a blood transfusion, the first of many. She needed a bone marrow biopsy to confirm the leukemia. Soon, she would begin chemotherapy.

Despite what seems now to be obvious symptoms, we ALL – parents and doctors - were surprised by the leukemia diagnosis. I think there was an assumption on our parts that Sarah simply couldn't be diagnosed with any more problems. She'd had her share. No more allowed. But, this is not how it works…

After the leukemia diagnosis, I cut back my work hours to part time. Mark continued on his leave from his job. We had the impression that once Sarah was through the first six months or so of treatment, treatment would no longer be a big deal, and life would, in most ways, be back to normal. So, we decided we'd hang in there a while with our adjusted schedule in the hope that chemotherapy would become predictable for our family.

Let's just say, it didn't work out like that. Sarah has not had a typical course of treatment, and has experienced a number of unusual complications. As Mark's approved leave from the county drew to an end, we made the decision that he would return to work and I would leave my position as service coordinator. It was an easy decision to make because it was the right decision. It was a good decision. Mark has been back to his county job since July, 2004, and I have been home being Sarah's mom.

I don't know what the future holds.   I have learned, kicking and screaming, that I am not in control. But, I have also learned that there is a great God. He cares. He sees. He knows. He controls.

And in His mighty hands, whatever will be will be ok.

For He has plans…

Plans to prosper us…

Plans to make us useful…

Plans that are good and right and perfect…

And I anticipate sweetly what He will do as the years go by.

Have Your own way, Lord, in these lives which You have given.

NOVEMBER 19

For my students, Lord, I pray.

The Word has been sown in their lives.

Protect their hearts.

Their minds.

For that is the soil in which the seeds of truth have been sown.

Satan wants to rob them of what You have given.

Satan wants my students to have stony ground in the soil of their hearts, ground in which seeds refuse to grow deep roots.

Stony ground destroys endurance, and it is endurance which is needed on the rough road of life.

Satan wants my students to be among the thorns, caught up in the cares of the world, the deceitfulness of riches, the lusts of the flesh.

Thorns distract and choke the Word and kill the seeds. And without seeds, there will be no fruit.

Prepare in my kids, Lord, good ground, soil that is plowed up and fertile, soil that goes deep and bears fruit.

May my kids know, Lord, how much You love them.

May they know how much I, too, love them.

Protect them, for this is a dangerous world, this world in which they now go forth.

NOVEMBER 20

From *Total Truth: Liberating Christianity from its Cultural Captivity* by Nancy Pearcey [44]

Christianity out of Balance.

"(A) comprehensive vision of Creation, Fall, and Redemption allows no room for a secular/sacred split....

"Consider the typical evangelistic message: 'You're a sinner; you need to be saved.' What could be wrong with that? Of course, it's true that we are sinners, but notice that the message starts with the Fall instead of Creation. By beginning with the theme of sin, it implies that our essential identity consists in being guilty sinners, deserving of divine punishment. Some Christian literature goes so far as to say we are nothing, completely worthless, before a holy God.

"This excessively negative view is not biblical, however, and it lays Christianity open to the charge that it has a low view of human dignity. **The Bible does not begin with the Fall but with Creation: Our value and dignity are rooted in the fact that we are created in the image of God, with the high calling of being His representatives on earth**. In fact, it is only because humans have such high value that sin is so tragic. If we were worthless to begin with, then the Fall would be a trivial event. When a cheap trinket is broken, we toss it aside with a shrug. But when a priceless masterpiece is defaced, we are horrified.

"It is because we are the masterpiece of God's creation that the destructiveness of sin produces such horror and sorrow. Far from expressing a low view of human nature, the Bible gives a far higher view than the dominant secular view today, which regards humans as simply complex computers made of meat – products of blind, naturalistic forces, without transcendent purpose or meaning.

"If we start with a message of sin, without giving the context of Creation, then we will come across to nonbelievers as merely negative and judgmental...

"We need to begin our message where the Bible begins – with the dignity and high calling of all human beings because they are created in the image of God."
From *Total Truth: Liberating Christianity from its Cultural Captivity* by Nancy Pearcey [44]

NOVEMBER 21

I woke up early today.

On purpose.

Quiet time with God.

I decided to go outside for a walk. Coffee in hand. Wind blowing. As I was walking near the creek, which is running high thanks to recent rainy days, I was drawn into memories of my childhood… Walking in our woods. The back pond. The sound of running water in the creek. Dad, perched on a red International tractor, baling hay in the back field. The sweet aroma of freshly mowed timothy and clover. The damp smell of ploughed earth. Sweat running down our faces as we stacked hay high in the hay mow. The clickety-clackety metal sound of the hay elevator… Such good memories and simple safe times that seemed, then, as if they would go on forever. And yet, somehow the day came, unnoticed, that this chapter in my life closed.

Why was I in such a hurry to grow up?

Walking by the creek today, I longed for the good old days. Melancholy. Homesickness for days now gone.

Then, I started thinking about that chapter in my life titled, "Sarah's stroke." Seemed like a heartbreaking chapter at the time. But, the funny thing is, I don't look back at it that way now. Don't get me wrong, I don't want to relive it, but when I remember it, it is not with a feeling of dread or anger or anything even remotely negative.

And, the only reason that I can now have good memories from a bad time is that God brought good to me out of the bad we went through.

He brought more than good to me. He gave me Himself, and I will be forever thankful that such a time as that came into my life.

Not a time I would have chosen.

Not a time I wanted.

But, surely a time I needed.

That dark, selfish heart that thought life was all about getting what I wanted and being comfortable and that God is just some sort of big guy in the sky...it was this heart that needed healing and redemption and truth.

The days following Sarah's stroke were so lonely.

Yet I now know I was not alone.

This was when I met God.

He carried me then.

He carries me now.

He will continually carry me as the days go by and through whatever may come.

And, someday, He will carry me home.

NOVEMBER 22

We all know at least one. They are in our lives, they are in our families, they are in our churches, and sometimes they are us.

Who?

I am speaking of the person who claims the name of Christ but is not producing fruit for the Kingdom of God. The person who calls himself a "Christian" yet looks very much like the world.

How can this tragedy be?

How can one receive God's forgiving grace through the shed blood of Christ and then fail to bear fruit?

How can a person believe that he was rescued from eternal hell but then neglect to proclaim the Good News of salvation?

How can one accept Jesus as Savior, the only way to the Father, and yet continue to ignore the Word of God?

How can one be made clean and whole through Christ and yet hoard one's time, talents or money, thus robbing God of what He rightfully owns?

How can one be saved and yet be silent?

Did God save us so that we can stay like we are? Selfish. Proud. Controlled by untamed tongues that continue to curse or lie or gossip. Led by uncontrolled appetites for wealth and possessions or alcohol or recognition. Demanding what we want and want now. Ignorant of His Word. Too busy for prayer. Too tired for church. Too indifferent to the needs of the lost and hurting around us.

How can it be that we can be saved by God's mercy and grace and yet remain the same old creature?

I submit to you that if God is the vine and we are the branches, as the Bible tells us clearly in John 15 we are, then fruit we must bear! We must pray. We must fellowship. We must be in the Word. We must seek to serve. We must bear a burden for the lost. We must sacrifice our lives for the Kingdom of God. We must seek first His righteousness. We must yield to the direction and rebuke of the Holy Spirit.

If we have surrendered our souls to the merciful, Creator God who sent His Son to die for us, then we must also surrender our lives.

Every part of our lives...not just when it is convenient. Not just when we feel like it. Not just when we will benefit from it. Not just when we will get pats on the back. But always! We were, after all, bought with a price, the price of Christ's blood, and we are no longer our own!

And, the fruit we bear, just like the salvation we freely received, is produced by God's grace in our lives, fruit which is the evidence and the assurance of the salvation freely given.

Am I bearing fruit?

Are you?

It's a question worth considering.

It's a question with which to wrestle.

It's a question that deserves an honest answer.

NOVEMBER 23

How thankful I am for the gift of Christ.

Lord, You removed the natural deadness within which I was lost.

You removed the blindness and gave me sight.

You washed clean the scarlet stains of sin.

This is the gospel!

Thank You that the gospel is real and powerful to me.

It is foolishness to many, to those who are yet spiritually dead. But, to me, because of You, I know it is the power and wisdom of God, my God!

Lord, there are many natural people yet in my family. People who deny or ignore Your power and wisdom. People who trust in themselves and often their religion, but not in You. To them, the cross is foolishness.

Wake them from slumber!

Remove the blindness.

Alert them to spiritual dangers.

Blaze forth light into darkness and turn night into day as only You can do. Help them, Lord, to accept the things of the Spirit of God. Help them to hear and see and know that the gospel is the really good news!

The gospel is the power of God for salvation to everyone who believes and embraces the unleashed truth of who Jesus Christ is and what He has fully accomplished. May each person in our family seize the Savior and be saved.

Thank You, Lord, for the good news.

Thank You for salvation.

Thank You for who You are and for Your finished work.

In Jesus' Good and Complete Name...

NOVEMBER 24

"This may be the happiest, most wonderful verse in the Bible!" I thought to myself as my eyes traveled over the words...

But God raised Jesus from the dead (Acts 13:30).

Translation: "***But*** (no matter what else is going on, no matter how difficult life may seem right now) ***God*** (who is all-powerful, all-knowing, all-present, sovereign, eternal, immutable, merciful, gracious, loving, perfectly holy and always righteous) ***raised Jesus*** (the sacrificial Lamb who died for my sins and fulfilled the Law and the Prophets) ***from the dead*** (forever victorious over sin, the grave, and hell for all who come to Him in faith believing He is who He says He is and embrace Him as Lord of lords and King of kings)."

Nothing else matters the way this matters.

Is there any better news than this?

From this good news, gratitude must flow…

Thanksgiving.

Where do I begin? So many blessings, so undeserved.

I am grateful that God spoke and the universe came to be. That He hung each star in its place, that He calls each out by name and not one is missing.

That He formed man from the dust of the ground and breathed into man's nostrils the breath of life and man became a living soul.

I am grateful that God has knit me together and has given me life and purpose. That He sees me in my low estate, so often struggling, and He cares.

I am grateful that the Word was made flesh and dwelt among us…that the Creator God stepped into skin and time to become the Redeemer God.

I am grateful for the shocking humility of God who stretched out calloused hands to die for me.

I am grateful that the tomb is empty and victory is certain and the hope is real.

I am grateful that He is my Jehovah Nissi who has raised up a standard, and when the enemy comes in like a flood, I am safe – no matter what happens to my physical body – under His banner.

I am thankful that when my heart grows hard, God ploughs up the fallow ground.

I am thankful that in a world swiftly changing, God is the same yesterday, today, and forever. When I turn on the news and I see chaos...or in those moment when my own life seems broken and out of control...I know the truth.

The LORD God omnipotent reigneth!

I am grateful for who God is and for what He does.

I am thankful for all He has given me.

And, for all He has taken away.

Blessed be the name of the LORD.

NOVEMBER 25

Abiding...gratitude for God in the details. How can it be that the all-powerful Creator God – the One who inhabits eternity and spoke the universe into being, the One who is high and lifted up – how can it be that He cares about me and the details of my life?

Yesterday, 4 year old Ruby, for no real reason at all, grabbed my face between her tiny hands and, looking straight into my eyes, spontaneously blurted out, "Grandma, I love you!"

This was a special gift.

My own child was never able to tell me she loved me with words. Yes, Sarah expressed her love for me in other ways. But every mother wants to hear those sweet words from the lips of the child she bore. I never did. It was one of those details in which sorrow lingered. Ruby didn't know this. She didn't know that she was giving me a gift at all, much less one of significant value.

But God knew.

God understands the heart of a mother. God understands the nature of sorrow. And yesterday He used 4 year old Ruby to bless my heart with words I've hungered to hear.

God has been very good to me.

NOVEMBER 26

I'm writing this on a beautiful Sunday afternoon. There is a Mets game on TV. Sadly, my poor Mets are losing. Again. Mark is dozing in the recliner. The cat is napping under the bed. All is quiet, all is well in the Hanson household.

In the stillness of my home, my heart smiles remembering a memory made yesterday, a memory made right here.

Somehow – the blessing of God – I have the privilege of being a grandma. Granddaughters Kaygan and Ruby, 4 years old and 2 years old respectively, came for a visit. It was a warm and sunny afternoon.

We ate ice cream cones. Life is always better when ice cream is involved…

Soon after, Kaygan, Ruby, and I were running across the front yard with our arms stretched out wide. We were "running like the wind" and every once in a while we would spin in a circle. We girls, spinning and laughing and holding arms up high, were filled with joy (and perhaps a little vertigo)!

I watched my girls, realizing in ways that they don't, that it won't be long and they will no longer be satisfied to simply run across the yard, arms outstretched, running through the breeze and smelling wildflowers. Before long, they will join the hectic race and pace of mankind. But for today, they are simply enjoying the simple things.

This is beauty.

This is joy.

This is grace.

This is a memory…spinning in circles with precious grandchildren.

Seasons of life…each given by God, God who is good and good all the time!

NOVEMBER 27

A note to my students…2010

I have much to learn.

But one of the things I have learned over the years to be true is this: the Lord expects us to be a thankful people, for He is worthy always of our praise! I have learned that when I face a problem, whether great or small, one of the first steps in solving that problem (or growing through it) is gratitude.

Gratitude is one of the ways we magnify God, remembering that He is truly bigger than the problem, whatever the problem may be. The greater the challenge, the greater the need to be thankful immediately and consistently.

Seven years ago, Sarah was diagnosed with leukemia. I wish I could tell you that my first response was to be thankful.

It wasn't.

But, God, in His grace and mercy, patiently revealed Himself to me as the One worthy of thanksgiving and trust even as I watched my child suffer. Seven years later, I thank the Lord for Sarah's life. I thank Him that she is still here with us, but acknowledge that her number of days is in His hands.

And, what better hands to be in! Hands that are strong and mighty and able.

Yes, I am thankful for my child...both her life and her struggles.

And, I also want you to know this Thanksgiving, that I give thanks to the Lord for you.

You have blessed my life, sweet students, and for you I raise hands of gratitude.

Love in Christ,

Mrs. Hanson

NOVEMBER 28

Lord,

You are God of the impossible.

You accomplish mighty feats!

There is nothing too hard for You...and that includes breaking stubborn, selfish hearts and softening them so that You can save and then mold them.

Lord, salvation is always a miracle.

Whether world-hardened or sweet and kind, all souls are lost apart from You...and salvation, of even the sweetest soul, is a miracle of the highest order.

Jesus, You are the merciful, obedient Lamb of God. You alone can satisfy the Father's righteous wrath.   I praise You for choosing me to be one who confesses that You are Lord of lords and King of kings. Thank You that I share in the heavenly calling.

May every person in my family and in my classroom, now and in the generations to come, be called and share in the calling, and embrace You as the great High Priest upon whom we place our faith and fix our thoughts.

Lord everything exists for You, and through You.

Save those who are lost.   And then, bless them with an exalted, accurate view of You.

Whether we admit or deny it, the truth remains that You are great, and we exist because You allow us to.

May we love to exist through You and for You. May we love to exalt You and glorify Your Name.

In Jesus' Name, the Author and Perfecter of our faith...

November 29

I am thankful for my backyard.

It is a special place, a place where I have met regularly with God for many years and through many seasons.

It's been a place of joy and a place of sorrow.

Tears have been shed there, and laughter has been heard.

It is a place where I have struggled against plans and losses I did not understand, a place where I have bared my confusion and my exhaustion to God who carries the load with me and often for me.

It is a place where I have stood in awe of Him, looking up at the stars hung high by Him in the sky. It is a place where I have literally fallen to my knees and crumpled in brokenness, pouring out my heart and bitter sorrows before my God who hears and cares and knows always what is best.

It is a place where relationships have been cultivated and memories made...raking leaves and jumping into the damp, earth fragrant pile, first as a newlywed, then as a mother, and now as a grandmother.

My backyard, disheveled creek running through it, a small place in a big world, a simple place in a complicated world, a silent place in a loud world, a speck of the world where I have walked intimately with my Great God and have grown in knowledge of Him.

God through whom all blessings flow, whose name is a strong tower, whose blood was shed for me...Praise You!

NOVEMBER 30

From Total Truth: Liberating Christianity from its Cultural Captivity Nancy Pearcey [45]

Rise of the Sovereign Self

"In many churches, the individual alone with his Bible is regarded as the core of the Christian life. A poll taken in the mid-1990s by sociologist Wade Clark Roof found that 54 percent of evangelical Christians said, 'to be alone and meditate' was more important than 'to worship with others.' And more than half agreed that 'churches and synagogues have lost the real spiritual part of religion.' Roof concluded that 'the real story of American religious life in this half-century is the **rise of a new sovereign self** that defines and sets limits on the very meaning of the divine.' In other words, instead of challenging modern liberalism's notion of the autonomous self, evangelicalism tends to reflect the same theme in religious language.

"As Wolfe puts it, 'In every aspect of the religious life, American faith has met American culture – and American culture has triumphed.' Evangelicalism has largely given in to the two-story division that renders religion a matter of individual experience, with little or no cognitive content...

"The overall pattern of evangelicalism's history is summarized brilliantly by Richard Hofstadter in a single sentence. To a large extent, he writes, 'the church withdrew from intellectual encounters with the secular world, gave up the idea that religion is a part of the whole life of intellectual experience, and often abandoned the field of *rational studies on the assumption that they were the natural province of science alone.'...*

"Sadly, many Christians live much of their lives as though the naturalist were right. They give cognitive assent to the great truths of Scripture, but they make their practical, day-to-day decisions based only on what they can see, hear, measure, and calculate....in ordinary life, they walk over and sit in the naturalist's chair, living as though the supernatural were not real in any practical sense, relying on their own energy, talent, and strategic calculations. They may sincerely want to do the Lord's work, but they do it in the world's way – using worldly methods and motivated by worldly desires for success and acclaim.

"The Bible calls this living in the 'flesh' instead of in the Spirit, and Paul addresses the problem in the book of Galatians: 'Having begun in the Spirit, are you now being perfected by the flesh?' (Galatians 3:3). Many believers act as though becoming a Christian were a matter of faith, but being a Christian afterward were a matter of their own drive and willpower. They are striving to be 'perfected by the flesh.'

"Working in the flesh, they may well produce impressive results in the visible world. Churches and parachurch ministries may generate a great deal of publicity, hold glamorous conferences, attract huge crowds, bring in large donations, produce books and magazines, and wield political influence in Washington. But if that work is done in the flesh, then no matter how successful it appears, it does little to build God's Kingdom. When the Lord's work is done in merely human wisdom, using human methods, then it is not the Lord's work any longer."

From <u>Total Truth: Liberating Christianity from its Cultural Captivity</u> Nancy Pearcey [45]

November's Apologetic Moment...Contend for the faith

Fossil Fuels – Are They Moral?

From <u>*The Moral Case for Fossil Fuels*</u> *by Alex Epstein* [66]:

"This book is about morality, about right and wrong. To me, the question of what to do about fossil fuels and any other moral issue comes down to: What will promote human life? What will promote human flourishing – realizing the full potential of life? Colloquially, how do we maximize the years in our life and the life in our years?...

"And there is an incredibly strong correlation between fossil fuel use and life expectancy and between fossil fuel use and income, particularly in the rapidly developing parts of the world...Consider the fate of two countries that have been responsible for a great deal of the increase in fossil fuel use, China and India. In each country, both coal and oil use increased by at least a factor of 5 (between 1970-2010), producing nearly all their energy.

"The story is clear – both life expectancy and income increased rapidly, meaning that life got better for billions of people in just a few decades. For example, the infant mortality rate has plummeted in both countries – in China by 70%, which translates to 55 more children living per 1000 births. India has experienced a similar decrease, of 58 percent

"Not only in China and India, but around the world, hundreds of millions of individuals in industrializing countries have gotten their first lightbulb, their first refrigerator, their first decent-paying job, their first year with clean drinking water or a full stomach...(W)hen we look at the data, a fascinating fact emerges: As we have used more fossil fuels, our resource situation, our environment situation, and our climate situation have been improving, too...

"Overall, the improvement is incredible. Of course, there are places such as China that have high levels of smog – but the track record of the rest of the world indicates that this can be corrected while using ever increasing amounts of fossil fuels.

"Once again, the anti-fossil fuel experts got it completely wrong. Why?

"Again by not thinking big picture, by paying attention to only one half of the equation – in the case of fossil fuels, focusing only on the ways in which using them can harm our environment. But fossil fuels can also improve our environment by powering machines that clean up nature's health hazards, such as water purification plants that protect us from naturally contaminated water and sanitation systems that protect us from natural disease and animal waste. Pessimistic predictions often assume that our environment is perfect until humans mess it up; they don't consider the possibility that we could improve our environment. But the data of the last forty years indicate that we have been doing exactly that – using fossil fuels…

"I hold human life as the standard of value, and you can see that in my earlier arguments: I think that our fossil fuel use so far has been a moral choice because it has enabled billions of people to live longer and more fulfilling lives, and I think that the cuts proposed by the environmentalists of the 1970s were wrong because of all the death and suffering they would have inflicted on human beings.

"Not everyone holds human life as their standard of value, and people often argue that things are right or wrong for reasons other than the ways they benefit or harm human beings…Many leading environmental thinkers, including those who predict fossil fuel catastrophe, hold as their standard of value what they call 'pristine' nature or wilderness – nature unaltered by man.

"For example, in a 'Los Angeles Times' review of The End of Nature, Bill McKibben's influential book of twenty-five years ago predicting catastrophic climate change, David M. Graber, research biologist for the National Park Service, wrote this summary of McKibben's message: *'McKibben is a bio-centrist, and so am I. We are not interested in the utility of a particular species or free-flowing river, or ecosystem, to mankind. They have intrinsic value, more value – to me – than another human body, or a billion of them. Human happiness, and certainly human fecundity, are not as important as a wild and healthy planet. I know social scientists who remind me that people are part of nature, but it isn't true. Somewhere along the line – at about a billion years ago, maybe half that – we quit the contract and became a cancer. We have become a plague upon ourselves and upon the Earth. It is cosmically unlikely that the developed world will choose to end its orgy of fossil-energy consumption, and the Third World its suicidal consumption of landscape. Until such time as Homo sapiens should decide to re-join nature, some of us can only hope for the right virus to come along.'*

"In his book, McKibben wrote that our goal should be a 'humbler world,' one where we have less impact on our environment and 'Human happiness would be of secondary importance.'

"What is of primary importance (to McKibben)? Minimizing our impact on our environment. McKibben explains: *'Though not in our time, and not in the time of our children, or their children, if we now, today, limited our numbers and our desires and our ambitions, perhaps nature could someday resume its independent working.'* This implies that there should be fewer people, with fewer desires, and fewer ambitions. This is the exact opposite of holding human life as one's standard of value. It is holding human nonimpact as one's standard of value, without regard for human life and happiness…

"Ultimately, the moral case for fossil fuels is not about fossil fuels; it's the moral case for using cheap, plentiful, reliable energy to amplify our abilities to make the world a better place – a better place for human beings….we are at one of those points in

history where we are at a fork between a dream and a nightmare and the nightmare side is winning, thanks to decades of underappreciation of fossil fuels' benefits and massive misrepresentations of fossil fuels' risks. But the dream is absolutely possible. It just requires that we truly, to our core, understand the value of energy to human life…

"We don't want to 'save the planet' from human beings; we want to improve the planet for human beings. We need to say this loudly and proudly. We need to say that human life is our one and only standard of value. And we need to say that the transformation of our environment, the essence of our survival, is a supreme virtue. We need to recognize that to the extent we deny either, we are willing to harm real, flesh-and-blood human beings for some antihuman dogma…

"We just need to be clear on what is right, then take the time and sometimes social risk to try to reach the people who matter most to us. I wrote this book so you could hand it to the people who matter most to you – and so that you could take its ideas and make them your own, telling the people who matter to you how you think and feel.

"I wrote this book for anyone who wants to make the world a better place – for human beings – including many, many people who would start this book opposed to or at least suspicious of fossil fuels. Having held that position myself before, I know it can be well motivated. The idea of ruining the world for the less fortunate and, even worse, for our children or grandchildren is horrifying to us. Thus, when someone tells us of a major risk that our behavior is causing, we want to do something about it.

"What we are not taught is that the biggest risk is not using fossil fuels, and that using them is incredibly virtuous. We are not taught that we're building a civilization that serves us and the future, that we're creating knowledge and resources that can enrich everyone around the world. We're not taught that the choices we make often reflect an extremely rational calculation that balance benefit and risk. We're not taught that some people truly believe that human life doesn't matter, and that their goal is not to help us triumph over nature's obstacles but to remove us as an obstacle to the rest of nature.

"Make no mistake – there are people trying to use you to promote actions that would harm everything you care about. Not because they care about you – they prioritize nature over you – but because they see you as a tool.

"The unpopular but moral cause of our time is fossil fuels. Fossil fuels are easy to misunderstand and demonize, but they are absolutely good to use. And they absolutely need to be championed.

"There are many specific battles to be fought. The venue and strategy for each is ever changing, which is why the specific actions we take need to be timely and coordinated. That's why this book has a Web site, www.moralcaseforfossilfuels.com, which will let you know about the latest opportunities to fight for energy liberation, whether it's promoting a series of debates over fossil fuels, writing a public comment on the EPA's attacks on coal, or sharing inspiring stories about industrial progress around the world.

"But no matter what you read, the need for moral clarity will always be timely. Here, in a sentence is the moral case for fossil fuels, the single thought that can empower us to empower the world: Mankind's use of fossil fuels is supremely virtuous – because human life is the standard of value, and because using fossil fuels transforms our environment to make it wonderful for human life."

From The Moral Case for Fossil Fuels by Alex Epstein [66]

For God, who commanded the light to shine out of darkness, hath shined in our hearts, to give the light of the knowledge of the glory of God in the face of Jesus Christ.
II Corinthians 4:6

December

"All along, let us remember we are not asked to understand, but simply to obey..."
— Amy Carmichael, <u>Candles in the Dark</u>

DECEMBER 1

For You created my inmost being; You knit me together in my mother's womb. I praise You because I am fearfully and wonderfully made; Your works are wonderful, I know that full well. My frame was not hidden from You when I was made in the secret place. When I was woven together in the depths of the earth, Your eyes saw my unformed body. All the days ordained for me were written in Your book before one of them came to be. How precious to me are Your thoughts, O God! How vast is the sum of them! Were I to count them, they would outnumber the grains of sand (Psalm 139:13 – 18).

Written from Sarah's perspective...

I suppose, perhaps, my life could be considered, well, controversial. So, might as well start right out with some good old controversy. What better place to begin my story than with making everyone uncomfortable?

The uncomfortable, controversial truth is that, had I been conceived in the womb of a mother who didn't want me or had been afraid of the consequences my life might bring to hers, I might not be here. The uncomfortable, controversial truth is that I was considered a "baby" in the womb because I was wanted. In the eyes of the world, the "desire" to have me made me a living being. Had I, and my many disabilities, not been wanted, I would have been a "fetus".

Yes, truth is controversial when it makes people uncomfortable. Or challenges them. Or causes them to have to do something that they would rather not do or not do something they would rather do. But, truth is truth nonetheless and regardless of folks' feelings about it.

And, the plain simple truth of the matter is that I, yes I with my extra chromosome, am fearfully and wonderfully made. God knit me, yes birth-defected me, together in the womb. I am no surprise to Him. I am no disappointment to Him. I am no accident or error of nature. Nope. My frame, imperfect and weak as it is, was woven together by the same God who spoke the universe into being. God intentionally designed me. Yes, me.

Would you like a little description? If there were such a thing as the "baby in the womb store," I would be on the shelf with the following description: "*Caucasian girl with Down syndrome, hydrocephalus caused by aqueductal stenosis, atrial-ventricular canal heart defect requiring surgery soon after birth, impending moyamoya syndrome with a guaranteed cerebral vascular accident (i.e. stroke) to be followed by spastic quadriplegia, seizure disorder, neurogenic bladder, and an eventual diagnosis of acute lymphocytic leukemia.*" Sounds like a possible manufacturing mistake, huh? Let's go on and read the fine print of me: *"blond hair and lots of it, button nose as cute as can be, eyes that twinkle with the excitement of the simple things in life, a trusting attitude, a grateful heart, and joy unspeakable and full of glory. This is someone who will touch all those around her without ever speaking a word. This is someone who will cause others to examine their own gripes and complaints and wonder if, perhaps, they have more to be grateful for after all. This is someone who will make you happy if you let her!"*

But, the finest print of all is that I really, truly, and without a doubt am "*fearfully and wonderfully made.*" Mom always is telling me that God "knit me together" and saw my substance and knew and knows my frame and all the days ordained for me before even one of them came to be. She tells me that God was right there, weaving into my very being that extra chromosome that gave me the gift of Down syndrome. Mom says that God knew I would have hydrocephalus and a heart defect and that the blueprint for moyamoya and stroke and cancer was sketched and included for a purpose by a great and good, always good, God who was and is in control of it all, then and now and forever.

Mom agrees, there are days when we sure can get tired. There are days when things don't go as planned or as smoothly as we, if we were writing the script of our lives, would author it. And, things don't always make sense in as clear a way as we might like. Sure, there are unanswered questions. But, such is the beautiful mystery of life and of God. Yet, we know what we need to know to serve and love and enjoy Him forever. The rest, well, really doesn't matter, or at least it doesn't matter as much as we sometimes make it matter.

And, there is icing on this sweet cake of life. The icing is that all my days were ordained and written in God's book before even one of them came to be! He knows them all. Every single one.

DECEMBER 2

Written from Sarah's perspective...

WHY?

The typical question. The expected question. The universal question when something happens suddenly, unexpectedly, tragically. The common question when disappointment or failure or discouragement come along.

Why?

Why Down syndrome?

Why atrial-ventricular canal heart defect?

Why hydrocephalus?

Why birth defects and medical diagnosis and even more struggles to come?

Why me?

Mom tells me the story of how she wrote a letter to her sister-in-law, Sheila. My Aunt Sheila and her family live in Maryland, right on the beautiful Chesapeake Bay. Back when Mom was carrying me with her, she didn't have a computer, internet or e-mail and long-distance phone calls from a landline phone cost extra money. So, back then, Mom often wrote letters. That was how she told Aunt Sheila the news about my birth defects. She told her in a letter before I was born.

A few days after dropping the letter off at the post office, the telephone rang in our kitchen. It was probably on a Saturday or the weekend sometime because Mom was at home to pick it up. It was Aunt Sheila. She had read Mom's letter, and she seemed to be more troubled and upset by all this than Mom was! She asked repeatedly, "But, why?" Now, my Mom, ever the deep thinker type, had a profound answer: *"I don't know."*

Gee whiz, would somebody please let me out of this womb so that I can give them the real and reasonable answer! The real answer is *"Why not me?"* Why is it that we take the good and easy things from the Lord's hand without a second thought, often without even giving Him any credit or thanks? Like we deserve the good stuff, right? Maybe we don't say that, but we sure act like that's what we believe when we take and take and never say, "Why me" while we're taking. Then when a struggle comes along, all of a sudden that three letter word hunts us down and we let it beat us up instead of taking the sword of God's Word and putting it in the place it belongs.

If it's absolutely necessary to know "why," here it is. Always. No matter what the circumstances. No matter how weary, dreary, scary the day or the diagnosis may be: *...call upon me (the LORD) in the day of trouble: I will deliver thee, and thou shalt glorify me (Psalm 50:15).*

We are here to glorify God. That's why.

Whether healthy or sick.

Whether safe and secure or trembling in fear.

Whether happy or sad.

Whether an optimist or a pessimist.

Whether in plenty or need.

We are here to glorify the LORD. I and my extra chromosome, my history of stroke and cancer, and the shunt in my head are here to glorify the LORD.

Whatever else we and I may need to know about "why" will be shown to us as the need arises.

Until then, *Whoso offereth praise glorifieth me (Psalm 50:23),* the LORD says!

I can guarantee you, that I will not be disappointed with the outcome of my afflictions if my desire is to glorify the LORD!

DECEMBER 3

Written from Sarah's perspective...

Really?

Let's see if you can guess. What do you think was one of the most common comments that Mom and Dad heard during the days of rough sailing on stormy medical seas with me?

Take a minute and see if you can guess it. No peeking!

I'll even give you a hint. Church going people were more likely to speak these words than others. Does that help at all?

Well, here it is: *"God will never give you more than you can handle."* Or something along those lines. Sometimes it's the same idea in a different package: *"God is honoring you by this trial because He knows you can handle it."*

Oh, yeah? Really?

Is that really in the Bible? I mean, is this, um, "doctrinally correct?" Come on, I'm waiting! Show it to me in the Word of God!

I'll bet some of you, those who are familiar with Scripture, may be thinking of Paul's words to the Corinthians: *There hath no temptation taken you but such as is common to man: but God is faithful, who will not suffer you to be tempted above that ye are able; but will with the temptation also make a way to escape, that ye may be able to bear it (I Corinthians 10:13).*

Who's making the "way to escape?" God is!

It's all about God.

Our perseverance, our endurance, our pressing on in the face of difficult circumstances is not about our strength or our abilities. It's not about us handling anything.

It's all about God.

And guess what? It seems to me that God frequently, consistently through-out the Bible was giving people more than they could handle! Could Abraham really handle leaving his home and family to sojourn into unknown land and believe, despite his advanced years, that his descendants would be as numerous as the grains of sand on the sea shore or stars in the sky? Could he really surrender his son through whom these very descendants were to come?

Could Joseph really resist Potiphar's wife and handle being in jail for a crime never committed? Could Joseph really forgive his brothers who had sold him into slavery?

Could Moses really handle the entire Egyptian army on one front and the sea on the other? Could He really put up with the grumbling Israelites in the wilderness for forty years?

How about Joshua, could he really handle the hostile inhabitants of the walled fortress city of Jericho?

Could David really handle the giant Goliath? Was it really possible for him to endure the hatred of Saul and of his own son, Absalom?

Could Elijah really handle years of isolation and only enough provision for one meal at a time? Could Elijah truly conquer the hundreds of prophets of Baal?

Could Jonah really preach repentance to the Ninevites?

Could John the Baptist really preach repentance to the people of Israel? Could he really live on locusts and wild honey? Could he really handle being beheaded?

Could Stephen really handle the stones hurled at him?

Could Saul of Tarsus really handle the blinding light on the road to Damascus and become Paul the Apostle who died for the cause of Christ?

Could John the Apostle really handle abandonment to the Isle of Patmos?

How did Christ handle the mocking, the beating, the loneliness, the nails, the weight of sin, death on a cross?

Does God really give us only what we can handle and no more?

I say NO! He gives us much more than we can handle, and then HE HANDLES IT!

Then the word of the LORD came to Jeremiah: 'I am the LORD, the God of all mankind. Is anything too hard for me?' (Jeremiah 32:26, 27)

Is anything too hard for the LORD? (Genesis 18:14)

Then the LORD said to him (Moses), 'Who gave man his mouth? Who makes him deaf or mute? Who gives him sight or makes him blind? Is it not I, the LORD? Now go; I will help you speak and will teach you what to say.' (Exodus 2:11, 12)

DECEMBER 4

Written from Sarah's perspective...

Scars.

There are scars all over my body. Literally. My head. My chest. My tummy. My back. My neck. My arms. My thighs. My legs. My feet.

I want to share the story of three of these scars...

The first one is a scar on my face. It's on my right cheek, and it runs from my ear toward the middle of my cheek. These days, this scar is pretty hard to see. But it's still there. Most people don't see it. But, Mom sees it every day when she's washing my face and cleaning me up. This is a scar that somebody else gave to me out of carelessness.

When I was in the intensive care nursery, I had to have this thing called an NG tube. That stands for "nasal gastric" tube. That's the medical term for this long tube thingy that gets shoved down your nose, into your stomach, hopefully not ending up in your lungs. The purpose of this tube is for feeding. This tube can have food sent down it. Well, not real food, but some kind of formula food. Yucky smelling stuff as I barely recall. Well anyway, this old NG tube doesn't just stay in place all by itself. It needs a friend. That friend is called "tape." Lots of tape. Tape wrapped in a Y shape around the tube and then stuck on the face. Sticky medical tape. My face. Tape strong enough to keep that tube in place for a few days before it needs to be replaced.

This would not be my last experience with NG tubes. Since I was in the intensive care nursery, most of the day to day care was done by the nurses in there. Actually back then, Mom would not have been able to provide this kind of care. She could now. But, back then, she was a mere rookie learning the medical ropes. So, the changing of the NG tube fell upon a nurse. A busy nurse. A nurse who had done this so many times that the squirms and cries of a newborn baby as the tape was being removed and the tube pulled out and replaced no longer pierced her ears or her heart.

People in a hurry. Don't you love 'em? Yep, scars can be caused by people in a hurry, who don't mean to cause pain or injury, but that's what happens sometimes. Avoidable pain. Unnecessary injury. An unintentional scar. Obvious scars on the physical body or less obvious scars on the heart and the mind. Such is the scar on my face. A nurse in a hurry to get the tape off. Gave it a yank. Task complete. Schedule kept. Scar remains.

Next scar is a scar on my chest that runs up and down. Mom tells me that is officially called "vertical." I like that word. Vertical. This vertical scar is right in the middle of my chest, between my ribs. It's faded, but still a very obvious scar. This one was also given to me by another person, but not because of being in a hurry. This scar is there on purpose. Now in this case, it was put there with a good purpose. I know there are some out there who have scars put there by others on purpose, and not with good intentions. I don't really know that much about those kind of scars, although I know someone who does.

Anyway, this "good-intentioned, put there on purpose by someone else" scar was made because of my heart surgery. I'm glad for this scar. And, I'm glad for Dr. Rosenkrantz who gave it to me. He saved my life. And, this scar reminds me that sometimes pain is good for us. I had pain after my heart surgery. It was no fun at all. But, it was necessary for me to live and for me to grow. Dr. Rosenkrantz fixed up my heart, but he couldn't do it without leaving marks that it needed to be done in the first place.

The next scar to tell you about is a scar on my foot. Actually, on my feet. On my heels. They're kind of mostly callous and scar all mixed together. The reason I have these scars is because of me. I gave these to myself. By constantly pushing my heels into the back of my casts (after I had surgery to lengthen my hamstrings) and later into the backs of my sneakers, I hurt my own feet. I hurt myself. There's lots of ways we can hurt ourselves for sure. None of us, even me, is immune from that. Mom had to spend lots of time soaking my feet, putting pasty stuff on my heels, and watching for infection. See, my scars affected her, too. Not just me. But someone else. She doesn't have these scars on herself, but they still touch her life.

So, those are the stories of three of my scars. They don't hurt me anymore. Just remind me. They are a part of who I am now and each one has a story to tell.

Jesus has scars. Put there by other people, by people with the intention of hurting Him. Killing Him. He is God made flesh who came in truth and light to redeem the lost. *Herein is love, not that we loved God but that He loved us and sent His Son to be the propitiation for our sins (I John 4:10)* Propitiation. Great word. It means "satisfactory payment." Complete. Settled account. Made acceptable to the Father through the sacrifice of the Son.

He has the scars to show for it, too.

Nail pierced hands.

Riven side.

Those nails were driven in by people with the intent of inflicting injury, wounds, death.

Who drove the nails in?

Sinners. That would be all of us.

I'm thankful for my scars.

But, I'm more thankful for His.

I needed that hasty nurse.

I needed Dr. Rosenkrantz.

But most of all, I need Him.

We all need Him.

Propitiation.

Beautiful propitiation.

DECEMBER 5

Abiding...believing that it is never about success or failure. Only obedience. Whether my obedience to God results in success or failure in the eyes of the world is God's business.

In the King's economy, obedience to Him is always success.

Abiding means I make plans rooted in obedience, not ideas of success or failure...for in a Kingdom in which the first will be last and the last will be first, sometimes our deepest failure can be transformed into our greatest success.

Abiding means asking God every day to put me where He wants me to be. And then, actually being there, eyes wide open to His planned purpose for me, not my own. It involves risk and not always knowing all the details or the outcome, but going forth nonetheless, led by His Spirit and confident in Him.

Obeying the Spirit.

Following where He leads.

And on the road of obedience, there will be moments in which Goliaths show up, and we wonder if we are on the right road or not. Abiding believes, by faith, that all of life's Goliaths are small compared to the greatness of God, a God who see us in our low estates and stoops down to set us upon His Rock.

Boldly obey.

Live the life He has for you.

DECEMBER 6

Dear Father,

Thank You!

Praise You!

Glory to God in the highest...Christ has come.

God became flesh and dwelt among us. *"And can it be that I should gain an interest in the Savior's blood. Died He for me who caused His pain. For me, who He to death pursued. Amazing love, how can it be? That Thou my God hast died for me!"*

His birth was perhaps as painful as His death...for consider what He gave up to come and walk with man...consider where He was to go 30 some years after that night in a stable...How humble our Savior is!

May we realize that You, O Lord, gave as much on the night of Your birth as You did on the day of Your death!

Father, You became man and blood flowed through Your veins. Your heart beat and pumped red blood cells, hemoglobin, platelets, white blood cells and plasma through Your veins and arteries. The eternal God put on my mortality and spilt His blood for me...and gain did I...at the cost, steep and sharp, of Your life's blood. Your blood bought my salvation and my victory.

You pursued me all the way to Your death.

A sinner was I, yet You demonstrated love beyond love by dying for me. And for all.

Despite the fact that not all will come and embrace the gift of eternal life that You alone purchase. You died for all...those who come to Your side and are saved and those who refuse and must face the wrath of God.

Your sacrifice, the sacrifice that began at Your birth, is completely sufficient to save all, although not all will come.

Thank You that in Your grace and timing, I came to You, the One who came to me.

In Your grace and timing, may every person in my family and in my classroom, now and in generations yet to be, come to You...the One who came to us.

Manger.

Cross.

Empty tomb.

Coming again as Conquering King!

O What a Savior!

DECEMBER 7

December 7, 2006...my beloved Dad died.

Suddenly.

Unexpectedly.

He was only 61.

He was my good friend.

I miss him.

Christians are not exempt from sorrow, are we?

Just like the rest of the world, Christians experience sorrow and loss and sickness and death. Sometimes we have valleys of deep sadness to pass through. We should not be surprised by this. Jesus told His followers that, yes, we would experience troubles in life (John 16:33).

But, He doesn't stop with that reality. Jesus goes on in John 16:33 to encourage us that while we will have troubles and problems to deal with, we can "Take heart" because Jesus overcomes the world. Hope. That's what Christians have. That's what the world needs. And, that's just one of the many gifts that Christ offers us...hope.

We have hope because of Christ's finished work of salvation on the cross.

We have hope of health and wholeness in heaven.

We have hope of purpose and meaning in our struggles as we seek to serve the Lord through them.

We have hope because our trials are temporary and salvation, through the shed blood of Christ, is eternal for the repentant sinner.

Christians have hope because Christ is victorious. *...thanks be to God! He gives us the victory through our Lord Jesus Christ! (I Corinthians 15:57).*

And, we have hope because we are not alone.

Jesus suffered, too.

He knows what it feels like to be in physical pain.

He knows what it's like to experience emotional pain.

He anguished. Groaned.

As a result, He is really, really able to understand and to help. *For we do not have a high priest (Jesus) who is unable to sympathize with our weaknesses, but we have one who has been tempted in every way, just as we are - yet was without sin. Let us then approach the throne of grace with confidence, so that we may receive mercy and find grace to help us in our time of need (Hebrews 4:15, 16).*

DECEMBER 8

Dear Father,

Bless the Lord, O my soul and all that is within me.

Bless Your holy name!

As we near Christmas, there is tendency in our flesh to rush. We speed up in a frazzled attempt to be caught up with all the supposed demands of the holiday. Help us, Father, to deliberately, simply, and with conviction say, "NO."

No, I am not going to agree to participate in every request and event.

No, I will not lose track of the baby in the manger in this rush.

As Pastor said in the message today, there are many kinds of distractions and many of the distractions are good. Good causes, good intentions, good programs, good people. But, don't give up the BEST for the good! Don't lose that intimate time and connection with the Savior.   Christmas is about HIM! Even in the church, that is so often lost in hustle and bustle.

May I remember HIM!

May our family and our church remember HIM!

I pray for my family and my students to know the baby in the manger, to know Him well and to know why and for whom He came. He came in obedience to the will of the Father. He came to call sinners, me and you, to repentance. He came as the remission for sin. Without blood and repentance, there is no remission for sin. He gave the blood. We must bring the repentance.   If you have no change of mind and heart, the gift given at Christmas is not yours. The gift is for the repentant.

Father, may an understanding of, desire for, and spirit of repentance grip me, my husband, our family, and my students. Today and through the years.

In the Name of Jesus, the Gift of God…

DECEMBER 9

"High places."

That's how the Bible refers to those places where the Israelites went to worship idols. Worthless idols. The opportunity to worship the true and living God was offered to them, and so often, they chose instead to go to the high places and worship idols of no use made by the hands of men. Who knows, maybe some of the idol worshippers had even gone to the temple in the morning to worship the true and living God who had rescued His people from the oppressive land of Egypt, but now it was afternoon, and they were on their way to the high places.

Maybe they thought the high places were more fun. Maybe it was a social thing. Maybe they thought they could have it both ways...worship both God and idols. Maybe they didn't think God would see their disloyalty. Maybe they thought a little disloyalty wasn't a big deal. Maybe a good friend showed up and suggested they go to the high places and have a party and good time around the Asherah pole or the alter of Baal.

But, God tells us very plainly we cannot worship both Him and an idol. Check out commandments numbered one and two. Check out the books of Isaiah and Jeremiah and the minor prophets who warn repeatedly against the perils of idol worship. The warnings are all over the place...it is impossible to properly worship God if we are sneaking off to the high places to bow to Baal with our buddies.

And, those warnings were not just for the ancient Israelites. The Old Testament has extremely practical value for today's world and societies. High places still exist, you know. They are still here. Maybe we don't use the phrase "high places" today, and maybe we are not worshipping Baal or Molech or Asherah.

Today's modern world may try to disguise the high places behind sophistication. Yet, disguise does not extinguish their existence. Whenever we are worshipping anything other than God the Creator, Sustainer, Savior, Righteous Judge and King to come, we are standing on a high place. And, a high place is a dangerous place upon which to stand.

There is no benefit in trusting anything in this world more than we trust the Lord. No benefit at all. Maybe temporary pleasure, but no long term benefit and certainly no safety.

Have you a Baal on a high place in your life that you bow down to?

Money?

Possessions?

Career?

Relationship?

Alcohol?

Reputation?

Ungodly entertainment?

Peer pressure?

Gossip?

Lust?

Self?

Convenience?

Anger?

Appearance?

Intellect?

Selfish ambition?

Government?

Environmentalism?

Moral relativism?

Church tradition?

"Religion?"

The list of high places is long. And real.

DECEMBER 10

From The Quest for More by Paul David Tripp [46]

"What is the big thing that you are living for right now?"

"The transcendent glory that every human being quests for, whether he knows it or not, is not a thing; it is a person, and His name is God."

"We were never meant to be self-focused little kings ruling miniscule little Kingdoms with a population of one."

"We are meant to live for the ONE who IS GLORY."

"We must never shrink the size of our glory focus to the narrow glories of our own little lives."

"Have you treated the size of GOD'S GRACE as if it were no bigger than the size of your personal concerns?"

"The inertia of sin is always away from the Creator and toward ourselves."

"The ongoing tendency (inertia) is to treat my life as if it were no bigger than my life."

" 'Good' is the enemy of great."

"Few people attain great lives because it is just so easy to settle for a good life."

"Have you settled for living too small?"

"Have you settled into a self-focused enjoyment of the good life?"
From The Quest for More by Paul David Tripp [46]

DECEMBER 11

Father,

May I be less and You be more.

Be exalted, Lord.

May I be small and You big.

In You, You only, is my joy complete.

May I rejoice when I am small or weak or inadequate...fully aware that Your power depends not at all on me. May I be less, and You more.

All of You and none of me!

You are light. In You resides no darkness.

You are Immanuel – God with us - the light has come and visited the darkness of man.

May Your light burst through blind eyes, hard hearts, proud thoughts, strong lusts, dull senses - and shine – shine Your truth into the lost lives of mankind.

The light has shone in the darkness.

Many have not comprehended the light. Many have closed their eyes, intent and content to remain in the darkness.

Blaze, blaze into the lives, the wills, the hearts of mankind in all places, one man at a time.

The Kingdom advances one man at a time...but advance, it will!

In the Name of Christ, Immanuel…

DECEMBER 12

Except the LORD of Hosts had left unto us a very small remnant, we should have been as Sodom, and we should have been like unto Gomorrah (Isaiah 1:9).

Lord, may we be the generation of them that seek You, that seek Your face.

Lord, it is nothing with You to help, whether with many or with them that have no power: help us, O Lord our God, for we rest on Thee, and in Thy name we go against this multitude. O LORD, Thou art our God. Let not man prevail against Thee.

Help us to remember that we need to rely on You.

For Your eyes run to and fro throughout the whole earth to show Yourself strong in behalf of them whose heart is perfect toward You.

You, Lord, are our light and our salvation.

Whom shall we fear? What can mere mortal man do unto us?

Behold, Your eye, Lord, is upon those that fear You, those who trust in Your mercy.

You deliver our soul from death and keep us alive in famine.

You are our help and our shield.

Put them in fear, O LORD; let not man prevail. Put them in fear, O LORD; that the nations may know themselves to be but men (Psalm 9:20).

DECEMBER 13

God is a God of extremes.

He hung the stars in place. Out of the vastness of His power, He spoke the vast universe.

This same God who breathed the stars, breathed too our cells. He twisted DNA into a double helix and within its complex structure, He stores information…the blueprints of life.

This is the God of gravity and the God of protons, neutrons, and electrons. This God who designed both the vast and the minute with complexity and order and purpose.

I am grateful that God, Creator of all, the Great I AM who holds all together in His mighty power and everlasting mercy, recognizes me.

In the vastness of this universe, I am insignificant.

Yet, to the 'beyond vast' One who created this vast universe, I am significant.

I am more than matter…I actually do matter…to Him.

The electrons, protons, and neutrons that make up the atoms that make up the molecules that make up me have been designed with a purpose and woven together in His image.

I, made of matter, do matter, to the only One who really matters, the Great I AM.

And for that, I am forever grateful.

DECEMBER 14

Earlier this month, a 20 year old man went into an elementary school in Danbury, Connecticut. He had guns. He killed 20 students, ages 5 – 10, six adults…then himself. As I write these words, I'm sitting in my home. I am safe and comfortable. Meanwhile there are parents this night in Connecticut who are consumed with the horror of this evil and heart-wrenching loss.

Lord, the only answer to all of this is You.

Increasing security, stricter gun laws, more funding for mental health programs are not the solutions.

Because the problem is the human heart.

This is about the reality of evil. This is about spiritual warfare and powers of darkness. And the only real solution is the Light of the world, Jesus Christ.

God forgive us that as a nation we fail to pursue Your spiritual solutions to the problem of the human heart. We have forgotten to commit our ways to You, and instead we lean on our own understanding. We develop our own solutions...solutions based on government programs and funding and more laws...and all the while the true problem – wickedness in the heart of man – is ignored.

As a people we have become spiritually shallow, a nation heading into darkness. Have mercy on us, Lord.

You, Father, are the Lord of the harvest. I pray for You to send Your labourers into the field of hurting, grieving, shocked parents and families. Help the saved know how to comfort the hurting. Equip the brethren to bind wounds with truth and love. Help us to pray and to ever point hurting hearts and lost souls, Lord, to You.

You are the God of Redemption.

Buy us back, Lord, buy us back.

DECEMBER 15

From Foxe: Voices of the Martyrs [47]

Immanuel Andegeresgh and Kibrom Firemichel (October 17, 2006)

"Night had fallen as the men left their houses, silently closing the doors behind them. They each stood still a few frozen, breathless seconds and looked cautiously both ways down the street before they dared move. Confident of their concealment, they quietly and carefully set off in the direction of the meeting place, following the contours of shadows and dark lanes to veil their journey.

"When they arrived, they were greeted by the warm and familiar faces of their brothers and sisters who had also gathered here to fellowship together. For all of them, including two men, Immanuel Andergeresgh and Kibrom Firemichel, this was the only opportunity to worship their Savior together in a community, their only hope for true fellowship, and they were entrusting their lives to all of those present. They had become all too accustomed to the laws forbidding open worship in Eritrea. The fear and hesitation melted away as they began to worship and share together.

"It came as both an intrusion and a distress when a loud hammering at the door broke their praise. The singing stopped. The gathered believers exchanged wide-eyed and knowing glances. They knew immediately what it meant: Their meeting had been

discovered, and they would be arrested, detained, and possibly tortured for breaking the law.

"Since 2002, only the Orthodox, Roman Catholic, and Lutheran churches have been recognized in Eritrea, along with Islam. Numerous evangelical Christians have been arrested for practicing what officials call a 'new religion.' Since that time, thousands of Christians have been placed in prisons where they face deplorable conditions, some held in metal shipping containers in temperatures that can soar above 100 degrees Fahrenheit or drop below freezing.

"Within moments the door was forced open to reveal several uniformed security police, members of a task force specifically established to eradicate all 'menfesawyan,' or 'spirituals,' a term often used to describe Christians not belonging to one of the recognized churches.

"Immanuel, twenty-three years old, Kibrom, thirty, and eight others were arrested and taken to a military confinement camp. There they were subjected to torture and 'furious mistreatment,' according to one of the other believers. At the end of two days, Immaneul and Kibrom both died of severe dehydration and injuries sustained in the torture.

"In the end, the two men dared to gather with other believers because they understood the life-giving effects of sharing in the bonds of brotherhood. They understood the risks, but could not deny that to be united with Christ meant to be bound to one another in love and encouragement, gifts that far outweighed the risks."
From Foxe: Voices of the Martyrs [47]

DECEMBER 16

Dear Lord,

May my family know that Jesus is the Christ, the Son of God.

May my students know that Jesus is the Christ, the Savior of the world.

May they believe and have life in His name.

My soul glorifies You. My heart is Yours.

May You, my Lord, occupy the highest throne in my heart.

Be forever my King, my all in all.

Lord, there are so many distractions in our world.

Things that look fun.

Things that glitter and boldly beckon.

But within, these things of the world are rotten and rotting.

Deliver me, us, from the lust of the eyes, the lust of the flesh and the pride of life.

Reveal to me, to us, the truth about how subtle and deceptive are our lusts and the glittery trinkets of the world and its ways.

Give us clear thinking to examine even the dusty corners of our hearts and thoughts to discover any impure and rotting tentacles of the world.

May we love those who are perishing…may we love them with the love of Christ. As He was, may we be slaves to the Father, slaves to the brethren, and lights to the perishing. May we love compassionately the lost sheep without loving sinful ways.

In the Name of Jesus, Son of God…

DECEMBER 17

Dear Father,

Praise Your Name…

My soul glorifies You! Praise You, Lord, for Your goodness to me! Mark and I just visited Sarah's grave. I stood next to the grave, and tears rolled down my cheeks. They roll still as I write these words. But, praise be to God, who always causes me to triumph in Christ Jesus!

Hope. You, Lord, are so many things, not the least of which is hope. And the hope that flows from You to me is a great hope. It is no mere fantasy. Hope, founded and grounded in You, is a living hope, an eternal hope, a saving hope, a victorious conquering hope!

I do not yet see You face to face. But all around me exists evidence of You! The day is coming in which I will be privileged to behold Your beauty. In this I hope and wait patiently. I can walk by faith today because my hope is real, my hope is You.

Lord Jesus, be the hope of all my family. Be the One, the only One, that each of my beloved family rests upon and trusts in. I pray for deliverance for them from the devouring jaws of any hope they have that is not real and that cannot save.

I can sing a new song because I know that I know that I know I am saved by the blood of Christ, risen Savior, living hope.

In the Name of the Hope of Israel...

DECEMBER 18

Dear Lord,

May I have a heart like Philip. When You said to him, "Follow me," Philip followed You.

Thank You, Lord for saying to me, "Follow Me." Help me to do just that, Lord. Without fear, without complaining, without hesitation, may I follow You, Jesus, with hand to the plow and no looking back.

Call, I pray, all people in my family, now and in the generations to come, call them to follow. Speak their names, and may their hearts be willing and their feet ready to follow wherever You lead. Call. Equip. Enable consistent disciples, those who will endure, press on, and know from what they have been rescued.

May we be a persistent, enduring family that understands salvation and recognizes the real battles and dangers we face...the lust of the flesh, the lust of the eyes, the pride of life, deception and apathy from within and without.

May we be people who understand that Your wrath, mighty God, is just and while it is held back at this moment, the time is coming when it will be revealed to all...and the unsaved will be consumed by the all-consuming fire that You, Lord, are. And the saved will be purified and stand and live in eternal safety with joy complete in Your presence.

We need You.

Help each one of us to really, really grasp that truth.

In the Name of Jesus, the One who came, the One who calls, the One who will come again...

DECEMBER 19

I've been thinking about the word, "self." It is a word that can cause us much grief.

In the world, the word, "self" often comes attached to other words: *self-esteem, self-love, self-fulfillment, self-respect, self-confidence, self-expression, self-identity.*

As I turn my thoughts toward God's written Word in Scripture, I realize that these terms are not to be found.

Instead, God reveals value in such concepts as *self-denial, self-sacrifice, self-surrender, and self-control.* He teaches us that we are to lay down our self-perceived rights and instead pour ourselves out in lives of love and service for the purpose of HIS glory. He instructs us that we, made in His image, are to find our identity in HIM, not in ourselves. In other words, we are to die to self and live to HIM.

Such ideas are foreign in our culture. Often, these ideas are more than neglected, they are disdained. And yet, as I think on this, I come to the conclusion that it is not only the world that neglects and disdains God's wisdom regarding self, but it is I, too, who often disregard and rebel against God's counsel. I, a born again Christian, have the tendency - and a strong one at that - to move readily in the direction of self-promotion. I, a Christian who claims Jesus as my Savior, daily must recognize that my spiritual inertia is ever toward the idol of self.

Truth be told, I do want things my way. Now. I do want to be recognized and important and comfortable. And when God - the God who suffered and died for me - challenges me to give these things up, I bristle and complain.

I am an ungrateful child.

I look through self-righteous eyes at the world and condemn it because of its inexcusable and inexhaustible emphasis on self. And yet it is not this enemy that poses the greatest threat. It is I and the enemy of self within that poses the greatest threat to spiritual truth and growth in my life. I compare myself to the world, and I smirk with self-satisfaction, for I look pretty good in such a comparison.

But God...

In His everlasting love for me, He, in His perfect timing, draws my eyes, my attention, my heart toward His holiness. His perfection. His purity. And suddenly, I do not look so good, and my self-righteousness becomes filthy rags.

And thus I know I need Him.

And I know He will not fail, but will clothe me in the pure, white robes of HIS righteousness. My self-righteous filthy rags cast aside!

Daily, I fall short.

Daily, the idol of self creeps back in.

Daily, He is faithful to me.

My prayer is that He will this day make me weak so that He can show Himself strong and lead me on the path of self-denial.

Only by Him can this be accomplished.

DECEMBER 20

From **The Quest for More** by Paul David Tripp [48]

"Are you trying to build your own kingdom? Each of our lives is shaped by the war between the Kingdom of God and the kingdom of self."

"Little kingdom living turns life into an endless search for earthly treasure and an unending focus on personal need."

"You can't squeeze the large-vision lifestyle of the Kingdom of God into the small-vision confines of the kingdom of self. It will simply never fit."

"What makes your day a good day?"

"What are the things that you faithfully pursue?"

"Whose rules get the most attention and the quickest response in your life and relationships?"

"In the little kingdom of one, the highest law is the law of self."

"In the little kingdom of one, the highest will is the will of self."

"But, the little kingdom of one is not God's Kingdom."

"The little kingdom of one is a dangerous place to be..."

"*Whom are you seeking to satisfy?*"

"*The big question in the little kingdom of one is 'Am I satisfied?'*"

"*The big question in the Kingdom of God is 'Am I honoring God with my life?'*"

"*Whose glory motivates you to do what you do and to say what you say?*"

"*The daily war between the little kingdom of one and the Kingdom of God is a battle for competing glories.*"

"*Don't settle for the shadow glories of the physical earth.*"

From <u>The Quest for More</u> by Paul David Tripp [48]

DECEMBER 21

It seems I am continually letting the Lord down, continually falling short of His glory.

Yet, He is continually loving me, forgiving me, conforming me, making me His vessel.

He continually has a vision greater than mine.

He continually frames my life and my failures within His purpose and plan.

And while I am often distraught, my God never is.

My faith in Him is not what it ought to be. He deserved pre-eminence in my life. He deserves to be everything and the only thing to me, and I know He is not. How that must pain His all-knowing, pure, and beautiful heart.

Yet, He continually continues, working in my broken life, creating from the pieces a testimony of His greatness, chiseling from the rough-hewn rock of this life a soul, spirit, and body made in His image who will one day reflect His glory as I ought.

All because of Christ.

Yes, all because of the One who gave Himself for me, who died so I could live, and who now lives in victory, a victory that I, in Him, share.

DECEMBER 22

What a beautiful winter day. Feet of pure white snow covering the ground and hanging low and deep on the pine trees and over the roof top of the house. Today the sky is a perfect deep shade of blue after yesterday's persistent and constant gray.

There was neither school for Sarah (in her second year in Pioneer High School) nor for me (in my first year teaching at Central Baptist Christian School) thanks to the blustery blizzard and snow clogged roads. Mark was off to work at 3:30 AM. That left the house to me and Sarah and our black cat, sweet little Jo.

After working on lesson plans and taking a trek out doors to shovel off the steps and to enjoy God's amazing creativity in everything from a single snowflake to the heavens above, I decided it was a good day to put up our old Charlie Brown Christmas tree. Sarah was just waking up. I got the tree pulled out and the plastic branches shaped and placed on the "trunk". I got Sarah up and in her wheelchair so she could participate. Christmas music played in the background.

The cat was absolutely beside herself about this whole Christmas tree thing. I thought briefly she might have a heart attack. She stared, crouched, waved her tail and ran around. At one point, she took a flying leap into the middle of the tree from the middle of the floor. A verbal scolding was all that was necessary to cause her to pout and head for the spare room and a nap under the bed, leaving Sarah and I to the remaining ornaments and tinsel.

And then I heard it. Quietly, peacefully from the CD player into the living room and surrounding us with a reminder of the reason for Christmas and the reason for rejoicing every day of the year and in all circumstances...

> *O holy night, the stars are brightly shining.*
> *It is the night of the dear Savior's birth.*
> *Long lay the world in sin and error pining.*
> *Till He appeared and the soul felt its worth.*
> *A thrill of hope, a weary world rejoices,*
> *And yonder breaks a new and glorious morn.*
> *Fall on your knees....*
> *O hear the angel voices!*
> *O night divine,*
> *O night when Christ was born*
> *Surely He taught us to love one another.*
> *His law is love and His gospel is peace.*
> *Chains shall He break for the slave is our brother,*
> *And in His Name all oppression shall cease.*
> *Sweet hymns of joy in grateful chorus raise we...*

Let all within us praise His Holy Name!
Christ is the Lord, O praise His Name forever!
His power and glory ever more proclaim,
O night, O holy night, O night divine!

DECEMBER 23

Lord,

I buried a child this year.

And, my heart is broken.

But, I buried her with hope and assurance of seeing her again because of You.

Yes, it is sad that my child died, but not as tragic as the dying people around me who do not know the Savior.

So many people in the world who deny You. Ignore You. Reject You. So many who have committed themselves to idols that cannot save.

So many yet lost in their sin and the uncircumcision of the flesh.

Lord, may they feel the flames licking at them. May they sense the darkness pressing in and smell the stench of hell while there is yet time to flee.

Lord, replace stubborn stony hearts with hearts of flesh.

You, alone, Lord, know what it will take to draw a person to You. With the full awareness that it may take some very difficult and trying times and experiences, I ask You to do what You must to reach the lost.

You know who they are.

Do not abandon these works of Your hands to their own choices and demands!

They are, in their pride, demanding their own way.

Oh, Lord, do not give them their own way. Do not abandon them as they may want You to. Do not send leanness into their souls!

May the Holy Spirit be mighty to reveal You to the lost.

Grip each heart, Lord, in Your perfect way and timing. May there be no peace, no rest, no assurance, no contentment for the lost until each is driven to You and fall in brokenness and repentance before You and call You "Lord."

Then, once saved, may each live in freedom...forgiven, clean, new...

Victorious in You.

Lord, show us Your glory.

 In the Name of Jesus, the One who restores...

DECEMBER 24

Dear Father,

I pray for Your strength and grace for this night and tomorrow as we face our first Christmas without Sarah.

I pray for every broken heart in my family.

I pray for each person who has suffered a loss, a sorrow, a discouragement, a trial this year.

Lord, draw each broken heart near and speak Your love and truth into their lives.

My life.

And may ALL of us in this family, whether broken hearted or not, be broken before You. May we bow before You and call You Lord.

Lord of all.

Lord before all. Help each of us in our family, wherever this Christmas Eve may find us, come and adore You...Christ the Lord!

How worthy You are of all our adoration, yet how very little we truly give You. We are busy. We are sad. We are happy. We are tired.

Whatever we are, wherever we are, there is no excuse to adore You only half-heartedly.

Help us to adore You.

Wholeheartedly.

Tonight.

Tomorrow.

Forever.

Savior. Immanuel. God with us.

O Night Divine!

In the Name of the Incarnate Christ who dwelt among...

DECEMBER 25

How great is God!

The same powerful, mighty God Who spoke and breathed out the stars and who calls them each by name...the same all-knowing, all-wise God who designed the unfathomable complexity of DNA, information written in a 4-letter nucleotide alphabet, stored efficiently in a double-helix home, and copied effectively as cells reproduce...this same sovereign, immutable, eternal God knit me and you together in the womb.

He knows our names.

He knows our needs.

He knows our sins.

And, this great God, the glory of which the vast universe cannot contain but only reflect, this same great God clothed Himself in human flesh.

Deity added to Himself humanity, and Jesus Christ, who is from everlasting to everlasting, humbled Himself to live upon a small, pale blue dot called "earth."

The God of all glory and power became a babe in a manger... and grew into a man with calloused feet walking the dusty roads of Galilee and Judea.

He experiencing what we do. Life.

Only He without sin.

This same mighty God, star-breather and universe creator, felt His flesh ripped from His back by men wielding whips with sharp barbs dragged, like a plough, across bare skin. Deity felt nails sear through epithelial, connective and bone tissue of wrist and feet. Nerves were severed, and bare dendrites bore waves of pain throughout His body.

Perfect babe in the manger now perfect man impaled upon a Roman cross.

Not only was He perfectly innocent, He was completely powerful to stop the torture.

But, He didn't. Because He is love, and He knew, even from all eternity past, even before He spoke the world into existence, that this was and is still humanity's only hope.

His blood spilt and shed for ours.

He paying the price of our sin. The greatest exchange of all, God in my place, settling my account and giving me new life and eternal hope.

How I love the babe in the manger!

How I need Him!

How I love the bleeding man, God in torn flesh!

For I know the depth of my need, I know my vain attempts at goodness and religion can never satisfy the righteous wrath of the God I have wronged....but Christ's sacrifice can...and His sacrifice is now mine and His robes are now upon me. What joy unspeakable! How I love the Risen Savior, Mighty Conqueror, Everlasting King, Lion of the Tribe of Judah.

For He has won the victory.

Forever.

I am His. He is mine.

My prayer for all this Christmas is that we will truly Behold the Man and proclaim Him Lord of lords and King of kings of our lives!

Praise God for His indescribable gift...Merry Christmas!

DECEMBER 26

Consider Mary.

A teenage girl to whom a message was delivered… "You - a virgin - shall bear a Son and shall call His name Jesus: for He shall save His people from their sins." Mary knew the consequences of pregnancy under her circumstances in her culture. She could be stoned. Her response to this message of redemption? Mary humbly said, *Behold the handmaid of the Lord; be it unto me according to thy word…My soul doth magnify the Lord, and my spirit hath rejoiced in God my Saviour (Luke 1:38, 46-47).* She did not have all the answers. She didn't understand everything that was going on. But, Mary had faith, and that faith gave her the courage to surrender to the LORD and that surrender birthed joy.

Consider the Shepherds.

Lowly, nameless, unknown men keeping watch over their flock by night. *And, lo, the angel of the Lord came upon them, and the glory of the Lord shone round about them: and they were sore afraid. And the angel said unto them, Fear not: for, behold, I bring you good tidings of great joy, which shall be to all people. For unto you is born this day in the city of David a Saviour, which is Christ the Lord…And suddenly there was with the angel a multitude of the heavenly host praising God, and saying, Glory to God in the highest, and on earth peace, good will toward men. And it came to pass, as the angels were gone away from them into heaven, the shepherds said one to another, Let us now go even unto Bethlehem, and see this thing which is come to pass, which the Lord hath made known unto us. And they came with haste, and found Mary, and Joseph, and the babe lying in a manger…And the shepherds returned, glorifying and praising God for all the things that they had heard and seen, as it was told unto them (Luke 2:9-20).* The Shepherds came face to face with Emmanuel, God with us. Redemption Himself. And their response was one of joy unspeakable.

Consider the Wise Men.

They had been studying, waiting. And then they saw it, the star rising in the east. And when they saw the star, they rejoiced with exceeding great joy. You see, redemption had come. And from redemption flows joy (Matthew 2).

Consider Jesus Christ…*Wherefore seeing we also are compassed about with so great a cloud of witnesses, let us lay aside every weight, and the sin which doth so easily beset us, and let us run with patience the race that is set before us, Looking unto Jesus the author and finisher of our faith; who for the joy that was set before Him endured the cross, despising the shame, and is set down at the right hand of the throne of God (Hebrews 12:1-3).*

DECEMBER 27

1998 was our year without a Christmas tree.

Sarah was so sick and irritable following her stroke earlier that year.

Most of my time was spent directly caring for her. The rare free moments I had were reserved for sleep.

Sadly, I had no energy or heart to decorate a tree or to enjoy the holiday and all the meaning of Christ's birth.

This year, 1999, we have a Christmas tree.

This year I am experiencing the beauty of Christmas more than I ever have all my life.

This year, I clearly feel the joy of the essence of Christmas: that Christ came to our world in human flesh, full of love for us and ultimately to die for our sins.

Sarah still struggles in her recovery. She still cannot sit or roll, and using her arms is very difficult. Despite this, it seems to me that our prayers have been answered and our needs have been met. Sure, there have been some improvements in Sarah's physical skills – better head control, some use of her left arm, ability to bear weight on her legs. She is starting to use a computer with a touch screen. She is beginning to use pictures and eye gaze to tell us what she wants. She is sleeping all night, finally. She smiles and laughs.

But, the biggest and the best improvements have been in what we define as important – it is important that we trust in the Lord rather than ourselves; it is important that we enjoy Sarah and every moment with her; it is important that we appreciate the little gifts that each day brings.

I have learned that life is not about being entitled to good health and prosperity.

Rather, it is about being grateful when we have these things and grateful when we don't.

It is about holding on tightly to the Lord and His promises even when He seems silent and distant.

We have a Christmas tree this year because we feel the joy of Jesus in our lives.

We have joy in our hearts because we have Jesus in our lives.

DECEMBER 28

Dear Father,

How amazing to call You, "Father."

You who created all things with such ease and perfection, desires to hear my voice crying out to You and calling You, "My Father."

Truth.

May we seek truth.

And that truth begins with the reality that while all mankind is Your creation, not everyone, O Lord, is Your child.

O, Lord, the flawed idea that we are all Your children destined for heaven tears at my heart. So many believe this new age lie, and as a result they do not seek. They do not find You. They are on the broad path that leads to literal hell.

The way to heaven and eternal life with You is narrow. It begins and ends with Christ.

Yes, this is an exclusive claim. Offered freely to all.

There is no other way!

Jesus ONLY saves.

Not Allah.

Not Buddha.

Not our own good works.

Not our religion or our baptism or our church membership.

Not the idol in our minds that refuses to believe that hell is real.

Not the idol we create that suits our own tastes, an idol that does not require repentance, an idol that does not punish sins or sinners.

Not positive thinking.

These cannot save.

Jesus ONLY saves.

Hear the truth.

Come and drink deeply of this truth.

In the Name of Jesus, The Way, One and Only Way…

DECEMBER 29

I remember when I graduated from high school. Oh, how glad I was to be done!

It really is a big deal. It really is a closing of one chapter and the walking into another, as yet unwritten, chapter. It is exciting and scary all at the same time.

I took a walk this morning, and I remembered. I remembered being young and idealistic and full of myself. I remembered that I knew and loved God, but I also had utopian ideas about what I, apart from Him, could accomplish.

I remembered how I believed heaven on earth could be pursued and could be created…if just people would all pull the load in the same direction…if just everyone shared what they had with those who did not and if the right laws and regulations were implemented to ensure justice.

And I remembered the disappointment and defeat I experienced when I realized that heaven on earth would not become a reality.

We live in a fallen world.

We live in a world that routinely ignores or rejects God.

We live in a world in which even Christians often behave like a practical atheist.

We live in a world in which the hearts of men are desperately wicked….and no law or regulation or social service program can fix this…only the gospel offers enduring hope…and the gospel has been banished and ousted from our schools and our government and our science laboratories and our interpretation of history and even sometimes from our church pulpits.

No, we will not establish heaven upon earth. And if we could, then that would become the idol we worship, for we are a people prone to worship idols.

I remembered the slow evolution of my understanding….that it's ok that paradise is not possible on earth…that it's ok that my efforts will not produce perfection. It's humbling to realize that it's all about the Great I AM…. *"Not MY WAY….but YAHWEH"* (thanks, David, for that one!).

To learn humility before God requires failures and disappointments and defeats…these are the very things that usher us into victory…these are the very things that produce conquerors.

Victory is ours when we humbly learn that victory is Him.

I remembered hope being born in my life.

As you close this chapter, be excited.

But also be ready…aware that what you have planned may not be what God has planned…aware that you need Him in all places at all times and through all things…aware that struggles and trials and apparent defeats can be redeemed in God's mighty Kingdom and through His sovereign, even if mysterious, goodness and power.

Stand up.

Get out of the boat.

Go forth!

With Him.

<u>DECEMBER 30</u>

From <u>The Quest for More</u> by Paul David Tripp [49]

"What gives you HOPE? TRUE HOPE is never hope in a thing, but hope in a person."

"There are two classes of people in the world. The first is people who are living in temporary, soon-to-be disappointed hope. They have attached their hope to something that will ultimately fail, and so it is just a matter of time before their hope is undone."

"The second is people who are living with valid reason for hope. They have placed their hope in someone who will never fail...JESUS."

"In our broken world, one of the most radical things about the Big Kingdom of God is that it is a Kingdom of bright, shining, eternal HOPE!"

"God's grace gives us reason to be hopeful even in the middle of suffering."

"Big Kingdom living is living with guarantees...God's Kingdom WILL come! His will WILL be done! Every promise He has made WILL be fulfilled!"

"Your hope is absolutely attached to what kingdom you are serving."

"If your life is defined by how many of your little kingdom purposes you can realize, you will tend to be stressed, controlling, anxious, disappointed, and fearful. But if your hope no longer rests on your personal wisdom, strength, and character, if it no longer rests on the acceptance and performance of other people, and no longer rests on the belief that circumstances, institutions, and situations will not fail you, then you are beginning to move toward reliable hope."

"Big Kingdom hope rests on one place and one place alone – GOD."

"Big Kingdom hope is about entrusting my past, present and future, my identity, meaning and purpose, and my motivation for daily functioning to God and resting unafraid in Him. Sure, I will still face the disappointments of life in this fallen world. But, I will not panic, I will not run, and I will not quit, because my God is present even in my disappointment, and He will never change!"
From <u>The Quest for More</u> by Paul David Tripp [49]

DECEMBER 31

As we come to this last journal entry, this last devotional, I struggle.

What shall I say on this last page?

And I realize the time has come to be still.

To be quiet.

Enough of my words.

It's now time for you to find your voice, the voice that God has given you.

The last page....or rather the first page....is yours....

I love you guys.   Simply and truly, I pray for you.

Think.

Strive.

Remember.

Go in the strength that you have.

Meet with God.

He is good. He is great.

And, for you He has plans, plans for which He will equip you.

Walk with Him.

Be ye the salt of the earth.

With all my heart. And with fervent prayers….from me to you.

December's Apologetic Moment...Contend for the faith

Ready?

From <u>*What's So Great About Christianity*</u> *by Dinesh D'Souza* [67]

"Christians are called upon to be 'contenders' for their faith. This term suggests that they should be ready to stand up for their beliefs, and that they will face opposition. The Christian is told in 1 Peter 3:15, 'Always be prepared to give an answer to everyone who asks you to give the reasons for the hope that is within you.' But in order to give reasons, you must first know what you believe. You must also know why you believe it. And you must be able to communicate these reasons to those who don't share your beliefs. In short, you must know what's so great about Christianity.

"This is the arena in which many Christians have fallen short. Today's Christians know that they do not, as their ancestors did, live in a society where God's presence was unavoidable. No longer does Christianity form the moral basis of society. Many of us now reside in secular communities, where arguments drawn from the Bible or Christian revelation carry no weight, and where we hear a different language from that spoken in church.

"Instead of engaging this secular world, most Christians have taken the easy way out. They have retreated into a Christian subculture where they engage Christians concerns. Then they step back into secular society, where their Christianity is kept out of sight until the next church service. Without realizing it Christians have become post-modernists of a sort: they live by the gospel of the two truths. There is religious truth, reserved for Sundays and days of worship, and there is secular truth, which applies the rest of the time.

"This divided lifestyle is opposed to what the Bible teaches. The Bible tells Christians not to be of the world, sharing in its distorted priorities, but it does call upon believers to be in the world, fully engaged. Many Christians have abdicated this mission. They have instead sought a workable, comfortable modus vivendi in which they agree to leave the secular world alone if the secular world agrees to leave them alone...

"This is not a time for Christians to turn the other cheek. Rather, it is a time to drive the money changers out of the Temple. The atheists no longer want to be tolerated. They want to monopolize the public square and to expel Christians from it. They want political questions like abortion to be divorced from religious and moral claims. They want to control school curricula so they can promote a secular ideology and undermine

Christianity. They want to discredit the factual claims of religion, and they want to convince the rest of society that Christianity is not only mistaken but also evil. They blame religion for the crimes of history and for the ongoing conflicts in the world today. In short, they want to make religion - and especially the Christian religion – disappear from the face of the earth.

"The Bible in Matthew 5:13-14 calls Christians to be the 'salt of the earth' and the 'light of the world.' Christians are called to make the world a better place. Today that means confronting the challenge of modern atheism and secularism....

"It is impossible to remain neutral about these things. This is the message I have been trying to convey in this book. What can be said about Christ can also be said about Christianity. It matters. It is the very core and center of Western civilization. Many of the best things about our world are the result of Christianity, and some of the worst things are the result of its absence, or of moving away from it. Christianity's central claims about God and the nature of reality are supported by the greatest discoveries of modern science and modern scholarship. There are good intellectual and moral reasons to embrace Christianity. For all its eloquence and vehemence, the atheist attack fails. Despite all this, there remains an all too human resistance on the part of many people to becoming Christians. They want to know what's in it for them. This question may shock some Christians, but it is not a bad one. In a low sense, it can be taken to mean, How will Christianity give me financial success and a problem-free life? Christianity offers no such formula. The lives of Christians, far from being problem free, are often infused with struggle and sacrifice. In a higher sense, the undecided person is quite right to wonder how Christianity will make his life better. After all, he is considering not only whether to believe something but whether to base his life on it. Addressing myself specifically to unbelievers who possess an open mind, I conclude this book by enumerating some concrete ways in which Christianity can improve our lives.

"First, Christianity makes sense of who we are in the world. All of us need a framework in which to understand reality, and part of Christianity's appeal is that it is a worldview that makes things fit together. Science and reason are seamlessly integrated in a Christian framework, because modern science emerged from a Christian framework. Christianity has always embraced both reason and faith. While reason helps us to discover things about experience, faith helps us discover things that transcend experience. For limited, fallible humans like us, Christianity provides a comprehensive and believable account of who we are and why we are here.

"Christianity also infuses life with a powerful and exhilarating sense of purpose. While atheism in most of its current forms posits a universe without meaning, Christianity makes of life a moral drama in which we play a starring role and in which the most ordinary events take on a grand significance. Modern life is typically characterized by gray disillusionment. Christianity gives us a world that is enchanted once again. This is not a return to the past or a denial of modern reality; rather, it is a reinterpretation of modern reality that makes it more vivid and more meaningful. We now see in color what we previously saw in black and white.

"What produces this change of orientation? Christians live 'sub specie aeternitatis,' in the 'shadow of eternity.' Life can be terribly unfair, and this is for many people a natural source of cynicism and frustration. In the 'Gorgias' and in other Platonic dialogues, Socrates strives to prove that 'it is better to suffer wrong than to do wrong.' The proof is a failure because there are bad people in the world who prosper and there are good people who undeservedly come to grief. But Christianity produces an enlargement of perspective that prevents us from being jaded by this realization. Christianity teaches that this life is not the only life, and there is a final judgement in which all earthly accounts are settled. The Christian know that 'sub specie aeternitatis' it is better to suffer wrong than to do wrong.

"The business tycoon or law partner who cheats people and runs out on his wife may be viewed as a successful man of the world, but the Christian perceives him, 'sub specie aeternitatis,' as a truly lamentable figure. By contrast, the poor peasant who crawls to the altar on his knees – a failure by all the world's standards – is one who is preparing to receive his heavenly reward. 'Sub specie aeternitatis,' he is the truly fortunate one. Here we have the meaning of the phrase, 'the last shall be first.' It simply means that the standards of worldly success and divine reward are quite different. Without the perspective of eternity, this necessary inversion of values would be lost to us. Seeing things in a new light, the Christian can face life and whatever it brings with a sense of peace and hopefulness that are rare in today's world.

"Contrary to what secular critics say, the Christian does not and cannot hold our life on earth to be unimportant. Indeed, it is of the highest importance. The reason is startlingly obvious, and yet often goes completely unnoticed: it is this life that determines our status in the next life. Our fate for eternity hinges on how we live now. So living 'sub specie aeternitatis,' far from being a way to escape the responsibilities of life in this world, is actually a way to imbue life with a meaning that will outlast it. It is to give life much greater depth and significance because it is part of a larger narrative of purpose and truth.

"Christianity also offers a solution to the cosmic loneliness we all feel. However successful the secular life, there comes to every thinking person the recognition that, in the end, we are alone. Christianity removes this existential loneliness and links our destiny with God. Our deepest relationship is with Him, and it is a relationship that is never-ending and always faithful. The secular person may wonder what this relationship feels life. It is an enduring experience of the sublime. Have you ever had a moment with someone you love in which you are transported into a transcendent realm that seems somehow outside space and time? Ordinarily, such experiences are rare and never last for long. For the Christian, the sublime is a part of everyday life. Milton terms this a joy surpassing Eden, 'a paradise within thee, happier far.' Another benefit of Christianity is that is helps us to cope well with suffering and death. 'Time' magazine reported on the case of a woman who suffered a series of tragedies. Her husband was laid off. She had a miscarriage. A month later her first cousin was diagnosed with cancer. Then two hurricanes struck her hometown. Finally, one of her best friends died from a brain tumor. Here is the woman's reaction: 'We're putting our lives in God's hands and trusting He has our best interests at heart. I've clung to my faith more than ever this year. As a consequence, I haven't lost my joy.' Joy under these conditions simply isn't natural, and that is this woman's point – only the supernatural can produce enduring joy in the face of life's tragedies. When we are in pain and feeling hopeless, Christianity raises our spirits. We don't know why we are in this situation, but we have faith that there is a reason, even if only God knows what that is. Perhaps God is trying to teach us something, or to draw us closer to Him by intimating to us our mortality. Christianity also gives us the hope that when someone dies, we will see that person again.

"Then there is the matter of our own death. Ordinarily we do our best to avoid thinking about mortality, and many of us resist going to funerals. Funerals remind us of our own extinction, and the notion that we will one day cease to exist is a source of anxiety and terror. But Paul writes, 'Oh death, where is thy sting? Oh grave, where is thy victory?' For Christians, death is a temporal end but not a final end. The secular person thinks there are two stages: life and death. For the Christian, there are three: life, death, and the life to come. This is why, for the Christian, death is not so terrifying.

"Finally, Christianity enables us to become the better persons we want to be. The decent and honorable things we do are no longer a matter of thankless routine. This isn't just a morality we made up for ourselves. Rather, we are pursuing our higher destiny as human beings. We are becoming what we were meant to be.

"Christianity not only makes us aspire to be better, but it also shows us how to be better. In marriage, for example, Christianity teaches that marriage is not merely a contract. If we treat it that way and use it for our own benefit, it doesn't work very well. For Christians, marriage is a covenant not merely between the two parties but also between them and God. The operating principle of Christian marriage is agape or sacrificial love. This means that marriage functions best when each partner focuses primarily on the happiness of the other. This can be attempted as a secular proposition but human selfishness makes it very difficult. Christian marriage is much easier, because God is now a central part of the relationship. So when there are hardships in marriage, we pray to God and He gives us grace. Agape is not so much human love as it is God's love shining through us. This is a bountiful resource that is available for the asking, and when we make agape the ground of our marriages and relationships, we find that the whole system works and we are much happier as a result.

"We want to be better parents, and what better examples can we provide for our children than the Christian dad and mom practicing the sacrificial love of agape? We want to be good citizens, and can we find a more inspiring model of genuine compassion and charity than Mother Teresa? A man who saw her embrace a leper told her he wouldn't do that for all the money in the world. She replied that she wouldn't either; she was doing it for the love of Christ. This is the same motive that seems to have propelled humanity's greatest acts of heroism and sacrifice.

"We want to raise the level of our personal lives, bringing conscience into harmony with the way we live. Christianity gives us a reason to follow this interior guide; it is not simply our innermost desire but the voice of God speaking through us. We want to be good because virtue is God's stamp in our hearts, and one way we relate to Him is by following His ways. As Thomas More said, in the final analysis we are good not because we have to be but because we want to be. Seemingly incorrigible criminals, alcoholics, and drug addicts have reformed their lives by becoming Christians. Earlier in this book I quoted Steven Weinberg's claim that 'for good people to do bad things – that takes religion.' Actually, the exact opposite is true: for bad people to do good things – that takes religion.

"Ultimately we are called not only to happiness and goodness but also to holiness. Christ says in the Sermon on the Mount, 'Blessed are the pure in heart, for they shall see God.' What counts for God is not only our external conduct but also our inward disposition. Holiness does not mean merely performing the obligatory rituals on the outside; it means staying pure on the inside. Yet holiness is not something we do for God. It is something we do with God. We couldn't do it without Him. In order for us to be more like Christ, we need Christ within us. In the words of that disheveled prophet John the Baptist, standing waist deep in the river, 'He must increase and I must decrease.' Paul says the same thing in Galatians 2:20: 'It is no longer I who live, but Christ who lives in me.' This is Christ's countercultural challenge to us. In a society based on self-fulfillment and self-esteem, on looking after yourself and advancing yourself, Christ calls us to a heroic task of self-emptying. He must increase and we must decrease. This we do by allowing His empire an ever greater domain in our hearts. Goodness and happiness flow from this.

"For the Christian, human joys are a small foreshadowing of the joys that are in store. Terrestrial happiness is only a foretaste of eternity. As the book of Revelation 21:4 puts it, 'God will wipe away every tear, and there will be no more death, neither sorrow, nor crying, neither shall there be any more pain, for the former things are passed away.' It is in this spirit that the Christian awaits this final moment of destiny, relishing the gift of life while everyday proclaiming, 'Even so, come, Lord Jesus. We are ready.'"

From **What's So Great About Christianity** *by Dinesh D'Souza* [67]

Appendices

Apologetic Resources

Scripture Relating to Fear

Scripture Relating to Thoughts and Words

Scripture Regarding the New Life

Scripture Regarding Moral Purity

Thoughts About Marriage

A Special Message for Wives-to-be

When There is Grief

Promises Found in Scripture

Works Cited

About the Author

Appendix A
Apologetic Resources

Apologetics *(from Greek ἀπολογία, "speaking in defense") is the discipline of defending a position through the systematic use of information.*

www.answersingenesis.org

www.creation.com

www.icr.org   (Institute for Creation Research)

www.crossexamined.org

www.impactapologetics.com

www.reasons.org

www.privilegedplanet.com

www.equip.org

www.rzim.org   (Ravi Zacharias International Ministries)

www.stephencmeyer.org

www.discovery.org

www.reasonablefaith.org

www.americanminute.com (William Federer)

www.moralcaseforfossilsfuels.com

www.drroyspencer.com

www.heartland.org (conservative principles)

www.jbs.org (John Birch Society – conservative principles/freedom)

www.thenewamerican.com

www.prageru.com

APOLOGETIC BOOKS

Total Truth: Liberating Christianity from its Cultural Captivity (Nancy Pearcey)

How Now Shall We Live? (Charles Colson and Nancy Pearcey)

What's So Great About Christianity? (Dinesh D'Souza)

Your Mind Matters (John Stott)

Love Your God with All Your Mind: The Role of Reason in the Life of the Soul
 (J.P. Moreland)

More Than a Carpenter (Josh McDowell)

Evidence That Demands A Verdict   (Josh McDowell)

The Case for a Creator (Lee Strobel)

Cold Case Christianity: A Homicide Detective Investigates the Claims of the Gospels
(J. Warner Wallace)

Evolution's Achilles Heels (Robert Carter – editor/Creation Book Publishers)

Evolution Exposed: Biology (Roger Patterson)

Evolution Exposed: Earth Science (Roger Patterson)

Men of Science – Men of God (Henry M. Morris)

Science and the Bible (Henry M. Morris)

Many Infallible Proofs: Evidences for the Christian Faith
(Henry M. Morris and Henry M. Morris III)

Scientific Creationism (Henry M. Morris)

The Biblical Basis for Modern Science (Henry M. Morris)

The Answers Book (Ken Ham, Andrew Snelling, Carl Wieland)

Creation: Facts of Life (Gary Parker)

Bones of Contention: A Creationist Assessment of Human Fossils (Marvin L. Lubenow)

The Mythology of Modern Geology: A Refutation of Evolution's Most Influential Argument (Wayne Jackson)

Darwin's Enigma: Fossils and Other Problems (Luther D. Sunderland)

I Don't Have Enough Faith To Be An Atheist (Norman Geisler and Frank Turek)

Christianity and the Nature of Science (J.P. Moreland)

The Face That Demonstrates the Farce of Evolution (Hank Hanegraaff)

Science and Evidence for Design in the Universe (Stephen C. Meyer)

Of Pandas and People: The Central Question of Biological Origins (Stephen C. Meyer)

God and Design: The Teleological Argument and Mldern Science (Robin Collins)

Reason for the Hope Within (Robin Collins)

Darwin's Black Box: The Biochemical Challenge to Evolution (Michael Behe)

Darwin on Trial (Phillip E. Johnson)

Reason in the Balance: The Case Against Naturalism in Science, Law, and Education (Phillip E. Johnson)

The Wedge of Truth: Splitting the Foundations of Naturalism (Phillip E. Johnson)

The Mystery of Life's Origin (Charles Thaxton, Walter Bradley, and Roger Olsen)

Icons of Evolution (Jonathan Wells)

Evolution: A Theory In Crisis (Michael Denton)

Charles Darwin and the Problem of Creation (Neal Gillespie)

The Design Inference (Willam A. Dembski)

No Free Lunch: why Specified Complexity Cannot Be Purchased Without Intelligence
(William A. Dembski)

Mere Creation (William A. Dembski)

Privileged Planet: How Our Place in the Cosmos Is Designed for Discovery (Guillermo
Gonzalez and Jay Wesley Richards)

Rare Earth   (Peter Ward and Donald Brownlee)

The Myth of Religious Neutrality: An Essay on the Hidden Role of Religious Belief in
Theories (Roy Clouser)

Truth to Tell: The Gospel as Public Truth (Lesslie Newbigin)

Foolishness to the Greeks: The Gospel and Western Culture
(Lesslie Newbigin)

The Bone Peddlers (William Fix)

The Moral Case for Fossil Fuels (Alex Epstein)

Climate Confusion (Roy Spencer)

Why Scientists Disagree About Global Warming: The NIPCC Report on Scientific
Consensus   (Craig D. Idso, Robert M. Carter, S. Fred Singer)

Climate Change: The Counter Consensus (Robert M. Carter)

Descent into Slavery and Fourth Reich of the Rich (Des Griffin)

Appendix B
Scripture Relating FEAR

Deuteronomy 31:6
Be strong and courageous. Do not be afraid or terrified because of them, for the LORD your God goes with you; He will never leave you nor forsake you.

Psalm 56:3,4
When I am afraid, I will trust in You. In God, whose word I praise, in God I trust; I will not be afraid. What can mortal man do to me?

Psalm 27:1
The LORD is my light and my salvation - whom shall I fear? The LORD is the stronghold of my life - of whom shall I be afraid?

From Psalm 121
I lift up my eyes to the hills - where does my help come from? My help comes from the LORD, the Maker of heaven and earth. He will not let your foot slip - He who watches over you will neither slumber nor sleep....The LORD will keep you from all harm - He will watch over your life; the LORD will watch over your coming and going both now and forevermore.

Proverbs 3:5-6
Trust in the LORD with all thine heart; and lean not unto thine own understanding. In all thy ways acknowledge Him, and He shall direct thy paths.

Proverbs 18:10
The name of the LORD is a strong tower; the righteous run to it and are safe.

Isaiah 40:31
But they that wait upon the LORD shall renew their strength; they shall mount up with wings as eagles; they shall run and not be weary; and they shall walk and not faint.

Isaiah 41:10
So do not fear, for I am with you do not be dismayed, for I am your God. I will strengthen you and help you; I will uphold you with my righteous right hand.

Matthew 6:25, 32, 33

Jesus said, Do not worry about your life, what you will eat or drink or about your body, what you will wear. Is not life more important than food, and the body more important than clothes? Look at the birds of the air; they do not sow or reap or store away in barns, and yet your heavenly Father feeds them. Are you not much more valuable than they?.....Your heavenly Father knows that you need them. But seek first His kingdom and His righteousness, and all these things will be given to you as well.

Matthew 11:28-30

Jesus said, Come unto me, all ye that labour and are heavy laden, and I will give you rest. Take my yoke (burden) upon you and learn of me: for I am meek and lowly in heart: and ye shall find rest unto your souls. For my yoke is easy and my burden is light.

Luke 12:6,7

Jesus said, Are not five sparrows sold for two pennies? Yet not one of them is forgotten by God. Indeed, the very hairs of your head are all numbered. Don't be afraid; you are worth more than many sparrows.

Romans 8:37

....in all these things we are more than conquerors through Jesus that loved us.

Romans 8:38-39

For I am persuaded that neither death, nor life, nor angels, nor principalities, nor powers, nor things present, nor things to come, nor height, nor depth, nor any other creature, shall be able to separate us from the love of God which is in Christ Jesus our Lord.

II Corinthians 12:9

Jesus said, My grace is sufficient for thee: for my strength is made perfect in weakness.

I Corinthians 14:33

For God is not the author of confusion, but of peace....

Ephesians 6:10-17

Finally, be strong in the Lord and in his mighty power. Put on the full armor of God, so that you can take your stand against the devil's schemes. For our struggle is not against flesh and blood, but against the rulers, against the authorities, against the powers of this dark world and against the spiritual forces of evil in the heavenly realms. Therefore put on the full armor of God, so that when the day of evil comes, you may be able to stand your ground, and after you have done everything, to stand. Stand firm then, with the belt of truth buckled around your waist, with the breastplate of righteousness in place, and with your feet fitted with the readiness that comes from the gospel of peace. In addition to all this, take up the shield of faith, with which you can extinguish all the flaming arrows of the evil one. Take the helmet of salvation and the sword of the Spirit, which is the word of God.

Philippians 3:13-14
Brothers and sisters, I do not consider myself yet to have taken hold of it. But one thing I do: Forgetting what is behind and straining toward what is ahead, I press on toward the goal to win the prize for which God has called me heavenward in Christ Jesus.

Philippians 4:4-9
Rejoice in the Lord always. I will say it again: Rejoice! Let your gentleness be evident to all. The Lord is near. Do not be anxious about anything, but in everything, by prayer and petition, with thanksgiving, present your requests to God. And the peace of God, which transcends all understanding will guard your hearts and your minds in Christ Jesus. Finally, brothers, whatever is true, whatever is noble, whatever is right, whatever is pure, whatever is lovely, whatever is admirable - if anything is excellent or praiseworthy - think about such things. Whatever you have learned or received or heard from me, or seen in me - put it into practice. And the God of peace will be with you.

II Timothy 1:7
For God hath not given us the spirit of fear, but of power, and of love, and of a sound mind.

Hebrews 10:39
But we are not of those who shrink back and are destroyed, but of those who believe and are saved.

Hebrews 12:2
Let us fix our eyes on Jesus, the author and perfecter of our faith, who for the joy set before Him endured the cross, scorning its shame, and sat down at the right hand of the throne of God. Consider Him....so that you will not grow weary and lose heart.

I Peter 5:6,7
Humble yourselves, therefore, under God's mighty hand, that He may lift you up in due time. Cast all your anxiety on Him because He cares for you.

I John 4:4
Ye are of God, little children, and have overcome them: because greater is He that is in you, than he that is in the world.

Appendix C
Scripture relating to
THOUGHTS AND WORDS

Thoughts

I Chronicles 28:9
And thou, Solomon my son, know thou the God of thy father, and serve him with a perfect heart and with a willing mind: for the LORD searcheth all hearts, and understandeth all the imaginations of the thoughts: if thou seek him, he will be found of thee; but if thou forsake him, he will cast thee off for ever.

Psalm 86:11
Teach me thy way, O LORD; I will walk in thy truth: unite my heart to fear thy name.

Psalm 119:11, 16
Thy word have I hid in mine heart, that I might not sin against thee…..I will delight myself in thy statutes: I will not forget thy word.

Isaiah 26:3-4
Thou wilt keep him in perfect peace, whose mind is stayed on thee: because he trusteth in thee. Trust ye in the LORD for ever: for in the LORD JEHOVAH is everlasting strength.

Matthew 5:28
But I say unto you, That whosoever looketh on a woman to lust after her hath committed adultery with her already in his heart.

Romans 12:1-3
I beseech you therefore, brethren, by the mercies of God, that ye present your bodies a living sacrifice, holy, acceptable unto God, which is your reasonable service.   And be not conformed to this world: but be ye transformed by the renewing of your mind, that ye may prove what is that good, and acceptable, and perfect, will of God.   For I say, through the grace given unto me, to every man that is among you, not to think of himself more highly than he ought to think; but to think soberly, according as God hath dealt to every man the measure of faith.

II Corinthians 10:5
Casting down imaginations, and every high thing that exalteth itself against the knowledge of God, and bringing into captivity every thought to the obedience of Christ.

Ephesians 4:22-24
That ye put off concerning the former conversation the old man, which is corrupt according to the deceitful lusts; And be renewed in the spirit of your mind; And that ye put on the new man, which after God is created in righteousness and true holiness.

Phillipians 3:8
Let nothing be done through strife or vainglory; but in lowliness of mind let each esteem other better than themselves.

Phillipians 3:5-8
Let this mind be in you, which was also in Christ Jesus: Who, being in the form of God, thought it not robbery to be equal with God: But made himself of no reputation, and took upon him the form of a servant, and was made in the likeness of men: And being found in fashion as a man, he humbled himself, and became obedient unto death, even the death of the cross.

Colossians 3:1-2
If ye then be risen with Christ, seek those things which are above, where Christ sitteth on the right hand of God. Set your affection (mind) on things above, not on things on the earth.

II Timothy 1:7
For God hath not given us the spirit of fear; but of power, and of love, and of a sound mind.

Hebrews 4:12-13
For the word of God is alive and active. Sharper than any double-edged sword, it penetrates even to dividing soul and spirit, joints and marrow; it judges the thoughts and attitudes of the heart. Nothing in all creation is hidden from God's sight. Everything is uncovered and laid bare before the eyes of him to whom we must give account.

Hebrews 12:1a-3
And let us run with perseverance the race marked out for us, fixing our eyes on Jesus, the pioneer and perfecter of faith. For the joy set before him he endured the cross, scorning its shame, and sat down at the right hand of the throne of God.   Consider (think about) him who endured such opposition from sinners, so that you will not grow weary and lose heart.

I Peter 1:13
So brace up your minds ("gird up the loins of your mind"); be sober (circumspect, morally alert); set your hope wholly and unchangeably on the grace (divine favor) that is coming to you when Jesus Christ (the Messiah) is revealed.

Words

Our words reflect the condition of our heart…..

Matthew 12:33-37
Jesus said, Make a tree good and its fruit will be good, or make a tree bad and its fruit will be bad, for a tree is recognized by its fruit.   You brood of vipers, how can you who are evil say anything good? For the mouth speaks what the heart is full of.   A good man brings good things out of the good stored up in him, and an evil man brings evil things out of the evil stored up in him. But I tell you that everyone will have to give account on the day of judgment for every empty word they have spoken.   For by your words you will be acquitted, and by your words you will be condemned.

Be deliberate and purposeful with our words……

Colossians 4:6
Let your speech be always with grace, seasoned with salt, that ye may know how ye ought to answer every man.

Titus 2:1
But speak thou the things which become sound doctrine:

II Timothy 2:15-16
Do your best to present yourself to God as one approved, a worker who does not need to be ashamed and who correctly handles the word of truth. Avoid godless chatter, because those who indulge in it will become more and more ungodly.

II Timothy 4:1-5
In the presence of God and of Christ Jesus, who will judge the living and the dead, and in view of his appearing and his kingdom, I give you this charge: Preach the word; be prepared in season and out of season; correct, rebuke and encourage—with great patience and careful instruction. For the time will come when people will not put up with sound doctrine. Instead, to suit their own desires, they will gather around them a great number of teachers to say what their itching ears want to hear. They will turn their ears away from the truth and turn aside to myths.   But you, keep your head in all situations, endure hardship, do the work of an evangelist, discharge all the duties of your ministry.

Psalm 19:14
Let the words of my mouth, and the meditation of my heart, be acceptable in thy sight, O LORD, my strength, and my redeemer.

Avoid rash words…..show restraint….

Psalm 141:3
Set a watch, O LORD, before my mouth; keep the door of my lips.

Proverbs 10:19
In the multitude of words there wanteth not sin: but he that refraineth his lips is wise.

Ecclesiastes 5:2
Be not rash with thy mouth, and let not thine heart be hasty to utter any thing before God: for God is in heaven, and thou upon earth: therefore let thy words be few.

I Peter 3:10
For he that will love life, and see good days, let him refrain his tongue from evil, and his lips that they speak no guile.

Ecclesiastes 3:7
A time to rend, and a time to sew; a time to keep silence, and a time to speak.

Ecclesiastes 10:11-14
Surely the serpent will bite without enchantment; and a babbler is no better. The words of a wise man's mouth are gracious; but the lips of a fool will swallow up himself.   The beginning of the words of his mouth is foolishness: and the end of his talk is mischievous madness. A fool also is full of words: a man cannot tell what shall be; and what shall be after him, who can tell him?

James 1:26
Those who consider themselves religious and yet do not keep a tight rein on their tongues deceive themselves, and their religion is worthless.

James 3:5-10
Likewise, the tongue is a small part of the body, but it makes great boasts. Consider what a great forest is set on fire by a small spark. The tongue also is a fire, a world of evil among the parts of the body. It corrupts the whole body, sets the whole course of one's life on fire, and is itself set on fire by hell.   All kinds of animals, birds, reptiles and sea creatures are being tamed and have been tamed by mankind, but no human being can tame the tongue. It is a restless evil, full of deadly poison.   With the tongue we praise our Lord and Father, and with it we curse human beings, who have been made in God's likeness. Out of the same mouth come praise and cursing. My brothers and sisters, this should not be.

Our words can make a positive difference to someone….

Proverbs 15:1-4

A gentle answer turns away wrath, but a harsh word stirs up anger. The tongue of the wise adorns knowledge, but the mouth of the fool gushes folly. The eyes of the LORD are everywhere, keeping watch on the wicked and the good. The soothing tongue is a tree of life, but a perverse tongue crushes the spirit.

Proverbs 25:11
A word fitly spoken is like apples of gold in pictures of silver.

Psalm 37:30
The godly offer good counsel; they teach right from wrong.

Do not take the name of the Lord in vain....no blasphemy

Exodus 20:7
Thou shalt not take the name of the LORD thy God in vain; for the LORD will not hold him guiltless that taketh his name in vain.

Ezekiel 35:12-13
And thou shalt know that I am the LORD, and that I have heard all thy blasphemies which thou hast spoken against the mountains of Israel, saying, They are laid desolate, they are given us to consume. Thus with your mouth ye have boasted against me, and have multiplied your words against me: I have heard them.

Do not lie....

Exodus 20:16
Thou shalt not bear false witness against thy neighbour.

Revelation 21:8
But the fearful, and unbelieving, and the abominable, and murderers, and whoremongers, and sorcerers, and idolaters, and all liars, shall have their part in the lake which burneth with fire and brimstone: which is the second death.

James 5:12
But above all things, my brethren, swear not, neither by heaven, neither by the earth, neither by any other oath: but let your yea be yea; and your nay, nay; lest ye fall into condemnation.

Titus 1:10-11
For there are many rebellious people, full of meaningless talk and deception, especially those of the circumcision group. They must be silenced, because they are disrupting whole households by teaching things they ought not to teach—and that for the sake of dishonest gain.

Do not flatter or exaggerate.....

Romans 16:17-18
I urge you, brothers and sisters, to watch out for those who cause divisions and put obstacles in your way that are contrary to the teaching you have learned. Keep away from them. For such people are not serving our Lord Christ, but their own appetites. By smooth talk and flattery they deceive the minds of naive people.

Jude 1:16
These people are grumblers and faultfinders; they follow their own evil desires; they boast about themselves and flatter others for their own advantage.

Do not grumble and complain......

Numbers 11:1
And when the people complained, it displeased the LORD: and the LORD heard it; and his anger was kindled; and the fire of the LORD burnt among them, and consumed them that were in the uttermost parts of the camp.

Philippians 2:14-15
Do all things without murmurings and disputings: That ye may be blameless and harmless, the sons of God, without rebuke, in the midst of a crooked and perverse nation, among whom ye shine as lights in the world;

James 5:9
Don't grumble against one another, brothers and sisters, or you will be judged. The Judge is standing at the door!

Do not gossip.....

Proverbs 18:6-8
The lips of fools bring them strife, and their mouths invite a beating. The mouths of fools are their undoing, and their lips are a snare to their very lives. The words of a gossip are like choice morsels; they go down to the inmost parts.

Proverbs 26:20-22
Without wood a fire goes out; without a gossip a quarrel dies down.   As charcoal to embers and as wood to fire, so is a quarrelsome person for kindling strife. The words of a gossip are like choice morsels;   they go down to the inmost parts.

Do not be coarse or perverse.....

Proverbs 4:24
Keep your mouth free of perversity;   keep corrupt talk far from your lips.

Proverbs 10:10-12
Whoever winks maliciously causes grief, and a chattering fool comes to ruin. The mouth of the righteous is a fountain of life, but the mouth of the wicked conceals violence. Hatred stirs up conflict, but love covers over all wrongs.

Ephesians 4:29-32
Do not let any unwholesome talk come out of your mouths, but only what is helpful for building others up according to their needs, that it may benefit those who listen. And do not grieve the Holy Spirit of God, with whom you were sealed for the day of redemption. Get rid of all bitterness, rage and anger, brawling and slander, along with every form of malice. Be kind and compassionate to one another, forgiving each other, just as in Christ God forgave you.

Ephesians 5:4
Nor should there be obscenity, foolish talk or coarse joking, which are out of place, but rather thanksgiving.

Be careful what you say when you are angry....

James 1:19-20
My dear brothers and sisters, take note of this: Everyone should be quick to listen, slow to speak and slow to become angry, because human anger does not produce the righteousness that God desires.

Matthew 5:22
But I say, if you are even angry with someone, you are subject to judgment! If you call someone an idiot, you are in danger of being brought before the court. And if you curse someone, you are in danger of the fires of hell.

Be grateful! Sing a new song.......

Psalm 116:17
I will offer to thee the sacrifice of thanksgiving, and will call upon the name of the LORD.

Hebrews 13:15
By him therefore let us offer the sacrifice of praise to God continually, that is, the fruit of our lips giving thanks to his name.

Psalm 22:3
But thou art holy, O thou that inhabits the praises of Israel.

Psalm 40:3
And he hath put a new song in my mouth, even praise unto our God: many shall see it, and fear, and shall trust in the LORD.

Psalm 86:12
I will praise thee, O Lord my God, with all my heart: and I will glorify thy name for evermore.

Psalm 95:1-4, 9
O sing unto the LORD a new song: sing unto the LORD, all the earth. Sing unto the LORD, bless his name; shew forth his salvation from day to day. Declare his glory among the heathen, his wonders among all people. For the LORD is great, and greatly to be praised: he is to be feared above all gods. O worship the LORD in the beauty of holiness: fear before him, all the earth.

Psalm 98:1
O sing unto the LORD a new song; for he hath done marvellous things: his right hand, and his holy arm, hath gotten him the victory.

Psalm 100
Make a joyful noise unto the LORD, all ye lands. Serve the LORD with gladness: come before his presence with singing. Know ye that the LORD he is God: it is he that hath made us, and not we ourselves; we are his people, and the sheep of his pasture. Enter into his gates with thanksgiving, and into his courts with praise: be thankful unto him, and bless his name. For the LORD is good; his mercy is everlasting; and his truth endureth to all generations.

Psalm 103:1
Bless the LORD, O my soul: and all that is within me, bless his holy name.

Psalm 107:1, 8
O give thanks unto the LORD, for he is good: for his mercy endureth forever. Oh that men would praise the LORD for his goodness, and for his wonderful works to the children of men!

I Thessalonians 5:16-17
Rejoice evermore. Pray without ceasing. In everything give thanks: for this is the will of God in Christ Jesus concerning you.

Colossians 3:16
Let the word of Christ dwell in you richly in all wisdom; teaching and admonishing one another in psalms and hymns and spiritual songs, singing with grace in your hearts to the Lord.

Some final thoughts........

Colossians 3:8-10
But now ye also put off all these; anger, wrath, malice, blasphemy, filthy communication out of your mouth. Lie not one to another, seeing that ye have put off the old man with his deeds; And have put on the new man, which is renewed in knowledge after the image of him that created him:

Ephesians 4:14-15
Then we will no longer be infants, tossed back and forth by the waves, and blown here and there by every wind of teaching and by the cunning and craftiness of people in their deceitful scheming. Instead, speaking the truth in love, we will grow to become in every respect the mature body of him who is the head, that is, Christ.

APPENDIX D
Scripture relating to the new life in Christ

Ephesians 4:17-24
With the Lord's authority I say this: Live no longer as the Gentiles do, for they are hopelessly confused. Their minds are full of darkness; they wander far from the life God gives because they have closed their minds and hardened their hearts against him. They have no sense of shame. They live for lustful pleasure and eagerly practice every kind of impurity. But that isn't what you learned about Christ. Since you have heard about Jesus and have learned the truth that comes from Him, throw off your old sinful nature and your former way of life, which is corrupted by lust and deception. Instead, let the Spirit renew your thoughts and attitudes. Put on your new nature, created to be like God—truly righteous and holy.

Galatians 5:22-25
But the fruit of the spirit is love, joy, peace, longsuffering, gentleness, goodness, faith, meekness, temperance: against such there is no law. And they that are Christ's have crucified the flesh with the affection and lusts. If we live in the Spirit, let us also walk in the Spirit.

Colossians 3:5-10
Mortify therefore your members which are upon the earth; fornication, uncleanness, inordinate affection, evil concupiscence, and covetousness, which is idolatry: For which things' sake the wrath of God cometh on the children of disobedience: In the which ye also walked some time, when ye lived in them. But now ye also put off all these; anger, wrath, malice, blasphemy, filthy communication out of your mouth.   Lie not one to another, seeing that ye have put off the old man with his deeds. And have put on the new man, which is renewed in knowledge after the image of Him that created him.

Romans 6:11-14
Likewise reckon ye also yourselves to be dead indeed unto sin, but alive unto God through Jesus Christ our Lord. Let not sin therefore reign in your mortal body, that ye should obey it in the lusts thereof. Neither yield ye your member as instruments of unrighteousness unto sin: but yield yourselves unto god, as those that are alive from the dead, and your members as instruments of righteousness unto God. For sin shall not have dominion over you: for ye are not under the law, but under grace.

Romans 12:1-3
I beseech you therefore, brethren, by the mercies of God, that ye present your bodies a living sacrifice, holy, acceptable unto God, which is your reasonable service. And be not conformed to this world; but be ye transformed by the renewing of your mind, that ye may prove what is that good, and acceptable, and perfect will of God. For I say, through the grace given unto me, to every man that is among you, not to think of himself more

highly than he ought to think; but to think soberly, according as God hath dealt to every man the measure of faith.

James 1:22-25
Do not merely listen to the word, and so deceive yourselves. Do what it says. Anyone who listens to the word but does not do what it says is like a man who looks at his face in a mirror and, after looking at himself, goes away and immediately forgets what he looks like. But the man who looks intently into the perfect law that gives freedom and continues to do this , not forgetting what he has heard, but doing it, he will be blessed in what he does.

I Peter 1:13-16
Therefore, with minds that are alert and fully sober, set your hope on the grace to be brought to you when Jesus Christ is revealed at his coming. As obedient children, do not conform to the evil desires you had when you lived in ignorance. But just as he who called you is holy, so be holy in all you do; for it is written: "Be holy, because I am holy."

Psalm 90:12
So teach us to number our days, that we may apply our hearts unto wisdom.

Luke 17:32
Remember Lot's wife. *(do not seek to return to or long for your old life. Flee your old life and run into the arms of Jesus, and continue daily to run to Him).*

I John 5:21
Little children, keep yourselves from idols. Amen. *(idols are anything that we want and think about more than God)*

I John 2:15-17
Do not love the world or anything in the world. If anyone loves the world, love for the Father is not in them. For everything in the world—the lust of the flesh, the lust of the eyes, and the pride of life—comes not from the Father but from the world. The world and its desires pass away, but whoever does the will of God lives forever.

James 4:1-4
What is causing the quarrels and fights among you? Don't they come from the evil desires at war within you? You want what you don't have, so you scheme and kill to get it. You are jealous of what others have, but you can't get it, so you fight and wage war to take it away from them. Yet you don't have what you want because you don't ask God for it. And even when you ask, you don't get it because your motives are all wrong—you want only what will give you pleasure. You adulterers! Don't you realize that friendship with the world makes you an enemy of God? I say it again: If you want to be a friend of the world, you make yourself an enemy of God.

Romans 13:13-14
Let us behave decently, as in the daytime, not in carousing and drunkenness, not in sexual immorality and debauchery, not in dissension and jealousy. Rather, clothe yourselves with the Lord Jesus Christ, and do not think about how to gratify the desires of the flesh.

I Corinthians 6:9-11
Know ye not that the unrighteous shall not inherit the kingdom of God? Be not deceived: neither fornicators, nor idolaters, nor adulterers, nor effeminate, nor abusers of themselves with mankind, Nor thieves, nor covetous, nor drunkards, nor revilers, nor extortioners, shall inherit the kingdom of God. And such were some of you: but ye are washed, but ye are sanctified, but ye are justified in the name of the Lord Jesus, and by the Spirit of our God.

I Corinthians 6:13b
........Now the body is not for fornication, but for the Lord; and the Lord for the body.

I Corinthians 6:18-20
Flee fornication. Every sin that a man doeth is without the body; but he that committeth fornication sinneth against his own body. What? know ye not that your body is the temple of the Holy Ghost which is in you, which ye have of God, and ye are not your own? For ye are bought with a price: therefore glorify God in your body, and in your spirit, which are God's.

Galatians 5:16-21
So I say, walk by the Spirit, and you will not gratify the desires of the flesh. For the flesh desires what is contrary to the Spirit, and the Spirit what is contrary to the flesh. They are in conflict with each other, so that you are not to do whatever you want.   But if you are led by the Spirit, you are not under the law. The acts of the flesh are obvious: sexual immorality, impurity and debauchery; idolatry and witchcraft; hatred, discord, jealousy, fits of rage, selfish ambition, dissensions, factions and envy; drunkenness, orgies, and the like. I warn you, as I did before, that those who live like this will not inherit the kingdom of God.

II Timothy 2:22
Flee also youthful lusts: but follow righteousness, faith, charity, peace, with them that call on the Lord out of a pure heart.

Titus 2:11-14
For the grace of God that bringeth salvation hath appeared to all men, Teaching us that, denying ungodliness and worldly lusts, we should live soberly, righteously, and godly, in this present world; Looking for that blessed hope, and the glorious appearing of the great God and our Saviour Jesus Christ; Who gave himself for us, that he might redeem us from all iniquity, and purify unto himself a peculiar people, zealous of good works.

II Peter 2:19-22

While they promise them liberty, they themselves are the servants of corruption: for of whom a man is overcome, of the same is he brought in bondage. For if after they have escaped the pollutions of the world through the knowledge of the Lord and Saviour Jesus Christ, they are again entangled therein, and overcome, the latter end is worse with them than the beginning. For it had been better for them not to have known the way of righteousness, then, after they have known it, to turn from the holy commandment delivered unto them. But it is happened unto them according to the true proverb, the dog is turned to his own vomit again; and the sow that was washed to her wallowing in the mire.

APPENDIX E
Striving to live a life of moral purity

Well, what can I say? You are going to face temptations. Lots of them. Brace yourself for that. Satan wants to render you useless. He wants to distract you. He wants you to give in to the lusts of the flesh, the lust of the eyes, and the pride of life. Fight. And when you fall down, repent. Then stand up and fight again! Remember, you do not fight alone. Even when it feels like it.

Completely, totally, utterly immerse yourself in God.
Seek Him with passion.
Deuteronomy 6:4-9
Hear, O Israel: The LORD our God, the LORD is one. Love the LORD your God with all your heart and with all your soul and with all your strength. These commandments that I give you today are to be on your hearts. Impress them on your children. Talk about them when you sit at home and when you walk along the road, when you lie down and when you get up. Tie them as symbols on your hands and bind them on your foreheads. Write them on the doorframes of your houses and on your gates.

Confess, seek forgiveness, repent.
I John 1:9
If we confess our sins, he is faithful and just and will forgive us our sins and purify us from all unrighteousness.

Fear the lord. It all begins with a right understanding of God.
Tremble before Him, for He is holy and we are not.
Proverbs 1:7
Fear of the LORD is the foundation of true knowledge, but fools despise wisdom and discipline.

Deuteronomy 6:13-19
Fear the LORD your God, serve Him only and take your oaths in His name. Do not follow other gods, the gods of the peoples around you; for the LORD your God, Who is among you, is a jealous God and His anger will burn against you, and He will destroy you from the face of the land. Do not put the LORD your God to the test as you did at Massah. Be sure to keep the commands of the LORD your God and the stipulations and decrees He has given you. Do what is right and good in the LORD's sight, so that it may go well with you and you may go in and take over the good land the LORD promised on oath to your ancestors, thrusting out all your enemies before you, as the LORD said.

Fear the Lord and cleave to Him.
Deuteronomy 10:20
Thou shalt fear the LORD thy God; Him shalt thou serve, and to Him shalt thou cleave, and swear by His name.

Fear the Lord and stand in awe of Him.
Psalm 33:8
Let all the earth fear the LORD: let all the inhabitants of the world stand in awe of Him.

Store up treasures in heaven.
Matthew 6:19-21
Don't store up treasures here on earth, where moths eat them and rust destroys them, and where thieves break in and steal. Store your treasures in heaven, where moths and rust cannot destroy, and thieves do not break in and steal. Wherever your treasure is, there the desires of your heart will also be.

Seek first the Kingdom of God.
Matthew 6:33
Seek the Kingdom of God above all else, and live righteously, and He will give you everything you need.

Abide in the vine.
John 15:6-11
Yes, I (Jesus) am the vine; you are the branches. Those who remain in Me, and I in them, will produce much fruit. For apart from Me you can do nothing. Anyone who does not remain in Me is thrown away like a useless branch and withers. Such branches are gathered into a pile to be burned. But if you remain in Me and My words remain in you, you may ask for anything you want, and it will be granted! When you produce much fruit, you are My true disciples. This brings great glory to My Father. I have loved you even as the Father has loved Me. Remain in My love. When you obey My commandments, you remain in My love, just as I obey my Father's commandments and remain in His love. I have told you these things so that you will be filled with my joy. Yes, your joy will overflow!

Count it all joy.
James 1:2-4
Count it all joy, my brothers, when you meet trials of various kinds, for you know that the testing of your faith produces steadfastness. And let steadfastness have its full effect, that you may be perfect and complete, lacking in nothing.

Work out your salvation ("exercise" your salvation...spiritual strength and spiritual muscle training). You are not working to be saved...you are working because you are saved and want to live a fruitful and obedient life.

Philippians 2:12-13

Therefore, my dear ones, as you have always obeyed [my suggestions], so now, not only [with the enthusiasm you would show] in my presence but much more because I am absent, work out (cultivate, carry out to the goal, and fully complete) your own salvation with reverence *and* awe and trembling (self-distrust, with serious caution, tenderness of conscience, watchfulness against temptation, timidly shrinking from whatever might offend God and discredit the name of Christ). [Not in your own strength] for it is God Who is all the while effectually at work in you [energizing and creating in you the power and desire], both to will and to work for His good pleasure *and* satisfaction *and* delight.

Know God's Word.
Hide God's Word in your heart.
Psalm 119:9-11
How can a young person stay on the path of purity? By living according to Your word. I seek You with all my heart; do not let me stray from Your commands. I have hidden Your word in my heart that I might not sin against You.

Know God's Word.
Choose to make His Word a light for your path, the way to walk.
Psalm 119:105
Your word is a lamp for my feet, a light on my path.

Know God's Word.
Pray for understanding. Pray for an obedient and repentant heart.
Pray for eyes that turn away from worthless things.
Psalm 119:33-37
Teach me, LORD, the way of Your decrees, that I may follow it to the end. Give me understanding, so that I may keep Your law and obey it with all my heart. Direct me in the path of Your commands, for there I find delight. Turn my heart toward your statutes and not toward selfish gain. Turn my eyes away from worthless things; preserve my life according to Your word.

Submit to God, resist the devil, draw near to God.
James 4:7-8
Submit yourselves therefore to God. Resist the devil, and he will flee from you. Draw nigh to God, and He will draw nigh to you. Cleanse your hands, ye sinners; and purify your hearts, ye double minded.

Grab and hold tightly the truth that Jesus has come to rescue you.
There is an enemy, and he wants to steal, kill, and destroy.
Jesus wants to give you truth and fullness.
John 10:7-10
Therefore Jesus said again, "Very truly I tell you, I am the gate for the sheep. All who have come before me are thieves and robbers, but the sheep have not listened to them. I am the gate; whoever enters through me will be saved. They will come in and go out, and

find pasture. The thief comes only to steal and kill and destroy; I have come that they may have life, and have it to the full.

Be humble. Be aware that there is an enemy that wants to devour you.
The way to resist him is to stay steadfast in the faith.
I Peter 5:6-11
Humble yourselves therefore under the mighty hand of God, that He may exalt you in due time: casting all your care upon Him: for He careth for you. Be sober, be vigilant; because your adversary the devil, as a roaring lion, walketh about, seeking whom he may devour: whom resist stedfast in the faith, knowing that the same afflictions are accomplished in your brethren that are in the world. But the God of all grace, who hath called us unto His eternal glory by Christ Jesus, after that ye have suffered a while, make you perfect, stablish, strengthen, settle you. To Him be glory and dominion for ever and ever. Amen.

Beware of false teachers. Beware of believing things that are false.
Guard your conscience and make sure it does not become seared and desensitized to sin and to lies.
I Timothy 4:1-2
Now the Holy Spirit tells us clearly that in the last times some will turn away from the true faith; they will follow deceptive spirits and teachings that come from demons. These people are hypocrites and liars, and their consciences are dead.

Believe the promise that God will make a way of escape from temptation.
He will help you to bear it and get through it.
I Corinthians 10:13
There hath no temptation taken you but such as is common to man, but God is faithful, who will not suffer you to be tempted above that ye are able; but will with the temptation also make a way to escape, that ye may be able to bear it.

Know the truth about temptation and sin. Know the consequences.
James 1:13-15
When tempted, no one should say, "God is tempting me." For God cannot be tempted by evil, nor does He tempt anyone; but each person is tempted when they are dragged away by their own evil desire and enticed. Then, after desire has conceived, it gives birth to sin; and sin, when it is full-grown, gives birth to death.

Ask God for wisdom. Then trust Him to pour His wisdom into your life.
James 1:5-8
If you need wisdom, ask our generous God, and he will give it to you. He will not rebuke you for asking. But when you ask Him, be sure that your faith is in God alone. Do not waver, for a person with divided loyalty is as unsettled as a wave of the sea that is blown and tossed by the wind. Such people should not expect to receive anything from the Lord. Their loyalty is divided between God and the world, and they are unstable in everything they do.

Lean on the Lord, trust in Him with all your heart. Submit to Him.
Do not trust in your own wisdom.
Psalm 3:5-7
Trust in the LORD with all your heart and lean not on your own understanding; in all your ways submit to Him, and He will make your paths straight. Do not be wise in your own eyes; fear the LORD and shun evil.

Be clothed in God's armor.
Know what God's armor is, and every day, put it on.
Ephesians 6:10-18
Finally, my brethren, be strong in the Lord, and in the power of His might. Put on the whole armor of God, that ye may be able to stand against the wiles of the devil. For we wrestle not against flesh and blood, but against principalities, against powers, against the rulers of the darkness of this world, against spiritual wickedness in high places. Wherefore take unto you the whole armour of God, that ye may be able to withstand in the evil day, and having done all to stand. Stand therefore, having your loins girt about with truth, and having on the breastplate of righteousness; and your feet shod with the preparation of the gospel of peace; Above all, taking the shield of faith, wherewith ye shall be able to quench all the fiery darts of the wicked. And take the helmet of salvation, and the sword of the Spirit, which is the word of God: praying always with all prayer and supplication in the Spirit, and watching thereunto with all perseverance...

Know God, know His Names, run to Him.
Proverbs 18:10
The name of the LORD is a strong tower; the righteous man runs into it and is safe.

Glory in His Name and seek His face.
I Chronicles 16:10-11
Glory in His holy name; let the hearts of those who seek the LORD rejoice. Look to the LORD and His strength; seek His face always.

Psalm 27:8
When Thou saidst, Seek ye My face; my heart said unto Thee, Thy face, LORD, will I seek.

God has given us sound minds.   Be thankful and use your sound mind to glorify Him.
II Timothy 1:7
For God hath not given us the spirit of fear; but of power, and of love, and of a sound mind.

Take your thoughts captive.   Replace immoral thoughts or deceptive thoughts and beliefs with truth. Speak truth from God's Word inside your mind.
II Corinthians 10:4-5
(for the weapons of our warfare are not carnal, but mighty through God to the pulling down of strong holds;) Casting down imaginations, and every high thing that exalteth

itself against the knowledge of God, and bringing into captivity every thought to the obedience of Christ.

Fix your thoughts on God, the eternal rock.
Isaiah 26:3-4
You (GOD) will keep in perfect peace all who trust in You, all whose thoughts are fixed on You! Trust in the LORD always, for the LORD GOD is the eternal Rock.

Fix your eyes upon Jesus.
Hebrews 12:1-3
Therefore, since we are surrounded by such a huge crowd of witnesses to the life of faith, let us strip off every weight that slows us down, especially the sin that so easily trips us up. And let us run with endurance the race God has set before us. We do this by keeping our eyes on Jesus, the champion who initiates and perfects our faith. Because of the joy awaiting Him, He endured the cross, disregarding its shame. Now He is seated in the place of honor beside God's throne.

Think about those things from above.
Colossians 3:1-2
If ye then be risen with Christ, seek those things which are above, where Christ sitteth on the right hand of God. Set your affection on things above, not on things on the earth.

Look upon things that are true, just and pure.
Philippians 4:8 (KJV)
Finally, brethren, whatsoever things are true, whatsoever things are honest, whatsoever things are just, whatsoever things are pure, whatsoever things are lovely, whatsoever things are of good report; if there be any virtue, and if there be any praise, think on these things.

Always remember that God's grace is enough.
II Corinthians 12:9-10
But He said to me, "My grace is sufficient for you, for My power is made perfect in weakness." Therefore I will boast all the more gladly about my weaknesses, so that Christ's power may rest on me. That is why, for Christ's sake, I delight in weaknesses, in insults, in hardships, in persecutions, in difficulties. For when I am weak, then I am strong.

Remember...you are never alone.
Hebrews 13:5-6
Keep your lives free from the love of money and be content with what you have, because God has said, "Never will I leave you; never will I forsake you." So we say with confidence, "The Lord is my helper; I will not be afraid. What can mere mortals do to me?"

Beware that it is easy to forget all that God is and all that He has done.

Deuteronomy 6:12
Then beware lest thou forget the LORD, which brought thee forth out of the land of Egypt, from the house of bondage.

Remember.
Numbers 15:37-41
The LORD said to Moses, "Speak to the Israelites and say to them: 'Throughout the generations to come you are to make tassels on the corners of your garments, with a blue cord on each tassel. You will have these tassels to look at and so you will remember all the commands of the LORD, that you may obey them and not prostitute yourselves by chasing after the lusts of your own hearts and eyes. Then you will remember to obey all My commands and will be consecrated to your God. I am the LORD your God, who brought you out of Egypt to be your God. I am the LORD your God.'"

I Chronicles 16:15
Be ye mindful always of His covenant; the word which He commanded to a thousand generations;

Psalm 20:7
Some trust in chariots, and some in horses: but we will remember the name of the LORD our God.

Psalm 77:9-14
Has God forgotten to be gracious? Has He slammed the door on His compassion? And I said, "This is my fate; the Most High has turned His hand against me." But then I recall all You have done, O LORD; I remember Your wonderful deeds of long ago. They are constantly in my thoughts. I cannot stop thinking about Your mighty works. O God, Your ways are holy. Is there any god as mighty as You? You are the God of great wonders! You demonstrate Your awesome power among the nations.

Psalm 78:35
And they remembered that God was their rock, and the high God their redeemer.

Luke 24:8
And they (the disciples) remembered His (Jesus') words,

Give praise. Be thankful. Cultivate gratitude in your life and in your thoughts.
Psalm 100
Shout for joy to the LORD, all the earth. Worship the LORD with gladness; come before Him with joyful songs. Know that the LORD is God. It is He who made us, and we are His; we are His people, the sheep of His pasture. Enter His gates with thanksgiving and His courts with praise; give thanks to Him and praise His name. For the LORD is good and His love endures forever; His faithfulness continues through all generations.

Psalm 95:1-7
Come, let us sing for joy to the LORD; let us shout aloud to the Rock of our salvation. Let us come before Him with thanksgiving and extol Him with music and song. For the LORD is the great God, the great King above all gods. In His hand are the depths of the earth, and the mountain peaks belong to Him. The sea is His, for He made it, and His hands formed the dry land. Come, let us bow down in worship, let us kneel before the LORD our Maker; for He is our God and we are the people of His pasture, the flock under His care.

I Thessalonians 5:16-24
Rejoice always, pray continually, give thanks in all circumstances; for this is God's will for you in Christ Jesus. Do not quench the Spirit. Do not treat prophecies with contempt but test them all; hold on to what is good, reject every kind of evil. May God Himself, the God of peace, sanctify you through and through. May your whole spirit, soul and body be kept blameless at the coming of our Lord Jesus Christ.
The one who calls you is faithful, and He will do it.

IF YOU ARE BORN AGAIN, KNOW YOUR VALUE. You are a precious treasure to God. You're are acceptable to him. You are deeply loved and fully known. You are no longer condemned. Given all of these beautiful truths, there will be fruit in your life. You will grow to despise sin in your life and sin in the world. You will be a changed person.

IF YOU ARE BORN AGAIN, KNOW YOUR POSITION. You are now a child of God. You are called to a holy life under the lordship of Jesus Christ. He will equip you to live such a life. Jesus is praying for you at the right hand of God. You have the Holy Spirit within you to teach, guide, strengthen you. You are not alone. All of God's promises are now yours. All of God's promises are yes in Jesus Christ. In Him you are more than a conqueror. In Him is victory. The proper position for a child of God is a position of victory over the flesh, sin, and the world.

Appendix F
Some thoughts on marriage

From my journal...

Marriage requires work. Lots of it. Mark and I have had good days and bad days in marriage. It's been worth it...

> *Every good day.*
> *Every grueling day.*
> *Every joy.*
> *Every challenge.*
> *It's been worth it.*
> *Not because everything has turned out as I expected it to. It hasn't.*
> *But because I have grown and my husband has grown.*
> *And our roots have gone deep. Together.*

Yes, it has been good even when it's been hard.

If I felt free to share anything at all, what would I share with you about marriage?

Two words. **LEARN. NOW.**

You may say, "Learn what?"
Learn from my mistakes.
Learn from God's Word.
Learn to nourish your marriage.

WHAT WERE MY MISTAKES?
Faulty assumptions....
Marriage would be easy.
My husband would always adore me.
Life would turn out exactly as I expected it to.

Poor priorities....
I spent more time preparing for my wedding day and the party to follow than I did preparing for my marriage

Weak foundation...
"God? Who needs God? He's busy and I've got it all under control
because I'm pretty smart and I know what I want and how to get it."
My foundation was built on the world's, not God's.

Small and deficient view of marriage...
I failed to take seriously the sacred nature of marriage.

Marriage is not just an event.
It is a framework by which you live your life.
It changes everything.

LEARN FROM GOD'S WORD.
To learn from God's Word, you must know God's Word.

To know God's Word, you must read God's Word.

Read from God's Word every day....even when you don't want to.

Decide to spend time in His Word every day, and then just do it*!*

What does God say about marriage in His Word?

Marriage is a PRECIOUS TREASURE
Marriage is SACRED because it was instituted by God.
Marriage is SACRED because it's source is God.
Guard this precious treasure.
Be vigilant and diligent to protect it despite living in a culture that minimizes the value of marriage and a culture that considers marriage optional and disposable.

> ***Stand and fight for your marriage against any Goliaths that come up against it!***

Marriage is a PERMANENT COMMITMENT
Marriage means, "I am yours and you are mine."
Marriage is not to be tossed aside lightly when it gets hard.
Marriage is not be quickly abandoned when you get tired.
We all know divorce happens.
Most of us have probably been affected by it one way or another.
We can't ignore this reality.

But a high and accurate view of marriage "surely requires that divorce be a last resort for the purpose of avoiding great disaster."

> ***Stand and fight for your marriage against any Goliaths that come up against it!***

Marriage is a PICTURE OF THE RELATIONSHIP between God and His people. Consider this paraphrase from John Piper:
The gospel is underestimated in its power to make marriages beautiful. Jesus intends to be the bridegroom of the church. And God designed marriage to display that. And very few of us do that well. The gospel is the power for a husband to become Christ-like. The gospel is the power for a wife to be responsive to Christ and responsive to her husband who is the representative of Christ. Marriage is huge. It's huge in ministry. It's huge in parenting. It's huge in the next generation. And it's huge culturally. The gospel – the

Good News that Jesus died for our sins and shed His blood for us — is the very essence of marriage. Marriage is intended to portray something true about Jesus Christ and the way He relates to His people. **It is the display of the covenant-keeping love between Christ and His people.**
(This Momentary Marriage: A Parable of Permanence by John and Noel Piper)

Stand and fight for your marriage against any Goliaths that come against it!

LEARN TO NOURISH YOUR MARRIAGE.
A good marriage doesn't "just happen."
It needs to be pursued on purpose.
HOW do you do this?
You have to do a lot of CHOOSING and then a lot of DOING...

> Choose to PRAY and then PRAY
> Choose to PRAISE and then PRAISE
> Choose to PREPARE and then PREPARE
> Choose to pursue PURITY and then PURSUE IT
> Choose to PERSEVERE and then PERSEVERE
> Choose the PRESENCE AND PEACE OF THE LORD

Have a BIG view of marriage! This is the most important earthly relationship you will ever have. Marriage is the foundation of the home. And the home is the foundation of the next generation. It is a high calling. Have a BIG view of God! Exalt Him above all else. Live your life sold out to Him, fully surrendered to Him.   Live your life palms up, giving Him everything.

Appendix G
A special message to wives-to-be...

I'd like to begin with a quote from a book called the <u>Names of God</u> by Ann Spangler... "God is not content to be known merely as Creator, Lord, or even Father. Incredibly, He reveals Himself also as Bridegroom or Husband. The Hebrew Scriptures contain numerous allusions to (God) as Israel's divine Husband, and the New Testament presents Christ as the church's Bridegroom. (Christ) is the Holy One who did not cling to His divinity but left His Father's house to dwell among us, calling us to become one with Him...To all of us, Christ offers Himself as our Provider and Protector, the One who has forever pledged Himself in faithfulness and love."

In our world today, marriage is very "me" centered, and is considered optional and conditional. There's this tendency to believe the distortion that "marriage is for me...it's too make me happy...it's too fulfill all my wildest dreams." To our detriment, we easily overlook God's magnificent and exalted view of marriage. Our tendency is to nurture a very small view of marriage..."it's about me"....rather than embrace the high and lofty view of marriage..... that it's about God.

A few weeks from now, you will be standing at an altar proclaiming, before God and many others, your commitment to another. On that day, many pictures will be taken of a beautiful bride and a handsome groom. And in the days and years to come, you will enjoy those pictures. As you grow older, you will smile knowingly at the memories of the young couple looking back at you in those snapshots. And yet, there is a bigger picture to consider. For marriage is not merely a picture of two people. The wedding day is not merely about a bride and a groom. Marriage is a sacred reflection of God's everlasting covenant with His people. It is a picture of His everlasting covenant with you.

My prayer for you is that you will always have God's glorious perspective on your marriage. Marriage is more than an agreement. It is a covenant intended to endure through good times and bad, through thick and thin, through happy and sad, through years of plenty and years of leanness. My own marriage started out very "me" centered. It has taken years of the Lord chiseling away at the hardness of my heart to carve out a person who now understands that my marriage is not about me. It is not about my happiness. It is about the Lord. It is about His holiness. You are starting out your marriage already possessing knowledge of this great truth. Protect it! Praise the Lord for it and protect it from the enemy who would love to steal such truth from you.

There is a word in the Bible that today's culture at best rejects and at worst absolutely despises. That naughty little word is "submission." Yes, it's true, the Bible does direct wives, shockingly, to submit to their husbands. May I share with you that I am not a wife for whom submission came easily. I remember reading that word in the book of Ephesians and thinking, "No way! That can't be for today!" In the early years of my marriage, I was quite clueless about what the Bible means when it speaks of "submission." I was married in a church, I stood at an altar, but no one told me how to be a godly wife. No one explained to me that Biblical submission is a beautiful gift under which we wives can find shelter and protection from the storms and stresses of life.

There is often a shallowness in our understanding of submission. We hear that word and immediately tend to recoil, falsely believing that it means "to be made inferior" or "to be mistreated and taken advantage of." That's not at all what submission means from God's point of view! God is the all-wise, all-powerful, amazing and mighty Lord of Lords and King of Kings. And yet despite such greatness, He takes the time to nourish and provide us with practical advice about how to live, including how to be married.

God knows that a body, such as a marriage, cannot exist and be healthy, with two heads. Thus, husbands are commanded to lead and to love their wives as Christ loved the church. May I suggest, that is no easy task! God has set a high standard for husbands! And, let's admit it, we wives are not always all that loveable! We have our days when we make it very difficult for our husbands to follow God's instructions to love us sacrificially. Nonetheless, God tells husbands to love, and commands wives to follow their husband's leadership, showing great respect as we do so. Ultimately, both husband and wife are to submit to the Lord's authority in their lives. In a marriage, it is not about who is superior and who is inferior. It is about the roles in a home that, when properly filled, lead to a satisfying, God-honoring life. Life is hard. But we often make it harder by ignoring God's practical instructions to us.

Another idea floating around these days is the flawed idea of, "I'll give 50% IF he will." Or, from a Christian point of view, it may sound something like this: "I'll submit to his leadership IF he loves me like he was told to. He was told to love me like Christ loved the church. Well, as soon as he starts doing that, I'll start submitting." Sarah, it's not about you giving 50% and Jonathan giving 50%. It's about each person giving 100%. And, it's about each person giving 100% even if the other is not. It's not about demanding your rights. It's about laying down your rights, just as Christ did. It's not about proudly promoting yourself. It is about humbly dying to self, just as Christ did. There is something special about marriage that makes it a unique place where we can be conformed more and more into the image of Christ.

Giving 100%, laying down our rights, dying to self, and becoming Christlike...let's be honest with one another, and those ladies here who have been married for many years will agree, these are not easy things to do. These things do not come naturally to these bodies of flesh within which we live. In the flesh, these are not things that we can do consistently. But in the Spirit, we can do all things through Christ who strengthens us. So, put on the full armor of God and prepare to press on toward the prize of the high calling of God in Christ Jesus.

All of us sitting here know that life is frail and fleeting. We have all laughed. And cried. We are each acquainted with joy as well as with sorrow. To each of us have come unique triumphs and unique trials. You will face challenges in life, the details of which are yet unknown. When Mark and I married, we had no idea the valleys we would walk through. None of us do. Decide now, before the challenges come, how you will respond to them. Purpose in your heart to cleave to God and to one another as husband and wife no matter what. Decide now to be faithful to God and one another no matter what. Be prepared to face the challenges before the challenges come. Be well-grounded in the truth that when the enemy comes in like a flood, the Lord will raise up a banner under which you can find shelter and safety. Go deep in the truth that God's grace is sufficient always and under all circumstances. He and He alone is enough. Be prepared to reflect the glory of God and proclaim His goodness. No matter what.

As I look back at my own marriage, I am thinking about some of the pieces of practical counsel I'd like to share as you begin this exciting new season in your life...

> Study your husband to know his heart. He's going to make mistakes. He's going to fall short of your expectations. He's not always going to say the right things. But, if you know his heart, you will be able to patiently extend grace.

> Be slow to speak, swift to hear, and slow to anger

> No matter how busy you are, make time for him. Be a good listener. It's easy to be interested in all that your husband has to say when you are first married. But the tendency is to lose that interest over time. We just get so busy sometimes! But, purposefully strive to always be interested in what your husband has to say. He will know you respect him if you do.

> Don't ever lie....even about the supposed "little" things

> Don't try to manipulate your husband with your tears

> Never, ever joke about him at his expense

> Do not share your disagreements on Facebook

> Make sure you have someone in your life who will speak truth to you even if you don't want to hear it

> Don't let little things unnecessarily become big things. I look back at most of the moments when Mark and I have struggled in our marriage, and almost always, the problem started as something very small that became big. And, it didn't have to.

> Remember, we do face an enemy. There will be days, believe it or not, when you may be tempted to think the enemy is your husband. But, it's not your husband. The enemy we face is Satan and this adversary would love to destroy your marriage. Satan is a thief and a liar and wants to kill, steal and destroy all

that is good.   So, be prepared to fight the good fight and know that you do not fight it alone. The same God who created the universe and all that is therein, has promised to never leave you nor forsake you. The same God who sustains this universe and holds it together in His mighty power is the same God who has promised that, in Christ, we are more than conquerors.   So, fix your gaze intently upon Him, and He will help you.

And always, trust in the Lord with all your heart and lean not on your own understanding. In all your ways acknowledge the Lord and He will make your paths straight.

In my marriage, Lord, help me...
To esteem my husband better than I
To respect my husband
To follow my husband and to encourage him in the difficult task of leading
To bring my husband good, not harm, all the days of his life
To be willing to overlook an offense
To be longsuffering
To remember that love is patient and love is kind
To remember that love is not rude nor is it self-seeking
To remember that love keeps no record of wrongs and it keeps hoping
Lord....
Guard my heart
Guard my mind and my thoughts
Guard my mouth
Protect me from having an unforgiving heart
Protect me from having an unrepentant heart
Protect me from any roots of bitterness taking hold
Protect me from pride

And, forgive me, Lord. I am not a perfect wife.
I am not always even a good wife.
But, I love my husband and I love You, Lord, and I want to honor You.
I want to be the wife that you expect me to be, the wife that you will help me to be through the power of the Holy Spirit. Forgive me when I fall short and help me to press on in Christ.

And now, as I close, I do pray for each person here. I pray for each marriage. I know all of us have scars, and many of us have wounds and scars in our marriages. But, there is hope and there is healing and it can be found in the truth of Jesus Christ. I pray that, today, you are able, through the blood of Christ which makes us acceptable to God, to stand and say to the Lord, "I am Yours and You are mine." And if today you are sitting there, and you can't say that, I pray that you will hunger and thirst for righteousness. I pray that you will diligently seek the Lord with all your heart, soul, mind, and strength until you find yourself on your knees at the foot of the cross pouring out your heart in full repentance before Jesus, the only Lord and Saviour, all sufficient to cleanse, to save, to heal, to make whole, to give us beauty for ashes.   There is hope because of Him.   There is victory to be found in Him.   There is joy in His presence.

May all your days together be filled with peace that passes all understanding and with abiding love for one another and for the Lord.

Appendix H
When there is grief...

What is the right adjective? Is it "unique?" Is it "difficult?" Is it "heartbreaking?"

We find ourselves in a difficult and heartbreaking situation. At almost the exact same time that Sarah was diagnosed with leukemia, James was diagnosed with acute lymphocytic leukemia. But, Sarah is a girl and James was a boy and Sarah was seven and James was nearly fifteen. Same disease, but different risk categories.

James and Sarah were on the 8th floor of Women and Children's Hospital of Buffalo together. Only for a few days. James ultimately ended up receiving most of his treatment at Roswell Park Cancer Institute, and Sarah, due to her young age and other medical complications, ended up receiving her treatment at Women and Children's Hospital.

James and Sarah never actually met. But we moms to James and Sarah met briefly. I don't know for sure what I looked like, but I can guarantee it wasn't pretty. I do remember what James' Mom looked like. Tired. Shocked. Sad. We didn't get to know each other all that well. Trying to establish a friendship in the midst of these early days of chemotherapy would be just too exhausting. But, when we passed in the hall, each one of us knew what the other was going through, and words were not necessary.

James got to go home from the hospital much sooner than Sarah. Sarah was battling a blood infection, and that delayed the start of chemo and thus the escape home. Both James and Sarah had to have a central line put in for chemo. James got a mediport (under the skin), and Sarah got a broviac (a line hanging out of her chest). James' Mom said he was pretty sore after surgery to place the mediport, and she was surprised because the doctors didn't really make it sound like it would be too painful. Doctors forget things sometimes. James was an athlete. He needed the mediport, not a broviac swinging from his chest.

After James and his Mom went home from the hospital, I lost track of them.

After a couple weeks, Sarah, too, escaped from the hospital. We dealt with low platelets, low white counts, blood and platelet transfusions, broviac dressing changes, heparin flushes, chemo administration, frequent nursing visits, mouth sores, hair loss, sorrow, and upset stomachs.

Time went by, good days and bad days existing side by side, as they do for everyone, but more intensified for cancer patients.

Pneumonia. Sarah on a ventilator. Sarah finally off the ventilator and able to come home. Back on the chemo bandwagon. Another half year of chemo under our belts, when Epstein Barr Virus (i.e. mononucleosis) attacked and overwhelmed Sarah's lungs and liver. Back in the ICU. Eventually feeling better and another escape from the hospital. Recover for a few days, and get back on track with chemo. That was life for Sarah and us.

We were about 28 months into chemotherapy (with another 8 to go), when my Mom told me she had read in the paper about a 17 year old boy named James who had just died from leukemia. He'd had to have a bone marrow transplant. His sister had donated the marrow. He'd been battling the disease for about the same time as Sarah.

Was it the same James?

It was.

James, strong and athletic, had died. Little Sarah already so disabled and frail prior to being diagnosed with leukemia, still alive and actually doing pretty well. I felt sad, grateful and guilty all at the same time. I was so sad for James' Mom. That could easily be me. It may someday be me. I was so grateful that my little girl is still here. And guilty. What is a parent of a living child battling the same disease to say to the parent of a child who has passed away?

I don't know for sure what the right thing to say is.

If I were preparing to lay my child in the grave, nothing would irritate me more than someone with a cliché. Especially if the intention of the cliché is to wrap the entire matter up in a neat little package with no loose ends, and make them (i.e. the speaker) feel better. There are loose ends swinging all over the place! The death of your child is a tangled mess of loose ends and unanswered questions and unbearable grief and no simple sentence from a well-intentioned person is going to wrap it all up in a neat and comfortable package.

Two paragraphs ago, I asked the question, "What is a parent of a living child battling the same disease to say to the parent of a child who has passed away?" That's a bad question because there is no good answer. My question should have been, "What is the parent of a living child battling the same disease NOT to say to the parent of a child who has passed away?" I may not know what to say, but I do have some idea of what not to say or do……

Do not minimize the pain. I think, sometimes, we who are not experiencing the loss first hand, tend to minimize the pain because it makes us feel more comfortable. If there is a hurting, grieving parent or sibling near you, do not be arrogant enough to think you have all the right words to balm the wounds….thus making you feel better. The right balm applied at the wrong time will bring no healing. I do not have the power to take away your pain. But, I do have the ability to join you in it, and to stand by your side (with few words) and be with you while you go through it.

Do not assume the hurting person wants to share the pain. I think most people want comfort when they are grieving. But, not all do. Some people want privacy. The only way to figure it out is to be sensitive to the grieving person's stance and words, and if you're not sure, then ask. It is ok to say to someone, "You know what, I want to do whatever I can to help you through this. I'm not sure how to do that. If I were in your shoes, I'm not sure if I would want company or if I would want to be left alone for a while. If I get it wrong, please tell me."

Do not talk non-stop just because you are nervous and unsure what to say. Remember, admitting that you do not know what to say to a grieving parent is a good thing to do. Refusing to allow silence doesn't help. Get over feeling uncomfortable about those "awkward silences." When we are uncomfortable with silence, that's when we (or at least I) say the most stupid things. Ever so slowly I'm learning (mostly as the result of embarrassing myself frequently over the years) that silence has gotten a bad rap. Maybe the best thing we can do at the funeral home is to stand with the Mom who has just lost her child and hold her hand and hug her. The old stand-by standard comment of, "She looks so peaceful and good....they did a great job," falls like an ax sharply on the ears of a parents burying their child. Do not tell them how good their dead child looks! They don't care if their child looks peaceful. They are not supposed to look peaceful...they are supposed to look alive.

Do not avoid the grieving family...unless they have indicated that they prefer privacy. It is very tempting to avoid people when we don't know what to say or do. Despite the potential awkwardness, make the phone call, stop to visit, keep in touch after the funeral. As is true whenever we suffer the loss of a family member, those weeks following the hectic activity of wakes and funerals are the most lonesome. Those are the times when we wander into the quiet room of someone now gone, and mourn. That is when the kind reminder that someone remembers (us and our child) and cares and is willing to share the sadness by showing attention is most needed.

Do not avoid the child's name and bringing up memories of the child to the parents...unless the family has indicated that is their wish. I know the arguments here...we think it's "sensitive" to be cautious when around the grieving parents, and to be careful not to bring up a sad subject. That's not a good argument. It's a bad excuse. Grieving parents are well tuned in to the people's reactions around them. If they sense you are being overly cautious, it becomes a barrier. The grieving parent then starts to feel obligated to avoid their own child's name so that you don't feel uncomfortable. You have just helped build a wall around a lonely person. My experience with Moms who have lost a child has taught me that most Moms want to talk about their child. Dads seem a little harder to figure out. But, I have noticed a common thread with the Moms.....most of them have told me that people avoid bringing up the name of their child or memories of their child.

Do not avoid laughter! Parents who have just lost a child want to feel like their child made a difference in this world, and that their child's life (vs. just their death) will be remembered. These parents are full of memories. Tremendous and powerful memories of a life that they loved. Laughter is a reminder and a reassurance that the child's life was not all about disease or disability or a sudden accident or loss or suffering. Laughter is a reminder that there were beautiful and full days that are being and will continue to be remembered by the people who knew the child. Sometimes when someone dies, especially a child, there is a tendency to narrow the memories of the life to those few moments at or around the time of death and the circumstances of that experience. Broaden the memories. This was a whole life, no matter how short it may have been, with abundant and varied memories.

And then there are the spiritual. God bless spiritual people. I love them, but they don't always know what to say to grieving parents. I, too, am a Christian who doesn't always know what to say. I certainly have a track record of many errors and faux pas when interacting with the grieving. There have been times when I wished my tongue would fall out of my mouth to prevent me from saying something stupid or phony or cliché. Why do we think we have to come up with something brilliant to say, something that will take away the pain? We do not have the power to take away the pain. The best we can hope to do is to stand with the grieving and share the pain.

Christians have God given tools in their tool box of social interaction to use. But so often, these tools of God's truth and love either stay in the box while we rely on our secular and independent selves or they come out at the wrong time. In order to be familiar with these tools and to develop skills to properly use them, it is necessary to read the directions first. These most important directions are found in the Bible. Everything I write from this point on is useless to you if you do not spend time in the perfect word of the Lord. I strongly urge you to read the manual!

Christians have the tool of the Holy Spirit available to them. The Holy Spirit (God Himself) woos people to Him. As huge as it is to comprehend, the great designer of this entire universe wants a relationship with us! The Holy Spirit keeps busy trying to get the attention of non-believers. If a person believes in and receives Christ as his Savior, then that same Holy Spirit that had been wooing him and knocking at the door of the heart and the mind, moves in. God Himself, in the form of the Holy Spirit, moves into your life and into your heart, and lives inside you. That same Holy Spirit whose main goal before had been to get your attention now focuses on filling you up, comforting you, encouraging you, teaching you, guiding you, interceding for you. Have you any idea of the power of the Holy Spirit to lead you in ALL circumstances? The power of the Holy Spirit is completely yours! But you MUST YIELD your will to His and allow Him to lead. And lead He will if you let Him. Including giving you the words to say and the timing to say them to a grieving person. *"Let your conversation be always full of grace, seasoned with salt, so that you may know how to answer everyone" (Colossians 4:6).*

Christians have the tool of prayer in the name of Jesus. There is power in the name of Jesus, and most Christians don't bother to open the door to that power. How many of us have sent a card and wrote in it, "You are all in our prayers every day." Or, how many of us have stood at a funeral home comforting a hurting person and using the words, "We will be praying for you." And then, after making such bold claims, never pray? Are you guilty of that? My hand is in the air! I am guilty of this, and I hang my head in shame at that truth. If you tell a hurting person that you are going to pray for them, then PRAY FOR THEM! When we pray for another person in faith, we are helping to *"quench the fiery darts of the evil one" (Ephesians 6:16).* The "evil one" (that would be Satan) hates us and wants to hurt us. He looks for weak moments. Weak moments are opportunities for him. Parents who have lost a child are so vulnerable to Satan's fiery darts. Satan wants to destroy faith in the true and living God. He wants to destroy families and wreck marriages. The loss of a child is potentially fertile ground for these further tragedies. If you tell a grieving parent that you are going to pray for them and their family DO IT! And, do it frequently and fervently. The Bible tells us in the Book of James that *"The effectual fervent prayer of a righteous man availeth much."*

Christians have the tool of the Good News. We keep it to ourselves a lot, but the fact is Christians have Good News to share with the world in general and with hurting people in particular. What is the Good News? Jesus Christ is the Good News. God has no pleasure that suffering, sorrow, and death exist. In fact, we are told in Romans 8:22 that the entire planet and all of creation is "groaning" in expectation of God returning to restore the world to His original intention. The Good News is that God wants to *"wipe every tear from their eyes" (Revelation 21:4).* This Good News is available to all who call on the name of Jesus....Jesus, the one who died on the cross for the sins of the world and was raised to life by God the Father victorious over sin and death for all who believe and receive Christ's gift and sacrifice.

Now, such Good News needs to be properly timed. To walk into a funeral home and start preaching to a grieving person that their beloved child is in a better place and that God knows best, and that *"all things work together for good,"* and that God has a plan that is better than our plans and that we should *"rejoice in our sufferings, because we know that suffering produces perseverance; perseverance, character; and character hope" (Romans 5: 3, 4)* is not wise. In Proverbs 25:20, God tells us, *"Like one who takes away a garment on a cold day, or like vinegar poured on soda, is one who sings songs to a heavy heart."* Although, as the song says, we are "Christian Soldiers," God does not want us marching into funeral homes rubbing salt in open wounds. He is well aware of the importance of timing. Perhaps this is a family that is desperate for the word of God. If that is the case, then what they really need is someone who is mature in the faith who can be in a relationship with them and share God's truth over time. They need commitment from you.

Christians have the tool of Christ's experiences of suffering. We don't always include this in the Good News message, but it is of vital significance to a family suffering loss or sickness. Jesus personally knows about pain and suffering. He is not a God who sits in heaven merely telling us how to handle pain. Jesus is our God who went through what we go through. God came to earth. He came as a human being. As mysterious as this truth is, Jesus was fully God and FULLY HUMAN. Being fully human, He experienced and felt temptation. He experienced and felt betrayal. He experienced and felt denial. He experienced and felt abandonment. Those nails that pierced His hands and feet, He felt those the same way we would have. Those thorns that pressed into the flesh of His scalp, hurt him just the same as they would hurt us. Hanging from the cross, He struggled to breath just like we would. The words of mocking that were hurled at Him broke His heart just like ours would break. He was spit upon. He was scourged. He had to carry a cross upon which He would be nailed. He died. And, not only did He die a horribly painful death, He died with our sins......mine, yours, the sins of all who have ever walked the earth......upon His shoulders. He took the punishment willingly. His suffering was a choice He made upon our behalf. Can you see Him in the Garden of Gethsemane right before His arrest? He knew what was coming. He was praying.....in anguish.

"He withdrew about a stone's throw beyond them, knelt down and prayed, 'Father, if you are willing take this cup from me; yet not my will but yours be done.' An angel from heaven appeared to Him and strengthened Him. And being in anguish, He prayed more earnestly, and His sweat was like drops of blood falling to the ground" (Luke 22:41-44).

"For we do not have a high priest who is unable to sympathize with our weaknesses, but we have one who has been tempted in every way, just as we are - yet was without sin. Let us then approach the throne of grace with confidence, so that we may receive mercy and find grace to help us in our time of need" (Hebrews 4:15, 16).

"He was despised and rejected by men, a man of sorrows, and familiar with suffering. Like one from whom men hide their faces He was despised, and we esteemed Him not. Surely He took up our infirmities and carried our sorrows, yet we considered Him stricken by God, smitten by Him and afflicted. But He was pieced for our transgressions, He was crushed for our iniquities; the punishment that brought us peace was upon Him, and by His wounds we are healed" (Isaiah 53:3-5).

Pain is no stranger to our God. As a result, He truly understands and He truly can and longs to comfort the hurting.

Christians have the tool of personal experiences of suffering. Christians have not been shielded from hurting and sickness and death. We are all born into a diseased and fallen world. Being a Christian does not guarantee a pain free life. The Bible actually instructs Christians to be prepared to face suffering, and that one of the positive results that can come from our pain is our ability to help others who are going through the same or similar circumstances. *"But in your hearts set apart Christ as Lord. Always be prepared to give an answer to everyone who asks you to give the reason for the hope that you have" (I Peter 3:15a).* If you're a Christian and have suffered sickness or loss or tragedy, when you feel ready, pray for God to help make you useful to someone else going through similar sorrows.

Christians have the tool of promises. God's Word includes His promises to His people. These are promises to ponder in our hearts and to look forward to. And, these are promises to share at the right time with hurting people who are hungry for truth. If you are a Christian who has experienced heart breaking, gut wrenching pain and loss, then you have meaningful work to do. If you can take your pain and hang tightly to God's promises in the midst of it, then you have a story to share.

Appendix I
Promises in Scripture

The promise of salvation.
That if thou shalt confess with thy mouth the Lord Jesus, and shalt believe in thine heart that God raised Him from the dead, thou shalt be saved. For with the heart man believeth unto righteousness; and with the mouth confession is made unto salvation. For the scripture saith, 'Whosoever believeth on Him shall not be ashamed.' For there is no difference between the Jew and the Greek: for the same Lord over all is rich unto all that call upon Him. For whosoever shall call upon the name of the Lord shall be saved (Romans 10:9-13).

The promise of forgiveness and cleansing.
If we say that we have no sin, we deceive ourselves, and the truth is not in us. If we confess our sins, He is faithful and just to forgive us our sins, and to cleanse us from all unrighteousness (I John1:8,9).

The promise that once our sins are forgiven, they are removed and remembered no more by God.
Bless the Lord, O my soul: and all that is within me, bless His holy name. Bless the Lord, O my soul, and forget not all His benefits: Who forgiveth all thine iniquities; who healeth all they diseases; who redeemeth thy life from destruction; who crowneth thee with lovingkindness and tender mercies; who satisfieth they mouth with good things; so that thy youth is renewed like the eagle's...The Lord is merciful and gracious, slow to anger, and plenteous in mercy. He will not always chide: neither will He keep His anger forever. He hath not dealt with us after our sins; nor rewarded us according to our iniquities. For as the heaven is high above the earth, so great is His mercy toward them that fear Him. As far as the east is from the west, so far hath He removed our transgressions from us (Psalm 103:1-5, 8-12).

The promise of abundant life and eternal life.
Jesus said, I am the door: by me if any man enter in, he shall be saved, and shall go in and out, and find pasture. The thief cometh not, but for to steal, and to kill, and to destroy: I am come that they might have life, and that they might have it more abundantly. I am the good shepherd: the good shepherd giveth His life for the sheep...My sheep hear My voice, and I know them, and they follow me: And I give unto them eternal life; and they shall never perish, neither shall any man pluck them out of my hand (John 15:9, 10, 27, 28).

The promises of an eternal home, comfort, and the Holy Spirit.
Jesus said, Let not your heart be troubled: ye believe in God, believe also in me. In my Father's house are many mansions: if it were not so, I would have told you. I go to prepare a place for you. And if I go and prepare a place for you, I will come again, and receive you unto myself; that where I am, there ye may be also....And whatsoever ye

shall ask in My name, that will I do, that the Father may be glorified in the Son. If ye shall ask any thing in my name, I will do it. If ye love me, keep my commandments. And I will pray the Father, and He shall give you another Comforter, that He may abide with you forever; Even the Spirit of truth; whom the world cannot receive, because it seeth Him not, neither knoweth Him: but ye know Him; for He dwelleth with you, and shall be in you. I will not leave you comfortless: I will come to you. Yet a little while, and the world seeth me no more; but ye see me: because I live, ye shall live also. At that day ye shall know that I am in my Father, and ye in me, and I in you.....These things have I spoken unto you, being yet present with you. But the Comforter, which is the Holy Ghost, whom the Father will send in My name, He shall teach you all things, and bring all things to your remembrance, whatsoever I have said unto you. Peace I leave with you, my peace I give unto you: not as the world giveth, give I unto you. Let not your heart be troubled, neither let it be afraid (John 14:1-3, 13-20, 25-27).

The promises to see us again, to hear our prayers, to ultimately overcome.
Jesus said, And ye now therefore have sorrow: but I will see you again, and your heart shall rejoice, and your joy no man taketh from you. And in that day ye shall ask me nothing. Verily, verily, I say unto you, Whatsoever ye shall ask the Father in my name, He will give it you. Hitherto have ye asked nothing in my name: ask, and ye shall receive, that your joy may be full....These things I have spoken unto you, that in me ye might have peace. In the world ye shall have tribulation: but be of good cheer; I have overcome the world (John 16:22-24, 33).

The promise to wipe away every tear and make all things new.
And I saw a new heaven and a new earth: for the first heaven and the first earth were passed away; and there was no more sea. And I John saw the holy city, new Jerusalem, coming down from God out of heaven, prepared as a bride adorned for her husband. And I heard a great voice out of heaven saying, 'Behold, the tabernacle of God is with men, and He will dwell with them, and they shall be His people, and God Himself shall be with them, and be their God. And God shall wipe away all tears from their eyes; and there shall be no more death, neither sorrow, nor crying, neither shall there be any more pain: for the former things are passed away.' And He that sat upon the throne said, 'Behold, I make all things new.' And He said unto me, 'Write: for these words are true and faithful.' And He said unto me, 'It is done. I am Alpha and Omega, the beginning and the end. I will give unto Him that is athirst of the fountain of the water of life freely' (Revelation 21:1-6).

The promise to intercede on our behalf.
Who is He that condemns? Christ Jesus, who died - more than that, who was raised to life - is at the right hand of God and is also interceding for us (Romans 8:34).

The promise of grace and mercy when we come to God.
Let us therefore come boldly unto the throne of grace, that we may obtain mercy, and find grace to help in time of need (Hebrews 4:16).

The promise that God's grace is sufficient.
Paul wrote: To keep me from becoming conceited because of these surpassingly great revelations, there was given me a thorn in my flesh, a messenger of Satan, to torment me. Three times I pleaded with the Lord to take it away from me. But He said to me, 'My grace is sufficient for you, for my power is made perfect in weakness'   (II Corinthians 12:7-9a).

The promise that we are never alone, and Jesus is always reliably the same.
...for He hath said, 'I will never leave thee, nor forsake thee.' So that we may boldly say, 'The Lord is my helper, and I will not fear what man shall do unto me...Jesus Christ the same yesterday, and today, and forever (Hebrews 13b, 6, 8).

The promises that the devil will flee, God will come near and God will lift us up.
Submit yourselves, then, to God. Resist the devil, and he will flee from you. Come near to God and He will come near to you....Humble yourselves before the Lord, and He will lift you up (James 4:7, 10).

The promise of rest.
Jesus said, Come to me, all you who are weary and burdened, and I will give you rest. Take my yoke upon you and learn from me, for I am gentle and humble in heart, and you will find rest for your souls. For my yoke is easy and my burden is light (Matthew 11:28-30).

The promise to renew our strength.
Hast thou not known? Hast thou not heard, that the everlasting God, the Lord, the Creator of the ends of the earth, fainteth not, neither is weary? There is no searching of His understanding. He giveth power to the faint; and to them that have no might He increaseth strength. Even the youths shall faint and be weary, and the young men shall utterly fall: But they that wait upon the Lord shall renew their strength; they shall mount up with wings as eagles; they shall run, and not be weary; and they shall walk and not faint (Isaiah 40:28-31).

The promise of victory over death.
I declare to you, brothers and sisters, that flesh and blood cannot inherit the kingdom of God, nor does the perishable inherit the imperishable. Listen, I tell you a mystery: We will not all sleep, but we will all be changed— in a flash, in the twinkling of an eye, at the last trumpet. For the trumpet will sound, the dead will be raised imperishable, and we will be changed. For the perishable must clothe itself with the imperishable, and the mortal with immortality. When the perishable has been clothed with the imperishable, and the mortal with immortality, then the saying that is written will come true: 'Death has been swallowed up in victory. Where, O death, is your victory? Where, O death, is your sting?' The sting of death is sin, and the power of sin is the law. But thanks be to God! He gives us the victory through our Lord Jesus Christ (I Corinthians 15:50-57).

The promise of inheritance.
Now if we are children, then we are heirs—heirs of God and co-heirs with Christ, if indeed we share in his sufferings in order that we may also share in his glory (Romans 8:17).

And He (Jesus) said unto me, It is done. I am Alpha and Omega, the beginning and the end. I will give unto him that is athirst of the fountain of the water of life freely. He that overcometh shall inherit all things; and I will be his God, and he shall be my son (Revelation 21:6-7).

The promise that God supplies our needs.
But my God shall supply all your need according to His riches in glory by Christ Jesus (Philippians 4:19).

If God is for us, who can be against us? He who did not spare His own Son, but gave Him up for us all - how will He not also, along with Him, graciously give us all things? (Romans 8:32).

The promise of Christ's return.
They (the disciples immediately following Jesus' ascension into heaven) were looking intently up into the sky as He was going, when suddenly two men dressed in white stood beside them. 'Men of Galilee,' they said, 'why do you stand here looking into the sky? This same Jesus, who has been taken from you into heaven, will come back in the same way you have seen Him go into heaven' (Acts 1:10,11).

The promise of Christ's glorious riches and love.
For this reason I kneel before the Father, from whom His whole family in heaven and on earth derives its name. I pray that out of His glorious riches He may strengthen you with power through His Spirit in your inner being, so that Christ may dwell in your hearts through faith. And I pray that you, being rooted and established in love, may have power, together with all the saints, to grasp how wide and long and high and deep is the love of Christ, and to know this love that surpasses knowledge - that you may be filled to the measure of all the fullness of God. Now to Him who is able to do immeasurably more than all we ask or imagine, according to His power that is at work within us, to Him be glory in the church and in Christ Jesus throughout all generation, for ever and ever! Amen (Ephesians 3:14-21).

The promise that all will be well; nothing can separate us from the love of Christ.
And we know that in all things God works for the good of those who love Him, who have been called according to His purpose...Who shall separate us from the love of Christ? Shall trouble or hardship or persecution or famine or nakedness or danger or sword?...No, in all these things we are more than conquerors through Him who loved us. For I am convinced that neither death nor life, neither angels nor demons, neither the present nor the future, nor any powers, neither height nor depth, nor anything else in all

creation, will be able to separate us from the love of God that is in Christ Jesus our Lord (Romans 8:28, 35, 37-39).

This list is just a few of God's promises to His children. God is not a genie in the bottle at the whim of our beck and call. He is God. He is big. He is unfathomable. He wants what is best for us. What is best for us is to be in a relationship with Him through Christ. Thus, the wonderful, marvelous promises of God are never intended to be dispensed like magic. No. Instead they are arrows pointing toward Christ. The promises of God are intended for the children of God. May we be faithful to pray for those who do not know God, the great author of these beautiful promises.

WORKS CITED

1. Andrew Murray, <u>The Deeper Christian Life</u> (Grand Rapids, MI: The Zondervan Corporation, 1985). 15 – 16.

2. John Foxe, et al., <u>Foxe: Voices of the Martyrs</u> (Alachua, FL: The Voice of the Martyrs and Bridge-Logos, 2007). 54 - 55.

3. Murray, <u>The Deeper Christian Life</u>, 61.

4. Murray, <u>The Deeper Christian Life</u>, 83 – 84.

5. John Charles Ryle, <u>Holiness: Its Nature, Hindrances, Difficulties, and Roots</u> (Webster, NY: Evangelical Press USA, Reprinted with new foreword 2004). 51, 64.

6. Foxe, <u>Foxe: Voices of the Martyrs</u>, 65 – 66.

7. Ryle, <u>Holiness</u>, 194 - 196.

8. Ryle, <u>Holiness</u>, 203 – 204.

9. Horatius Bonar, <u>Night of Weeping: Words for the Suffering Family of God</u> (Chicago: Moody Press, 1958).

10. J.I. Packer, <u>Knowing God</u> (Downers Grove, IL: Intervarsity Press, 1973). 82 – 83.

11. Foxe, <u>Foxe: Voices of the Martyrs</u>, 135 – 136.

12. Packer, <u>Knowing God</u>, 90 – 92.

13. Packer, <u>Knowing God</u>, 158 – 159.

14. Charles Colson, <u>A Dangerous Grace</u> (Dallas, TX: Word Publishing/Prison Fellowship Ministries, 1994). 12 – 13.

15. Foxe, <u>Foxe: Voices of the Martyrs</u>, 173 – 174.

16. Colson, <u>A Dangerous Grace</u>, 15 – 16.

17. Colson, <u>A Dangerous Grace</u>, 244 – 245.

18. C.S. Lewis, <u>The Problem of Pain</u> (New York, NY: Harper Collins, edition 2001, original 1940). 33, 34, 35.

19. Foxe, <u>Foxe: Voices of the Martyrs</u>, 197 – 198.

20. Lewis, <u>The Problem of Pain</u>, 39, 40, 41.

21. Lewis, <u>The Problem of Pain</u>, 106, 107, 108.

22. Philip Yancey, <u>Where is God When it Hurts?</u> (Grand Rapids, MI: Zondervan Publishing House, 1990). 68 – 71.

23. Foxe, <u>Foxe: Voices of the Martyrs</u>, 216 - 217.

24. Yancey, <u>Where is God When it Hurts?</u>, 107 – 109.

25. Yancey, <u>Where is God When it Hurts?</u>, 233 – 234

26. Eric Metaxas, <u>Bonhoeffer: Pator, Martyr, Prophet, Spy – a Righteous Gentile vs. the Third Reich</u> (Nashville, TN: Thomas Nelson, Inc., 2010). 136 - 138

27. Foxe, <u>Foxe: Voices of the Martyrs</u>, 231 – 234

28. Metaxas, <u>Bonhoeffer: Pastor, Martyr, Prophet, Spy – a Righteous Gentile vs. the Third Reich</u>, 196, 208 – 210.

29. Metaxas, <u>Bonhoeffer: Pastor, Martyr, Prophet, Spy – a Righteous Gentile vs. the Third Reich</u>, 469, 471, 472.

30. Corrie ten Boom, <u>The Hiding Place</u> (Uhrichsville, OH: Barbour Books, 1971). 193 – 194.

31. Foxe, <u>Foxe: Voices of the Martyrs</u>, 240 - 242.

32. ten Boom, <u>The Hiding Place,</u> 199 – 200.

33. ten Boom, <u>The Hiding Place</u>, 231 – 232.

34. W. Phillip Keller, <u>A Shepherd Looks at Psalm 23</u> (Grand Rapids, MI: Zondervan, 1970). 26-27, 55-56.

35. Foxe, <u>Foxe: Voices of the Martyrs</u>, 251 – 252.

36. Keller, <u>A Shepherd Looks at Psalm 23</u>, 138 – 142.

37. Keller, <u>A Shepherd Looks at Psalm 23</u>, 142 – 145.

38. L.B. Cowman, <u>Streams in the Desert</u> (Grand Rapids, MI: Zondervan, 1997). 158-159.

39. Fox, <u>Foxe: Voices of the Martyrs</u>, 252 – 254.

40. Cowman, <u>Streams in the Desert</u>, 455-456.

41. Cowman, Streams in the Desert, 316-318.

42. Nancy Pearcey, Total Truth: Liberating Christianity From Its Cultural Captivity (Wheaton, IL: Crossway Books and Good News Publishers, 2004). 34, 35, 44, 45.

43. Fox, Foxes: Voices of the Martyrs, 315 – 316.

44. Pearcey, Total Truth: Liberating Christianity From Its Cultural Captivity, 87-88.

45. Pearcey, Total Truth: Liberating Christianity From Its Cultural Captivity, 292, 323, 362.

46. Paul David Tripp, A Quest For More: Living For Something Bigger Than You (Greensboro, NC: New Growth Press, 2008). Selected quotes from chapters 1 and 3.

47. Fox, Foxes: Voices of the Martyrs, 336 – 337.

48. Tripp, A Quest For More: Living For Something Bigger Than You, selected quotes from chapters 4 and 5.

49. Tripp, A Quest For More: Living For Something Bigger Than You, selected quotes from chapter 17.

50. Charles Colson and Nancy Pearcey, How Now Shall We Live?, (Carol Stream, IL: Tyndale House Publishers, Inc., 1999). Selected quotes from the introduction and chapters 2 and 3.

51. David Hull, "The God of the Galápagos", *Nature (magazine),* 352:485–86, 8 August 1991.

52. Norman Geisler and Frank Turek, I Don't Have Enough Faith to be an Atheist, (Wheaton, IL: Crossway Books, 2004). 73.

53. Geisler and Turek, I Don't Have Enough Faith to be an Atheist, 80.

54. Geisler and Turek, I Don't Have Enough Faith to be an Atheist, 92-94

55. Choi, Charles Q. "7 Theories on the Origin of Life." *LiveScience.* TechMedia Network, 24 March. 2016. Web. 22 Apr. 2016

56. Richard Dawkins, The Blind Watchmaker: Why the Evidence Reveals a Universe Without Design (New York, NY: Norton, 1987). Cover, 1-3, 5.

57. Michael J. Behe, Darwin's Black Box: The Biochemical Challenge to Evolution (New York, NY: The Free Press, 1996). 46.

58. Charles Darwin, On the Origin of Species, (Mineola, NY: Dover Publications, Inc., 2006). Chapter IX.

59. Robert Carter (editor), <u>Evolution's Achilles' Heels</u> (Powder Springs, GA: Creation Book Publishers, 2014). From chapter 4: "The Fossil Record" by Dr. Emil Silvestru. 113.

60. Robert Carter (editor), <u>Evolution's Achilles' Heels</u>, From chapter 4: "The Fossil Record" by Dr. Emil Silvestru. 120.

61. Carter (editor), <u>Evolution's Achilles' Heels</u>, (Powder Springs, GA: Creation Book Publishers, 2014). From chapter 4: "The Fossil Record" by Dr. Emil Silvestru. 131.

62. Carter (editor), <u>Evolution's Achilles' Heels</u>, From chapter 4: "The Fossil Record" by Dr. Emil Silvestru. 144.

63. Carter (editor), <u>Evolution's Achilles' Heels</u>, From chapter 4: "The Fossil Record" by Dr. Emil Silvestru. 146.

64. Carter (editor), <u>Evolution's Achilles' Heels</u>, From chapter 4: "The Fossil Record" by Dr. Emil Silvestru. 148.

65. Geisler and Turek, <u>I Don't Have Enough Faith to be an Atheist</u>, Selected quotes from chapter 1.

66. Alex Epstein, <u>The Moral Case for Fossil Fuels</u> (New York, NY: Penguin Group, 2014). 13, 15, 16, 20, 21, 30, 31, 34, 35, 201, 208, 209.

67. Dinesh D'Souza, <u>What's So Great About Christianity</u> (Carol Stream, IL: Tyndale House Publishers, Inc., 2007). Excerpts from the preface and from 303 – 308.

ABOUT THE AUTHOR

Brenda Hanson was born in 1969 and was raised on a dairy farm in Western New York. There was something wonderful about farm life and working side by side with family through the seasons of the year and the seasons of life. As a farm girl, she learned the value and beauty of hard work. In 1994, she graduated from Daemen College in Amherst, NY with a degree in history/government and education. This was also the year that she married her beloved husband, Mark. In 1996, they became the joyful parents of Sarah. For many years, Brenda was a stay-at-home mom, a role she treasured. On April 13, 2011, the Lord called Sarah home to heaven. As Mark and Brenda said "goodbye" to their precious girl, they leaned hard upon the Lord and each other.

In 2009, Brenda joined the teaching team at Central Baptist Christian School in Yorkshire, NY. Teaching is a high calling and a profound privilege that Brenda embraces with joy and enthusiasm.

She is a wife, mother, daughter, sister, grandmother, aunt, and teacher….all roles she cherishes…

But above all, she is a child of the Most High God.
Redeemed.
And she loves to proclaim it!

Contact Information
brendahanson10@gmail.com

Made in the USA
Columbia, SC
20 May 2021